BE

D0271570

Le

PEMBROKE
Invoice : 05/1679 Price EUR29.09
Title: Haw-Haw the tragedy o
Class:

940.5488743

Withdrawn from Stock
Dublin City Public Libraries

HAW-HAW

THE TRAGEDY OF WILLIAM AND MARGARET JOYCE

Also by Nigel Farndale

A Sympathetic Hanging

Last Action Hero of the British Empire:
Commander John Kerans 1915–1985

Flirtation, Seduction, Betrayal:
Interviews with Heroes and Villains

HAW-HAW

THE TRAGEDY OF WILLIAM AND MARGARET JOYCE

NIGEL FARNDALE

MACMILLAN

First published 2005 by Macmillan
an imprint of Pan Macmillan Ltd
Pan Macmillan, 20 New Wharf Road, London N1 9RR
Basingstoke and Oxford
Associated companies throughout the world
www.panmacmillan.com

ISBN 0 333 98992 9

Copyright © Nigel Farndale 2005

The right of Nigel Farndale to be identified as the
author of this work has been asserted by him in accordance
with the Copyright, Designs and Patents Act 1988.

Picture credits: Corbis: 7; Deutsches Rundfunkarchiv: 18 (bottom);
Forman Archive: 18 (top left and right), 24, 31; Fox: 12; Heather Iandolo: 1, 3,
14, 17; Hulton: 8, 21, 22; The Imperial War Museum: 26, 28, 29; Courtesy of
the National Archives of the United Kingdom: 10, 15, 16, 19, 23, 25;
PA Photos: 27, 30; Popperfoto: 2, 11; Tully Potter: 4

Every effort has been made to contact all copyright holders
of material in this book. If any have been inadvertently overlooked,
the publishers will be pleased to make the necessary
arrangement at the first opportunity.

All rights reserved. No part of this publication may be
reproduced, stored in or introduced into a retrieval system, or
transmitted, in any form, or by any means (electronic, mechanical,
photocopying, recording or otherwise) without the prior written
permission of the publisher. Any person who does any unauthorized
act in relation to this publication may be liable to criminal
prosecution and civil claims for damages.

1 3 5 7 9 8 6 4 2

A CIP catalogue record for this book is available from
the British Library.

Typeset by SetSystems Ltd, Saffron Walden, Essex
Printed and bound in Great Britain by
Mackays of Chatham plc, Chatham, Kent

For my parents, Geoffrey and Barbara

ACKNOWLEDGEMENTS

Among those who have helped me with this book I would particularly like to thank Heather Iandolo, James Clark, Geoffrey Perry, the late Lady Mosley, Dame Vera Lynn, Tully Potter, Judith Joyce Ware, Francis Beckett and, for his sage advice and for agreeing to read the manuscript, Terry Charman of the Imperial War Museum. My thanks also to those who assisted me at the National Archives–Public Record Office, Kew, especially Sheila Knight, Tim Padfield, the copyright officer, and Janet Fennings, for helping me decipher Margaret Joyce's short-hand.

I am also grateful to Lawrence Aspden, curator of Sheffield University's Special Collections and Archive, Monty Kolsky and Sandra Clark at the Board of Deputies of British Jews, the researchers John Hope, Brian Clough and Dr David Turner, the authors Mary Kenny, Stephen Doril, Professor Colin Holmes and David Seabrook, the documentary-makers Brian and Virginia Gilbert, the lawyer Julia Braybrook, and the collectors Michael and Doreen Forman. My thanks as well to the staff at the London Library, the Wiener Library, the British Library, the Bodleian Library, the Travellers' Club library, the National Sound Archive, the Haus des Rundfunks, Berlin, the Bundesarchiv, Abteilung Potsdam and the Deutsches Rundfunkarchiv in Frankfurt and Berlin.

Thanks to the readers of the *Sunday Telegraph*, too, around a hundred of whom wrote to me with their memories of Lord and Lady Haw-Haw, including V. A. Kiralby, who made cups of tea for Joyce during his Blackshirt days, Peter Macey, who stood outside the prison as Joyce was executed, and Bill Steele, who remembers Joyce from when he looked after him as a child in Dulwich. Finally I would like to record my especial gratitude to my editors at Macmillan, George Morley, Stuart Evers and Nicholas Blake, my agent, David Miller of Rogers, Coleridge & White, and, for humouring me and acting as a single mother during the weekends I was working on this book, my wife Mary.

CONTENTS

PROLOGUE

The word tragedy comes from the Greek for goat (*tragos*) and song (*oide*). Goat-song. This mocking lament, sung in ancient goat-satyr plays, was heard again on 3 January 1946, the day William Joyce, better known as Lord Haw-Haw, became the last civilian in England to hang for high treason.

That was on a Thursday. By the Saturday, his wife Margaret had been spirited out of the country, under armed escort, to a military detention centre in Belgium. Two weeks later, Major J. F. E. Stephenson of MI5 sent an enigmatic memorandum to the head of the British Intelligence Bureau in Brussels: 'It has been decided by the authorities in the UK not to prosecute this woman, in effect on compassionate grounds. There is no lack of evidence implicating her in the treasonable activities of her late husband; but the authorities do not think that she need be punished further, and would like her to be returned to Germany as a German subject.'

So it was that an American husband was hanged as an Englishman, while his equally 'guilty' English wife was freed as a German.

Untangling this conundrum will be one of the endeavours of this book. For now, though, it should be explained that William Joyce, one of the most notorious traitors in British history, was indeed an American, born in Brooklyn, New York, on 24 April 1906. By definition then, it might be supposed, it was impossible for him to be a traitor to England, however hard he tried. What is more, he committed his act of treason – broadcasting Nazi propaganda to England – from Germany; and, as his defence lawyer pointed out, all legal authority insisted that 'an alien who was outside the King's dominions owed no sort of allegiance to the Crown'.

(It was equally impossible for Joyce to be a traitor to America, incidentally, because by the time the United States entered the Second World War in December 1941, he had taken German citizenship.)

Margaret Joyce, on the other hand, was born in Old Trafford, Manchester, on 14 July 1911. She was as English as warm beer.

William Joyce might seem an unlikely tragic figure, in the colloquial sense. After all, he died an unrepentant fascist and anti-Semite, and though his *Germany Calling* radio broadcasts were considered a good laugh by many, some found them sinister and frightening, while others still were angered by them. But, in the literary sense, a tragedy is what his death most definitely was. Indeed, when I first began researching Lord Haw-Haw several years ago, I was surprised that no one had ever thought to write a play based on the high drama and low farce of his life, not least because it conforms in almost every particular to Aristotle's definition of a tragedy.

'The change in the hero's fortunes must lie not in depravity but in some great error on his part,' Aristotle wrote in *The Poetics*. 'It should contain incidents arousing pity and fear, wherewith to accomplish its catharsis of such emotion.'

By any standard definition, Joyce was depraved, that is, morally corrupt, because he was a fascist, an anti-Semite and, in spirit if not in deed, a traitor. But his political beliefs do have to be considered in their historical context. In the 1930s, according to Sir Oswald Mosley's reckoning at least, as many as half a million ordinary British citizens, as well as a large percentage of the aristocracy, considered themselves to be fascists of one kind or another, as well as anti-Semites. It can only be presumed that many of them held these poisonous views naively. Anti-Semitism especially was a woolly, almost abstract concept to most, a debating term divorced from an Englishman's everyday experience of the world. William Joyce, for example, never met a Jew until he was a student in London in the 1920s, and the first time he encountered one wearing a yellow star on his coat, in Berlin, he felt deeply perturbed. All but the most backward British fascists, then, would have been appalled to think that their views, in another country, in another context, could lead to the systematic murder of six million people.

As for Joyce's treachery to his adopted country, well, it is possible, with some effort, to regard aspects of this in an almost sympathetic light. The cloven hoof of fascism, as the left-wing thinker Cyril Joad called it, was protruding from beneath Joyce's coat from his teenage years onwards. He never wavered in his loyalty to his chosen cause, even when it would have made his life a lot easier to do so. The doggedness with which he stuck to his convictions does not render them any less repellent, of course, but it does suggest that the man was prideful and steadfast.

Equally he was sincere, and correct, in his warnings about what he called the 'Red Menace' threatening Europe, a term that was to catch on during the Cold War. And he always regarded himself as a patriotic Englishman, believing from the early 1930s onwards that it was in the best interests of the British Empire to form an alliance with Germany against the forces of world communism. He made a grotesque mistake. He chose evil over good; the damnation of Nazi tyranny over the salvation of British liberal democracy and freedom. And in doing so he committed that most icy of sins, treason. Yet I'm not sure even this constitutes 'depravity' in the Aristotelian sense.

The tragic hero, Aristotle stated, was not 'pre-eminently virtuous and just', rather he was guilty of *hamartia* or an error of judgement. 'For it is the perpetual tragic irony of the Tragedy of Life that again and again men do laboriously contrive their own annihilation, or kill the thing they love . . . For the most poignant tragedy of human life is the work of human blindness – the Tragedy of Errors.' Joyce's decision to lie about his true nationality in his application for a British passport in 1933 was a fatal error. As the historian A. J. P. Taylor wrote, he was hanged for making a false statement when applying for a passport, the usual penalty for which was a £2 fine.

Aristotle also believed that the tragic hero must undergo a *peripeteia*, or turning point. The manner in which the young Joyce acquired the scar on his cheek – a Jewish communist, he claimed, slashed him with a razor – certainly provides this. The hero must also have a tragic flaw to his character, such as *hubris*, an overweening self-confidence which leads him to disregard a divine warning or to violate an important moral law. The proud and arrogant Joyce had plenty of *hubris*. It was the reason he became, as a teenager in Ireland, an informer for the Black and Tans (the despised auxiliaries with whom the British tried to quash Irish insurgency). It was the reason, too, that he became a ruthless street fighter and celebrated soapbox orator during his time as deputy to Sir Oswald Mosley.

It was also the reason he found phenomenal fame and notoriety in Berlin, when, along with Churchill, Hitler and Tommy Handley, he became one of the best-known radio voices of the Second World War. Such was Joyce's 'vaulting ambition' he took sole credit for the Lord Haw-Haw persona, regardless of the consequences, when, to begin with, Haw-Haw was in fact a composite of several broadcasters.

In almost every tragedy there is an atmosphere of doom from the beginning: the prologue assures us that all will not end happily; that what is willed by the characters is itself part of a larger will, something already written. The tragic hero must undergo an *anagnorisis*, or moment of discovery about this predestiny. Chillingly, one of Joyce's teachers at school predicted: 'That boy will either do something very great in the world, or he will finish on the end of a rope.' Joyce himself had many presentiments on this subject, from the mid-1930s onwards. He used to refer sardonically to the drinks cabinet in the corner of his Berlin office as the 'Hanging Judge', his own personal pub. This *anagnorisis* criterion, then, was met on a number of levels. And it culminated in an entry he wrote in his diary in Hamburg on 22 April 1945, just days before the British army captured the city: 'I realised this morning so clearly that in the eyes of Englishmen, I have forfeited all claim to live in their land or consider myself English. I am sorry; for I have now nothing left. Long before Germany's defeat became certain, I knew that I could never be at home here. Has it all been worthwhile? I think not. National Socialism is a fine cause, but most of the Germans, not all, are bloody fools. England means so much to me, and now I am old. Well, in that spirit, I can take any punishment that is coming to me, but I am sorry for Margaret, whose outlook is quite different.' Hitler identified himself with the German people, though in his final days he considered them weak and unworthy of him. Joyce had no such fantasy to comfort him. He was a mongrel. He could no more identify himself with the German people than he could the American, Irish or British.

At the end of a Greek tragedy, order must be restored to the kingdom through a cleansing, or *catharsis*. This was Aristotle's final criterion and Joyce – a scapegoat of sorts – satisfied it the moment he stepped up to the gallows.

The tragic hero must fall to disaster, then, through a combination of personal failing and circumstances with which he cannot deal. But, as

Aristotle knew, he would most effectively evoke both our pity and terror if he was neither thoroughly good nor thoroughly evil, but a mixture of both. Even Macbeth and Richard III, for all their determination to be villains, are not outside our sense of humanity's range. They have redeeming qualities: a certain dignity and courage when forced to confront their own mortality; a glimmer of nobility, even. And Joyce had these, too. There are several accounts of how he would continue working at his desk during air raids on Berlin, seemingly indifferent to the bombs falling around him. At his trial he showed no self-pity; on the contrary, he was calm and stoical, declining to pass the blame or deny his motives. When the hour of his death came, he met it with a steady eye.

He accepted, too, with ironic detachment, the contradictory ways in which he had been caricatured in the British press: as either a puny, monocled ass of the Bertie Wooster type, or a sneering Nazi bully boy for whom hanging was too merciful a punishment. He also accepted the mythic status granted him by the jittery British public. Nearly everyone from the war generation has a Haw-Haw story, often involving the clock in their town hall running a quarter of an hour slow – detailed information, of course, that could only have reached the diabolical Haw-Haw through his network of fifth columnists and spies. Almost always these stories are apocryphal. Few if any Haw-Haw rumours had their origins in any German broadcasts. They were the manufacture of war nerves, arising spontaneously. Curiously, it always seemed to be the most remote and boring English villages which Haw-Haw declared would be bombed to oblivion. In the fevered summer of 1940, for example, when a German invasion looked imminent, Newton Poppleford in Devon was, according to one Home Office report, 'a hotbed of Haw-Haw rumours'. In other parts of the country, depriving the sweet-toothed English of their pleasures seems to have been a Luftwaffe priority: in Keynsham, near Bristol, for instance, production at the Fry's chocolate factory ground to a halt after a rumour began that Haw-Haw had said: 'By the way, we know all about Fry's!' And in November 1940, Mr J. E. Faber, Managing Director of British Fondants Ltd of East Molesey in Surrey, telephoned the Ministry of Information in London to enquire about supposed threats made by Lord Haw-Haw to his confectionery business. Workers at the Chivers Jam factory in Cambridge, meanwhile, were convinced they had been 'promised a visit'.

Few people have been so mythologized in their own lifetime as Lord Haw-Haw. And few have been as paradoxical as William Joyce. As Maxwell Knight, the head of B5(b), an autonomous department within MI5, wrote in a secret report in 1934: 'William Joyce is certainly a very complex character.' Knight would know. He was pretty complex himself: an anti-Semitic bisexual oddity who kept dozens of wild animals in his house, including a bushbaby, a bear and several snakes and parrots. Knight, on whom Ian Fleming is thought to have based the character 'M' in the James Bond novels, had an intriguing friendship with Joyce.

Behind the crude Haw-Haw caricature was a man of subtlety, texture and wild contradiction. Joyce could rant, lose his temper and be obnoxious, but he could also be polite, thoughtful and amiable. His lawyers and prison guards, for example, all confessed to having been beguiled by him, and he inspired intense loyalty in his friends. He had a first in English from London University. His passions in life were Wagner, chess and the poetry of Dryden, Shelley and Tennyson, which he could and would quote effortlessly, at length, from memory. Yet he was an unthinking racist bigot.

Joyce was a stranger to self-doubt and angst, and could be volatile, boorish and bloody minded. But he was also whimsical, impulsive and insanely optimistic, not only about the outcome of the war – even after D-Day – but also about his doomed appeal to the House of Lords as he awaited execution. As a soapbox orator he was said to be electrifying. As a broadcaster, he could be both droll and hypnotic. He had a tender side, too, as the copious love letters he wrote to Margaret from his condemned cell show.

Above all, Joyce was an eccentric, a textbook example of one, in fact. Literally, the word eccentric means off centre, or outside the circle, and, according to Dr David Weeks, a clinical neuropsychologist who has done extensive research into eccentricity, nearly all true eccentrics have the following characteristics in common: they are nonconforming, quixotic, intelligent and curious (in addition to the academic areas he specialized in, Joyce acquired a certain expertise in anatomy, chemistry and Old Norse). Eccentrics are opinionated, outspoken and happily obsessed with one or more hobbyhorses, convinced that they are right and that the rest of the world is out of step. They are, moreover, not interested in the opinions of others (Joyce once said he found cocktail parties boring because he always knew what other guests were going to say before they said it). From an early age eccentrics know that they are different. They are prone to use their own words and spellings (Joyce would refer to Christtide instead of Christmas, and would often use a Germanic 'k' instead of 'c', as in sarkastik, or a 'kw' instead of a 'qu', as in kwarrel. Like his more famous and very distant cousin James Joyce, he simply preferred his own spellings). Eccentrics also tend to be scruffy, unembarrassable, healthy, and unmotivated by greed (Joyce was completely indifferent to money). They are usually the eldest or an only child (Joyce was both, in a way, because he was six before he had a sibling). They are aware that others find them strange, but they don't really care. In addition, they have the sort of buoyant positivism that comes from being comfortable in their own skin.

And eccentrics, Weeks believes, are always possessed of a mischievous sense of humour. William Joyce suffered from what he himself termed 'compulsive levity'. When a woman heckler at a Blackshirt rally shouted out: 'You're a right bastard!' Joyce didn't miss a beat. He gave a cheery wave and said: 'Thank you, Mother.' To make Margaret laugh, he would goosestep around their bathroom in Berlin. In his expression of red-meat political views he was like a shock-jock: tasteless, rude and often funny. But Joyce also belonged to a British satirical tradition which dated back to Defoe, Swift and Hogarth. He would refer to 'that liquorish stick de Gaul', and to Churchill as that 'caterwauling snake with an Oedipus complex'. George VI and Elizabeth he memorably called 'your stammering King and your bandy-legged Queen'. His motto, he once said, was never give offence unintentionally.

Joyce couldn't help devising childish nicknames for places and people. He dubbed the Funkhaus (the Reichsrundfunkhaus, the German equivalent of the BBC's Broadcasting House) the Skunk House. He renamed Ribbentrop, Ribbontripe. Mosley, the Leader, he called the Bleeder. Sir Hartley Shawcross, the Attorney-General prosecuting at his trial, became Hotcross Buns. He was ruder about the judge: he called Mr Justice Tucker, Mr Justice 'Ucker. He used a similar abbreviation to describe Hunt, the policeman who testified at his trial.

As his day in court approached, Joyce's dry sense of humour did not desert him. When his legal advisers visited him in prison, the question was discussed whether he should exercise his right to challenge any Jewish jurors who might be called to the Old Bailey.

'How does one know them?' Joyce asked.

'Oh, when they take the oath they put on a hat or put their hand on their head,' he was told.

'I see,' Joyce said. 'Well, if six of them do it, wouldn't it be a good idea if I took the oath the same way?'

Greek tragedies usually contain moments of tragicomedy. It follows, then, that it wasn't always Joyce who was making the mischief, but the gods who were toying with him for their sport. Joyce was such an English patriot, for example, that when he briefly joined the British army in the early 1920s, his fellow soldiers would amuse themselves by whistling 'God Save the King' whenever he was lying on his barrack-room bed. He would always jump off it and stand to attention. And when he first moved to Berlin the same thing happened, only with 'Heil Hitler', the standard form of greeting at the time. In cafes he would stand to attention every time someone said Heil Hitler, which was every few minutes. Berliners, who would remain seated, looked on bemused. Later, in custody, Joyce had his false teeth confiscated and his scalp painted with a green scurf ointment. To his credit he saw the funny side of all this; he joked about his various indignities in his letters. Indeed he seems to have regarded his whole trial as an elaborate joke at his own expense.

Every tragic hero, or anti-hero, needs a heroine. This then is also the story of Margaret Cairns White, the rangy, auburn-haired woman who married Joyce, twice (they divorced and remarried in Berlin). Theirs was a complicated relationship, romantic and passionate at times, violent at others. She would characterize him as her sexual slave; he would describe his love for her as pathological. When referring to each other, they used affectionate nicknames: he called her Mother-Sheep, a reference to a Shakespearian sonnet. She called him the Old Ram. She would stand up to him in arguments, mock him and sexually torment him, and he in turn would sometimes lose his temper, verbally abuse her and even, very occasionally, hit her. Often when he dithered she would be the one to push him into a decision, as was the case when they couldn't decide whether to go to Dublin or Berlin on the eve of war. As can be revealed for the first time in this book, they were very much partners in crime. Lady Haw-Haw's propaganda work for the Nazis was much more extensive than has previously been assumed. She began broadcasting in October 1939 and continued until April 1945. Her commitment to fascism ran nearly as deep as her husband's; and MI5 considered her to be just about as much a traitor.

The Joyces became a celebrity couple in Berlin. Both had affairs. Both were partial to schnapps and opium. Hitler awarded him the Cross of War Merit, her the Civil Merit Medal. William once wrote in a letter to Margaret that he was Tristan to her Isolde. (Wagner's opera is about the stoical importance of a good death in a godless world: death as an expression of love.) But actually, a better comparison might be with Bonnie and Clyde. Margaret and William were, after all, outlaws in the end, hiding out on the Danish border for nearly a month after the war ended, on the run from the British army.

In one of its reports on her, MI5 rather coyly described Margaret Joyce as 'an extremely attractive woman'. Like her husband she was a rather nonchalant, flippant character, who also had a fiery side and could drink most people under the table. But she was more bohemian than he. More capricious. More flirtatious, too — indeed she was described by one of her former colleagues at the Funkhaus as 'a rather fast woman' and by MI5 as a 'good time girl', for which read 'promiscuous'. She craved distraction. She loved to dance. She was easily bored and prone to bouts of listlessness. When she was interned at the end of the war, the exasperated commander in charge of her camp notified MI5: 'Margaret Joyce has a biting tongue with a very good control of language. She is a very strongly sexed woman who demands notice and attention and would not hesitate to use her sex to get what she wants. She is a good actress. She has never shown any sign of cracking.'

In many ways, the lives of William and Margaret Joyce are manna to a biographer. Margaret told her story through her (unpublished) memoirs, as well as through the daily diaries she kept throughout the war and the extensive interviews she gave to her interrogator and later confidant John Alfred Cole, a British army officer, while interned in Germany after the war. Joyce's best friend and business partner Angus Macnab left behind what amounted to a William Joyce archive of notes and manuscripts and these now form part of Sheffield University Library's Special Collection. Also held at Sheffield are the reminiscences of A. K. Chesterton, a cousin of the novelist G. K. Chesterton, who knew the Joyces well from their Blackshirt days. He wrote vivid unpublished accounts of their last months in London and their first in Berlin. Many of the other central players in

Joyce's life wrote memoirs or diaries, notably Sir Oswald Mosley and Josef Goebbels, his mentors; Commander Burt, the man who charged him; Lord Shawcross, the man who prosecuted him; and Albert Pierrepoint, the man who executed him. The most evocative account of Joyce's wartime life is to be found in the epic *Berlin Diary* written by the American CBS correspondent William Shirer. More recently, intriguing new light has been shed on Joyce's formative years in Ireland by the Irish author and journalist Mary Kenny. In her book *Germany Calling* she reveals, among other things, that the IRA had attempted to assassinate Joyce when he was fifteen. The most vivid account of Joyce's trial was penned by Rebecca West for the *New Yorker* in 1946. In the same year, the Old Bailey published a full transcript of the trial as part of its Notable British Trials series. These accounts, then, form the bones of this book.

The flesh on them is provided by Joyce himself, in his own words, as recorded in his semi-autobiographical volume *Twilight Over England*, his newly declassified Berlin diaries, held by the National Archives–Public Record Office, his broadcasts and the hundred and fifty or so letters he wrote in prison. A person's self-identity, even the extent to which they reinvent themselves for the outside world, is central to any psychological portrait. Joyce's view of himself, then, forms a significant part of this book. In Berlin, for instance, he seemed to be aware of his role as a player in an unfolding tragedy. He had a running joke with Eduard Dietze, his boss at the Reichsrundfunkhaus, that he had made a pact with the devil – that he was Faust to Dietze's Mephistopheles.

Life is breathed into this flesh by material, much of it previously unpublished, taken from the dozens of detailed files which MI5 kept on William and Margaret Joyce, which were declassified in 2000. In William's case, the files were compiled over a twenty-five-year period.

In addition to these sources I have been greatly helped in this book by conversations with Heather Iandolo, Joyce's daughter, born in 1928, who also allowed me to draw upon her archive, which includes copies of her father's prison letters. Although she is a devout Catholic, Heather occasionally visits synagogues to atone for her father's bigotry. Eerily, she resembles William Joyce, or rather, with her high cheekbones, she looks like how you imagine he might have looked had he grown old. Like him, she is a former schoolteacher with a very precise way of talking, and a wry sense of humour.

I have also talked to as many of the people connected with the Joyces' story as is still possible, including James Clark, an urbane man who bears a resemblance to the older Laurence Olivier. In his late teens he read the nightly news bulletins that preceded Lord Haw-Haw's broadcasts, indeed he sometimes even stood in for 'His Lordship', until he became disillusioned with Nazism in 1942 and was interned by the Germans for the remainder of the war. He was subsequently charged with treason at the Old Bailey and bound over to keep the peace for two years. Other contemporaries of the Joyces who helped me include Geoffrey Perry, the army officer who wounded Joyce as he was capturing him; Dame Vera Lynn, whose shows were broadcast by the BBC at the same time as Haw-Haw's, to try and lure listeners away; and the late Lady (Diana) Mosley, who, with the elegant bluntness for which she was known, suggested to me that: 'As Joyce was sentenced to death on a quibble I thought his "trial" was a disgraceful injustice. The authorities were determined to kill him, and it might have been more honourable to do so without the farce of a trial. War and justice cannot co-habit.'

My research has taken me to America, Ireland, Germany, Norway and, of course, Joyce's many haunts in England. In fact, when he first moved to London he lived across the Common from where I live now. And from the loft where I have my study, I can see the prison where he was hanged.

Sitting contemplating this prison I have sometimes asked myself whether William and Margaret Joyce are worthy subjects for a joint biography. Readers will have to make up their own minds, but I would say this: William's xenophobia was contemptible, certainly; and he was an odd fellow, no question: but I do find his story – and that of the feisty, funny temptress he married – enthralling.

And it is not just me, it seems. To this day, William Joyce retains a strange hold on the British national psyche, perhaps because he is still a useful hate figure, perhaps because the nation still feels a sense of guilt that he might have been hanged for the sake of vengeance rather than justice. At his treason trial, Sir Hartley Shawcross mocked Joyce with the words: 'I daresay that in the years to come in the pages of history it will count for nothing what happens to William Joyce in the course of this trial. He will leave no mark upon those pages.' Yet, in 1990, Sir Hartley was asked to write an entry for Joyce in the *Dictionary of National Biography*. He refused.

Four years later, the term Lord Haw-Haw was deemed unparliamentary language by the Speaker of the House of Commons, and so joined a list of banned terms including 'ruffian', 'Pharisee', 'cad', 'jackass' and 'Pecksniffian cant'. And as recently as 2002, Lord Haw-Haw topped the *Sun* newspaper's list of '100 Britons we love to hate', quite an achievement for a German who was born in America. William Joyce, I'm sure, would have been amused.

PART 1

CAPTURE

'I think, from the point of view of his own character and even of his consciousness of its need for salvation, the defeat of Germany and of himself were welcome experiences. After all, it was not England that had to be purged and chastened before salvation, it was William Joyce.'

Commander Leonard Burt of Scotland Yard,
the man who charged Lord Haw-Haw with high treason

PEMBROKE BRANCH TEL. 6689575

ONE

'You wouldn't happen to be William Joyce, would you?'

As the shadows lengthened on 28 May 1945, two British army officers drove their lorry deep into a forest on the Danish–German border, parked in a clearing and began gathering kindling for their stove. At first they ignored the weary-looking, underfed man who limped towards them out of the trees.

'*Excusez-moi,*' he called out, pointing his walking stick at some branches in a ditch. '*Il y en a encore des brindilles par ici.*'

One of the officers, Lieutenant Geoffrey Perry, was a young German-Jewish interpreter who had been advised to change his name, Horst Pinschewer, while serving with the Allies against the Nazis. Distractedly, he replied in German: '*Ja, ja. Danke.*'

The man was wearing a threadbare tweed suit. He had a dimpled chin, slicked-back hair that was shaved at the sides, and a deep scar running from the corner of his mouth to his right ear. Perry noticed this as the man smiled at him, picked up one end of a branch, dragged it over to the truck and tossed it in the back. He continued on his way but, after a few yards, stopped, turned and said, this time in English: 'Here are three or four more logs.'

The voice was clipped, refined, one of the most famous of the war. Captain Bertie Lickorish, the other officer, recognized it instantly. 'You know,' he whispered to Perry, 'that voice sounded terribly like Lord Haw-Haw.' The officers straightened their backs and eyed the man as he gathered up a log in both hands and began walking towards them again, muttering about the difference between coniferous and deciduous trees.

'When he reaches us,' Lickorish said quietly, 'ask him his name. I'll cover you.'

As the man tipped his load, Perry said simply: 'You wouldn't happen to be William Joyce, would you?'

Half turning round, the man delved into his trouser pocket with his left hand. Perry, thinking he was reaching for a gun, drew a Walther pistol he had confiscated a few weeks earlier, aimed low and shot him in the right buttock. A second shot glanced off the shoulder of his jacket. As he collapsed to the ground clutching his backside, the man moaned: 'My name is Hansen.' He withdrew his hand from his pocket to show that what he had in it was not a gun but a Reisepass. 'I'm not armed,' he said, his face contorted in pain. Lickorish grabbed the passport. It was, indeed, in the name of Wilhelm Hansen. Under occupation it read 'teacher'. The captain frisked the wounded man for weapons and found instead a Wehrpass, or service book, which showed that the man was a member of the Volkssturm, the German Home Guard. The name on it was William Joyce.

Lieutenant Perry's apparent trigger-happiness was understandable. It was four weeks since Adolf Hitler's death amid the rubble and carnage of Berlin. A month had also passed since the drunk yet philosophical Lord Haw-Haw made his final, slurring broadcast from Hamburg. In his last command, Hitler had handed control of what was left of the Third Reich to Grand Admiral Dönitz, who had already transferred the government rump from Berlin to Flensburg, a naval dockyard in the north of Germany overlooked by a medieval castle. Considered quaint because of its quays, kiosks and tree-lined fiords, Flensburg was the last Nazi bolthole. The streets were crowded with staff cars filled with German officers. From the North Sea to the Baltic, the Danish frontier was closed. Perry and Lickorish had been ordered to stay out of Flensburg, which was why they were patrolling the forests around the town rather than going in.★

★ The Dönitz Government was short-lived, effectively ending on 23 May, the day Dönitz was formally arrested. When he and his batman came down with his luggage packed, the arresting British officer said: 'You're not going on holiday, you know. You're going to prison. You have the choice of one suitcase.' Dönitz chose badly. When his luggage was examined at Luxembourg it contained nothing but vests and underpants.

The whole border area had been full of senior Nazis on the run, many of them armed and fanatical enough to want to die fighting. A week earlier, Heinrich Himmler had committed suicide not far from the forest where Perry and Lickorish were collecting firewood. Indeed William and Margaret Joyce had seen the SS leader passing through their hotel lobby just days before he died. Himmler had been captured in disguise: he had shaved off his moustache and donned a sergeant major's uniform and an eyepatch. He had been searched and stripped. A British doctor, still not satisfied, had taken him over to a window to look more closely into his mouth. Immediately Himmler bit on the tiny cyanide capsule hidden there and died within a minute. Admiral von Friedeburg, the man who had signed the surrender on the Western Front, had also recently killed himself nearby. After being captured he had gone back to his quarters under escort to get clothes. While there, he had asked permission to go to the lavatory. Before his escort realized what was happening, von Friedeburg had locked himself in. They broke down the door to find he had taken poison. He, too, was dead within a minute.

Joyce must have been aware of these cases because as he lay on the ground he composed himself and said to Perry: 'I suppose in view of recent suicides, you were expecting me to reach for a phial of poison? Don't worry, I'm not that sort of person. I ask for one favour, will you tell my wife what happened?'

The officers, impressed by Joyce's sangfroid, administered first aid: an army-issue bandage pad. Because it had been fired at such close range, the bullet had passed through both buttocks, leaving four wounds. Lickorish asked again if William had a gun. 'Yes,' Joyce said. 'But I left it under my pillow.' The two officers then lifted their prisoner into the back of the truck, carefully laying him face down on the twigs and branches. 'I felt rather sorry for him, actually,' Perry said later. 'I asked him what he was doing in the wood. He said he'd had a row with his wife.' They returned to their camp a short drive away and handed him over to the Military Police.

The capture of Lord Haw-Haw could not have been more poignant or more appropriately tragi-comic. Goebbels' most famous broadcaster, the 'superpropagandist' as he was known, the wag who, during the blackout, had been a laughing stock to some, a fiend to others, had been rumbled by a man called Bertie Lickorish out collecting firewood. He had, moreover, been shot in the buttocks by a Jew, a cruel irony for an anti-Semite.

The Joyces were among the last on the 'most wanted list' to be captured – Speer, Keitel and Jodl having all been rounded up along with Dönitz. They had been getting by on starvation rations for three weeks as they kept low profiles, changing addresses, going for long walks in the woods around the Danish border. They had even crossed the border at one stage, only to turn back when they heard that the British were already in Denmark. They had disguised themselves to get back through the border checkpoint: William had worn a major's greatcoat, Margaret the jacket of a woman signals auxiliary. As they crossed over into Germany the guard nevertheless recognized them and said with a grin: 'Ach! The Family Haw-Haw!'

Back in the German countryside they had found a certain tranquillity in their predicament, enjoying the spring sunshine after a hellish winter spent among the black, smouldering ruins of Berlin. According to Margaret, William was being 'very sweet'. They would sit for hours on the soft pine needles in the forests, talking, reflecting, waiting. Margaret had an idea for a novel set in Berlin. William began writing a book about the war. They listened to BBC news reports on the wireless. One afternoon a fortnight before their capture they met two British soldiers and William played a game of what he called Russian roulette with them: he struck up a conversation with them in English. They were, according to an entry Margaret made in her diary, 'very angry about the Blitz, bug bombs and Buchenwald.' The Joyces had been told by Goebbels' staff that they would be transported first to Copenhagen then across the narrow sea to neutral Sweden. Their ultimate plan was to try to get to Ireland. But the British had occupied Denmark and the back door to Sweden had closed. Lord and Lady Haw-Haw had been trapped.

Lieutenant Perry felt a mixture of awe and fear when he came face to face with this particular famous Nazi. More than the other remote figures in black uniforms and jackboots, Joyce had come to personify the enemy. On the Home Front nearly as many people had listened to Lord Haw-Haw's broadcasts as to the BBC. He had become a British national institution. Even the young princesses used to listen to him. Like everyone else they considered him a national joke, a figure of fun; he was, after all, much parodied by comedians. His broadcasts, it was said, were designed to lower British morale but instead had the effect of cheering everyone up. But that was only half the story. During the dark days of the Blitz the laughter had been uneasy. Haw-Haw had got under people's skin. Preternatural powers had been attributed to him. His agents were thought to be so widespread they could keep every public clock in Great Britain under constant supervision, and report back to Berlin instantly with unnerving details of any that were running fast or slow. Haw-Haw had, it was said, accurately predicted British troop movements as well as the postings of minor civil servants. He had also commanded the Luftwaffe to target cities according to his whim. Everyone claimed they had heard him mention their town or village by name, even if, when pressed, they would admit that they hadn't actually heard the broadcast themselves but rather had heard about it from a friend, or a friend of a friend. In other words, Lord Haw-Haw had been mythologized in the public imagination. Perry was not going to take any chances with such an omnipotent enemy.

Less understandable is Joyce's reason for speaking to Perry and Lickorish in his unmistakable aristocratic – or rather fake-Oxbridge – drawl, and thereby effectively giving himself up. He could surely have lain low for a couple of years and disappeared into a neutral country. It may be that, with his appetite for mischief, he had been playing another game of roulette with himself. Or perhaps it was because punishment is the only cure for a guilty conscience. More likely, he wanted, consciously or unconsciously, to be captured in order to make a martyr of himself. As a student of the romantic poets, he wanted to fulfil what he saw as his destiny. He wanted to play the tragic hero, to be heroic, to be Miltonic. This would be the prelude to his final dramatic scene.

Later that night, Joyce was given the news he had been dreading. His wife Margaret had also been arrested. She – a slim, well-spoken, handsome, thirty-three-year-old with auburn hair cut in a bob – had gone out to the forest looking for her husband when he had not returned. She had even bleated like a lost sheep, their pet signal to each other.

A lieutenant, supported by ten soldiers, two Bren carriers and a lorry, had turned up at the house where she and Joyce had been staying for the past week. It was in the hamlet of Kupfermühle, a short walk from the forest (the soldiers had soon found out from the locals where their mysterious English prisoner had been living). They asked if she was Mrs Joyce. She bowed by way of an answer. They then described the man they had just arrested and asked if that was her husband. Thinking William might have tried using his false passport, Margaret said she didn't think it sounded like him. They then told her he had admitted who he was. Margaret's voice was clipped and round-vowelled. In her broadcasts as Lady Haw-Haw she sounded like the actress Celia Johnson. 'We've been expecting this to happen for weeks,' she said to the officer who arrested her, 'so we mustn't make a fuss about it now.'

A search of drawers, overcoat pockets and tweed trousers revealed 9,635 German Reichsmarks, 1,280 Swiss francs, 500 US dollars, 65 Danish kroner and 10 Russian roubles. (The Reichsmarks were valueless because trading in them was by then illegal. But during the war they would have been worth about £500. The Swiss francs and US dollars would have been worth a total of £192 18s 11d. The total value of their savings in today's money would be about £13,000.)

The arresting officers also found two typewriters and two packed cardboard suitcases. Each was tipped out onto the bed and itemized. Margaret's included a swastika ring, a bottle of pills, a pair of spectacles, a sewing set, a diary, a 7.65mm automatic with eight rounds, and 150 snapshots (some of her in swimming costume, others of athletic-looking German soldiers in their swimming trunks posing at the Berlin lidos). There was also an edition of Shakespeare, a collection of poetry, some American newspaper cuttings about Lord Haw-Haw and a copy of *Lord Haw-Haw of Zeesen*, a spoof biography illustrated with cartoons. This was written by Jonah Barrington, the *Daily Express* journalist who had coined the name Haw-Haw on 18 September 1939.★

Her husband's suitcase contained neatly folded shirts (blue), trousers (checked), singlet (white), pullover (grey) and pyjamas (striped). There was also a pair of metal foot supports, one box of condoms, three phials of Redexon vitamins, a ten-pfennig piece, a box of digestive tablets, a nail file, two odd slippers, two hair brushes, two tooth brushes, one enamelled mug, a tin of toothpaste, three German tobacco coupons, shaving soap and razor, a metal ashtray, six soft collars, one stiff collar, three hair slides and a Smith & Wesson revolver with five rounds of ammunition. There

---

★ Barrington wrote: 'A gent I'd like to meet is moaning periodically from Zeesen. He speaks English of the haw-haw, dammit-get-out-of-my-way variety, and his strong suit is gentlemanly indignation.'

were also slim editions of Marlowe and Horace, and two other books: *Portrait of a Village*, and *Armies of the Revolution*.

Whatever their motivation for treachery, it certainly hadn't been material gain. All the Joyces' worldly goods were meticulously listed, and many of them then promptly disappeared into the pockets of souvenir-hunting soldiers. Even Margaret's stockings were taken.

The only possession she had been able to grab as she was led out of the house was a fur coat and, wrapped in this, despite the warm weather, she was brought to the same guard house as Joyce. No sooner had she sat down than a door was opened and soldiers emerged carrying Joyce on a stretcher. As the party passed, he looked up and smiled ruefully. Margaret gave an uncertain wave and, as he reached the door, she called out, 'Erin go bragh' – Ireland forever. He was placed in a waiting ambulance. It was the last they were to see of each other for six months. Both had wanted to make amends. They had had an argument, which is why Joyce had gone for his walk on his own. That night in her diary Margaret wrote: 'Quarrelled with Will and let him go out alone and he was arrested and shot at. I was arrested with all the Asmussens [the family they were staying with], but they let them go. Some of the officers came to jeer at me, but some were nicer.'

This economic entry did not convey the extent of her indignities that night. In making light of them she seems to have been playing up to an English stereotype: grace under pressure. The riddle of her citizenship would prove almost impossible for the authorities to solve, but, for the moment, she was content to play at being the phlegmatic Englishwoman. She was taken to the police station in Flensburg and put in a cell which had recently been vacated by Himmler. All it had was a decaying mattress on the floor. A hastily scribbled sign had been stuck on the door which described the occupant as Mrs Hansen, alias Mrs William Joyce. Under 'reason for arrest' on her charge sheet it read: 'Danger to security'.

The guard on duty in the station that night entered Margaret's cell and stared. After a while he said: 'I just wanted to see what a traitoress looked like.' Other soldiers craned their heads around the cell door. 'Come on in, gentlemen,' Margaret said. 'Have a good gawp.' One soldier asked if she felt guilty about Belsen. Like the majority of Germans, she replied, she knew nothing about it. The soldiers shuffled to one side as a major and an army chaplain entered the cell. The major looked around, sniffed the air and told her that she reeked. The chaplain asked her when she had married Joyce – assuming that she had, that is. Margaret gathered her fur coat around her and said that unless he put his questions in a more becoming manner, she would refuse to answer them. She then requested a glass of water. The major ordered the guard to make sure it was laced with typhus, like the water the inmates of Belsen were forced to drink. Margaret looked at him impassively and asked: 'Don't you mean typhoid?' At this the major lost his temper, called her a bitch and shouted: 'I should knock your pretty teeth out for saying that.'

'I don't mind if you hate me,' Margaret countered, 'so long as you do it politely.'*

For several hours, a steady procession of soldiers came to stare at her. When they eventually left her alone, almost alone, she began to weep. As she was on suicide watch, a guard had to sit in her cell and watch her as she slept. A female guard was assigned to keep an eye on her when she visited the lavatory.

William Joyce was taken to the 74th British General Hospital, a red-brick block close to the British Second Army Headquarters in Lüneburg, near Hamburg, a seven-hour drive away. By now news of his arrest had filtered out. Soldiers, some with cameras, crowded around the ambulance, hoping for a glimpse of the demonic aristocrat with the sinisterly funny voice. At 5 feet 6 inches, Joyce was shorter than everyone had imagined. Lying on a stretcher, with a grey blanket draped over him, wearing blue-and-white-striped pyjamas, he wasn't quite as dapper as everyone thought he would be, either. For one thing, he wasn't wearing the monocle which cartoonists had always depicted him with. And his face, though pallid and gaunt, wasn't contorted into a permanent sneer, as folklore suggested it would be. In fact his face appeared sunken because his false teeth had been confiscated in case they contained a secret cyanide capsule – and this made him look much older than his thirty-nine years. As he was being carried in to the hospital some of the soldiers began taunting him with shouts of 'Jairminny Calling! Jairminny Calling!' His comeback silenced them, briefly: 'In civilized countries wounded men are not used for peepshows.'

Diaries of the time capture the mood: part indignation, part amusement that Lord Haw-Haw had been caught with his trousers down. The Countess

---

* This episode was related to the author by a source who wishes to remain anonymous.

of Ranfurly records: 'After dinner we were joined by Mr Sulzburger [sic] of the *New York Times* who had just returned from Russia. We had a laugh over Lord Haw-Haw being captured.'

'WE'VE GOT HAW-HAW!' was the banner headline in the *Star* on 29 May. 'CAUGHT IN MANHUNT: WIFE, TOO.' At least the *Star* accepted Margaret *was* Joyce's wife. Most papers described her as 'a woman who claims to be his wife' as if they thought it impossible that people as depraved as the Joyces could actually be married. Some described the nine-year-old dress she was wearing as being an item 'that would have caused women to turn round and admire her had she walked down Regent Street'. The papers were scandalized by the comforts she was afforded. The *Daily Express* and *Daily Mirror* especially made much of the fact that she had been allowed a volume of Shakespeare from her bag.

Brigadier Roscoe Harvey was the first to interview Margaret Joyce. She was sent down to his headquarters on a nearby lake. 'When I got there I found a car drawn up with a British officer and this bird,' Harvey was to recall. He approached her and said: 'I hear you're Mrs Joyce?'

'Yes.'

'What nationality are you?'

'I think a wife takes her nationality from her husband,' she said with a raised eyebrow. 'But I understand that there is considerable doubt what nationality my husband is.'

The next day, Lieutenant Perry flew to London on compassionate leave: his father had had a heart attack. At the airport he was repeatedly asked for his autograph. He also gave an impromptu interview to the press which he later discovered ruined his chances of receiving an MBE – Field Marshal Montgomery quashed a recommendation for one on the grounds that Perry had not asked permission to talk to journalists.

Margaret, meanwhile, was taken to Lüneburg, where she made a formal statement to Captain William Skardon of MI5. 'I came to Germany on 26 August 1939,' she said, 'having left England because I felt that, as I was morally unable to assist in Britain's war effort, it would be unfair to remain in the country. Having observed England's attitude since Munich in 1938, I regarded the outbreak of war as inevitable. It was my opinion that a war between Britain and Germany would be a national tragedy for both nations and did not regard it as a war against two opposing nations but against opposing political faiths . . . While in Germany I worked for the Reichsrundfunkgesellschaft [the RRG, the German equivalent of the BBC]. From September 1939 until April 1945 I have written and spoken talks but have always refrained from making attacks on the British people . . . I did of course attack British politicians with whose views I profoundly disagreed. The RRG authorities provided me with false papers and offered me assistance to get out of Germany but, as proved to be the case, I thought that my chances of leaving the country were very small and therefore fully expected to be arrested by the British authorities.'

On 31 May, with the pain from his wounds ebbing, it was William Joyce's turn to be visited by Captain Skardon. The officer introduced himself and came straight to the point. He had already been to the radio station in Hamburg and there he had found records of Joyce's employment, his salary slips, his diaries and typed notes from his talks. He had also visited Joyce's flat in Berlin and found Joyce's order of the Cross of War Merit (first class) signed by Hitler in facsimile. 'I am charged with the duty of making enquiries into the activities of British subjects employed by the enemy during the course of the war,' Skardon said. 'There is abundant evidence to show that you have been working for the German Broadcasting Services, and it is proposed to present a case to the Director of Public Prosecutions.'

The officer cautioned Joyce but he brought no charge, largely because the authorities in Britain were still trying to work out what they could actually charge him with. From his hospital bed, he answered Skardon's questions as best he could and, after a break for lunch, he dictated a statement which, judging by its fluency, he had rehearsed many times in his head.

'I was in Ireland from 1909 to 1921,' it began. 'I acquired German nationality on 26 September 1940. I take this opportunity of making a preliminary statement concerning the motives which led me to come to Germany and to broadcast to Britain over the German radio service. I was actuated not by the desire for personal gain, material or otherwise, but solely by political conviction. I was brought up as an extreme Conservative with strong Imperialist ideas but, very early in my career, namely in 1923, became attracted to fascism and subsequently National Socialism . . . One of my dominant beliefs was that a war between Britain and Germany would be a tragedy, the effects of which Britain and the British Empire would not survive . . . When in August 1939 the final crisis emerged I felt that the question of Danzig [the German name for Gdansk in Poland] offered no just cause for a world war ... It remained my undeviating purpose to attempt as best I could to bring about a reconciliation, or at least an understanding, between the two countries ... I became certain that Britain, even though gaining a military triumph over the Germans, would in the event be confronted with a situation far more dangerous and complicated than that which existed in August 1939 and thus until the very last moment I clung to my hope of an Anglo-German understanding, although I could see that the prospects thereof were small.'

He concluded: 'I know that I have been denounced as a traitor and I resent the accusation as I conceive myself to have been guilty of no underhand or deceitful act against Britain, although I am also able to understand the resentment that my broadcasts have, in many quarters, aroused. Whatever opinion may be formed at the present time with regard to my conduct, I submit that the final judgment cannot be properly passed until it is seen whether Britain can win the peace. Finally I would like to stress the fact that in coming to Germany and in working for the German radio system my wife was powerfully influenced by me. She protests to the contrary but I am sure that if I had not taken this step she would not have taken it either.'

The intelligence officer read the statement over and gave it to the prisoner to sign. It was intriguing for several reasons: first, it reflected Joyce's belief that he was a patriot rather than a traitor. Secondly, it shows the store he placed upon consistency: whatever else he might be accused of he wasn't politically fickle. He had believed in fascism since 1923 and had never wavered, indeed he thought to be a conscientious objector would be hypocritical. Third, most of the two hundred or so British renegades who had been rounded up after the war, some of whom had broadcast propaganda or joined the British Free Corps, a Waffen-SS unit composed entirely of British subjects, said they had changed sides to spy on the Germans or to sabotage German propaganda. Joyce accepted his guilt unequivocally. Fourthly, the fate of his wife Margaret weighed heavily on his mind, and, as we shall see, was to have a great influence on the conduct of his trial.

Finally the statement is revealing in the one crucial fact it leaves out. One of the most notorious traitors in British history wasn't British at all. He was American.

TWO

'I'm not the thug people always think I am.'

By the time she was flown from Lüneburg to the military detention barracks in Brussels a week later, Margaret had firmed up her story. She was still wearing her fur coat but had no head scarf, and so when she was taken to the airport in an open-top jeep her hair was tousled. There were photographers waiting and, feeling sick at the prospect of flying, and looking dishevelled, she had to pose for them beside the jeep. Reporters noted that she was 'prinking her hair', taking it as a sign of her vanity. In fact it was a nervous gesture. She had only flown once before, from Oslo to Berlin in 1942, and she had hated the experience. The flight to Brussels proved to be a white-knuckle one. According to Robert Bruce, who was serving with the signals section of an RAF squadron at Wunstorf, the Dakota she was flying in was forced to do an emergency landing following 'engine trouble'. In due course, a car arrived at the guardhouse with 'a female prisoner' under army escort. 'Until the following morning it was my responsibility to look after the prisoner,' he later recalled. 'A cell with a bed and a table was found and Mrs Joyce was secured within. She was tall and thin and wearing a two-piece suit of tweed material. She had applied a liberal dash of perfume. I asked if she had eaten and when she said she hadn't I arranged for Spam, bread and tea to be sent to her cell. She then said that while she was in custody a guard was always present in case she used her knife for a suicide attempt. Accordingly I sat at the table and conversed with her. She revealed that although English by birth she was now a German citizen, as was her husband William Joyce, and she was confident they would be treated as such by British justice. She also said that in due course she and her husband would move on to South America. She spend a restless night and in the morning thanked me for our interesting conversation.'

Margaret was then flown the rest of the way to Brussels, where she was met by an escort of Military Police, two male and two female. When they escorted her to a cell in Forrest Prison on the Avenue Louise, she cooperated as best she could. She had learned to be polite to her captors. Had she known how many months she was to remain there, in solitary confinement, without being charged, she might not have gone so quietly.

Three days later, William Joyce, his wounds having responded well to penicillin, was also moved from Lüneburg to Brussels, though he wasn't told that his wife was already there. He did find out about his mother, though, from a *Daily Mail* article he was handed. It revealed that she had died in April. In fact she had died the previous September.

In a jaunty letter to Margaret, which wasn't delivered for a month, William described the conditions at the detention barracks: 'Main disadvantages are lack of sunlight and exercise, and having to sleep – or lie – on a board without mattress or pillow. No good for four wounds. But the food good and plentiful, while the NCOs, though they sound demented, are efficient, just and conscientious. As a glass-house, the place is A1.'

At times the flippant vernacular of Joyce's letters reads almost like a parody of P. G. Wodehouse, as if he had decided to play up to the Wooster stereotype that had been foisted upon him in his role as Lord Haw-Haw, the aristocratic fop. But it was fashionable at the time to play up to another stereotype, that of the Englishman in extremis who wore the mask, affected a stoical, ironically detached manner and kept the upper lip stiff. Tellingly, when Wodehouse himself was captured (by the Germans, in 1940), he described his prison in a tone similar to the one in which Joyce described his: 'Summing up my experience as a gaol-bird,' he wrote, 'I would say that prison is all right for a visit, but I wouldn't want to live there if you gave me the place. On my part there was no moaning at the bar when I left Loos. I was glad to go. The last I saw of the Alma Mater was the warder closing the door of the van and standing back with the French equivalent of "Right away". He said "Au revoir" to me – which I thought was a little tactless.'

Joyce remained in Brussels for a week, while the authorities in Britain continued to search for a charge that would hold up at trial. MI5 was especially worried. While searching the Joyces' flat in Berlin, Captain Skardon had also found papers proving that Joyce had been born in New York. It prompted T. M. Shelford of MI5 to write an anxious internal memo: 'If he is in fact only an American citizen and he became a naturalised German before the outbreak of war between the USA and Germany, he is not presumably a traitor?'

The reputations of government ministers as well as crown prosecutors were in the balance. If William Joyce was allowed to walk away from the Old Bailey a free man, there would almost certainly be a public outcry. The thirst for revenge against the Nazis had to be slaked. The dilemma of the British judiciary was straightforward enough. How do you try an American citizen for being a traitor to Britain? A rumour began to circulate that Joyce wasn't made a German citizen until 1943, in other words until after America had entered the war, and this offered some hope of a conviction. An MI5 report, written by Lieutenant Colonel Cussen, read: 'An acquittal whether at the Old Bailey, or by the Court of Criminal Appeal or House of Lords, must invariably create a public outcry, which no amount of legal argument will be able to silence. The only thing which might mollify the public would be if Joyce immediately on his acquittal were re-arrested for extradition to the USA on a charge of treason to be preferred there.'

But the hope offered by this rumour proved false. An MI5 investigation showed that Joyce had indeed, as he declared in his statement, become a German citizen in September 1940.

Pressure was also beginning to mount on the international stage. The Foreign Office was concerned about the reaction of the Soviet Union to an acquittal, as there had already been critical comment in the Soviet media concerning this and other treason cases. The pressure for a speedy resolution to the Lord Haw-Haw case was compounded by Fleet Street, which had now worked itself up into a frenzy of indignation: all the papers were demanding that Joyce be hanged. The Director of Public Prosecutions felt obliged to agree, suggesting that Joyce could be indicted for high treason. But the Attorney-General, Sir Donald Somerville, said he was 'incredulous' at the suggestion. There did not appear to be sufficient grounds or evidence for the charge, he argued. If any proceedings could be taken against Joyce, he went on, they would more reasonably be based upon breaches of the wartime Defence Regulations, for which he could then be given a fourteen-year prison sentence.

There was another hitch. The prosecution only had one witness, Albert Hunt, a detective inspector who had heard Joyce speak in his Blackshirt days before the war. Hunt admitted that he had never actually talked to Joyce but he claimed he recognized his voice the moment he heard him broadcasting, which was, he thought, 'within a month of the outbreak of the war' and so before the time Joyce became a German citizen. The Treason Act (1351), however, required two witnesses to testify to an act of treason. A new Attorney-General, Sir David Maxwell Fyfe, was appointed, as part of Churchill's 'caretaker' government in advance of the July general election. He was more sympathetic to public opinion, or at least to the demands of the newspapers which were baying for some war crimes trials. Maxwell Fyfe agreed to a change of the Treason Act (1351). It would become the Treason Act (1945). The main difference, conveniently enough, would be that the new Treason Act would require only one witness.

There was still some doubt, though, as to whether it was Joyce's voice that Hunt had heard. It emerged that when Jonah Barrington had written his celebrated description of Joyce as having an officer-and-gentleman voice of the haw-haw variety, he had actually been listening to another Englishman, Norman Baillie-Stewart. No matter. The chances were that the defence team would not press this point, especially as Joyce had already happily confessed to being a broadcaster *after* the first month of the war.

It fell to Commander Leonard Burt, 'Burt of the Yard' as he was better known, to bring Joyce home. Burt, a quiet, dignified man to whom villains tended to confess, was working for the Intelligence Corps, on secondment from the Murder Squad of Scotland Yard. His mother had lived in Southampton and had died of a stroke when the city was heavily bombed. She had been a regular listener to Joyce's broadcasts and Burt was convinced that these had contributed to her stroke because she said they made her 'worry all the time'. She couldn't help listening, she said when her son told her not to, because she found Joyce's voice so compelling.

Early on the morning of Saturday 16 June – the day after the new Treason Act (1945) had been given Royal Assent – a message arrived for Burt from Army Intelligence, Berlin: Joyce was to be collected from the transit military prison in Brussels. Three hours later, Burt was landing in the Belgian capital in a Dakota. Joyce was brought limping out of his cell. 'I'm here to take you to England, where you will be charged with high treason,' Burt said. 'Collect your belongings. The plane is waiting.'

'I am at your service, sir,' Joyce replied. He was not an impressive sight. He had developed a skin disease affecting his scalp, and to treat this his hair had been shaved off and he had been daubed in green ointment. The buttons on his threadbare blue suit had been removed in case he tried to choke himself on one. His confiscated dentures had not been returned. But Burt, despite his memories of his mother, took an instant liking to his prisoner. He found Joyce to be friendly, cooperative and coolly reconciled to his fate.

Burt decided not to use handcuffs. He had an armed guard with him, but they kept their distance. It was Burt who carried the wounded Joyce onto the plane. The two men sat together, smoking and staring out the window and, as Burt later recalled, 'talking as though we had been boyhood friends.' Joyce, for his part, later said he found Burt a 'singularly fine chap.' Soon after take-off, as they flew through a cloud wrack, they glimpsed a field of crosses where lay British soldiers who had been killed in the First World War. 'Madness,' Joyce said to Burt. 'England and Germany at war with each other, the two countries which should be closest together, in blood, ideals, ambitions – madness, I tell you.'

Halfway through the flight, one of the guards, sitting several seats behind, came shyly forward with his autograph book. Joyce thought for a moment before writing in a firm, right-sloping hand: 'We are about to pass over the white chalk cliffs, England's bulwark. It is a sacred moment in my life – and I can only say, whatever my fate may be, God bless Old England on the lea.' As the Channel glinted below them he turned to Burt and said: 'I have the courage of my convictions, you know. I can stand up to the consequences.'

'I like you for saying that,' Burt said.

'I'm not the thug people always think I am,' Joyce continued. 'I remember before the war if it came out in conversation that I'd got a first at London University, people wouldn't believe me. I could see them disbelieving me.' Moments later Joyce craned forward and said: 'Look! The White Cliffs of Dover!' before adding under his breath, 'God bless old England. God bless old England.'

At 3 p.m., as the plane was coming into land at Odiham, Hampshire, Joyce turned to Burt a final time and said: 'My wife had nothing to do with anything I did. I know you won't try and pin anything on her.'

When the plane came to a halt, Joyce stepped onto English soil for the first time since August 1939. Waiting at the bottom of the steps was Lieutenant Colonel Cussen of MI5 and Detective Sergeant Fletcher. Burt handed over a medical file including X-rays of Joyce's bullet wounds. The report said: 'Joyce complains of stiffness of legs and has difficulty bending them. He has mild seborrhoeic dermatitis of the scalp and a gun shot wound in his right thigh.' He was taken to Brixton Prison where he was weighed, measured and photographed.

The next day, Joyce's oldest and dearest friend, Angus Macnab, turned up at Bow Street Magistrates' Court asking to see him. The two men had not met since the one had waved goodbye to the other from Victoria Station en route to Dover and Berlin six years earlier. Macnab had spent three of the past six years interned; after that, he had served as a volunteer ambulance driver. When told a visit was out of the question, Macnab asked if he could leave Joyce some money, cigarettes and beer. He was told he couldn't do that either.

On Monday 18 June 1945, Joyce appeared at Bow Street. A crowd had been queuing up for several hours to see him and to get good seats in the public gallery. Press photographers and reporters were already there, some crowded onto tenement windows overlooking the court in the hope of taking pictures of Joyce walking around in the exercise yard at lunchtime. A whisper went around the crowd that he was not an Englishman at all, but a German. He was remanded in custody for a week. Although he still did not know where Margaret was, he wrote her a letter in which, referring to their pet names for each other, Mother-Sheep and Old Ram, he commented on the barristers' wigs, taking the sight of so many fleeces herded together as a sign of good fortune. He joked about appearing in the Bow Street dock and, referring to his shaved and painted head, said that one Special Branch officer had asked most sympathetically what the matter was.

Joyce seemed to enjoy this moment of farce. And he was determined to see the funny side of his injury. The bullet, he explained, went through both buttocks, and lodged on the outside of the left thigh without injuring any bone. This he deemed 'a close call.'

On 25 June, Joyce returned to the Magistrates' Court, this time represented by C. B. V. Head, a short, blond, hunchbacked solicitor working on legal aid from the firm of Ludlow & Co. Head briskly raised the question whether there was any case for Joyce to answer, if indeed he was an American subject – or had been, prior to his German naturalization. The only people, Head argued, who can commit treason are those who owe allegiance to the Crown, namely: a) British subjects by birth; b) the children of British subjects born abroad; c) naturalized British subjects; and d) aliens actually resident in the King's realm. Joyce was none of these. The prosecution had neither proved nor even attempted to prove that his father was a British subject when Joyce was born in New York in 1906. And it was legally and logically impossible for him, while he was in Germany, to commit high treason against the King, to whom he owed no allegiance whatever, once he had left the British Isles.

Head's arguments were brushed aside, and three days later, Joyce was committed for trial at the Central Criminal Court. Head appealed for an adjournment until September so that, among other things, a copy of Joyce's birth certificate could be sent over from the United States. This was granted. On the other side of the Atlantic, J. Edgar Hoover himself was asked to lead the FBI investigation into Joyce's US nationality.

MI5 was now taking it for granted that Margaret would be prosecuted. An internal memo about her stolen possessions noted: 'Unless her property can be traced, their loss may be the subject of comment in the press and at her trial.' But a Home Office memo to the Director of Public Prosecutions suggested that the process of charging Margaret was proving a legal head-ache: 'Is it proposed to prosecute Mrs Joyce in this country?' it asked. 'Would a visit by Mrs Joyce to her husband *cause legal embarrassment?* . . . Her British passport did not expire until 27 September 1943, unlike Joyce's [which expired in September 1940]. She made her first broadcast, according to her diary, on 3 October, 1939. She was awarded a War Service Medal by Hitler on 1 Sept, 44.'

Joyce, meanwhile, was visited in prison by his twenty-seven-year-old brother Quentin. They talked about the deaths of their parents, who had lived in Dulwich. William had heard vague details about his father, that he had supposedly died in a bombing raid in 1941, aged seventy-four, but now he heard the whole story: it hadn't been the bomb that killed his father. The family had heard the bomb coming and Joyce's sister Joan had said: 'This is ours!' Everyone had dived under the big table in the dining room. The ceiling fell in but everyone survived. The shock put a strain on his father's heart, though, and he had to give up his job, as a door-to-door vacuum-cleaner salesman, and died a few months later. The priest had refused to bury him until the press had withdrawn from the precincts of the church. Some papers had claimed he died of a broken heart, so ashamed of his son was he. Others made much of the irony that Lord Haw-Haw's father had died at the hands of the Luftwaffe. As for his mother, she had died of bronchitis and Quentin told his brother that her last words had been: 'Tell William I'll always be with him.' William said he was grateful his mother had been spared the ordeal of the trial. She was a brave and gallant woman, he concluded, but it was a kind providence that relieved her of this imposition.

Joyce told Quentin he was worried about his wife's whereabouts. Quentin duly wrote to Margaret. 'My dear Margaret, I know that your main source of anxiety will be over William. Well, as you may have heard by now I see him almost every day and his spirit is absolutely magnificent. I have always been considered a fairly cheerful sort of character myself; but by comparison with him I must appear a real Dismal Desmond. I was amazed by his cheerfulness and complete indifference to his immediate surroundings. His only worry was that he had not been able to get any news of you, and he was anxious for your sake.'

He need not have worried unduly about Margaret's material comforts: she had worked out a deal whereby she did her prison officer's darning in return for items procured on the Brussels black market. But William had good grounds to worry about Margaret's future. Captain Skardon had just filed a report on her to Major Stephenson at MI5 HQ in London, which had in turn passed it on to the DPP. It had an ominous conclusion: that to all intents, she was just as much a traitor as her husband. 'Margaret Joyce is a person with a somewhat independent mind, and it was of her own volition that she actually assisted in the work of the RRG. In her political beliefs she echoes the views of her husband, though she claims to be independent in thought, and asserts that her opinions are her own. It is not clear to what extent she may have aided the enemy; but she was a persistent speaker and writer for the German radio. Because of her employment she led a comfortable life in Germany during the war. Her case is only less serious than that of William Joyce because she was less well known and was not so frequently heard in England as her husband.'

A curious memo from Major Stephenson followed a few days later, on 2 July. Having earlier made it clear it intended to charge her with treason, MI5 was now suddenly suggesting that she be allowed to escape, perhaps because a deal of some sort had been made with her husband in the interim. 'We are considering transferring her to 37 Reinforcement Holding Unit in Brussels,' it read. 'There she would have the opportunity of making away with herself, if she felt so inclined. Captain Spooner, who has seen the conditions there, thinks this might be *a possible solution*.'

Unaware of this, Margaret wrote her first letter to William. It arrived in Brixton Prison a few days later. 'I was certainly good and left behind this time!' This was a reference to how she had sometimes missed trains when the two had travelled together. 'And now they can't read the markings on my fleece and don't really know to what flock I belong. Really, the young Intelli-gent who acted as postman came along yesterday and wanted to know who brought me here and why because they have no papers about me at the Intelli-gentsia and don't really believe in me . . . It would be nice to be in the same town or country as you but, on the other hand, an English prison, although more civilised, no doubt, would certainly not be so homely as this one. The nuns destroy the prison atmosphere . . . The Intelli-gents are evidently making themselves responsible for me, which is nice, because although in common with most of their fellow-countrymen, they may be "idiotes" they do know their own job and are always extremely courteous and even kind. Yesterday the postman brought along a nice ATS officer to see me in case there were any female oddments I needed . . . I wish I knew what was happening. Neither the postman nor the ATS had the slightest ideas as to whether you had been committed for trial or not . . . What has happened to old Quisling? Have they caught that swine Ribbontripe? What is Russia doing about Japan? . . . If I should be taken to England and charged, I shall get in touch with Head at once. I am the only one with a cell to myself and British officers come to see me. My social standing is something that would even get by in Boston. Your wife, Margaret.'

After this, William and Margaret were able to write letters every day. He addressed her by various nicknames, Mae, Meg, Meb, Freja, Mother-

Sheep, Ol and Little Ape Face. He would always begin them with 'greetings and Yp–Baa!', their private bleat. He would sign himself Will or sometimes Brixton Bill. He tried to reassure her that he was well and in good spirits. He used his comic spellings and a mixture of English and German. He often used the glib style of his broadcasts, referring to his capture, for instance, as 'the indecorous event' and treating his guards' fears about him committing suicide – or as he put it, breaking trade union conventions – as a joke: 'Some slight ill feeling seems to have arisen because I was unsporting enough to behave like the fox that, instead of running for its life, sat on a fence and smoked a cigarette. To crown all, I made no attempt at suicide. Dammit all, Sir, after such Nazi caddishness on my part, it is no wonder that poor Meg had an uneven reception.'

By 14 July, a month and a half after his capture, Joyce had put on half a stone and was keen to tell his wife. He seemed content generally. 'Except for my heartfelt concern for you,' he wrote, 'I am quite happy. I am keeping down the fat with exercise, which includes voluntary window-cleaning.' In contrast to his privations in Germany he now had food and shelter and was surrounded by the sort of unexcitable Englishmen he admired, an improvement on the hysterical Nazis he was used to. He had always liked the police – and they him – and his passion for order and discipline was met by the routines of prison life. He liked the prison uniform of shirt, underwear and socks, describing them as 'tasteful and well made'. He especially appreciated the sense of being in an organization which functioned flawlessly at every level. 'It is a mental tonic. Despite my grey hairs, I still, like you, dear, have some capacity for adaptation, which, however, reminds me uneasily of the chameleon that was placed on the Mackenzie tartan and, after a moment, burst!'

He brooded upon their turbulent relationship. 'I have just read Cronin's *Hatter's Castle*. Do you know it? It is the sordid epic of a lowland megalomaniac domestic bully – well told, if a trifle prolix in parts. It could be a classic and it should be studied by all bad-tempered and conceited husbands. Might be a set book for the marriage exam of the future social order! Anyhow, it has deepened my repentance.'

He discussed the Midland and Northern accents of the British soldiers who had guarded him in Brussels. They had hardly understood him. 'I thought my English clear if nothing else. So now I have concluded that even from a linguistic point of view I am obsolete.'

His thoughts kept returning to the *Heimat* (the homeland), as he always called Germany. He wrote that he still felt enormous affection for Berlin, what little remained of it. And he took a gloomy comfort in the thought that it was now beyond being hurt. In her reply to this, Margaret asked what London looked like after the Blitz. Joyce wrote back that he had seen nothing which veterans of Berlin would call real destruction. London, he thought, looked more like a former matinee idol who had run to fat and was now past caring about cleanliness.

(Coincidentally, P. G. Wodehouse, upon returning to New York under a cloud after the war, described the experience as being 'like meeting an old sweetheart and finding she has put on a lot of weight.')

Compared to what he had seen happen to Berlin, Joyce must have thought London had come off lightly. But his view of the former matinee idol was partial, limited to what he could glimpse from a Black Maria. Had he been able to walk around central London and breathe in the post-war atmosphere he would have found it disturbing, for it bore little resemblance to the city he left behind in 1939. Kerbstones were painted black and white to help pedestrians find their way during a blackout. The brick used for patching houses was bright yellow. Petrol shortages meant there was hardly any traffic on the roads. And the symbols of war were still in evidence: Anderson shelters, those folded corrugated iron sheets covered by earth, were still squatting in back gardens; barrage balloons still wallowed in the sky waiting to be taken down; iron railings that had been sawn off and used for the war effort had not been replaced. The Luftwaffe had left scars everywhere: craters, smoke-blackened buildings, spaces where houses used to be. Some streets looked like the mouths of men who had been in drunken brawls and were now missing teeth. Verges that had been dug up as part of the Dig for Victory campaign had yet to be paved over. Sandbags were still stacked outside shops. Blackout curtains were still hanging from windows. Glass panes not boarded up were still reinforced with crosses of tape.

The people were different, too. They were less tolerant and frivolous. Everyone had had experience of death. And social attitudes had changed: as demobilized soldiers melted back into civilian life, they found that women had taken their jobs in the factories and were now expecting to be treated as equals. There was indeed a sameness to people, thanks to the Board of Trade approved clothes designs. Men wore trilbies and ill-fitting demob suits. Pasty-faced women still painted seam marks down the backs of their legs to make it look as if they were wearing stockings. People were still hungry from rationing, which would remain in force for several more years. They still ate reconstituted eggs and Woolton Pies (meat pies without the meat). The grain of everyday existence had little changed with victory. London smelled of the coal still used in factories, homes and railways. The feeble gas lamps still in service in many streets barely penetrated the smog. Homeless people were living in temporary prefabricated houses or were sleeping on neighbours' floors. They were wearing the same threadbare clothes day after day. And because water was still restricted, with black lines around baths, Londoners smelled. If they no longer troubled to wash, it wasn't out of choice.

No wonder there was vengeance in their hearts. Joyce got a vague sense of this in the letters he received from members of the public. 'An Inverness fan', for example, wrote 'cheer up, the worst is yet to come'. Other letters dismissed him as a joke. A 'well wisher from Plymouth' wrote 'you were better than Tommy Handley'. But in his cell, isolated from the world, Joyce was largely unaware of this national mood. Already naturally prone to self-absorption, he now indulged in sentimental introspection. He claimed to Margaret that he was sure they would have many more joyful years together. This was the only prospect which made his life meaningful, he added. Poignantly, he also reassured her that she would remain beautiful in old age. He knew, in his heart, that he would not be around to see his wife grow old.

She had been trying to get pregnant for a year and she wrote to tell him that her period – which they called 'Mrs Thing' – came shortly after her arrest. Joyce wrote back: 'Fate did not play the joker!'

Although the case was now sub judice the press did not miss the chance to print stories about the need for vengeance against Nazis generally and traitors in particular. The *Daily Mail*, which famously, in 1934, had run the headline: 'HURRAH FOR THE BLACKSHIRTS!', was the most vehement. Among the letters which the *Evening Standard* ran was one from a woman who demanded that after the conviction of the surviving Nazi leaders they should be hanged upside down along the Thames. But a survey by the BBC suggested that the majority of the general public was much less keen to see Haw-Haw executed.

All Joyce's family and defence correspondence, as well as transcripts of all his conversations with visitors, including with his lawyers, was being intercepted by MI5 and handed on to the prosecution team. This illegal practice continued throughout Joyce's trial. One example which was noted down and passed on to the prosecution concerned a visit from Quentin Joyce on 5 September. Quentin told his brother that there was talk of prosecuting him on the technical grounds that he committed his acts of treason in England, through the medium of the receiving wireless set. William was quoted as saying: 'In that case they should hang the voice, not the throat from whence it came. It's like the geometrical theorem, a part you can never make a whole.' There was, the transcript noted humourlessly, 'loud laughter on both sides and the visit ended.'

Joyce's defence team, of course, was given no reciprocal tip-offs about the state of mind of either the prosecution or the Home Office. What would it have made, for instance, of a memorandum written by a senior Home Office official to the Director of Public Prosecutions, which effectively admitted Joyce was German? 'In view of the notoriety of the case, there can be no doubt that the public will expect immediate action by the Home Office if the man is acquitted. I therefore propose, if approved, to instruct the Commissioner of Police, in the event of Joyce's acquittal, for his immediate arrest for internment as an enemy alien and his conveyance to Brixton prison to await repatriation to Germany.' (The DPP in turn decided on 5 September, two weeks before the trial, that Joyce was 'almost certainly a German national'.) His case was discussed in Cabinet, which was unusual indeed.

Let us get a picture of our man as he sits in his cell in Brixton awaiting trial. His hair has now been cropped very short because of his scalp infection. He is able to walk, with sticks. He takes exercise: toe touching is part of the cure for his wounds. He assures his wife that he is protected from prisoners who try to get at him, yet this is not true because he is regularly jeered at when he exercises alone in the yard, and he is sensible of the effect his presence has on his fellow inmates: when it is suggested that he should go to the prison chapel he says his appearance would probably distract the devout from their meditations. He is cheerful and sleeping well. He plays chess every day with his guards. He writes letters. He takes visits from his solicitor and jokes with his guard: 'It will be amusing if my defence can get away with it.' He is also visited by his family. His sister Joan, who worked as a tram conductor during the war, is almost unrecognizable to him, having shed most of what he calls her puppy fat. She expects to get married before long: Joyce jokes that he knows nothing of the victim. He reads novels from the prison library (John Buchan, C. S. Lewis and E. M. Forster are his favourites; he also reads a book by Dennis Wheatley, whom he had known before the war). He draws strength from his belief that he has committed no crime by his own morality. He broods upon his extraordinary time in Berlin, his days as a Blackshirt, his childhood in Ireland. He contemplates the fates of Hitler, Goebbels and Himmler and those awaiting trial in Nuremberg. He considers his own destiny. To the outside world he seems optimistic that he will win his case. But the strain of waiting shows between the lines of his correspondence. As the trial date approaches, Joyce tries to give his wife some hope, while preparing her for the worst. He thinks she will be relieved when the day of his trial dawns. The waiting, he suggest, is much harder for her than for him.

On 17 September 1945, the wait was over. With large crowds milling outside, a jury of ten middle-aged men and two women walked up the steps of the Old Bailey in London. Like everybody else in England at that time, Rebecca West noted, they looked 'puffy and haggard'. Like everyone else they were fatigued from six years of war, of food shortage, of uncertainty.

It was an overcast Monday morning. The area around the court had been levelled by German bombs so the pillared building rose from a wasteland of charred rubble overgrown with weeds. Some of the courts were burnt-out shells and were sealed off by a makeshift brick wall. The corridors and stairs inside were in perpetual dusk because of the blackout paint still on the windows.

On their left, as the jury entered the court and took their seats, they saw the witness box, the bench and the small box in which an official shorthand-writer was sitting waiting. Before them, on a row of reserved seats, sat the world's press. So many journalists had turned up, an extra row of seats in the public gallery had been commandeered to accommodate them. Then the jury saw the solicitors' table, where Head sat, as well as police officers and representatives of the department of the Director of Public Prosecutions. On that table there were also members of MI5 wearing army uniforms, as was the custom for intelligence officers during and immediately after the war.

Beyond them was the counsel's bench at which was seated the new Attorney-General, Sir Hartley Shawcross (the second appointed since proceedings had started against Joyce in June). A couple of months later, Shawcross was to make his name as the presiding prosecutor at the Nuremberg trials. Behind him were a number of barristers in wig and gown, including Gerald Slade, the KC leading Joyce's defence. Still further back privileged members of the public sat on the benches retained by the Common Council of the City of London. Before the front row of counsel, a special shelf had been fitted to hold some of the books to which they would be referring in the course of the trial; other volumes overflowed onto their desks. Between the solicitors' table and the judge's platform was a raised desk at which the clerk of the court and his assistant were sitting and, beside them, the Director of Public Prosecutions. On their right was a raised dock.

Three taps on the floor behind the platform were heard, like the signal in a theatre for the raising of the curtain. Everybody stood and faced the bench. The door opened and a small group of aldermen and sheriffs in their robes passed through. They turned and bowed to the judge, Sir Frederick Tucker, as he entered in his red robe, carrying in his hand a pair of white gloves and a strip of black cloth – the 'black cap'. Tucker reached his desk in the centre, while an usher intoned a proclamation in Latin. When he finished, the judge turned and bowed to the alderman, then to the clerk and the counsel, and, finally, to the jury. He sat down and placed the black cloth unobtrusively behind a row of books where the prisoner would not see it, until, perhaps, the end of the trial. Under the new Treason Act (1945), the punishment for high treason was death by hanging – there was no alternative sentence if a defendant was found guilty. (This was a marginal improvement on the old Treason Act, which stipulated that the condemned prisoner should be 'drawn on a hurdle to the place of execution, and, after execution, shall have the head severed from the body, and the body divided into four quarters.') Also by virtue of the new Act, three judges were no longer required to sit. One would do.

The wheels of justice had been set in motion. The jury was about to hear the life story of a man who had become a myth. They were to be taken on a journey that would begin in America and end in Germany, with stops in Ireland and England on the way.

'Put up William Joyce,' the clerk called.

The jury craned forward in their seats for their first glimpse of the infamous Lord Haw-Haw. Footsteps were heard on the steps at the back of the dock. The air in the Old Bailey seemed to tighten. The moment of reckoning, and truth perhaps, had arrived.

PART 2

THE EARLY YEARS: AMERICA, IRELAND, ENGLAND

'You see me, men of Argos, you understand that my crime is wholly mine; I claim it as my own, for all to know, it is my glory, my life's work, and you can neither punish me nor pity me. That is why I fill you with fear.'

Jean-Paul Sartre, *Les Mouches*

THREE

'That boy will either do something very great in the world, or he will finish on the end of a rope.'

On 7 May 1906, Alfred E. Shipley, the secretary of the Board of Health of the City of New York, issued a birth certificate declaring that William Joyce had been born a fortnight earlier at 1377 Herkimer Street, Brooklyn, New York. The child's mother was named as twenty-six-year-old Gertrude Emily Joyce; the father as Michael Francis Joyce, a thirty-six-year-old building contractor, born in Ireland.

In fact Michael Joyce had been born on 9 December 1866, which meant he was thirty-nine, not thirty-six – a genuine mistake perhaps, or a wilful touch of self-invention. The son of an illiterate farmer from Killour, County Mayo, Michael Joyce had followed a wave of Irishmen emigrating to the United States and settling in New York. On 25 October 1894, at the age of twenty-eight, Michael had taken American citizenship. Gertrude Joyce, née Brooke, known to her family as Queenie, had been born in Crompton, Lancashire, into a middle-class Protestant family. Her father was a doctor, her brother a solicitor. They had disapproved when she moved to America and, on 2 May 1905, married Michael Joyce – especially as the marriage meant their daughter automatically became an American citizen, too.

Although William Joyce, rather grandly, later described his father as an architect and 'a man of independent means', in fact Michael Joyce was little more than an odd-job man who was by turns an electro-type operator, labourer, lock maker and coachman. But his work in the building trade paid reasonably well and by October 1909 he had saved enough money to return to Mayo as a conquering hero, or at least as a modestly successful businessman. His main reason for returning seems to have been homesickness; his reason for not returning sooner, pride. Michael sailed back first and Queenie followed a month later with her small, three-year-old son − according to family folklore, William had weighed no more than a bag of a sugar at birth.

In his first year back in Ireland, Michael Joyce found work as a publican, and William's earliest memory related to this period: he crept downstairs one night at the age of four and ate some cheese. He smoked the butt of a cigar, too. The resulting sickness gave him an aversion to cheese, he said later, but not tobacco. He was a precocious child who could read fluently at five. He was also still, at that age, an only child and prone to the usual egomania associated with being the centre of parental attention. His attendance at a local convent school was irregular and, at the age of six, he was briefly struck off the register.

Michael Joyce was not a popular landlord, at least not after he ejected an unconscious drunk one cold night. The drunk died of hypothermia outside the pub and the locals never forgave him. This was partly the reason why, in 1913, when William was seven, the family moved to an area just north of Galway known locally as 'Joyce's Country' (the novelist James Joyce was also from the area). Along with other property, which he let out, Michael Joyce bought 1 Rutledge Terrace in Rockbarton, Salthill, a comfortable two-storey house with a small walled garden in a secluded position just off the promenade. Here, over the following twelve years, the Joyces had four more children: Frank, Quentin, Joan and Robert. They were so much younger than William that he referred to them as 'the children'. The children, in turn, idolized him, even when, in later life, their connection with him would cost them jobs and leave them ostracized. Quentin especially, who was born in 1917, hero-worshipped his oldest brother and followed him into fascism. He was interned during the war and became a tireless campaigner on William's behalf during his trial.

Michael Joyce, the proud father of five, began to prosper in Ireland, becoming manager of the horse trams in Galway, as well as the landlord of barracks occupied by the Royal Irish Constabulary. He doesn't seem to have had much time for his children, being a remote and authoritarian figure. Jesuit priests were a much bigger influence on William's early life. In 1915, as a short, fair-haired, blue-eyed boy, he was sent to the Jesuit-run St Ignatius Loyola College in Galway where, as he later recalled, 'the staff and the boys were tough, Latin was supreme, and an excitable Latin master banged boys' heads on the radiator.' The Jesuits instilled in him a sense of discipline and an acceptance of punishment, and perhaps traditional Catholic feelings of guilt about sex as well. Perhaps, too, they also instilled in him a little subliminal anti-Semitism. (As James Joyce once said: 'Ireland has the honour of being the only country which never persecuted the Jews – because she never let them in.') The Jesuits also left him with a love of language – his classmates would note how he used big and strange words – as well as a passion for debate. According to William's uncle Gilbert, the boy had 'a strong tendency to argue with his teachers'.

His time at St Ignatius certainly left him with a feeling of confidence in his own academic abilities. One of his essays, about a day out to Lough Corrib, was of such a high standard he was asked to read it out to the senior school. By the age of ten he had developed a quaintly ornate way of speaking. When he heard that his friend William Naughton had a cold, he earnestly said to the boy's mother: 'Do tell Billy to take care of himself, Mrs Naughton. After all, one's health is one's most precious possession.'

William's best subjects were English literature – especially poetry – and languages, specifically Latin, French and German. He played rugby but was clumsy and didn't make much of an impression at team sports, preferring instead to skate and sail, something he was taught to do by fishermen in Galway Bay. He also developed a passion for chess and would spend hours playing every day with his friend Miles Webb – that and practising hypnotism. He enjoyed the rough and tumble of the playground and broke his nose in one fight, after, it was said, another boy had called him an Orangeman. It left him with a nasal tone of voice. Already, it seemed, William was becoming the subject of rumours and urban myths. It was said that he produced a gun at school one day, procured from the RIC barracks of which his father was landlord.

Though he could be difficult and immature, he was generally considered popular. If anything, he was a gang leader. Other children were drawn to his precociousness, bombast, impatience, self-assurance and, above all, his enthusiasm. Such was the gusto with which he tackled everything, he once swung the censer so hard during a church service that the glowing incense was scattered down the aisle. But there was also a serious, brooding side to William's personality that belied his years. One of his class mates, E. L. Kineen, recalled: 'He was a morose and lonely little fellow . . . For all his brightness there was something missing in Willie. He would give impromptu speeches in the playground warning his playmates about the growing dangers of communism.'

Perhaps his slightly strained home life meant he had to grow up quicker than other boys. William had long felt divided loyalties between his mother's Protestantism and his father's Catholicism. But at the age of fourteen he became distinctly disillusioned with the Catholic Church. He asked his divinity master whether his mother, to whom he was devoted, was damned for eternity unless she converted to Rome. The master assured him she was. At this, young William declared that, if such was the case, he rejected the Catholic doctrine. 'If my mother is going to Hell, then so shall I.' The master, who thought highly of his academically gifted, if awkward pupil, was so upset by this wilful display of independent thought that he took young William to see the Bishop of Galway. The boy refused to budge on the subject; on the contrary, he put up a spirited defence of his position. The exasperated master apologized to the bishop and returned William to his mother with the prophetic words: 'That boy will either do something very great in the world, or he will finish on the end of a rope.'

Years later, when he was awaiting execution, his wife Margaret mentioned in a letter that she was considering converting to Rome and wondered if her husband minded. He claimed by way of reply that he laughed at the thought of his ovine wife convulsing with inner heterodoxy while being drawn into the maw of the Roman wolf. He didn't mind her turning Catholic if she wanted to, he wrote, and he did not fear for her prudence when making her confession. But much as he admired the Church, and much as he should like to rejoin it, he concluded that he simply could not.

It was no accident of timing that, within weeks of losing his faith in religion, William had found something new to believe in: politics. Ireland was a volatile and, for a child, exciting place to be growing up. He was ten at the time of the Easter uprising, an impressionable age, and he had seen first hand its bloody aftermath. A boy impatient to become an adult, he found the street fighting, the conspiracies and the intrigues exhilarating and romantic. They fired his childish imagination. One evening in a lane near his house he found the body of his neighbour, a policeman, with a bullet hole in his head. Soon afterwards he saw a Sinn Féiner cornered by police and gunned down. He seems to have been fascinated rather than haunted by these sights. Violence and bloodshed were becoming commonplace for him. One can only wonder at the psychological scars this was leaving on him.

In 1920, when William was fourteen, the violence escalated with 'the Tan War', which started when the British government reinforced the Royal Irish Constabulary with a paramilitary force, the Black and Tans, so called because their uniform was part police uniform, part khaki service dress. Michael Joyce, though a Catholic, was loyal to the Crown. William later wrote in his book, *Twilight Over England*: 'I was brought up by my parents in a creed of fanatical patriotism which the English people found very hard to understand. From my earliest days, I was taught to love England and her Empire. Patriotism was the highest virtue that I knew.' William not only shared his father's suspicion of Republicans, he went to the extreme of volunteering to act as a spy on behalf of the Black and Tans. Though it would have made sense to recruit a schoolboy as an informer – he would be able to listen in on adult conversations and tail people without arousing too much suspicion – there is no record of his service, and it may have been a schoolboy fantasy. After all, he had also claimed to be a Boy Scout and, though he did indeed learn the signals, and somehow managed to obtain a Scout uniform, there were no Scout troops in Galway. Nevertheless, there are various accounts of how William acted as a sort of cheerleader to the Black and Tans, sitting like a mascot on the front of their vehicles as they drove through Galway.

By the age of fifteen, William was spending nearly all his spare time in the barracks of the Black and Tans and at the headquarters of the Royal Irish Constabulary. On one occasion a British police officer was murdered while playing tennis. The military funeral was coming from Renmore Military Barracks and the troops were marching with reversed arms, the band playing. William and his friend Miles were there together in front of a crowd of people. As the coffin passed William sprang to attention and, although dressed in ordinary clothes, gave an elaborate and stiff salute, holding it with a grim set face for two or three minutes with everyone gaping as much at him as at the cortège. According to a statement he made to the police years later, Miles felt quite embarrassed because neither of the boys were soldiers and yet William had had the courage to do it, while Miles, although he felt the same, had not.

Douglas Duff, a Royal Irish Constabulary member fighting with the Royal Marines against the IRA, recalled in his memoirs how William once jumped on his unit's landing craft during a patrol. 'He was one of our greatest embarrassments in Galway City. His trouble was fanatical patriotism to England and a burning wish to fight against the Irish "rebels", as he always called them. He often tried to smuggle himself into our lorries ... we laughed at him, but we used to chase him fiercely for, if he had been killed or wounded, his ending would have caused the man in charge of the patrol a lot of trouble.'

By 1921, the IRA had firebombed several of Michael Joyce's properties, because he had been helping the police. The previous year they had set fire to his house, and Michael had been involved in protracted negotiations with the government to get compensation. It was time to get out. A truce was declared in July and the Black and Tans began withdrawing in October. William's protectors had gone and IRA lynch mobs were swearing that they would settle scores. At fifteen, the diminutive William still looked like a child, which would have made him an unusual choice as a target for the IRA. But there was a rumour that he had informed on a priest, Father Michael Griffin, who was subsequently killed by the Black and Tans. As revenge for his treachery, it has been claimed, the IRA ordered his assassination. A twenty-eight-year-old IRA 'lieutenant' was ordered to shoot him on his way home from school. He took up position on the route between the school and the Joyces' house in Salthill a couple of miles west. But the IRA's information was out of date because, for security reasons, Michael Joyce had just moved his family to another address, Victoria Place. The sniper waited in vain.

William Joyce later claimed that, at the behest of British Intelligence, the Foreign Office supplied him with a temporary British passport in which his birthplace was given as Galway, though no record of it was kept. Whatever the truth about his passport, and about the circumstances of his leaving, it is certain that the Joyce family had to leave Ireland in a hurry. According to Frank Joyce, William's brother: 'We were given a week's notice to clear out of the country or be shot.' On 8 December 1921, two days after the Anglo-Irish Treaty was signed and the Irish Free State declared, William was put on a train to Dublin, ahead of his parents and siblings. He caught the next ship to England.

FOUR

'There is something to be said for having a well-fed appearance.'

A fifteen-year-old boy crossing the Irish Sea on his own, about to start a new life in a strange land, would have felt a mixture of trepidation and wonderment. This one would also have had a sense of coming home: his father, after all, had filled his head for years with patriotic thoughts about Old England on the lea.

William Joyce's first journey on English soil was a short one. He took the train to Oldham in Lancashire where members of his mother's family still lived. Within days he had applied for a commission in the British army, with the Worcestershire Regiment, and had lied about his age to do so. When asked to prove he was eighteen he told them that he had never been issued with a birth certificate, as registering births wasn't compulsory in Ireland. The regiment, which bore an Irish harp on its colours, accepted this. Joyce took a medical and it was recorded that he weighed 8 stone 2 pounds.

The other recruits were amused by Joyce's fanatical patriotism and would tease him by whistling the National Anthem when he was lying on his bed so that he would leap to attention. Even after he realized what their game was, he would humour them by obliging. After four months' officer training, William developed rheumatic fever from wearing damp clothes and, in hospital, his real age was discovered. He was duly discharged from the army.

But he was not to be deterred. With typical precociousness he decided that his character could best be built by military discipline and self-improvement through academic work – and that the way to combine the two was to win a place at university and there join the Officers' Training Corps. And the only place for an ambitious young man to be a student, he reckoned, was London.

On 9 August 1922, at the age of sixteen, he wrote a letter to the officer commanding London University's OTC. His application, written in a neat hand and sent from 86 Brompton Street, Oldham, turned out to be a ghost image of actual events. Among other things, he claimed that he had worked for British Intelligence in Ireland – an exaggeration worthy of Walter Mitty.

Joyce went on to explain that he had been trained in the rudiments of musketry, bayonet-fighting and squad drill while serving with the Worcestershire Regiment, which would have been true enough. He then made a statement about his ambiguous nationality, in the hope that this would pre-empt any problems it might cause. He lied that he was born in America, but of British parents, and that he had left when he was two. He also said that when stationed in Ireland he had been told that he possessed the same rights as he would have done if he had been British by birth. He claimed he could obtain sworn statements as to his loyalty to the King and added that 'I am in no way connected with the United States of America, against which, as against all other nations, I am prepared to draw the sword in the British interest.' He concluded: 'I have always been desirous of devoting what little capacity and energy I may possess to the country which I love so dearly. I ask that you may inform me if the accident of my birth, to which I refer above, will affect my position.'

The tone of the letter is both pretentious and pompous, and dripping in false modesty. But William probably felt a bit chippy about his Irish-American roots – at the time, the English felt great prejudice against the Irish, dismissing them as second-class citizens, or worse (at his trial twenty-three years later, Rebecca West characterized Joyce as 'a queer little bog trotter with an Irish brogue'). Even so, the statement, which was to prove a damning admission in court, reflected what the young William regarded his true nationality to be. It ranged from the wilfully misleading – he must have known his parents weren't British – to the perhaps innocently mistaken – he was three, not two when he came to Ireland. His colourful literary flourish about being prepared to draw his sword in the British interest may seem comic and a little toe-curling but, to be fair, he was only sixteen when he wrote it. Most sixteen-year-olds commit offences against the English language. And there is something endearing about his self-aggrandizing reference to his having been 'stationed' in Ireland. He was stationed at his parents' house. And the accident of his birth, to which he refers, would indeed go on to affect his position, fatally. Nevertheless, London University's OTC sent him an enrolment form to fill in after he had matriculated.

He passed the London matriculation examination that autumn and registered as a student at Battersea Polytechnic, where he studied chemistry, among other subjects, trained as a featherweight boxer, and took up swimming and fencing. Fitness, he decided, was as important as mental discipline and so he began a regime in the gymnasium, building his upper body to the point of being barrel-chested.

He sent off his enrolment, giving his birthplace as New York. The OTC commander wrote to William's father, who had now followed his eldest son over to England and was living, temporarily, in Oldham. 'Your son William Joyce has seen me with a view to joining the University of London OTC,' the letter began, 'and has also spoken of his desiring to register as a candidate for a Commission in the Regular Army. It appears however that he is in doubt as to whether he is a British subject of pure European descent. From what he tells me I think he comes within this definition, as he says you were never naturalised as an American. Perhaps therefore you would confirm this point, and I shall be able to proceed with his enrolment and registration.'

Michael Joyce's reply was equivocal, ignoring the question about his being a naturalized American. 'With regard to my son William; he was born in America, I was born in Ireland, his mother was born in England.' So far so true. Then he added a lie: 'We are all British and not American citizens.'

The OTC did not press the point. William was enrolled and he enjoyed his image of himself as a young irregular soldier back from 'intelligence work' in Ireland. William moved to Clapham Common – 10 Longbeach Road – to be near his family, who had just moved to Dulwich and opened a grocer's shop. In the summer of 1923, at the age of seventeen, he passed four 'intermediate BA' exams – the equivalent of A levels – in Latin, French, English and history. That September, he began a degree course in English at London University's Birkbeck College.

That was also the year he became a fascist. His political activism began conventionally enough: he joined the University's Conservative Society. But then students began to discuss the exciting developments that were happening on the international stage. In Germany that year Adolf Hitler's ill-timed attempt at a putsch had failed, and while in prison he had begun writing *Mein Kampf.* In Italy, meanwhile, Mussolini had been much more successful. He had pioneered a new political movement called fascism. It had won massive popular support and was now being talked of as the antidote to communism, which, since the Russian Revolution in 1917, had been unnerving the Western democracies. The British aristocracy especially was worried by the implications of the Tsar's murder. An assumption was growing that the Bolsheviks who committed such atrocities tended to be Jewish.

Within two months of joining the Conservative Society, Joyce had effectively left it to join a newly formed group called the British Fascisti Limited. It had been founded by Rotha Lintorn-Orman, an eccentric spinster.* She had army in her blood, being the granddaughter of a field marshal, and she modelled her party on Mussolini's fascist movement. Its members were distinguished by a foppish black handkerchief in their breast pocket. In truth the British Fascisti Limited was a rather ramshackle outfit of retired army officers, mentally negligible old ladies, and young drones who wore plus-fours and were given to intervening, ineffectually, in strikes. The group, based in Battersea, had grandiose ideas about national mobilization, should the Reds reach British shores. The arrogant and combative young Joyce was in his element and, that summer, he had been reprimanded by the British Fascisti for immoderate language. He was warned formally in a letter: 'Had you been a member you would have been expelled for "ill considered and ill judged remarks," coupled with subsequent loud-voiced interruptions.'

Political meetings at the time were boisterous affairs, with much heck-ling and scuffling, but also grievous bodily harm. At one rally, according to Joyce, a communist stabbed a friend of his in the testicles with a rusty hatpin. The friend died of blood poisoning. Labour and Tory party rallies especially became violent following the publication of the infamous 'Zinoviev Letter', in which the Communist Internationale had supposedly

---

* With her enthusiasm for manly uniforms it has been suggested that Miss Lintorn-Orman was almost a caricature of a repressed lesbian.

instructed its British members to infiltrate the Labour Party and the trade unions. By the time the letter was revealed as a hoax, the damage to the Labour Party had been done. The Conservatives won the 1924 general election. Joyce was unable to celebrate the victory, though, because he was in hospital, recovering from what may have been a second attempt on his life.

On the evening of 22 October 1924, a week before polling day, he had led a squad of British Fascisti to the Lambeth Baths hall to protect the Conservative-supported candidate for Lambeth North, who was speaking at a public meeting. Joyce stationed his men around the hall in anticipation of a demonstration by communists. There was fighting, and afterwards, as Joyce was walking home, he was set upon by a gang of communists. They overpowered him and pinned him down on the pavement. One of them produced a razor and placed it in the corner of Joyce's mouth before slashing upwards to his ear. Joyce was taken to Lambeth Infirmary and, the next day, the eighteen-year-old undergraduate made the first of many appearances in a newspaper. The *Evening Standard* reported 'wild scenes by hooligans'. A photograph showed Joyce sitting up in bed with a bandaged face. Joyce later recalled that the photographer had approached his bed and, mistaking him for an anti-fascist, had sympathetically exclaimed: 'These fascist blackguards are damn swine to carve you up like that. They should be shot.' Joyce said: 'I laughed till I nearly burst my stitches.'

In his version of events, his attackers were 'Jewish-communists', though how he could have known this is not clear. Perhaps they had taunted him, or he them. Either way, the scar made Joyce a young hero to the fledgeling fascist movement, and it gave him a sense of purpose. It meant that Jewish communists had replaced 'Irish Rebels' as 'the enemy' in his imagination. 'An attempt was made to cut my throat,' he was quoted as saying, 'but the razor slashed a quarter of an inch too high. There is something to be said for having a well-fed appearance.' Thereafter he called his scar his 'Lambeth Honour'. Clearly he preferred to think of it as a battle scar sustained in an open fight, rather than the result of his being held down and humiliated.

For the rest of his life William Joyce bore this savage scar on his face, its thin weal too long and neat to pass for a distinguished duelling scar. It took on a totemic significance for him, a violent reminder every morning, when he looked in the mirror to shave, of who he was and what he stood for.

According to his friend Angus Macnab, Joyce needed twenty-six stitches and was on the danger list for two weeks. 'WJ asked for a discharge from hospital but the doctor refused it,' he wrote. 'On the morning of 11 November, he obtained some clothes, absconded from the hospital and took his place at the Cenotaph for the Remembrance Day service.'

Joyce laid a wreath, it was said, and shortly afterwards collapsed. Hazel Barr, a pharmacy student who recognized him from college, took him back to her parents' house in Chelsea so that he could recuperate. So began a two-year courtship. Without the injury, Joyce might never have met his first wife.

The scar seems to have made Joyce more serious minded. Not for him the frivolities of the Roaring Twenties: no wild student parties or nights spent dancing the Charleston with flappers in short shift dresses. Instead he took to wearing his khaki uniform to lectures and, one day, as he was entitled to do, he even turned up carrying his rifle – just as, according to Irish folklore, he had done at school. Joyce sat alone in the front row, his rifle across his knees, and stared at his English tutor Marjorie Daunt. She liked him, indeed she regarded him as her star student and was always impressed by his apparently photographic memory for poems and prose. But the fresh scar was livid on his cheek and, occasionally, the side of his face twitched. At the best of times, as Joyce himself liked to say, he had a 'queer dial', but the introduction of the twitching on top of this proved too much for Miss Daunt. 'I thought: if he's as mad as he looks he may well stand up and shoot me,' she said later. She asked him politely not to bring the gun into lectures in future, or at least, if he did, to leave it with the umbrellas in the corner of the room.

Miss Daunt persuaded Joyce to tone down the purple prose in his essays. He honed his writing skills further by contributing to the college magazine. In a parody of Augustan verse he attacked the decadence of modern culture, dismissing George Bernard Shaw as a 'sacrilegious lizard' and Noël Coward as a 'worm-eaten weakling'. (This was long before Coward wrote his controversial hit 'Don't let's be beastly to the Germans', which Joyce no doubt approved of.) Judging by the response the young writer's work generated in the letters page of the next issue, the other students were horrified. One letter primly read: 'Mr Joyce has been unable to restrain himself from gratuitous rudeness.' Another protested: 'The proper place for such ill-bred and unprovoked effusions is the editorial wastepaper basket.' Joyce was pleased with his rabble-rousing prose. He had found a way to get under people's skin.

His attempts at acting were even less popular. When the English faculty put on an obscure sixteenth-century play, Joyce was cast as a traveller armed with a stick who had to beat off two highwaymen. During rehearsals he got so carried away he knocked one of the highwaymen off the stage and caused the other to lose a tooth. He was removed from the cast. As with the swinging of the censer in church, Joyce simply did not know how to curb his natural exuberance. He always went too far.

By the summer of 1924, British Fascisti Ltd was claiming a hundred thousand members, though this seems unlikely. Perhaps whatever mass appeal it did have was related to its lack of policies. It saw itself simply as a force to defend 'King and Parliament'. After a time, Miss Lintorn-Orman withdrew to her country house in Somerset and the headquarters in London were taken over by a brigadier general called Blakeney. He changed the wording of the title to British Fascists, introduced a member-ship badge with the words 'For King and Country' encircling the initials BF, and found other high-ranking ex-servicemen to take over local leadership: there was a General Tyndal-Biscoe in charge of Bournemouth and an Admiral Tupper running the branch in Liss.

During 1925, when the threat of strikes was almost paralysing the government, the British Fascists flourished: there was talk of members forming paramilitary motor-cycle squads which could be rushed to the aid of government forces in an emergency. But while some members of the British Fascists condoned scuffles in the name of keeping public order, others balked at the thought of violence. The party split and a number of splinter groups emerged: the British Empire Fascists, the Fascist League, the Fascist Movement, the National Fascisti and the British National Fascists. The latter's speciality was breaking up Labour Party meetings.

Joyce tried to reform the party by drafting regulations for a disciplinary court, so that an accused could not get off on a technicality. He included the clause: 'The court shall have the power to define an offence.'* His new regulations made no difference: the party did not reform and Joyce returned to the Tory fold, becoming President of the Conservative Society

---

* When on trial for his life in 1945 he recalled with grim amusement this attempt at law-making to the disadvantage of the defendant.

and a frequent speaker in College Parliament. He also harboured an ambition to stand for Parliament as a Conservative MP.

The British Fascisti Limited had introduced Joyce to fascism. It also brought him into contact with a man who was to have a significant impact on his life: Maxwell Knight, known to his friends as Max, or M. The enigmatic Knight was a member of the British Fascisti Limited from 1923, becoming first its research officer then, when it became the British Fascists, its Director of Intelligence and a member of its governing council.★ He was shortly to become a senior figure in MI5, too, in which capacity he would employ Joyce as an undercover agent.

Knight cut a heroic figure. He was six years older than Joyce, had served briefly with the Royal Naval Reserve during the Great War and had cultivated a range of engaging eccentricities, such as smoking long, hand-made cigarettes from a tobacconist in Sloane Street. He had also developed a rather sinister fascination with the occult which he shared with his friends Dennis Wheatley and Aleister Crowley. Knight was tall with dark, bushy eyebrows and a Wellingtonian nose which he referred to as 'my limb', and he always dressed in slightly shabby tweeds. He had a hypnotic voice, was a keen jazz saxophonist and drummer, spending much of his time in bohemian jazz clubs where aristocrats mingled with prostitutes and drug dealers, and he had an obsession with exotic animals. He could recite trivia about them endlessly, from the correct method of mounting a llama to the breeding cycle of the laughing hyena. His daily help, Mrs Leather, would complain of the way grass snakes used to flop down the stairs of his flat in Chelsea. He kept them in the bath. He also kept a blue-fronted Amazonian parrot in the kitchen and a Himalayan monkey in the garden.

Knight was an eccentric who did not mind being 'considered a bit mad'. Visitors to his home might, as one recalled, 'find him nursing a bush baby, feeding a giant toad, raising young cuckoos or engaging in masculine repartee with a vastly experienced grey parrot.' For several years Knight also had a pet bear named Bessie who 'excited a great deal of attention and admiration' when he took her, sometimes accompanied by a bulldog

---

★ US National Archives show that in December 1923 Knight was representing the British Fascisti in informal discussions with the US Embassy in London. He was already a leading fascist by the time he was recruited by MI5.

or a baboon, for walks near his Chelsea home. Ian Fleming, who worked in the Department of Naval Intelligence, was fascinated by Knight's mysterious persona, and used him as the model for 'M', James Bond's boss.

Knight and Joyce had a mutual friend: Hazel Barr. Knight had courted her when she was eighteen and he twenty-four. They used to sit next to each other on the bus every morning: she on her way to Lady Margaret's, a private school in Fulham, he on his way to Willington School, a boys' prep school in Putney where he was teaching Latin and games. One day he had asked if he could visit her. She readily agreed and he turned up the following Sunday morning wearing riding clothes. He had, he explained, just been exercising his horse in Rotten Row. Hazel's father, a dentist who had served with the Scots Guards in the First World War, was impressed by Knight. Her mother was too, not least because he had already started writing detective stories and had had a couple published. Hazel would later recall: 'I was completely enamoured of him. I think the feeling was mutual.' She would tell him what she thought was wrong with his detective stories: the heroine in one would not wear red, she pointed out, because it would clash with her auburn hair.

But it wasn't to be, in part because Knight was bisexual, or rather homosexual and in denial about it. He married twice, and each marriage ended in disaster. In 1925 he married one of the Bright Young Things, Gwladys Poole, a twenty-five-year-old socialite, but he never consummated the union. They lived in a large flat in Sloane Street, bought with Gwladys's money – and it can be imagined how its value must have gone down when Knight moved his menagerie in. That year, Knight went to a dinner party at which Major General Sir Vernon Kell, the Director-General of MI5, was present. Kell discreetly asked Knight if he would come and see him in his office the next day. He was offered a job in MI5. Kell decided that Knight was 'extremely patriotic, highly versatile and bore himself with all the trappings of a country gentleman who not only hunted, shot and fished but was a witty and popular socialiser.' Kell made no real investigation into Knight's social background and therefore knew nothing of the menagerie that occupied his home. Nor did he discover that Knight used to poach (as in steal) salmon and hide them in his trousers.

But Kell almost certainly knew about Knight's involvement with the

British Fascists and, significantly, did not consider that there was a conflict of interests. In fact there is some evidence of collusion between MI5 and the British fascist movements of the inter-war years. As the British Fascists' Director of Intelligence, Knight was responsible for compiling intelligence dossiers on its communist enemies and fascist rivals; for planning its counter-espionage and covert-action operations; for establishing and supervising the fascist cells it set up and operated in the trade unions and factories; and for the movement's own internal security and disciplinary problems.

According to the testimony of Neil Francis-Hawkins, a flamboyant homosexual who was an influential member of the British Fascists, shortly after Knight left the movement in 1927 he revealed his identity as an MI5 officer and offered assistance to the BF in its work for the 'Clear Out the Reds Campaign' launched by Commander Oliver Locker-Lampson, Colonel John Gretton, Sir Henry Page Croft and Winston Churchill.*

That Knight's fascist sympathies did not constitute a barrier to his recruitment suggests that Kell, in the 1920s at least, did not regard the fascist movement as being hostile to the state. On the contrary, he saw it as an ally. To combat the Bolshevik danger, indeed, MI5 had been collaborating with a private right-wing intelligence agency operated by Sir George McGill, which was 'actively engaged in fighting the anti-Christ of Communism'. McGill's private intelligence network had also worked with Lieutenant J. F. C. Carter, Assistant Commissioner at Special Branch, who occasionally supplied it with funds and officers. To MI5, then, the British Fascists would have appeared merely as a more militant and aggressive version of an agency with which it was already colluding.

Knight had served an 'intelligence apprenticeship' in McGill's agency from 1923. He had learned to collect intelligence on communists, socialists

---

* Francis-Hawkins became Director-General of the British Union of Fascists and was also one of the earliest BUF members to be interned in May 1940. Appearing before the Advisory Committee on 18B Detainees in 1944, he informed it that Knight 'had been Director of Intelligence at the British Fascists'. This is substantiated by Foreign Office papers in which Knight's name appears on a list of the British Fascists' senior executives provided by two of the movement's members in September 1926 to Special Branch and Foreign Office officials. Knight's membership and position as the BF's Chief Intelligence Officer also appears in an intelligence report on British fascism submitted to the Australian authorities in November 1924, and discovered by the historian Dr Andrew Moore in the Australian archives.

and 'militant' trade unionists, as well as conduct sabotage operations against them. Knight's recruitment to MI5 was probably effected by McGill himself, who was a close friend of Kell. It was almost certainly not a matter of chance that Knight found himself attending the dinner party at which Kell was among the guests.

In 1927, Kell brought in Guy Liddell, who was married to an aristocrat, to train Knight. Knight was put in charge of infiltrating the Communist Party of Great Britain. To this end he recruited Tom Driberg, the (homosexual) writer and future MP, and ordered him to join the Communist Party while at Oxford. Knight was 'crazy for Driberg'. He also recruited Olga Grey and had her work for Harry Pollitt, the leader of the CPGB. Feeling humiliated by the attention Knight lavished on the beautiful Olga, and excluded by the way he spent all his spare time writing novels, Gwladys became depressed, took an overdose of barbiturates and died. There was an inquest which plunged Knight into scandal. An open verdict was recorded.

As Joan Miller, one of Knight's MI5 agents, noted later: 'The communist threat was something about which M felt very deeply indeed; his views on this subject, you might say, amounted almost to an obsession. He was equally adamant in his aversion to Jews and homosexuals, but prepared to suspend these prejudices in certain cases. "Bloody Jews" was one of his expressions. His vehemence against homosexuals was obviously to safeguard his reputation in the office. His tastes inclined him in the direction of rough trade. My role was to provide a cover for his shady infatuations. We lived together but never consummated.'

There was no such ambiguity about William Joyce's sexuality. He pursued the tall and shy Hazel, and in 1927, a week after his twenty-first birthday, he married her at Chelsea Register Office. The timing was significant because, since he had obtained the age of consent in law, he no longer needed parental approval. Hazel, too, had just turned twenty-one. Both sets of their parents were against the marriage. Hazel's mother even fainted when told that the deed was done. Such was the paucity of choice – the First World War having reduced the number of eligible bachelors considerably – she had longed for her daughter to marry Maxwell Knight. Hazel's two sisters were also astonished.

The choice of a register office was also significant. Though he still described himself as 'a believer', Joyce had now drifted so far from the

Roman Catholic Church that he was able to say: 'I can imagine no greater handicap upon any universal creed than that the Son of God should come to Earth as a Jew and His Church be left to the tender mercies of the Wops.' At Hazel's insistence, though, they did have an Anglican blessing, and this was followed by a lunch for two at Epping. After this they returned to their respective homes as though nothing unusual had happened that day.

A month later, William graduated with a first-class honours degree. His was one of only two firsts awarded in English at Birkbeck that year. He had written essays on Shakespeare, Dryden (satiric theory and practice) and Milton (from *Paradise Lost* to *Samson Agonistes*). Miss Daunt was so pleased she encouraged him to study philology as a postgraduate. He began an MA thesis on 'unrounded vowels in English'.

The following year, his MA uncompleted, Joyce applied for a post at the Foreign Office, the rule that candidates had to be born within the United Kingdom 'or one of the self-governing dominions' having been waived. On his rather gushing application one civil servant had scribbled: 'A little oily, don't you think?' As usual, Joyce had overdone the patriotism. His application was rejected at the interview stage, although he later claimed he took the examination and passed, only to be told that candidates were expected to have a private income. There was another reason he hadn't been accepted. The Principal at Battersea Polytechnic had written a damning reference: 'Mr Joyce held extreme views and upheld the use of violence in political action . . . Our very vivid recollection of Mr Joyce is that he was entirely unfitted for a responsible position, and particularly for the Foreign Office or Diplomatic Service.'

Despite his high intelligence, Joyce was unable to rationalize setbacks such as these without blaming others: he blamed his failure to complete his MA on a member of the faculty whom he alleged had stolen his research; his failure to join the Foreign Office he blamed on his not having an independent income. Unsure where his vocation lay, he drifted into work as a part-time tutor at a crammer. It provided him with a steady income – which was just as well, because, soon afterwards, Hazel announced that she was pregnant. Joyce's inadvertent career move proved fortunate for another reason – he discovered he was a natural pedagogue. He began looking for a full-time career in teaching.

Part of the appeal, for him, was in having impressionable young students treat him like the sage he always assumed he was. There was one pupil who was especially impressed: Mary Ogilvy, a bright and prepossessing young woman of fairly noble birth (her father was the younger son of a baronet). The two first met in 1927 when Mary was sixteen. Within months they had embarked upon an affair. It lasted for about a year.

Heather Joyce was born on 30 July 1928. The delivery was difficult – William wept at the sight of his wife in pain – and, though he was excited about becoming a father for the first time, the introduction of a baby to the house put an additional strain on his marriage. It was not long before Hazel found out about Mary. The two were members of the same branch of the Conservative Party, Chelsea – as indeed was William, who fancied his chances of being selected as the Tory candidate for that safe seat. Hazel, who was now working at a chemist's shop in Shepherd's Bush, tearfully confided in Mrs Marsden-Smedly, a senior member of the Chelsea Conservative Association, that William 'owned to having seduced one of his pupils, was in love with her and wanted a divorce to marry her'. Mrs Marsden-Smedly was scandalized. 'We pounced,' she later recalled. 'Moral pressure was brought to bear on [Joyce] and he was allowed to resign, which he did with customary flamboyance.' Joyce said he was resigning because he had tried to reform the Tory party but had found it 'unreformable'. He said he had 'lost his lemon' with the Chelsea Tories. But everyone knew the real reason.

The affair ended when Mary was sent abroad, first to Austria and then to Paris where she studied history of art and music. Later, when Joyce became famous as Lord Haw-Haw, Mary feared that the truth might come out about her affair. It did not. She married, had six children and, after the war, moved to South Africa. In the 1950s she confessed all to her son Tully. She had fallen under Joyce's spell, she said, and he had 'deflowered' her. She recalled especially that he had been obsessed with Wagner and that he played her his recordings constantly as a form of seduction. For his part, Joyce never quite got over Mary Ogilvy – in the final weeks of the war he referred to her wistfully in his diary, wondering what might have been.

In 1929, the lovelorn Joyce distracted himself with politics, showing ever more commitment to his chosen cause. He began to get noticed for his ebullient soapbox style. By this stage he wasn't anti-Semitic so much as race-conscious, and he regarded the right as the 'the upholders of

Anglo-Saxon tradition and supremacy'. The Wall Street Crash and the Great Depression that followed it heightened the political tensions of the time. In desperation, people looked to ideological extremes for answers, be they communist or fascist. Joyce flirted with a number of crackpot, fascist splinter groups. But his heart was not in any of them. He longed for a political heavyweight to come along and unite all the small factions into a single powerful whole. He was in luck – such a man was looming on the horizon, and he had the potential to become a political giant.

FIVE

'Hitler and Mosley, what are they for? Thuggery, buggery, hunger and war!'

For Joyce, a parvenu quivering with English patriotism, the attraction of Sir Oswald Mosley was obvious. Mosley – tall, handsome, urbane, titled, swashbuckling – was ten years older than Joyce and an Establishment figure with a capital E. He was a Wykehamist (an old boy of Winchester College), a war veteran (having served with the Royal Flying Corps), an Olympic fencer and, so clearly it seemed, a man of destiny. He moved easily among the rich and powerful. Indeed, such were his social bona fides, when he married the daughter of Lord Curzon in 1920, King George V and Queen Mary were among the guests.

He was also a rising star on the political stage. He had won a seat in parliament at the age of twenty-two, as a Coalition-Unionist (Conservative), and had then crossed the floor, first as an Independent and then as a member of the Labour Party (in protest about the use of torture to interrogate Sinn Féin prisoners). In 1929, he had been appointed Chancellor of the Duchy of Lancaster. Now, as the new decade dawned, Mosley resigned from the Labour Party to form the New Party.

He had, he said, become disillusioned by the government's failure to act on mass unemployment. But there was another reason. He had good political antennae; he sensed people were looking for a radical change in British politics. In a diary entry for 1930, his friend the diplomat and writer Harold Nicolson described a dinner party at the house of Oliver Stanley, a future Secretary of State for the Colonies. Among the future political heavyweights present were Bob Boothby, Walter Elliot and Mosley. The gentlemanly discussion centred on 'whether it would be well to have a fascist coup'. Mosley certainly thought so and within months he had welded all the cranky little fascist factions into one cohesive political movement.

By this time, Joyce had passed an examination to become a Licentiate of the College of Preceptors. It sounded grand but all it meant was that he was now qualified to teach full-time. This he proceeded to do, at the Victoria Tutorial College. He was feeling popular: his students admired him, in part because he was generous with his time, especially with any keen to learn the subtleties of chess. These were halcyon days for Joyce: he had the rhymes of the romantic poets on his tongue and their heroic ideals in his head. And, on the domestic front, things seemed to have stabilized: the Joyces had a second daughter, Diana, on 20 July 1931.

In January 1932, Mosley and Harold Nicolson visited Mussolini in Rome. They took note of what was happening in Germany: the Nazis had grown to become the largest party there, claiming 230 of the 608 seats in the Reichstag. The Foreign Office, though, was alarmed. Fascism was sweeping Europe: Mussolini in Italy, Hitler in Germany – and now Mosley, who had taken to wearing riding boots and a black shirt, was set to become the movement's torch bearer in Britain.

His plans for careers in the civil service and the army now shelved in favour of academia, Joyce registered for a PhD in philosophy and psychology at King's College, London. But he still had half an eye on a career in politics, and, though the Foreign Office door had been slammed in his face, an MI5 door had creaked open. Maxwell Knight was about to take charge of an ultra-secret autonomous section within MI5's B Branch, 'M Section', later called B5(b). It would be responsible for infiltrating extreme left- and right-wing political organizations. Knight had proposed the idea to the Director-General of MI5 by arguing that the strongest arm of counter-subversion was long-term counter-intelligence and infiltration. He had been given the approving nod and was now busy recruiting agents. In this context Knight wrote 'an appreciation of W Joyce from one who has known him for many years.' It amounted to a mini-biography. 'In Ireland he saw battle, murder and sudden death at a very tender age. When he came to England after the Irish trouble he commenced to educate himself and achieved comparatively brilliant success.

He was as fanatical in his studies as he is in other directions, and several times during his scholastic career he reduced himself to the verge of a nervous breakdown.' Knight was especially interested in Joyce's language skills, noting that he spoke several and was fluent in French and German. The spymaster also knew, from Joyce presumably, about the 'intelligence work' Joyce had done in Ireland and so, around this time, he sounded his friend out on whether he would be prepared go to Germany as a deep-cover British agent, become naturalized there and join the Nazi Party. It is not known how Joyce responded to this suggestion, but presumably, given that he had a young family, a steady job at home, and he considered the Germans sympathetic allies in the fight against world communism, it would not have appealed to him much, as a long-term venture at least. He did, however, agree to act as an MI5 agent charged with the task of passing on information to the Security Service about political extremism, both communist and fascist. And by now something else had come along to convince Joyce his destiny lay in Britain: Mosley's dynamic new political movement.

On 1 October 1932, Mosley founded the British Union of Fascists. By the end of the month the first acts of violence had taken place: at a meeting in Stoke a heckler challenged Mosley to a fight; Mosley jumped down from his platform to face him; a fracas ensued. Soon, whenever columns of fascists singing 'Rule, Britannia!' took to the streets they would be met by columns of communists singing 'The Internationale' in counterpoint. The two sides would hurl abuse and slogans at each other as they marched, and when they met they would trade punches.

Within months, BUF membership had reached ten thousand. The party created a paramilitary headquarters in Chelsea, the Black House, and posted uniformed sentries at its door. They copied the fascist salute. Members addressed Mosley as the Leader – in imitation of the Duce – and each other by surname only. In the yard stood military-looking trucks for carrying speakers to their venues, as well as squads for skirmishes with 'Red troublemakers'. When recruits joined the BUF they undertook to pay a monthly subscription of a shilling if employed, and four pence if unemployed. This being the Depression, most paid four pence. They were expected to buy their own black shirts from the Black House for seven shillings and sixpence but were given free a badge which was a representation of the fasces – a bundle of sticks bound together around a central axe – symbolizing that a single stick might be broken but a bunch could not be: this had been the symbol of the magistrates' office in ancient Rome, and was now the emblem of Mussolini's fascist Italy.

The early membership of the BUF included Jews. In January 1933, the month Hitler came to power, Mosley said: 'Racial and religious persecution are alien to the British character. We do not attack Jews because they are Jews, we only attack them if we find them pursing an anti-British policy: any Jew who is not anti-British will always get a square deal with us.' It wasn't to last. He would, like Joyce, soon come to regard Jews as synonymous with communists, and therefore a useful enemy to rally against. Whilst not actually fashionable among the intelligentsia, anti-Semitism was certainly not a taboo: Virginia Woolf, T. S. Eliot, George Orwell, Noël Coward, Graham Greene, Agatha Christie and John Buchan all held mildly anti-Semitic views at this time. And W. B. Yeats was virulent in this regard.

A reputation for fascist violence soon spread, and it played into Mosley's hands. He had recognized the importance of image in politics and his embryonic party was becoming known as much for its leader's bodyguards – muscular youth-club members who carried rubber truncheons and glared challengingly at audiences – as for its policies. BUF meetings were deliberately theatrical in presentation: in March 1933 Mosley took his followers to the Free Trade Hall in Manchester. He tried to restrain his stewards from being too obviously rough to a heckler; the police intervened to restore order and told Mosley's goons to leave the building. Mosley ordered them to obey and stood with arms folded while the police tried and failed to produce conditions in which his speech could be heard.

Many political figures had been attracted to Mosley's cause, John Strachey, Aneurin Bevan and Randolph Churchill among them. The attitude towards the BUF at Westminster seemed to be a matter of 'wait and see'. Joyce joined within months, possibly at Knight's behest. Although Knight was a sincere fascist, his modus operandi was to keep an eye on the BUF on behalf of MI5. In this capacity, he wrote a glowing report about Joyce: 'A born leader of men, and very loyal and sincere in his ideals. He is a rare combination of a dreamer and a man of action.'

The Leader recognized Joyce's potential, too, especially his oratorical skills. As a self-confident, energetic soapbox orator who could and would crack jokes as well as quote long passages of Virgil and Shakespeare from memory, Joyce had found his metier. Although he had had an audience as an academic – according to A. K. Chesterton, he was a 'brilliant if erratic lecturer who commanded a considerable following' – it had been captive. Now people were coming voluntarily to hear him speak, albeit with impure motives sometimes. He once spoke about fascism for four hours at Evesham and, according to Chesterton, 'people stayed on out of sheer curiosity to ascertain how long he could keep it up.'

For an ambitious, articulate and ideologically driven twenty-six-year-old, the BUF presented a thrillingly new and dangerous alternative to the dull old bourgeois order. Joyce was contemptuous of the mediocrity of the established parties and the effete liberalism of the intellectuals. 'Fascism,' he declared, 'is not a creed for the smug mice who choose to emerge from under Bloomsbury tea-cosies to have a nibble at it.' In other words, he kept a knuckleduster in his desk alongside volumes of Burke, Dryden and Pope.

The Reichstag fire in the late winter of 1933 enabled Hitler to assume greater powers and use force to quell opposition. Many of Mosley's grander supporters, such as Harold Nicolson, had backed away, unnerved by the direction Continental fascism was taking. When, in the summer of 1933, six months after Hitler had been appointed Chancellor, Mosley decided to visit Germany, Nicolson no longer wanted to be seen at his side. Mosley invited Joyce to accompany him instead.

For some time Joyce had been worrying about the embarrassment he might cause to the British Union of Fascists if it became known that he, one of its leading lights, wasn't actually British. Significantly, membership of the BUF was open to 'all *British* subjects irrespective of race'. No proof of nationality was needed, though. A candidate simply had to state that he or she was loyal to King and Empire. Joyce may even have feared that he faced deportation if his true nationality was discovered – a humiliating prospect for one who regarded himself as a patriotic Englishman. He needed a passport to get to Germany, and the risk of making a false statement, as opposed to admitting the truth, must have seemed negligible to him. Besides, by now he probably thought of himself as British. He certainly *felt* British. He had claimed to be British (enough) to join the OTC, was on the electoral register as British and for years his father had encouraged him to think of himself as British. (He must have told his father about his decision to apply for a British passport because, as Quentin Joyce later testified, his father took all his documents relating to his American naturalization out into the garden and burnt them on a bonfire. These may have included William's papers, too, because Michael Joyce had obtained a copy of his son's birth certificate from New York on 2 November 1917 and this seems to have disappeared. It did not matter, as it happened: a birth certificate was not needed for British passport applications, just two references.)

This, then, was the background to Joyce's decision to lie about his place of birth. It was to prove his tragic turning point, his *peripeteia*. Ironically the date of his passport application was 4 July, American Independence Day. His declaration of independence read: 'I, the under-signed, William Joyce, at present residing at 41 Farquhar Road, SE19, London, hereby declare that I am a British subject by birth, having been born at Rutledge Terrace, Galway, Ireland, on the twenty-fourth day of April, 1906, and not having lost the status of British subject this acquired, I hereby apply for a passport for travelling to Belgium, France, Germany, Switzerland, Italy, and Austria for the purposes of holiday touring.'

Joyce had unwittingly signed his own death warrant. From this moment on, he was a condemned man.★

As things turned out, Mosley could not go on the trip to Germany and so he sent Joyce in his stead, as part of a small BUF delegation. There is a photograph of Joyce taken at a Nuremberg rally on 31 August 1933, two months after he applied for his passport. It was printed in the official Nazi brochure to mark the occasion, and standing two away from him, wearing a tweed suit and black shirt, is Unity Mitford. The two got to know each other slightly. Whether Joyce also used this trip to do any work for Knight is a matter of speculation.

Mosley was otherwise preoccupied in the summer of 1933: busy setting out a statement of aims in a manifesto called *The Greater Britain*. British fascism, he wrote, was not a creed of personal dictatorship in the Conti-

---

★ The twenty-seven-year-old American later claimed he had given false information in order to be consistent with the 'special passport' he had signed to get him out of Ireland. If Joyce really had been given a passport by the Foreign Office in 1921 it would not have been valid in 1933. It is possible that it could have been renewed for a further five years in 1926 – in an interview with the author, Joyce's daughter Heather claimed that her parents had gone to Florence in the late 1920s – but as yet no records have emerged to support this.

nental manner. Nor was it anti-Semitic and violent in character. 'If the situation of violence is to be averted, the Old Gang Government must be overthrown and effective measures must be adopted before the situation has gone too far. The enemy today is the Old Gang of parliamentarians. The enemy of tomorrow, if their rule persists much longer, will be the Communist Party.' Mosley dismissed the old parties as 'organisations of old women, tea-fights and committees.' He protested that it was never the BUF's intention to cause violence – he claimed they were just trying to suppress Red anarchy and maintain law and order – but many assumed the brawling that accompanied his meetings was a deliberate attempt to destroy democratic procedures. In private he would refer to his 'biff boys' and say: 'We shall rely on the good old English fist.'

With success came the cranks. One, a conman called George Crellin, joined the BUF and promptly announced that he was the Director of Finance. On the strength of this he hired a large car and a horse to ride around Hyde Park on. He was only able to get away with this because the finance department at Black House was full of smoke and mirrors. Indeed, in August 1933, J. R. Clynes, a former Home Secretary, wrote that Mosley was becoming 'the Greta Garbo of British politics', because he was surrounding himself with a fog of mystery so dense that even his own followers must have found it difficult to penetrate. But the secrecy was understandable: Mussolini had begun financing the BUF and would continue to do so for the next two years.

Excited by his growing reputation as a speaker, Joyce decided to resign from his post at the Victoria Tutorial College, abandon his doctorate at King's College and accept an offer to work full time as the West London Area Administrative Officer for the BUF. Here was a chance to practise psychology rather than theorize about it. He had an intuitive grasp of the black magic of propaganda, engineering mass emotions by a precise psychological pressure. He was soon appointed the Director of Propaganda on a respectable salary of £300 a year. In this capacity he trained activists, wrote papers and delivered speeches, often while standing on the roof of a loudspeaker van. In the party magazine *Blackshirt* he described democracy as a psychopathic expression of inferiority.

On 20 November that year Mosley's recurring phlebitis caused him to drop out of a rally at Streatham, and he asked Joyce to make the 'leader's speech' in his stead. Joyce seized the opportunity and proved he could be just as mesmerizing a demagogue as Mosley. A week later he faced an audience of more than five thousand at Liverpool Stadium. When word of the rally got out, thousands of protesters armed with knuckledusters and potatoes embedded with razor blades turned up outside and chanted: 'Hitler and Mosley, what are they for? Thuggery, buggery, hunger and war!' Joyce took it all in his stride and delivered an electrifying speech. He was now being widely talked of as a possible successor to Mosley, in the event of the Leader's phlebitis proving fatal.

A. K. Chesterton, a cousin of the writer G. K. Chesterton, was a prominent BUF member at this time. A tall, thin man with piercing eyes, he was regarded as a hero among party members, not least because he was a man of action who had won a Military Cross for bravery in the trenches. 'William Joyce is a brilliant writer, speaker and exponent of policy,' he wrote after Joyce's triumph at the Liverpool rally. 'He has addressed hundreds of meetings, always at his best, always revealing the iron spirit of fascism in his refusal to be intimidated by violent opposition.'

Another who was impressed by Joyce's rhetorical skills was John Beckett, a former Labour MP who had acquired notoriety by attempting to remove the Mace during a stormy session at the House of Commons. He had became Publicity Director for the BUF and was known for his jokes and irreverent stories. Many BUF members remembered him telling the story of the Mace, and how it was so light that he almost fell over backwards. Joyce's six-year-old daughter Heather remembered hearing one of the adults tell her mother: 'That John Beckett, he's got a filthy tongue,' and the next time Heather met John, she watched him, hoping he would stick his tongue out so that she could see what a filthy tongue looked like. Beckett, whose mother was Jewish, loathed accepting orders. He seems to have considered Joyce a kindred sprit. 'I first met him in 1933 at a great and crowded meeting in Paddington Baths. I had left political life in disgust some years previously, and as I was much impressed with the fascist creed, a friend urged me to join the Mosley organisation. I asked who else they had to lead beside Mosley, and was taken to Joyce's meeting as an answer to the query. I have heard all those men who are claimed amongst our greatest speakers. Within ten minutes of this twenty-seven-year-old taking the platform, I knew that here was one of the dozen finest orators in the country. Snowden's close reasoning and unerring instinct for words were allied with Maxton's humour and Churchill's daring.* That great audience assembled to hear a speaker quiet unknown in the political world and the enthusiasm created was an eye-opener to me, and would have been to most of the Westminster hacks with whom I had previously associated public influence.'

1934 proved to be a heady year for the British Union of Fascists. Its membership rose to fifty thousand† and it seemed an unstoppable force. The mood at Black House was that the BUF would be in power within a year. Chilling and strange as it may now seem, William Joyce was being talked of as a future viceroy of India. To many British fascists it suddenly seemed as if they were no longer on the fringe, they were about to take centre stage. For one thing, their party had the swooning support of the *Daily Mail*. In a leading article Lord Rothermere himself declared: 'The Blackshirt movement is the organised effort of the younger generation to break this stranglehold which senile politicians have so long maintained on our public affairs. Being myself in the middle sixties, I know how stealthily and steadily that seventh decade saps one's powers and stiffens one's prejudices.'

And Rothermere wasn't the only member of the great and good to take Mosley seriously. Lloyd George said: 'Sir Oswald is a very able man and he is making considerable headway.' Ezra Pound and Wyndham Lewis were among the literary figures who supported Mosley, even if Lewis was a little nervous about being photographed at Black House – he would come hurrying in with his hat pulled down and his coat collar up around his ears. George Bernard Shaw, the great apologist for Stalin, now applied his skills as a judge of character to Mosley. In a lecture to the Fabian Society he said: 'Sir Oswald Mosley is a very interesting man to read just now – one of the few people who is thinking and writing about real things and not about figments and phases. I know you dislike him, because he looks like a man who has some physical courage and is going to do something and that is a terrible thing. You instinctively hate him because you do not know where he will land you, and he evidently means to uproot some of you.'

At a mass rally at the Albert Hall in April 1934, Mosley addressed an audience of ten thousand supporters. The evening began with an orchestra

---

* James Maxton and Philip Snowden were Labour MPs.
† Claims vary. Some sources say forty thousand. Special Branch put BUF membership at twenty thousand.

and choir playing the 'Horst Wessel' song, set to English words. According to the *Manchester Guardian*: 'Just before eight the spotlights were turned on to the long gangway leading through the arena to the platform and a procession of twelve standard bearers marched in carrying alternately Union Jacks and fascist banners. The standard bearers grouped themselves round the organ, the spotlights swung back to the main entrance, and there stood the Man of Destiny. Slowly he paced across the hall, chest out, handsome head flung back, while his followers, every man on his feet, cheered and cried "Hail Mosley! Hail Mosley! Hail Mosley!"'

Mosley spoke without notes for an hour and a half, declaring among other things that the British fascists were patriots fighting in the war against communism. He also said he believed fascists should take power using democratic means, then declare a dictatorship.

Mosley's son Nicholas recalled: 'There was always a large part of a speech by my father that was calmly and rationally presented: sometimes his critics said that this was too large a part – that he overestimated his audience by assuming it could follow the technicalities of his arguments. But the flow of fact and argument gave an impression of great control and authority. And then there would be a change; he would stand back from the microphone as if he were a boxer sizing up an opponent before a knock-out attack: he was coming to his peroration. There is still in existence a gramophone record of the end of this Albert Hall speech; my father's voice comes out lashing like some great sea: it is pulverising, it is also, from a human being, like something carried far away beyond sense. It sends shivers up and down the spine – of both wonder and alarm – what is it all for, this yell for immolation? People at the end of such a speech of my father's were on their feet and cheering; it was as if they had been lifted high on a wave; what did it matter if they were hurled against, or over the top of, a cliff?'

In May there was a large Blackshirt dinner at the Savoy Hotel with guests in full evening dress and Mosley and his mother photographed for *Tatler*. The first big Hyde Park rally came that summer. As the Blackshirts, their hair shaved at the sides, formed around Marble Arch, the communists arrived from the Bayswater Road accompanied by fife and drum. The two forces met. They jostled. The police tried to keep order. Then a phalanx of Blackshirts arrived from Park Lane marching in columns of three. At their head was Mosley, dressed in black, his toothbrush moustache twitching. The Blackshirts formed a tunnel and the arms went up in salute. Both Mosley and Pollitt were speaking and the event attracted sixty thousand people, by police estimates.

After that, massed ranks of two or three thousand Blackshirts would regularly parade in Hyde Park and White City. Joyce found such rallies exhilarating. The largest indoor one was on 7 June that year at Olympia. A crowd of fifteen thousand turned up. In the week before the meeting, the communist *Daily Worker* had published plans for a five-column march on Olympia and produced a road map to show readers how to get there. They were to merge in the Hammersmith Road at 6.30 p.m. About three thousand communist protesters, many armed with knuckledusters, converged on the venue while a cordon of five hundred policemen on horseback and on foot kept the path clear for ticket-holders. When guests such as Lord Trenchard arrived by car they were met with jeers.

According to Philip Toynbee, one of the spectators: 'The leader strode into the arc lights. He was flanked by four blond young men, and a platoon of flag-waving Blackshirts followed in their wake. The procession moved very slowly down the aisle, amid shouts, screams, and bellows of admiration; amid two forests of phallic, upraised arms. Sir Oswald held one arm at his side, thumb in leather belt: the other flapped nonchalantly from time to time as he turned a high chin to inspect us.'

A couple of hundred communists had infiltrated the crowd and they began jeering and chanting 'fascism is murder'. Mosley paused and waited, hands on hips, while searchlights played on the chaotic scene below him. When the heckler was identified, the Blackshirts chanted and the nearest squad of 'biff boys' advanced and ejected him aggressively. Two protesters climbed up into the roof and, while hanging from the girders, scattered communist leaflets on the crowd below. There were running fights. Hecklers were so brutally handled some were knocked unconscious and others had to be rushed to hospital. Film crews recorded the beatings.

The fascists may have won the fight that night, but over the next few days the communists won the propaganda victory. In the papers, one Conservative MP called it 'a deeply shocking scene' and accused the Blackshirts of behaving like 'bullies and cads'. He deplored the introduction into England of this 'vile bitterness, copied from foreign lands'. Another eyewitness, also an MP, was quoted as saying: 'Again and again as five or six fascists carried out an interrupter by arms and legs, several other fascists were engaged in hitting and kicking his helpless body.' A vicar supported this account: 'In the corridor a young man was being chased by a horde of Blackshirts: some collared him by the legs, some by the arms, and, held in this way, he was beaten on the head by any fascist who could get near him.'

Only Patrick Donner MP took the side of the fascists. In the *National Review* he wrote: 'The fact is that many of the communists were armed with razors, stockings filled with broken glass, knuckledusters and iron bars; that they marched from the East End, the police kindly escorting, with the avowed purpose of wrecking the meeting. Can it, in equity, be argued that the stewards used their fists, when provoked in this manner, with more vigour than perhaps the situation required?'

The *Daily Mail* thought so, especially after Hitler's 'Night of the Long Knives' in which eighty senior SA men were murdered. Prompted by this news, Jewish firms such as Lyons threatened to withdraw their advertising from the *Daily Mail* unless it in turn withdrew its support for the BUF. Rothermere agreed.

As a damage-limitation exercise, Mosley wrote to Rothermere: 'We have given our pledge that no racial or religious persecution will occur under fascism in Britain; but we shall require the Jews, like everyone else, to put the interests of Britain first. We no longer admit Jews to membership of our movement because a) they have bitterly attacked us; b) they have organised as an internal movement which aims at national organisation and revival. We certainly are not prepared to relax our attitude towards the Jews in view of the fact that in the last year 80% of the convictions for physical attacks on fascists were pronounced on Jews while the Jewish community represents only 0.6% of the population.'

Rothermere replied: 'My dear Mosley, as you know, I have never thought that a movement calling itself fascist could be successful in this country, and I have also made it clear in my conversations with you that I never could support any movement with an anti-Semitic bias, any movement that had dictatorship as one of its objectives, nor any movement which would substitute a "corporate state" for parliamentary institutions in this country. The assistance which I have rendered you was given in the hope that you would be prepared to ally yourself with the Conservative forces to defeat socialism at the next and succeeding elections.'

By no means all the Blackshirts thought it a bad thing to lose the *Daily*

Mail as an ally. A. K. Chesterton wrote: 'Lord Rothermere imagined, it seems, that Mosley was a Right-Wing Tory instead of a fascist revolutionary, and that his movement existed to bolster up big business in Britain. Incalculable harm was done by this intervention, and the large influx of recruits which resulted proved almost useless to a man.'

Mosley decided it was time to shed the party's reputation for violence and ill-discipline. He put Joyce in charge of 'I Squad', a 'defence force' who wore breeches, jackboots and peaked caps with their black shirts. They were trained in boxing, judo and self-defence. A leaflet was printed stating the required behaviour of a member of I Squad: 'He stands, together with his fellow stewards, smartly to attention with hands by his side. When the hecklers start, the speaker at first tries to calm them; but if this fails, and potatoes studded with razor-blades come sailing over, it is the steward's duty to stop the disturbance. Often he finds that these missiles are being thrown by women while their menfolk stand well out of harm's way singing. He is not allowed to harm any woman. If he is hit by a man he is entitled to hit back – not otherwise. If the police come upon the scene, any disorder is at once left to them. Fascists immediately drop their hands, even if they are in the act of being struck, and leave retaliation to the police.'

The new rules seemed to work. One night soon after they were issued, members of the BUF were attacked with stones down a side street in Manchester. Three were injured and they counter-attacked but stopped when recalled by a bugle. Records show that the police were impressed by this 'show of discipline'. One officer said: 'Joyce really had his men under control and he was always fair to us. We could never come to an understanding with the communists. But if I went to Joyce and told him that his men were doing something that wasn't fair to the police, trying us too hard or interfering with our time off, he'd have his men right off that job in half an hour and there'd be no grumbling.'

I Squad tended to socialize together. Eric Piercy, one of its members, became a friend to Joyce, and more than a friend to Joyce's wife Hazel. One reason why Joyce did not realize he was being cuckolded was that he was working long hours. The regime at the Black House was tough. According to a District Inspector at the National Headquarters: 'Day and night the Black House buzzed with activity. Typewriters rattled in administrative offices, printing presses clattered out the *Blackshirt* – the first

BUF weekly paper. In one lecture room, a lesson on election law would be in progress; in another aspiring speakers would be put through their hesitant paces; elsewhere the young tough men of I Squad were being taught their boxing and judo. Cars roared in and out of the transport yard, and all the time there was a constant stream of callers and enquirers, some of whom were well known figures in the literary, professional, business and sporting worlds. Those who went home after a mere eight or nine hours at their desks were labelled clock watchers and denounced as unworthy of the cause they served. As many of them had wives or young families, domestic unhappiness too frequently arose. Wife trouble became one of the recognised occupational hazards of British fascism.'

Maxwell Knight had by now taken to wearing a mackintosh and a brown trilby with a turned-down brim. Rarely a week went by without him adding fresh information to Joyce's file – indeed on 17 December 1934, he noted, perhaps a touch enviously, that 'EH Piercy is on intimate terms with Joyce's wife'. He wrote an admiring MI5 report about Joyce around this time: 'Although Joyce has much in common with Mosley he can be a much more likeable character in many ways. His political beliefs are probably very mobile, but it is considered that his fundamentals are quite sound. I should not think that anything could occur to shake his basic patriotism and he is violently opposed to what can be broadly described as bolshevism.'

Joyce was now living on the King's Road, near the Black House, and Knight would occasionally drop in on him at home. Hazel Joyce would get 'very excited' about these visits. Joyce seems to have been a model father to his daughters, who were now six and three. 'He used to do funny things to make us laugh,' Heather recalled. 'He would play the piano and sing silly songs: folk tunes and old Irish rebel songs, for a joke. And he liked to take us for boat rides in Battersea Park. He was affectionate. He loved his children. Loved his home. But he did have an awful temper. When he was annoyed he would habitually slam the door behind him. He would then go for a very long walk to Richmond Park and come back hours later in good humour. My mother would say "he has forgotten it all now".' He seems to have wanted to use his skills as a teacher on his own children. 'He would teach us about the Greek myths and would also take out his Bible in the evenings and read it to us.' But he must also have been filling their innocent heads with fascist thoughts.

Heather drew a cartoon of a Jew with a big nose one day and handed it to her father with the word 'Mazeltov!' And one day she heard her father singing 'Dulwich over Alice'; only years later did she realize he must have been singing: 'Deutschland über Alles'.

SIX

'The greatest Englishman I have ever known.'

Given that Mosley was nearly a whole foot taller than Joyce, they must have looked quite comical standing side by side in the dock at Lewes Assizes on a cold, windy day in December 1934. They had been arrested after a rally in Worthing, Sussex, and charged with assault and riotous assembly. The judge tried to establish what had happened. About a hundred fascists, it seems, had marched through the town and had been met by a gang of three hundred or so Reds, many of whom had arrived from London and were giving the clenched-fist salute. The crowd set off fireworks and chanted: 'To hell with the Blackshirts!' and 'Throw Mosley into the sea!' Mosley wasn't thrown, but he was struck. The police were called. The Blackshirts mounted a fighting retreat to a cafe and when they looked out of the window they saw a barrage of tomatoes and eggs being hurled. Mosley and Joyce tried to make a run for it but were spotted and, amid cries of 'There's Mosley! Let's get the bastard!' they were attacked and beaten up. Blackshirt reinforcements arrived and launched a counter-attack which left several anti-fascists bloody and unconscious in shop doorways. Two men ended up in hospital.

No witnesses were prepared to come forward and testify, but a policeman did commend Joyce for his discipline under provocation. The charges were dropped and Joyce felt intoxicated, convinced that he enjoyed the acquiescence of the Establishment as represented by the police, MI5 and the legal system. He also felt proud to be seen as Mosley's right-hand man, his admiration for him verging on hero worship. In a speech to a Brighton audience he gushed: 'We know that England is crying for a leader and that leader has emerged in the person of the greatest Englishman I have ever known, Sir Oswald Mosley.'

Joyce, too, was having a kind of greatness thrust upon him by his admirers. According to Peter Morris, a fellow Blackshirt: 'He was known as the Mighty Atom. He was an excellent speaker. He gave the impression of strength. He was short, and thick. He was broad as he was long. His chest was terrific, his waist was small, his legs were terrific, his arm muscles were terrific. He had worked his body. And he was such a charismatic character. Both on the platform and in little groups of people, he always dominated every group.'

And after his brush with the law in Worthing, he also became admired for his bravery among his fellow Blackshirts, who by this time included Joseph Hepburn-Ruston (Audrey Hepburn's father) and, possibly, Spike Milligan.* One enthusiastic former Blackshirt, Ronald W. Jones, recalled: 'Brave? Oh yes, Joyce was brave all right. I can so well remember plunging behind him into the heart of a mob literally howling (mobs do and it's frightening) with fury.'

Joyce's fame went to his head. In one delusion of grandeur he wrote to Goebbels to share his theories about the German economy. There is no record of Goebbels writing back. Perhaps Joyce felt he could identify with 'the gallant little doctor', as he called him: after all, both were short in stature, wildly optimistic and highly skilled at oratory. They were both from a Catholic, academic background and had a passion for Goethe and Shakespeare. And both were prone to hero-worship.

By 1935 Joyce had begun to follow events in Germany carefully and had become convinced that Mosley should forget about Mussolini and model himself on Hitler. To this end, he used his role as deputy chief speaker to try and bounce the Leader into a more pro-Hitler agenda.

Some of Mosley's aides sensed what Joyce was up to and urged caution on their man. G. S. Gerault wrote a report for the Leader: 'It should be

---

* Milligan claimed that he joined the Young Communist League around this time, but according to his biographer Humphrey Carpenter, several sources, including a policeman, have suggested that it was actually the British Union of Fascists he briefly joined. Perhaps Milligan, being Milligan, joined both. After all, in a television interview in the 1970s he said that he sometimes used to wear a black shirt in the 1930s just to see what reaction he would get.

realised that the country as a whole is 95 per cent against Hitler and all that he has done; and all the protests and explanations which may be made fall on deaf ears. We are definitely wasting time in any attempt to defend the Hitler regime, and we should have contented ourselves with saying that it is far too early for any intelligent man to form any sort of conclusion. There is an undoubted feeling throughout the movement that the leader is being jockeyed either knowingly or unknowingly into an impossible position by Assistant Administrative Officer Joyce; and there are those who say that he is now, to all intents and purposes, the Movement. This feeling is intensified when members see pamphlet after pamphlet on policy appearing over this officer's signature; when they should either be anonymous or signed by the Leader.'

For Joyce, being pro-Hitler meant being anti-Semitic. When, after a speech in Chiswick, he was asked about class war and the 'tea-for-twos', as he called the Jews, he said: 'I don't regard Jews as a class. I regard them as a privileged misfortune.' This was reported in the papers the next day alongside a photograph of Joyce in his black shirt. Mosley did not object.

Joyce admitted his pro-Hitler stance didn't always find favour among the British. In fact he said that when he made speeches people sometimes 'stared as if I was a hawker of ladies' underwear who had accidentally strayed into a monastery.' Although the term 'racism' was coined in 1935, 'anti-Semitism' in Britain was still something of an abstraction, based loosely on the feeling that Jews were running big business. The idea that Jews were both powerful and corrupt appealed to those who felt that life was treating them unfairly – it provided a useful, all-purpose conspiracy theory. There was a vague collective memory, for example, that an Attorney-General, Rufus Isaacs, had been implicated in the Marconi scandal of 1912/1913, but that was about the only impact Jews had made on the British national consciousness. In the East End, though, it was a different story. Jews had settled there after the Great War and had become associated with gangsterism. (The same was true of certain towns on the south coast, which was why Mosley and Joyce had gone to stir up trouble in Worthing. Brighton and Hove were other towns that were associated with Jewish settlement. In *Brighton Rock*, published in 1938, Graham Greene describes Pinkie being cornered: 'Semitic faces ringing him all round. They grinned back at him: every man his razor out.')

Joyce, then, found a more receptive audience for his anti-Semitic views when he took his soapbox into the East End. His targets were Jewish bankers and communists, but also the public schools, aristocratic decadence, the Stock Exchange and parliamentary democracy. He spoke about the need for hard work, discipline and national purification; about the plight of the unemployed, the farmers and the shopkeepers, as well as the need for Anglo-German agreement. His humour though sardonic and rude often had bite. He described Ramsay MacDonald as the 'Loon from Lossiemouth. The Bright Hope of Socialism installed as head of a Tory government amidst the ape-like grins of the City Financiers.' The Liberal Party, he declared in another speech, was 'formed out of the scum and dregs of all that was left in the worst elements of the Whig menagerie.' Winston Churchill was, after the Dardanelles disaster, 'an imitation strategist, the Butcher in Chief to His Majesty the King, willing to serve under any flag in order to improve fortune and minister to self-admiration.' Stanley Baldwin was 'the steel merchant metamorphosed into a squire by casual experiments in pig breeding.' Joyce also referred to the 'phenomenal freak whom it would be indecent to describe as Viceroy.'

A darker side to Joyce's oratory also emerged, as witnessed by Cecil Roberts, a writer who heard him at a political dinner at the Park Lane Hotel, London. 'After dinner we adjourned to the ballroom in which a member of the British fascist hierarchy was to make an address, in the unavoidable absence of Sir Oswald Mosley. The speaker, a person unknown to most of us, was thin, pale, intense, he had not been speaking many minutes before we were electrified by this man. I have been a connoisseur of speech-making for a quarter of a century, but never before, in any country, had I met a personality so terrifying in its dynamic force, so vituperative, so vitriolic. The words poured from him in a corrosive spate. He ridiculed our political system, he scarified our leading politicians, seizing upon their vulnerable points with a destructive analysis that left them bereft of merit or morality. We listened in a kind of frozen hypnotism to this cold, stabbing voice. There was a gleam of a Marat in his eyes, and his eloquence took on a Satanic ring when he invoked the rising wrath of his colleagues against the festering scum that by cowardice and sloth had reduced the British Empire to a moribund thing, in peril and annihilation.'

Joyce was pushing at an open door. Mosley never tried to discourage him from his racist views. They served his purpose because he had come round to Joyce's view that anti-Semitism was inseparable from anti-communism, because it was the Jews who were challenging the fascists at the rallies. 'I have encountered things in this country which I did not dream existed in Britain,' Mosley said in a speech at the Albert Hall. 'One of them is the power of organised Jewry which is today mobilised against fascism. They have thrown down their challenge to fascism, and I am not in the habit of ignoring challenges. Now they seek to howl over the length and breadth of the land that we are bent on racial and religious persecution. That charge is utterly untrue. Today we do not attack the Jews on racial or religious grounds; we take up the challenge that they have thrown down because they fight against fascism and against Britain. They have declared in their great folly to challenge the conquering force of the modern age: tonight we take up that challenge. They will it: let them have it!'

There was something comical about the Leader. Nancy Mitford lampooned him mercilessly in her novels of the time. P. G. Wodehouse recognized it, too. In *Code of the Woosters* (1938), Bertie Wooster tells Roderick Spode, the leader of the Blackshorts: 'The trouble with you, Spode, is that just because you have succeeded in inducing a handful of halfwits to disfigure the London scene by going about in black shorts, you think you're someone. You hear them shouting Hail Spode! And you imagine it is the Voice of the People. That is where you make your bloomer. What the Voice of the People is saying is "Look at that frightful ass Spode swanking about in footer bags! Did you ever in your puff see such a perfect perisher?"'

The fact that Mosley insisted on calling himself the Leader was enough to have the general population sniggering. When Hitler called himself the Führer no one laughed, even though he looked like Charlie Chaplin. When Mosley borrowed the title, everyone thought it hilarious. Even Joyce, one of his most devoted supports, took to calling him the Bleeder behind his back. Another popular joke was to call him the 'Lilliputian Führer'. A number of factors may explain why the British chose not to go down the fascist route taken by Italy, Germany and, after a fashion, Spain. One is that the movement, with its strange-sounding name and its sinister black uniform, just seemed too foreign for Little Englanders' tastes − in itself an entertaining twist given that the 'patriotic' BUF distrusted 'foreigners', and concentrated on Englishness rather than Britishness. Another reason may be that the English have a more developed sense of irreverence and irony than the Italians, Spanish and Germans. As Lord Haw-Haw was to discover to his cost in Berlin, the English sense of humour can be a dangerously subversive weapon. When the BUF symbol changed from the sticks bound together to a flash and a circle, it soon became known as the flash in the pan. The English urge to prick pomposity and mock those who take themselves too seriously proved in the end too strong.

George Orwell believed that if ever there was to be English fascism it would be sedate and subtle and, initially, unlikely to be referred to by the f-word. 'It is doubtful,' he wrote, 'whether a Gilbert & Sullivan heavy dragoon of Mosley's stamp would ever be much more than a joke to the majority of English people.' Sometimes the comedy was more a matter of being patronized. Just as the Nazis identified themselves with blood and soil, so the BUF always claimed a great affinity with farmers. One of the more bizarre charges against the Blackshirts was 'conspiring together to effect a public mischief'. This charge was levelled after BUF members dug ditches and built barricades to keep away bailiffs who wanted to carry away farm equipment and livestock. A crowd formed to watch. Police came to arrest them. They put up no resistance. At the Old Bailey, nineteen of them pleaded guilty and were discharged by the judge who rather sweetly said: 'I am told you are good fellows and I hope you will remain good fellows, realising how badly advised you were in this matter.'

Another example: the BUF candidate for Whitechapel was a professional boxer. Teddy 'Kid' Lewis was illiterate and could make only one speech, which he laboriously learned by heart. When word got out, wags would turn up to hear his speech and chant the lines along with him, while correcting any lapses of memory, and generally falling about laughing.

There was also something comical about the way the BUF was riddled with sympathetic MI5 spies. In addition to Joyce, the BUF intelligence officer P. G. Taylor, whose real name was James McGuirk Hughes, was on Knight's books. Another MI5 agent provocateur was Bill Allen, who had been an Ulster Unionist MP from 1929 to 1931 and was the heir to the W. H. Allen publishing empire. Allen, like Joyce, managed to spy on the BUF and be a committed fascist at the same time. Mosley even knew of Allen's MI5 connections. He let him continue working at the Black House, he said, because he considered Allen so eccentric he would be bound to provide unreliable information. 'Very much involved with MI5,' Mosley later said of Allen. 'Made no bones about it, that is why he wasn't imprisoned in the war, of course, because he had done so much for them.'

In 1935 a new Central Council was set up including John Beckett, William Joyce, A. K. Chesterton and Major General J. F. C. 'Boney' Fuller, a short, abrupt man who had been a celebrated military strategist in the First World War. Here there was another Maxwell Knight connection. Fuller was associated with Aleister Crowley, the self-styled 'apocalyptic beast', who was, in turn, associated with Knight. Crowley had been keen to help MI5 and had already passed on information on communism in Europe. Knight and Crowley had a mutual friend in the novelist Dennis Wheatley who shared their interest in the occult. Scandal followed Crowley wherever he went. He had run a community in Sicily where, it was said, a number of children had disappeared in connection with Satanic masses. Wheatley had met Crowley through the journalist Tom Driberg, another of Knight's agents.

Knight secretly applauded the anti-Semitism of Joyce and Mosley, and often made anti-Semitic jokes, regardless of the company. But there may have been another aspect of Blackshirt life that attracted him. The Black House seems to have been something of a haven for gay men. Neil Francis-Hawkins, the Director-General of the BUF, was an active homosexual, and at the party headquarters he surrounded himself with admiring young fellow travellers. It is tempting to think that the attractions of the BUF for gay men might have included the tight black uniforms, the body building, the male bonding and the choreographed drill. As the German Marxist critic Walter Benjamin put it: 'Fascism is the aestheticisation of politics.'

The BUF, of course, was consciously echoing the SS in its look and, as the historian Ian Kershaw has noted, the orchestrated might of the black-uniformed SS in the march-past scenes of Triumph of the Will elicits fear, but the image of the would-be master race intrigues at the same time. 'Fascination and repulsion are not far apart.' It may also have been that conservative-minded gays and lesbians felt socially excluded to some degree and so, as a compensation, they exaggerated their conservatism in order to feel included: a part of traditional, judgemental 'straight' society.

The presence of feisty young women, too, contributed to the sexually charged atmosphere at the Black House. The BUF, after all, prided itself

1. 'Willie' Joyce as a precocious ten-year-old schoolboy
(third from the right, back row) at St Ignatius College, Galway.

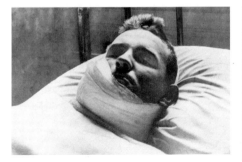

2. 'An attempt was made to cut my throat but the razor slashed a quarter of an inch too high. There is something to be said for having a well-fed appearance'.

3. As a young woman in Carlisle, Margaret White trained as a dancer. She spent her life fleeing boredom and, especially in Berlin, would often seek distraction on the dance floors of nightclubs.

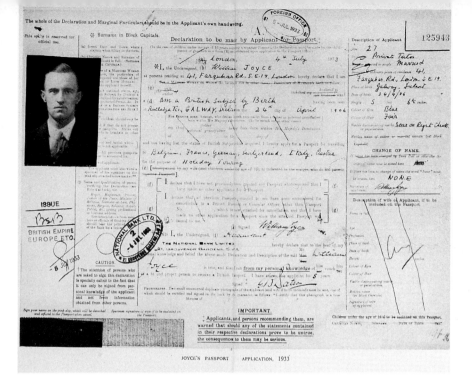

JOYCE'S PASSPORT   APPLICATION, 1933

4 (*left*). Mary Ogilvy was sixteen years old when she had an affair with the married William Joyce. They had met through the Chelsea Conservative Association and as soon as the affair became public knowledge Joyce was expelled from the Tory Party.

5 (*above*). Joyce's application for a British passport in 1933, essentially signing his own death warrant.

6 (*below*). Shortly after receiving the fraudulent British passport, Joyce (third from left) attended a Nuremberg rally with, among others, Unity Mitford (far left).

7 (*left*). Joyce in his black shirt with his scar showing. He was admired for his bravery among his fellow fascists, especially in street fights.

8 (*above*). British fascists on the march in London in 1934. Mosley had adopted the Nazi salute for his movement and had begun calling himself 'the Leader'. Joyce routinely changed this to 'the Bleeder'.

9 (*below*). Joyce sitting (at the end on the right) with the hierarchy of the British Union of Fascists in 1935. Seated second from left is Eric Piercy, the man who had an affair with, and later married, Joyce's first wife, Hazel.

10 (*left*). Margaret White dressed as a Blackshirt in 1936,
shortly before she married William Joyce.

11 (*above*). Joyce speaking at a BUF meeting in front of a table draped with
a Union Jack. An 'electrifying speaker', he once spoke for four hours.
People stayed on out of curiosity, to find out how long he could keep it up.

12 (*below*). Mosley cultivated an image of himself as a Man of Destiny.
By 1934 membership of the BUF had reached its peak of around 50,000
and he was convinced he would be in power within a year.

13. Maxwell Knight, an eccentric who kept snakes, parrots and a bushbaby in his home, employed Joyce as an agent in an autonomous department within MI5.

14. In 1937 Joyce took to wearing a trench coat like Hitler's . . .

on its sex equality – a third of its members were female, and both men and women wore the same uniform. Women members, presumably, were drawn to the same aspects of the Blackshirt cult that gay men were: the cut of the uniforms, the muscles, the virility of the symbols. And the fascists did present themselves as 'men of action'. Some of them, such as Joyce, had an obvious dark side, too. They were fighters. They were ruthless. And, as the poet Sylvia Plath noted in another context years later, women adore fascists; it is because fascists have 'brute hearts', apparently.

There were many affairs between male and female members of the BUF staff. As a district inspector wrote of the Women's Section at National Headquarters – 'Lady Mosley, Oswald Mosley's mother, had her office at NHQ: she entered fully into the life of the Movement and was popular with the girls; she kept a motherly eye on some of the less staid and prettier ones and warned them of the hungry looks being cast in their direction by appreciative Blackshirts and by one high-ranking officer in particular who was both an experienced politician and an experienced womaniser.'

She was referring to her son. Women found his brute heart irresistible. Even the diminutive scar-faced William Joyce was about to discover that fascism was an aphrodisiac.

SEVEN

'We can always undo it if we don't like it.'

Margaret Cairns White was a good-humoured, flirtatious woman with long legs, rosebud lips and knowing green eyes. With her tall, slender figure and her lustrous auburn hair, she tended to attract the attentions of men. In February 1935, when she was twenty-four, she organized a bus trip from her hometown of Carlisle to Dumfries to hear William Joyce speak. She had seen a photograph of him in *Fascist Week* and was intrigued to know what he would be like in person. She had already had contact with him, after a fashion, having written to him in his capacity as Propaganda Director of the British Union of Fascists, a position he had been promoted to the previous year. She had asked his permission to speak on behalf of the BUF at a public debate; he had replied with a curt letter of refusal. But Margaret was undaunted; she was a sexually confident woman who liked a challenge.

When she entered the hall at Dumfries, Joyce was already speaking. She closed the door quietly behind her and tiptoed forward. The black-shirted figure on the stage stopped talking and stared at her calmly, as though there was no one else in the room and he had been waiting for her to arrive. She froze. Everyone turned to stare at her. The silence was excruciating. She moved forward to an empty chair. Joyce continued to regard her thoughtfully. He waited until she had sat down and settled before he finally stopped staring at her, tilted his head up and continued with his speech.

Speaking fluently without notes, Joyce promised that if it came to power, the first priority of the BUF would be to tackle the chronic unemployment which the Great Depression had brought to Britain. He spoke against the decadence of 'aristocratic fops', the unfairness of private education, the dangers of cheap foreign imports flooding the market, and, inevitably, Joyce being Joyce, he contrived to blame the nation's economic woes on Jewish financiers in the City. His message went down well that night. The audience applauded and cheered, intoxicated by the speaker's combination of energy, invective and wit. Margaret in particular appreciated his lack of moderation. Joyce struck her as dangerous and exciting.

When the meeting adjourned for an interval before question time, Joyce appeared at her side and stood, shoulders squared, heels together, in the doorway. She was taller than him, but with his barrel chest and his erect posture he had a strong physical presence. Joyce was the first to speak: 'Whence came you?'

The curious, archaic phrase threw Margaret momentarily. 'Is that a Biblical quotation?' she asked.

Joyce nodded. 'Revelation.'★

'Well,' she said with a smile, 'I came from Carlisle.'

'For this meeting? I'm flattered.'

'My name is Margaret White. You wrote to me.'

Joyce blinked.

'You told me I wasn't allowed to take part in a debate, do you recall?'

Joyce frowned, then smiled. 'From your letters I thought you must be at least fifty!' He was laughing now. 'I imagined you as wearing glasses and carrying a tightly rolled umbrella!'

She laughed, too. They talked and parted with an agreement that correspondence between the Carlisle branch and the London headquarters would be more friendly in future.

On the bus home, the man sitting next to Margaret said he was so impressed by Joyce he was planning to drive the following evening to Kirkcudbright, the next stage in Joyce's speaking tour. On an impulse, Margaret asked if she could come with him. He probably couldn't believe his luck and agreed, mistaking her interest in Joyce for an interest in him. She arrived for the start of Joyce's speech this time but didn't get a chance

---

★ The quotation, from ch. 7 v. 13, was ironically appropriate: 'And one of the elders answered, saying unto me, What are these which are arrayed in white robes? and whence came they?'

to talk to him in the interval because he was surrounded by groupies, all eager to meet the political prodigy they had been reading about. But just as the second half of the meeting was about to start and she was heading back to her seat, Joyce loomed up beside her again. 'Call on me at the Black House next time you are in London,' he said casually, then disappeared back into the crowd. Margaret wasn't used to such cool treatment from men. Joyce's apparent indifference was proving seductive.

Margaret, an only child, had grown up in a terraced house on Nelson Street, Carlisle. She was educated at the Girls' County High School and she attended an Anglican church every Sunday. After leaving school she had trained as a dancer, but in 1934 had shelved her hopes of making a career on the stage in favour of a more conventional occupation: she took a typing course and went to work as a secretary at Morton Sundour Fabrics Ltd, the textile warehouse on Denton Hill in Carlisle where her father, Ernest Robert White, had worked as an assistant manager since 1915.* In a statement to the police years later, her boss at the warehouse, Donald Nicholson, described her as 'a capable girl, with plenty of initiative and a low, distinctive voice.' He might have added that she also had distinctive political views. She had inherited her fascist leanings from her father, an enthusiastic member of the British Union of Fascists. Though his forebears were part Irish, part Italian, both he and Margaret's mother Mabel had been born in London. It was at her father's prompting that she had begun selling copies of *Fascist Week* outside meetings in Carlisle. But she began speaking 'at the Cross' in the town's market square – the traditional place for free speech – of her own accord and, as she called one heckler 'a communist pig', it was clear her political views were her own. Indeed she soon became the head of the women's section of the Carlisle branch of the BUF. She seems to have been something of a feminist in outlook – she would wear trousers occasionally, which raised eyebrows, and she was more liberated sexually than most of her generation. At the time she first met Joyce she had had a number of casual flings as well as one or two serious suitors, including a doctor. But she felt trapped by her life in the provinces. She was bored. Joyce seemed anything but boring.

It was several months before Margaret was able to find an excuse to

---

* He was made redundant in 1937 and moved to Manchester, where he found work as a postman.

visit London. She called in at the Black House, but Joyce was not there. She went back the next day to find Joyce was there but that he didn't greet her with the enthusiasm she had hoped for. He seemed distracted, as indeed he was, by his seven-year-old daughter Heather, who was spending the day with him. Margaret discovered later that Joyce and his wife Hazel were separating after eight years of marriage and that Joyce and Heather were having their last few days together as father and daughter. He had taken Heather to see his office and show her all the Blackshirt parapher-nalia, including a packet of Blackshirt cigarettes, the favourite brand of the chain-smoking Joyce. (The BUF liked to cross-brand. It also ran Blackshirt holiday camps and the Blackshirt Automobile Club.) Afterwards, Joyce took his daughter to see the lights of Piccadilly Circus.

With the prospect of divorce had come the question of custody. At first, Joyce floated the idea that he and Hazel could look after one daughter each, with him taking Heather, or Heth as he called her. Hazel said the children couldn't be separated and Joyce accepted that she was right. He reflected on the matter and decided that his daughters needed a mother more that a father. They agreed Joyce would have no access, believing that a clean break would be best for the children.

A few days later, on his last evening with his children, Joyce played the piano for his daughters. He then took them to bed, and as he was tucking Heth in, she said in a worried voice: 'Uncle Eric wants to know how I would feel about one day having another baby sister, or a brother.' Joyce gave Heth a hug and then began to weep. She had never seen her father cry before. 'Don't worry, don't worry,' he said. 'It'll be all right.' It wasn't. Hazel and the children moved out of the family home in Chelsea and moved into Eric Piercy's house in Barnes. For the first few mornings after the move, Heth phoned her father, then her mother said: 'I don't think you should phone Daddy anymore.' And so she didn't. Joyce had seen his daughters for the last time. They were seven and four.*

As divorce proceedings began, Joyce moved into a flat in Bramerton Street, Chelsea, with Angus Macnab, a colleague from the BUF and a regular chess opponent. Their paths had crossed when they had been put jointly in charge of the public-speaking classes at the Black House. Because

---

* This account of the separation was conveyed to the author by Joyce's daughter Heather. At the request of her family, it has been slightly expurgated.

of their mutual love of language, and a shared sense of humour, they had become the closest of friends, in fact they were almost inseparable. Walking together, they were an incongruous sight: Macnab was much taller than the barrel-chested Joyce and had wrists and ankles as thin as lead piping. Where Joyce had a broken nose, hair shaved at the sides and a scar, Macnab had fierce black eyes that blazed behind thick glasses and a tiny fuzz of black hair fancifully arranged on his prematurely bald head. Macnab, who was a year younger than Joyce, was the son of a surgeon. His academic route was more conventional than Joyce's: he had been educated at Rugby and Christ Church, Oxford. He was a gifted translator of Latin and Greek poetry but chose teaching as a profession, becoming a classics master at a prep school in 1932. The two men amused themselves by conversing in Latin.

In February 1936, a year after seeing Joyce for the first time, Margaret left her job in Carlisle to work full-time in the Manchester branch of the BUF. When she read that Joyce was due to speak at a meeting in Leeds, she made sure she was there, arranging to drive to the venue with a friend in his sports car. Joyce gave no indication that he noticed Margaret from the platform, but during the interval he came over and invited her to see him in London in a few days' time. He would be speaking at a large rally at the Albert Hall. She could come to that, he suggested, and afterwards they could meet at a Mayfair party which was being hosted by the aunt of a titled member of the BUF. She accepted. That night, on the drive back over the Pennines from Leeds to Manchester, she and her companion became lost in a bank of fog on a moor. The sports car they were driving in was cold and damp, and it was almost dawn before they managed to get home. The next day Margaret fell ill with pleurisy and was of a mind to cancel her trip to London. But after a couple of days in bed she was feeling better, or at least well enough to travel. She was nothing if not determined.

Margaret was impressed by the sight of the fascists' banners flying outside the Albert Hall. She found the charged atmosphere thrilling, especially when a crowd of communists turned up and began chanting abuse. Afterwards, at the party, she was impressed further when she had her coat taken at the door by a liveried footman. Once inside, a butler handed her a whisky and she looked around the room hoping to recognize someone. To her relief, Joyce touched her arm, drew her to one side and asked what she was drinking.

'Whisky.'

'Nonsense,' he said, taking her glass away and signalling for a butler to bring champagne over.

The glasses arrived. They sipped. 'No doubt you've heard about my private affairs?' Joyce asked.

She had, as it happened: one of the Blackshirts had told her that Joyce was getting divorced. She nodded distractedly, looking at the other guests.

'When my affairs are settled I hope we can see each other more often.' She smiled, still looking around the room.

'In fact, I wondered whether you would consider marrying me.'

The background chatter in the room seemed to fade. Margaret stared at William in astonishment, unsure what to say. She hardly knew this man, and hadn't even been alone with him, and yet he was proposing marriage. She felt detached from her voice as she answered: 'Well, we can try. We can always undo it if we don't like it.'

Joyce lifted his glass to clink against hers and spilt champagne on her hand. It seemed to pierce the unreality of the scene and they both laughed. They looked at each other steadily and drained their glasses.

Joyce then took Margaret's hand and strode into the middle of the room. 'We have just got engaged,' he announced. There was a moment's silence before the other guests raised their glasses and offered their congratulations. John Beckett came over to shake Margaret's hand and, as he did so, he whispered in her ear: 'I do hope you'll be happy, but it may be uncomfortable being married to a genius. And William is a genius, you know!'

'Well, he's certainly impetuous,' she said drily.

Joyce would have to wait several more weeks before his decree absolute was granted. In the meantime, Margaret took a room in the same building as him and Macnab. For the benefit of neighbours she pretended she was the housekeeper. For the sake of her family, she persuaded Macnab to say, if asked, that he was her lover. Her parents were devout Anglicans and would have disapproved more if they had known it was the still-married Joyce she was sleeping with. The three of them, being short of money, spent most evenings together, entertaining each other: talking, drinking, smoking, playing cards. Joyce took to calling Macnab 'the Master', or 'Bonga' when he was being an absent-minded professor: 'John is being Bonga-ish,' he would say. He always called him by his first name, John,

even though Macnab called himself by his middle name, Angus – it seems
to have been a private joke between them, perhaps to do with the poacher
John Macnab, the John Buchan character popular at the time. But after
two months the cost of living separately was proving too high so all three
moved into a furnished flat owned by a doctor in Fawcett Street, just off
the Fulham Road, not far from the house where Joyce's hero Thomas
Carlyle had lived. They made an odd threesome: Macnab the tall and thin
egghead, Joyce the short but solidly built street fighter, Margaret the
willowy and pale femme fatale. The hit of the time was Jack Buchanan's
'I'm Still Dreaming', but such romantic ditties were not indulged in this
flat. Joyce and Macnab shared a passion for Wagner. Indeed, the neighbours would complain about them playing 'Teutonic operas' on their
gramophone well into the small hours. Margaret didn't seem to mind.
She, like them, had a sense of fun. They were young and reckless. The
amiable Macnab had been a member of the Oxford Alpine Club and
would shin up the drainpipe whenever keys were forgotten. They were
also mischievous. Joyce once led a midnight march of Blackshirts through
an area of Evesham in Worcestershire that was populated by Italian
labourers – and as his marching song he chose Mussolini's anthem
'Giovanezza'. Above all, Margaret seems to have regarded the two men as
her mentors. Macnab, especially, was such a good teacher he even
managed to interest her in geometry, a subject she thought she hated.

Not far away, in a flat in Dolphin Square, Maxwell Knight was busy
setting up his new HQ for B5(b). The flat belonged to the brother of his
new wife Lois and the name above the doorbell was Miss Coplestone, her
maiden name. He was yet to consummate this marriage and Lois soon
became alarmed at the young men, all B5(b) officers, who were constantly
hanging round their flat. One, John Bingham, said: 'M always had
something alive in his pocket. You never quite knew what.' He was
known to have raised a nest of adder eggs in his pyjama pocket.

Galvanized in part by Mussolini's successes in Abyssinia, Mosley
decided to target the East End, where a hundred and fifty thousand British
Jews lived. So it was that on 4 October 1936 the Battle of Cable Street
was fought. Mosley had planned a march from Royal Mint Street to
Shoreditch, Limehouse, Bow and Bethnal Green. At each district on the
way he would give a speech. His communist opponents, led by Harry
Pollitt, famously declared 'they shall not pass'. They waited for them

behind barricades in Cable Street. This was shortly after the outbreak of the Spanish Civil War, and communist feelings were running high. They arrived by the busload, armed with coshes and knuckledusters. Before Mosley arrived there was chanting and stone throwing. Some six thousand police were needed to keep order. Mosley's open-top Bentley arrived with a motorbike escort. He was standing up in it, giving the fascist salute. He got out and marched up and down the columns inspecting them while, beyond the police cordon, the communists tried to charge. Most were driven back but some pushed through and were arrested.

The main battle was between police and communists. The Blackshirts were hardly involved in any of the hand-to-hand fighting, which was probably just as well for them as there were seven thousand fascists against a hundred thousand communists.

The Commissioner of Police told Mosley not to start until his men had cleared the streets of barricades. In Cable Street a lorry had been used to construct a defence. The police tried to push their way through but were repelled. They attempted a baton charge. There was a running battle in which stones were thrown and truncheons and iron bars rained down on heads. The communists retreated to a second barricade, scattering broken glass and ball bearings as they went, to discourage police horses. The fighting lasted for two hours during which eighty-three communists were arrested and more than a hundred people were injured.

Joyce had prepared a speech. It was never delivered. The Commissioner telephoned the Home Secretary for permission to cancel the march. The request was granted and Mosley, keen to move on from his reputation as the leader of a gang of thugs, gave orders for his men to turn and march the other way, back down Queen Victoria Street towards the Embankment. Before dismissing his men at Charing Cross Bridge, Mosley made a speech in which he accused the government of surrendering to 'Red violence and Jewish corruption'.

It looked like a retreat. The communists had won. Harry Pollitt announced, with justification: 'This is the most humiliating defeat ever suffered by any figure in English politics.' The Battle of Cable Street took on historic significance and became part of left-wing folklore. The fascists did not pass, neither in Cable Street nor in the country as a whole. The momentum that had been building for fascism in Britain, in harmony with the fascist movements in Italy, Germany and, to a lesser extent, Spain, had come to a juddering halt. The BUF never recovered. Britain had been saved from the jackboot.

Mosley's behaviour struck many as odd, though. He could have encouraged his men to be honourably arrested, or he could have taken another route through the East End. Instead he had been seen to back away from a chance to cause havoc – and his party had become a laughing stock. Perhaps his mind was elsewhere. The next day he was flying to Berlin for his wedding to Diana Guinness, one of the Mitford sisters and, it was generally acknowledged, one of the most beautiful women of her generation. High society had known about their affair for months. Most of the Blackshirts had known, too – William Joyce called her 'the Huntress', after Diana, the Roman goddess of hunting. But the press had yet to catch up with the story. Diana Guinness and her sister Unity Mitford had stayed with Josef and Magda Goebbels for the Olympic Games in Berlin earlier that summer. Magda had suggested that if she and Mosley wanted to get married in secret they could do so in the Goebbels' drawing room. This they did on 6 October 1936. Adolf Hitler was one of the guests.

After Cable Street, Joyce became disillusioned with Mosley, seeing him as a weak leader. 'He would never say boo to a goose except when coppers were in front of him,' he said. He was mentally preparing himself to usurp Mosley. As Knight wrote in an MI5 report: 'Joyce is a greater force than Mosley himself. His personal vanity is great, and has incurred the hatred of many, but he never allows adulation to go to his head. He is highly suspicious and watchful. His brain is wonderful in its capacity for assimilation.' Joyce began to undermine Mosley. When Mosley introduced a new uniform of leather boots, breeches and Sam Browne belt that was meant to resemble the SS uniform, a caustic joke began to circulate that it seemed more like that of 'King Zog's Own Imperial Dismounted Hussars'. The comment had Joyce's dabs all over it. He was shifting his hero-worship to another man of destiny, Hitler.

And he was not alone. These were strange times in Anglo-German relations. The Olympic Games and Leni Riefenstahl's film *Triumph of the Will* had glamorized Berlin. *Country Life* ran an 'at home with Herr Hitler' feature. Lloyd George went to visit Germany to meet Hitler, having already gone on record as saying he thought the Führer a 'very great man'. The visit was spun as a meeting of great men. According to Thomas Jones, a biographer of Lloyd George, 'Hitler was forty-six, Ll G was seventy-three, alike only in their perfect grooming and the brilliance of their blue eyes, these two actors exchanged courtesies.' Hitler gave his guest a signed photograph, and Lloyd George said how honoured he was to receive the gift from the greatest living German. Back in England, Lloyd George wrote: 'He is a born leader of men. A magnetic, dynamic personality . . . The old trust him. The young idolize him.'

The King, too, was a Hitler fan, which is no doubt why the BUF became preoccupied with the impending abdication. Ever optimistic, the British fascists hoped that the beleaguered Edward VIII would solve his problems by dissolving Parliament and asking Sir Oswald Mosley to form a government. 'When the crisis became front-page news, Mosley was in Liverpool, and had to stay overnight for a conference,' John Beckett recalled. 'He telephoned to London and asked Joyce and I to drive there and discuss the position with him. A Bentley was placed at our disposal, and we reached his private suite at the Adelphi Hotel at about seven. Mosley was in a state of great excitement. He claimed to be in direct communication with the court. The King, he said, was strengthened by the knowledge of the support of him and his movement, and for this reason could accept Baldwin's resignation and call upon Mosley to form a government. Standing in the middle of the room, he detailed his plans for governing without parliament until the budget, pointing out that the financial estimates until then had already been passed. He strode about the room in excitement as he explained that millions of pounds would be available to fight an election in such a cause, and that as Prime Minister he could broadcast as often as he wished . . . We left that night convinced that he already believed himself in charge of the nation's affairs, and agreed that his powers of self delusion had finally conquered his sanity. He could not realize that nobody except himself and the comical little group of ex-pedlars and humourless ex-officers with whom he was surrounded took him seriously.'

Joyce, always an ardent monarchist, was a great admirer of Edward VIII. He gloomily recalled the time in November 1936, a month before the abdication crisis, when the King had visited the South Wales valleys and had been so appalled by the poverty and unemployment he had said something must be done. 'It was done,' Joyce now reflected, 'to him.'

Edward abdicated in December, became Duke of Windsor and married

Wallis Simpson. In this capacity he met Hitler at the Obersalzburg a few months later, while ostensibly on a tour to study German housing and social policies.

On New Year's Day 1937 a new Public Order Act came into force, aimed at the Blackshirts. It banned the wearing of political uniforms on public occasions, prohibited stewards at open-air meetings and gave the police powers to stop processions likely to cause a breach of the peace. Joyce took to wearing black sweaters of a shape calculated to recall the fascist black shirt.

Knight made a note in his by now bulging MI5 file: 'Joyce is apparently fed up about the loss of the uniform. From what I am told, I feel certain that Joyce has turned from the Napoleonic pose to a copy of a Prussian officer. I hear that his manner has steadily been becoming more parade ground like and that his hair is cropped closer than ever before.'

Briefly, Joyce grew a toothbrush moustache and also took to wearing a trench coat like Hitler's. It was in this coat that, five days after his decree was made absolute, William was married to Margaret. He was thirty, she twenty-five. The ceremony took place at Kensington Register Office on 13 February 1937. Angus Macnab was one of the witnesses. Margaret's cousin and aunt were present, but not her parents because her mother had flu, although this may have been a convenient excuse, given that they did not approve of their daughter marrying a divorcé. On the marriage certificate Joyce gave his job as university tutor (retired), which was not quite a lie, and his father's profession as 'of independent means', which was. A brief cocktail party followed, hosted by another of the witnesses, Mrs Hastings Bonora, a BUF member. Another friend brought along a wedding cake.

They did not go on a honeymoon, in part because they could not afford to. Instead they went canvassing in Shoreditch, a safe Labour seat where Joyce was standing as a BUF candidate in the local elections. Joyce warned his new wife that he might lose support if voters discovered he was a divorcé, and therefore asked her to pretend she was his first wife. 'If anyone comes up to you and says: "Good day, Mrs Joyce, and how are your children?" Keep your head!' Feelings ran high during the campaign. At one point the grandson of the female Labour candidate spotted Joyce putting up a poster and shouted something abusive at him. Joyce, it was said by Labour supporters, promptly emptied his paste pot over the child's head.

Labour won, as expected. But the established parties were shocked when it was announced that Joyce had polled 2,564 votes, almost half that of Labour.

Joyce chose to ignore the routine courtesies of congratulating his opponent, acknowledging it had been a fair fight and thanking his supporters. Instead he created a scene. Standing rigidly with his hands by his side he declared that it had been 'a thoroughly dirty fight'. Then he turned and marched from the platform. There were audible gasps in the hall. Margaret ran to catch up with him and told him his performance made him look like a bad loser. 'There is no point in pretending to be a good sport when both sides have been so rude to each other during the campaign,' he replied. 'When you think someone is wrong, it is dishonest to treat him as though he might be right.' The logic couldn't be faulted but the diplomacy could. He was similarly blunt a few days later when he casually announced to Margaret that, by the way, she had become an American citizen when she married him. After a minute she regained her composure and said: 'Fancy that.'

Margaret was fast discovering that her husband had 'a brilliant but warped brain', as Captain Mohan, a leading BUF member, memorably put it. He consisted almost entirely of logic, she concluded, and that could cause social discomfort. He was prone to 'fey' mood swings, she noticed. And he found it difficult to be tactful and to empathize with other people. He disliked jazz, for instance, because the Nazis had deemed it decadent and so, regardless of who was present, or whose house he was in, he would always turn off a wireless set that was playing it. (Quite how he coped when socializing with the jazz-loving Maxwell Knight, history does not record.) Another example: one day Margaret discovered, wrapped in a cloth in a cake tin, an unlicensed pistol. When she asked him about it he looked blank, as if he couldn't understand why anyone wouldn't keep a gun in their cake tin. She also soon came to realize how uncompromising he was: he refused to make small talk with people he found uninteresting. 'Why should I,' he would ask, 'when I know exactly what they're going to say?' He may have learned to cope with his 'warped' condition by regarding conversation as a performance, a chance to show off his erudition and wit. As was noted by Rebecca West: 'Everybody who met him agrees that he never talked for long without putting a twist on a sentence that surprised the hearer into laughter.'

There was something odd, too, about the way Joyce seems to have been able to cut himself off emotionally from his children. A few months after they saw him for the last time some toys arrived for his daughters from Harrods: a toy dog for Diana and a grey battleship for Heather. Heather rang up the store's toy department to ask who had bought them and was told by the assistant that it had been a gentleman with a scar. It was the last communication he had with them.

Perhaps he was able to transfer his feelings for his daughters to his adoring young siblings, whom he always referred to as 'the children'. He used to dress his brother Robert in a black shirt and would get his sister Joan to hand out fascist leaflets at her school. 'Poor Mrs Joyce!' one of their neighbours in Dulwich said. 'With all those terrible children in their black shirts!'

Macnab, too, had noticed his flatmate's single-mindedness, as he recorded in a pen portrait. 'He kept no files, diaries or notes of any kind, but he could recall the date, place and circumstances of remote events and meetings with people. He never forgot a face or a name and could give a full account, unhesitatingly, of almost anything that had ever happened to him. He could quote – always exactly – any poem he had ever read with attention, and even notable pieces of prose. As a Latin scholar his technical qualifications were inferior to my own; yet he was the one who could quote Virgil or Horace freely and always to the point, not I. He possessed no Latin books; but I have *The Oxford Companion to Classical Literature* which he gave me as a Christmas (I beg pardon, he called it "Christtide" in the dedication! Adding "No Popery!") inscribed with the following on the flyleaf: "*Bacchum in remotis carmina rupibus Vidi docentem*" This is a quotation from an ode of Horace and the appropriateness is delightful. "I have seen Bacchus teaching poetry amid remote crags"; when he and I were the joint conductors of speakers' schools we did ourselves fairly well in the matter of drinks at times.'

Macnab described his flatmate as a polymath, and it is easy to see why. His special subject at Birkbeck was Germanic philology, which included Icelandic, Old Norse and Gothic. In addition to these languages he was fluent in German, French and Latin, and had a reasonable command of

Italian. He played the piano by ear. He was also good at mathematics and taught himself chemistry, medicine, physics and even anatomy. When, the previous Christmas, or Christtide, he broke his collarbone while skating in the north of Scotland, he used his knowledge of anatomy to set it himself: according to Macnab's unpublished *Material for a work on William Joyce*, 'When he got back two days later and went to St Thomas's Hospital to have it dealt with, they were surprised to find that the bones were in a good position and on the way to joining properly. He had set the break himself and kept it in position by proper strapping.' And yet, Macnab went on, 'He had a total and abysmal ignorance and incompetence of [sic] anything mechanical. With machinery he was lost: a child and, moreover, extremely clumsy. He never learned to ride a bicycle, much less drive a car. He would have been fatal on a horse. He played the piano well but was unable to dance or sing.'

Joyce's passion was chess, a game popularized at the time by 'the Chess Machine', the Cuban player José Raúl Capablanca, who had been world champion for most of the Twenties (had Joyce known that by the Thirties Stalin had come to regard chess as the definitive socialist game, he might not have been so keen). Macnab noticed a peculiarity about Joyce's chess technique which was at odds with his character. 'At chess he was strange. With his extraordinary speed of brain and his mathematical bent, he should have been first-class. He seemed to play soundly, never making a crass blunder as even good players do at times; yet he almost always lost to me who am a very indifferent player by club standards. The reason was his complete lack of aggressiveness. Occasionally he won a game from me when he had the black pieces, if I launched an unsound blitzkrieg attack and gambled wildly; but he never, absolutely never won with the white pieces, because he would always go on the defensive with the very first moves. In this respect he showed a curiously defeatist mentality. To beat him all one had to do was to avoid making any howlers and to go on pressing home the attack; he would merely defend, and never make a counter attack. I find this perhaps the strangest thing in his whole mentality, for most people would describe him as somewhat aggressive in outlook – especially on the platform.'

It may simply have been a matter of him identifying more with the ranks of black (shirts) marching across the board. After all, his defensiveness in chess suggested a certain defeatism and fatalism in his character that was at odds with his bravado – although consistent with his eventual circum-spection, silence indeed, at his own trial. Perhaps, as Knight implied in one of his reports, egotism is not incompatible with self-doubt. 'Joyce is a very complex character. He is at times very calm and cunning, with a fanatical, boundless energy and moral courage. He never compromises, has little stability, an overdeveloped intellect, and is theatrical, with a marked conspiratorial complex. Likes wine. This is my character assessment.'

Knight also noted, with regard to Joyce's status at the BUF: 'The fact that Joyce has been forced into background is not to my mind that J's powers are waning but that the heads realise the worth of the man and the danger to themselves. It will suit J to see OM in the limelight preening himself and generally providing publicity. J can afford to wait. He works hard. He does not model himself on the lines of the ascetic Hitler. He drinks, plays about with woman and plans. It is easy to see that he is an expert in intrigue but temperament does not allow him to seek popularity. He is pleasant to those who do not oppose him but never what one should call friendly. He is irritated to the point of insanity by the men above him. Especially the old men ... If this movement does collapse, it will not mean the last of Joyce. If on the other hand the movement succeeded in coming to power, I fancy that one of the first things Joyce will try to do is bring about a purge of the party. Joyce knows what he wants in life, and is out to get it ... OM knows that J is probably the most efficient and skilful officer he has and cannot afford to lose him.' By this time Knight was affecting to dislike Joyce, perhaps as a way of distancing himself from one of his placemen. But he added presciently: 'In him there is someone who might one day make history. With all his faults he remains in my mind one of the most compelling personalities of the whole movement.'

The mood in Britain had turned against the fascists. Mussolini's brutal attack on Abyssinia, Franco's bloody civil war in Spain and Hitler's Nuremberg rallies had outraged British liberal opinion. Press support for the BUF was waning, too, with managers of halls and stadiums nervous about the inevitable fighting that came with fascist rallies. The rift between Mosley and Joyce about whether they should align themselves with Mussolini or Hitler widened. Joyce thought British fascism could not be allowed to share the same fate as Christianity in being left to 'the tender mercies of the Wops'. Its future, he was convinced, lay in forging close links with Nazi Germany. To this end he cultivated a friendship with Dr Christian Bauer, a young German working in London who spoke fluent English and wrote for *Der Angriff* (the *Attack*), a newspaper founded by Goebbels. He was also – presumably unknown to Joyce – a member of Goebbels' personal Intelligence Service.

Joyce, who had been as devoted to Mosley as Goebbels was to Hitler, now adapted a favourite line from Alexander Pope: 'He, like the Turk, bore no rival near the throne.' A policeman in a late-night train compartment asked a tired-looking Joyce what he really thought of Mosley. Joyce fixed the policeman with a cold eye. He was famous among the British fascists for his power to curse and, for the next ten minutes, quietly and steadily, he used it. The police officer paid Joyce the compliment of saying that he never once repeated himself.

Part of the tension between the two men was to do with the BUF's chiaroscuro funding arrangements. By 1937 Mussolini had stopped bankrolling the party, which as far as Joyce was concerned was another reason why the Union should no longer model itself on Italian fascism. Mosley was now having to pay for what amounted to a private army out of his own pocket. Joyce helped by cultivating regular contributors, including Alec Scrimgeour, a paralysed, retired stockbroker at whose grand country house near Midhurst, in Sussex, Joyce was to spend many a happy weekend. His friendship with him and with his sister Ethel, a tall handsome woman with an immense knot of hair twisted on the nape of her neck, was genuine. He enjoyed their company, and their hospitality – they would drink champagne and brandy as they discussed politics on their terrace – and he was enchanted by the landscape around their house, regularly going on walks through woodland before ending up in a country pub. He and Margaret also enjoyed riding bareback on a pony which the Scrimgeours kept in their paddock, though the maladroit Joyce rarely managed to stay on long.

But the funds from private donors were not enough to plug the gap left by Mussolini's bankers. In April 1937, Mosley assembled his paid staff and announced that he was going to have to make four-fifths of them redundant. He read out a list of names: Joyce and Beckett were the two highest-profile casualties. Mosley was probably relieved to have an excuse to let the increasingly antagonistic Joyce go.★ Macnab and Margaret resigned out of protest. Eric Piercy, who had by then married Joyce's ex-wife Hazel, remained loyal to Mosley.

Joyce, the perpetual outsider, had been expelled from the BUF, just as he had been from the Conservative Party, and from the army, and from Ireland and even from his school. He now had to find a part-time job that would allow him to continue in politics: a return to tutoring pupils for university entrance, in partnership with Macnab, seemed to be the obvious compromise. The unlikely threesome, Macnab and the Joyces, moved to a new flat suitable for taking pupils: 83 Onslow Gardens, South Kensington. They put up a small plate on the door which read MACNAB & JOYCE, PRIVATE TUTORS. At first there was no shortage of pupils but Joyce soon began turning away any potential students he felt he could not teach properly. He thought it would be 'deceitful'. Margaret argued that he should sacrifice principle for practicality: they needed to pay the bills. Eventually Joyce agreed to bring in extra income by expanding the tutoring service they offered to include teaching English to foreign students. But then he undermined this move by deciding that no coloured or Jewish clients would be allowed. Margaret, always the more common-sensical of the two, was furious. 'Apart from anything else,' she fumed, 'it's so bloody tactless.'

William did not know it yet, but this unexpected show of temper from his normally easy-going wife was a taste of things to come.

★ Years later, after the war, Mosley dismissed Joyce as 'that horrid little man'.

EIGHT

'A little trip to Deutschland in the morning.'

Shortly after being made redundant from the BUF, Joyce took the train to Sussex to visit Alec Scrimgeour. He returned with funds to form a new political party. John Beckett agreed to be its joint leader and, after much discussion, they decided to call it the National Socialist League. The name was chosen partly because it would be an English echo of the phonetic contraction Nazi, and partly because they had come to realize that the general public considered the word 'fascist' to be foreign and therefore a little suspicious.

About sixty members of the BUF joined them at first, including Chesterton, Macnab and Margaret, who was appointed assistant treasurer. They set up the party headquarters at 190 Vauxhall Bridge Road, designed a membership badge in the shape of a steering wheel with the words 'Steer Straight' underneath and wrote a manifesto in which they claimed to be 'the only 100 per cent *British* organisation working with *British* people and *British* funds for the rebuilding of *Britain* in a modern way.'

And by 'modern', presumably, they meant British.

One old BUF lag recalled going to see the NSL at their headquarters: 'Up several flights of uncarpeted stairs. The HQ was on the top floor in a single room, also uncarpeted, the only furniture a desk and two or three chairs. In a corner of the room were a couple of piles of leaflets. And Beckett and Joyce.' A few weeks later, the same former colleague saw the two men on a street corner with a portable platform. One of them was standing on it and speaking while the other was heckling – a standard way of trying to attract an audience to an open-air meeting. Joyce and Beckett had become close. Joyce, for example, appeared in Beckett's wedding photograph that year, even though Beckett was only pretending to be married. His first wife had refused to give him a divorce so he had simply arranged for a bogus wedding photograph to be taken – and his new 'wife' simply started calling herself Anne Beckett.

The two men collaborated on a seventy-one-page booklet, *National Socialism Now*, which was sold for a shilling at meetings. The main body of the text seems to have been written by Joyce, judging by the colourful flourishes and the long-windedness. On the subject of aristocratic decadence, for example, it reads: 'Champagne may bubble and rose petals bestrew the footwear of some itinerant scion of declining nobility, but no benefit will accrue to us.' National Socialism should be revolutionary in its methods, he argued, and aimed at freeing people from the twin shackles of Marxism and capitalism. It should, moreover, evolve out of the British soil. 'Therefore, in true respect for the German Leader's gallant achievement against international Jewish finance and its other self – international Jewish Communism – I would gladly say, "Heil Hitler!" and at once part company with him, realising what a pitiable insult it is to such a great man to try to flatter him with an imitation which he has always disdained. His way is for Germany, ours is for Britain; let us tread our paths with mutual respect, which is rarely increased by borrowing.'

Immediately after the First World War, the forged document *The Protocols of the Elders of Zion* had inspired a demented belief in an international Jewish conspiracy to take over the Western world. Paranoia was already fevered among the aristocracy, who saw what had happened to their counterparts in Russia and assumed it had been at the instigation of Jewish Bolsheviks. Joyce's booklet tapped into this mood by calling for a pact with Hitler against Bolshevism and Jewish international finance. But Britain should not persecute or hate the Jews, he concluded; instead she should recognize them as a foreign people like any other, 'with such exceptions as the state would make in the case of any well-disposed foreigner whose presence could harm nobody and benefit some.'

Beckett wrote an introduction in which he described Joyce as 'for politics, a very young man. Now only thirty-one, he will, in coming years, exercise a very great influence upon the life and thought of our people. He himself prefers the spoken word to the written, and his name

is already known as a fine and compelling speaker throughout the country.'
In a sideswipe at Mosley, Beckett added that arguments about leadership before there is anything to lead are stupid. 'Joyce and I do not set
up as people to be saluted and hailed on every possible and impossible
occasion. We merely come forward as instruments of a great policy . . .
What will happen to us when National Socialism attracts the thousands of
brilliant young men and women whom it must attract is a matter of great
indifference.'

It was just as well because the British version of the German National
Socialist Party was unlikely to hold any Nuremberg-style rallies – instead
it inspired great apathy, with its membership soon dwindling to barely two
dozen, and they not so much 'brilliant young men and women' as friends,
acquaintances and various oddities, such as Count Potocki, a long-haired
pretender to the Polish throne and former prisoner who had been
prosecuted for the publication of obscene poetry. The rest of the members
were undercover Special Branch officers sent to keep an eye on them. It
wasn't long before Beckett left this splinter group – after an argument
about leadership, naturally – to form a new splinter group.

Mosley, meanwhile, was experiencing a revival of fortune, having
found common ground with the appeasers. His slogan 'Mind Britain's
Business' could be seen chalked on walls everywhere. The Prime Minister,
Neville Chamberlain, seemed to agree with this sentiment. This sixty-
nine-year-old Victorian gentleman in a wing collar found it 'horrible,
fantastic, incredible' that Germany's desire to annex the Sudetenland in
September 1938 meant people in Britain were having to dig trenches in
public parks and try on gas-masks. Some thirty-eight million masks had
been distributed that week and with them came real fear. For many, the
smell of rubber would ever after fill them with a sick feeling of dread.

For Joyce the prospect of a war with Germany meant some stark
choices: it looked likely that conscription would soon be introduced and
he didn't want to be a conscientious objector as he considered it 'utterly
abhorrent to sabotage the national defence in any way'. Also, he regarded
conscientious objectors as 'lower than amoeba'. Yet he felt he couldn't
fight against National Socialism. He came up with a contingency plan: he,
Margaret and Macnab would move to Dublin, because it was assumed the
Irish Free State would be neutral in any coming war. With this in mind
he checked the five-year passport he had obtained by deception in 1933

and it had just expired. On 24 September, six days before the Munich
Agreement was signed, Joyce renewed his passport for one year. On the
same day, Margaret applied for a passport for the first time. In her signed
declaration, she knowingly lied. 'I hereby declare that I am the wife of
William Joyce and that my husband is a British citizen by birth, having
been born in Galway Ireland.' Her passport was issued a few days later. It
would not expire until 27 September 1943.

When Chamberlain returned from Munich on 30 September with a
piece of paper in his hand and proclaimed 'peace for our time', the Joyces
had perhaps more reason than most to feel relieved. They put their travel
plans on hold. But they also began to brood on the possibility of moving
to Germany. To this end they kept up their contact with Christian Bauer,
or perhaps it was Bauer who made sure he kept in with the Joyces.

MI5 was convinced that Bauer was an agent of the Abwehr, the
German equivalent of MI6. This suspicion was magnified when they
began to intercept cryptic messages from Bauer to Joyce: 'Q [Quentin
Joyce] will have told you that I am going to switch the old footlights on
and that I should be grateful for more information in that respect. You'll
understand. You can tell him, too, that Marseilles is OK. He'll know. I
am continuing this by handing on a letter for Q who will tell you about
the "scheme". This only of course if the Person in question.' Quentin
Joyce was eleven years younger than his brother William. According to
Rebecca West he was the better looking of the two, with 'a sturdy body,
a fresh colour, thick lustrous brown hair, and the soft eyes of a cow'. MI5
noted that he was employed in the Department of the Directorate of
Signals at the Air Ministry 'and in the opinion of D3 is in a position to
obtain information of a highly confidential nature.' As the Germans
invaded Czechoslovakia in March 1939, Quentin went to stay with Bauer
for seventeen days in Berlin. MI5 intercepted the letters the two men sent
each other after this and found there were many references to 'stamps',
which was a recognized code for maps.

As ever, though, Maxwell Knight had a remarkable degree of autonomy not only from MI6 and Special Branch but also from the rest of MI5.
According to Richard Darwell, a B5(b) agent, 'We had very much a free
hand to recruit anyone we thought might be useful.' It has been suggested
that around this time Knight may have proposed and even agreed that
William Joyce could go to Germany and, in the role of agent provocateur,

continue his intelligence work for B5(b). That didn't stop another department within MI5 obtaining a warrant to tap Joyce's phone and intercept his mail, though. If Joyce had an inkling that the Service he occasionally worked for was now opening his post and listening to his phone calls he didn't show it. In fact he was as incautious in his opinions as ever.

The doctor and his wife, the Joyces' landlords, were standing in their hall, aghast at the news of the German invasion of Czechoslovakia, when Joyce came home. They asked him: '*Now* what do you think of Hitler?' Joyce said without hesitation: 'I think him a very fine fellow.'

According to the MI5 files, Joyce now thought Mosley 'little more than a conceited popinjay'. Mosley, for his part, now thought Joyce: 'Intensely vain; a quite common foible in very small men.' Mosley was part right. Joyce was intellectually vain and was apt to pontificate with utter conviction on subjects with which he had only a passing acquaintance, usually from reading a single book. He combined exhibitionism, pedantry, egocentricity and fluency with a phenomenal memory for quotation. But he could hardly be described as physically vain. In fact, his appearance, even when he was trying to look smart and militaristic, rarely rose above mildly scruffy.

It may be that he simply could not afford new clothes. Alec Scrimgeour died shortly after the NSL was founded, and though he had left instructions in his will for his sister Ethel to continue funding the League, it was running into debt. The party moved to smaller premises where Joyce enjoyed running a bar which sold ale and 'three types of Cyprus sherry'. The plainclothed Special Branch officers attending meetings now outnumbered genuine members. Even the loyal and convivial Chesterton was coming to regard Joyce as being a little too eccentric for his tastes. After one informal meeting among friends, Chesterton wrote: 'Joyce brought the meeting to an end by calling for the National Anthem to be sung. That done, he shouted the Nazi cry of triumph: Sieg Heil! I did not attach much importance to the episode, if only because the unpredictable little man was quite as capable of closing the meeting in Icelandic or Old Norse, both languages, incidentally, which he had mastered . . . I expressed my concern at the growing danger of war. Joyce arose vehemently to dispute my contention. "There will be no war," he thundered. "I trust Adolf Hitler to see to that." Something had happened to Joyce's clarity of vision.'

The doctor's wife, already unnerved by the political views of her odd tenants, was alarmed at some of their late-night parties, especially after she encountered in the corridor the long-haired man who claimed to be the Polish monarch. He was wearing a scarlet cloak and a pectoral cross, which suggests that he was one of Aleister Crowley's sinister circle.

Some months earlier, the doctor's son had been taken ill and had had to miss two terms of boarding school. Macnab and Joyce had offered to coach him. When the boy now returned to school, his teachers were amazed at his grasp of mathematics, Greek and Latin. After this, the doctor and his wife warmed to their lodgers and would invite the threesome down for sherry parties. As they would later recall, guests found Joyce's conversation amusing, civilized and even charming. He would quote poetry, tell jokes at his own expense and, more importantly, stay off the subject of politics.

Joyce continued to enjoy his soapbox oratory, even when he had to compete with the sound of traffic. He delighted in goading passers-by and shouting at hecklers, who invariably shouted back: 'Bloody well go and live in Germany if you like it so much!' He still ended his meetings by singing – in his tone-deaf way – the National Anthem. Any Communists who happened to be passing would sing the 'Internationale' back at him. These encounters were usually good natured until 9 November 1938 – Kristallnacht – when the Nazis unleashed a wave of pogroms against Germany's Jews. After this the British became less tolerant of pro-Nazi cranks on street corners. There were scuffles and Joyce appeared on charges of assault again. He claimed he had given a heckler 'a tap on the head' with his stick. The charge was dismissed, while Macnab was fined £1 for obstruction. Following that court success Joyce, in mischievous mood, went with Macnab and others to the nearby Rochester Row police station and sang 'God Save the King' to the police. A few months later he was charged again, and again the charge was dropped. Far from regarding him as a nuisance, the police seemed to consider Joyce a harmless political eccentric in a mac.

As usual there were a plethora of small, swivel-eyed, right-wing splinter groups surfacing. Among the more prominent were the Nordic League, which had its inaugural meeting at Caxton Hall on 23 May 1939, with Joyce in attendance; the Anglo-German Fellowship, which included dozens of peers among its membership, as well as the anti-Semitic Duke of Westminster; the Link, which was founded by the pro-Nazi Admiral Sir Barry Domville; the British People's Party, founded by Lord Tavistock (the future Duke of Bedford); and, most significantly, the Right Club, founded by Captain Archibald Ramsay, an anti-Semitic Conservative MP who characteristically referred to the 'jewspapers' and 'refujews'.

The Right Club was intended as an umbrella group for all the various 'patriotic societies' and splinter groups. The members of the Right Club were listed in what became known as 'the Red Book', a stout ledger bound in red, with a brass lock. The entries were all in Ramsay's handwriting: 135 men and 100 women. Most prominent among the members were the Duke of Wellington and Lord Redesdale, father of the Mitford sisters. Joyce's name is entered in the notorious ledger twice, by mistake. With his application to join the Right Club he enclosed 5/-, along with an apology for not being able to afford more. His political activities, he wrote, were having an impact on his private finances.

In addition to joining all these clubs, Joyce even started up a new one of his own, a tiny offshoot of the NSL called the Carlyle Club, in tribute to one of his heroes, the historian Thomas Carlyle. (One of his favourite Carlyle quotations, incidentally, was: 'No one who has once wholly and heartily laughed can be altogether irreclaimably bad.')

In June 1939, Joyce wrote to his landlord to inform him that he was unable to honour his three-year lease, the number of his pupils having shown a marked decline. Soon afterwards, the doctor's wife met Margaret on the stairs and said she was sorry they were leaving for so sad a reason. To her astonishment, the normally stoical Margaret burst into tears, flung her arms round her landlady's neck, and sobbed out: 'You do not know how bad they are! You have no idea how bad they are!'

Angus Macnab, who had begun courting a fellow fascist, an Irish woman called Katherine Collins, moved to 6 Claverton Street, a flat in Pimlico. Under the influence of G. K. Chesterton and Hilaire Belloc, he embraced neo-scholasticism and Catholicism. The Joyces rented a basement flat in Kensington, 38a Eardley Crescent. It was in the shadow of Earl's Court, the venue for so many of the fleeting triumphs of British fascism, and was so small the Joyces called it their 'doll's house'. It must have been galling for Joyce to witness the massive rally held by Mosley at Earl's Court on 16 July. He couldn't ignore it: more than twenty thousand people attended. It seemed to symbolize his reversal of fortune: once the darling of the fascist movement, he was now impecunious, down on his luck and living in a flat the size of a cupboard.

The British fascist movement, as led by Mosley, was gaining strength again, despite the fact that he had become less cautious in his anti-Semitism. He had perhaps resigned himself to George Orwell's comment at the time, 'You can't say anything for or against the Jews without getting into trouble.' Mosley thought there might be some political capital to be gained from trouble.

Hitler, who had said he had 'great plans for Mosley', was intrigued and asked Herbert von Dirksen, Joachim von Ribbentrop's replacement as German Ambassador in London, to find out what the British felt about Jews. A growing number of people in Britain, Dirksen reported, thought that Jews were to blame for the looming war with Germany: 'Anti-Semitic attitudes are revealed more clearly by conversations with the man in the street than by press sources. Here, except in Leftish circles, one can speak of a widespread resentment against the Jews which, in some instances, has already assumed the form of hate. The view that the Jews want to drive Britain into war with Germany finds widespread belief.' It may have been a case of wishful thinking, of telling Hitler what he wanted to hear, yet this sentiment was echoed by no less a literary figure than E. M. Forster, who wrote about anti-Semitism in Britain that summer: 'Jew consciousness is in the air. Today the average man suspects the people he dislikes of being Jews, and is surprised when the people he likes are Jews. On the surface, things do not look too bad. Labourite and Liberal behave with their expected decency and denounce persecution, and respectability generally follows suit. But beneath the surface, things are not so good, and anyone who keeps his ears open in railway carriages or pubs or country lanes can hear a very different story. People who would not ill-treat Jews themselves, enjoy tittering over their misfortunes; they giggle when pogroms are instituted by someone else and synagogues defiled vicariously: "Serve them right really, Jews!"'

By the summer of 1939 Germany was threatening to march into Poland and the Joyces were now wondering seriously whether their destiny lay in Germany, not Ireland. They discussed the possibility with Macnab, who was planning a holiday to Berlin. Just as Macnab was leaving, Joyce gave him a note of introduction to Christian Bauer, his friend who was now working for Goebbels' Propaganda Ministry. As an afterthought he said:

'John, if you are willing, I want you to do something for me after you have got to know Christian. I want him to find out whether, in the event of my leaving England and going to Germany, Goebbels is able and willing to arrange for my immediate naturalisation as a German citizen, together, of course, with Margaret, if she accompanies me.'

Macnab saw Bauer over several meetings. Bauer spoke to Goebbels, or so he claimed, and the Joyces' German citizenship seemed guaranteed immediately upon their arrival – not only theirs but Macnab's as well because, at this stage, he was planning to go with them. Macnab returned to London on Monday 21 August 1939, and told the Joyces the good news. Reassured by Bauer's apparent guarantee of citizenship – it meant Joyce would not have to rely on his British passport and could not, therefore, be accused of treason – they all but made up their minds to move to Germany.

Two days later, Joyce was stunned by the news that Ribbentrop, who was now the German Foreign Minister, had signed a non-aggression pact with Molotov, his Soviet counterpart. Joyce felt betrayed. In his imagination he had cast Hitler as the far-sighted world statesman who had recognized the Bolshevik menace for what it was. So much for steering straight, he thought. Harry Pollitt, Joyce's opposite number in the British Communist Party, was also reeling from shock.

Joyce went for a long walk so that he could think clearly. As he brooded and smoked and walked he saw signs of London preparing for war: volunteers filling sandbags, tape being placed over windows to minimize shattering, trenches being dug, gas masks being distributed, posters going up about the evacuation plans for children, air-raid warnings being practised. He felt numb with indecision. Hitler had let him down, so perhaps he should revert to his original plan to escape to Ireland. Normally good sleepers, William and Margaret that night lay awake discussing whether to go to Berlin or Dublin. Margaret, who was the more decisive of the two, argued the case for Berlin. Like Lady Macbeth, she began screwing her husband's courage to the sticking-place. Eventually Joyce got out of bed and paced the floor. He chain-smoked, thought out loud, and read and re-read the newspaper report about the Soviet–German non-aggression treaty.

Such was Joyce's long-term hatred of Bolshevism he should have taken this opportunity to turn his back on Hitler, with honour, according to his own code. Instead he perhaps worried that a loss of nerve now might make him look weak and unprincipled in the eyes of his beloved Margaret. If he stayed, he was faced with a further decline into street-corner political obscurity, or, worse, imprisonment. Moving to Germany, he reasoned, would be an adventure and the place might even prove to be a land of opportunity. He tried to rationalize events: Hitler, he told Margaret, had been rebuffed by Chamberlain in his fight against communism so he had had to take this step to safeguard the Fatherland. 'There has to be a higher loyalty even than nationalism,' he said. 'Our war is with bolshevism so if that means fighting on the side of Germany, so be it.' Margaret agreed and added that it would be more logical and honest for them to go to Germany. 'And, anyway,' she said, 'once there, we can let fate decide the rest.'

The matter was all but settled. They would go to Germany if they could. But they both knew this decision was academic unless Joyce was able to renew his passport, which was only valid for one more month, and this would by no means be a straightforward process because, as well Joyce knew, his name was on various Home Office lists of political agitators.

It was now Thursday morning. They had talked through the night. As soon as they had finished breakfast, they set off for the passport office. Joyce filled out an application form for a renewed passport, valid for one year, the shortest period of time for which a passport could be issued. The Assistant Passport Officer on duty was Harold Godwin, a man with a nervous disposition who was to have cause to remember that day. He approved Joyce's application with a thump of his stamp.

Margaret then took both their passports to the German Consulate and asked for visas for a holiday. The building was full of anxious-looking German servants who were wanting to get back to the Fatherland before the war started. The official who issued the visas wished Margaret 'a good journey'. With their passports and visas, the Joyces now had the option to go to Germany, though a final decision was still to be made. Fate was to force their hand.

Just after midnight, the phone rang in the Joyces' flat. It was Maxwell Knight. He said something like: 'I should warn you, William, you are about to be arrested and interned.' Margaret listened to the other end of the conversation.

'When?' Joyce asked. A pause. 'Thank you, Max.'

It was a last favour – a payoff, perhaps, for services rendered – by a spymaster to his loyal agent. Later that day the Commons would pass the Emergency Powers Defence Act, under which Special Branch would be able to arrest Joyce and other political agitators who might be thought sympathetic to the enemy. Joyce told Margaret. Again, they sat up all night talking: William worrying about whether he should move to Berlin permanently, Margaret wondering what to pack and where to store their furniture and books. She decided to ask Miss Scrimgeour to look after them.

On Friday 25 August, Hitler issued orders for the invasion of Poland but cancelled them when told of a guarantee of mutual support between Britain and Poland. That morning Margaret set off for Midhurst, taking the automatic pistol which Joyce had given her to hide. She buried it under the spreading roots of a tree near Miss Scrimgeour's house. It was their favourite tree. The Joyces always attached great significance to certain trees. They associated them with the 'cosmic tree of life' which, in Nordic mythology, linked heaven and earth.

While she was away, Joyce withdrew all his savings from the bank. That night he gathered together the members of the National Socialist League and the Carlyle Club and announced that he was going away for some time and that the two organizations would therefore have to be suspended. He returned home and, with the help of his sister Joan and his brother Quentin, he packed his suitcase. Once everything was crammed in, Margaret tried to lift one of the cases. It was too heavy. She opened it up and found that William had repacked a heavy bronze eagle which she had removed once already.

When Macnab called round, Joyce took him by the arm and said: 'Margaret and I are making a little trip to Deutschland in the morning.'

'I want to come with you,' Macnab said.

'No,' Joyce said. 'This trip is not for you. I know your loyalty but it isn't fair to you, and, anyway, you're engaged to be married. I couldn't have asked you to come, and that's why I've delayed telling you until now. If I wait another day I fear it would be jail for yours truly and starvation for Margaret.'

'What if there is no war?' Macnab asked.

Joyce shook his head. 'I'm going to throw in my lot with Germany for good or ill. I am very sorry to leave England, which I love, but I have made my choice, and Margaret is of the same mind as myself. Our life in England is over.'

He later reflected in a book he wrote in Germany: 'For my part, the decision was easy to make. To me it was clear on the morning of 25 August that the greatest struggle in history was now doomed to take place. It might have been a worthy course to stay in England and incessantly work for peace: but I had one traditionally acquired or inherited prejudice, which many will think foolish and which may be logically difficult to defend. England was going to war. I felt that if, for reasons of conscience, I could not fight for her, I must give her up for ever. Such an argument I do not commend to anybody else, but man is guided by more than reason alone, and in this great conflict, I wanted to play a clear and definite part. In small matters, it is easy to be guided by conventional loyalty. In great matters, a man has the right to hold himself responsible to Higher Justice alone.'

On the morning of Saturday 26 August, the day he was due to be arrested, William and Margaret Joyce, accompanied by Macnab, set off for Victoria Station. On the way, they noticed the semi-blacked-out traffic lights and the lorries carrying troops. The station was seething with British citizens returning from the Continent. Walking against the tide, the porter who carried their luggage looked at their labels and said: 'Berlin! That's a rum place to be going right now.' He didn't know they had bought one-way tickets.

Michael Joyce did not come to see his son and daughter-in-law off. He hadn't attended their wedding, either, which suggests that relations between them were strained. But Joyce's mother and two of his brothers, Frank, a BBC engineer, and Robert, a recent school-leaver, turned up to see them off. (Frank, a former Blackshirt, was interned for eleven months during the war, before joining the army and becoming a quartermaster-sergeant. Robert also joined up later in the war and served in Italy.) The devoted Quentin couldn't be there to see his oldest brother off because he had just been sent to work for the Air Ministry in Bristol. It proved to be a temporary posting.

The family and friends made awkward small talk. Queenie gave Margaret a Brussels lace collar, a family heirloom, as a parting gift. Whistles blew, doors clanged shut and, after waving handkerchiefs from the windows, Joyce and his wife settled back in their seats, in silence. They brooded upon the train journey ahead of them to Dover and then, via ferry, to Ostend. Joyce was a great one for the dramatic exit. He only just managed to escape Ireland in time, now he was escaping England with just hours to spare.

The authorities would have been aware of his passport renewal. He was a wanted political activist whose name was on the police suspect lists at ports. Yet he and Margaret left the country publicly, just days before war was declared, with luggage clearly labelled 'Berlin' and one-way tickets for Berlin. It was a suspiciously easy exit.

At Dover the man checking passports seemed to hesitate when he looked up at them but then he stamped their documents and they boarded the ship unhindered. The sea was calm. Seagulls were wheeling and screeching overhead. Many of the German passengers on board were weeping as the ship cast off, but the Joyces showed no emotion. They merely stood on the stern deck, hands on the rail. Perhaps William was thinking about something he had written two years earlier: 'If it ever happens to us to see the chalk cliffs receding for the last time as the water widens between us and our homeland, then the memories will come in a choking flood, and we shall know our land when it is too late.'

PART 3

BERLIN

'I am consumed with pity for Joyce because it seems to me that he lived in a true hell: to have enough brains to discern that there was such a thing as political science, and to be inflamed with a passionate desire to be the instrument of political wisdom, and to be such a damn fool that all he could work up was a peculiarly idiotic variety of anti-Semitism; and to be puny and plain and be capable of the ardent and enduring love he showed for his wife in Berlin – there couldn't be anything worse.'

Rebecca West in a letter to Cyril Connolly

NINE

'Oh, let's stop messing about and just stay here.'

By the time William and Margaret Joyce arrived at the German frontier, they were tired and hungry. They had eaten only stale, unbuttered bread and salami, all that was on offer on the train. Their fellow passengers were civilians, Berliners hurrying home. As they waited to have their passports checked, they saw on the office wall a poster of Hitler. They had never seen one so openly displayed before and it brought home to them the cold reality of their situation. They were in another country now, and there could be no going back.

As the train pulled into Berlin's Friedrichstrasse station, they pressed their faces to the window to savour the architectural sights, but the buildings around the station looked shabby and neglected. At the echoing terminus, under a canopy of glass and iron, they looked around for a porter. It was a long time before one arrived and helped them take their bags to the taxi rank. When they stepped out into the balmy morning sunshine, they took deep breaths. The city, they decided, smelled of toothpaste. There was hardly any traffic. It was Sunday 27 August 1939, exactly one week before Britain was to declare war on Germany. To the Joyces it seemed impossible to believe that they were in the capital of a country hurtling towards war.*

* Margaret later recalled that at this point William implied that he had been to Berlin before. 'The place seems to have changed,' he said to her as they looked around. He would not elaborate. According to the unpublished 'Material for a work on William Joyce' by Angus Macnab, 'Before 1939 Joyce had only been to Germany once in his life. This was for a matter

There was a solitary taxi, which they loaded their bags into. They then headed for a small hotel that Macnab had recommended – it was near the Potsdamer Platz, a German Piccadilly Circus. Again they pressed their faces to the windows, taking in the broad, cobbled avenues lined with trees, the windowed flats, the grand hotels.

After checking in, they washed, changed and unpacked before going to the hotel's restaurant, where they ate breakfast in silence. After this they went for a walk, staring at the foreign-looking trams, the cafes with tables outside, the flower-sellers, a shop window with the word 'Juden' daubed on it, the newsagents with severe-looking papers with titles in Gothic script. They came to Berlin's vast central park, the Tiergarten, and decided to stroll through it. The park was designed in the baroque style, with mazes, avenues of trees, benches, bandstands and intersecting paths. The reds, golds and greens of the leaves presented an encouraging sight to the Joyces. There were swans on the river. They linked arms as they walked. Berlin, they agreed, was beautiful on the cusp of autumn.

To cool down, most Berliners had gone to the lakes surrounding the city to paddle, promenade and sunbathe, as well as enjoy the views across the water to the imperial palaces of Potsdam. There were pleasure steamers there, and brass bands and ice-cream stalls. Margaret had brought her swimming costume and was keen to join them but William said that recreation would have to wait until they had found jobs and sorted out their German citizenship.

They returned to their hotel so that William could telephone Christian Bauer. 'Hello, Christian. This is William. Margaret is with me. We have left England. Just arrived in Berlin.' There was a pause. 'That's right.' Joyce frowned. 'I see, I see. Tonight, then.' He replaced the receiver. William told Margaret that Christian had seemed surprised and said he couldn't see them until the evening. Joyce had imagined his arrival would have merited a more enthusiastic response from the German authorities.

To fill the time until evening, they went sightseeing. Middle-aged men in military uniforms were walking their dogs along the broad avenues. Young mothers were pushing prams. William bought a Sunday newspaper

---

of weeks only, and I think it was some time in the early 20s on a school or college vacation.' In fact it was in 1933.

and was shocked to read that food-ration cards were being issued that day. They maundered through the leafy Wilhelmsplatz and stared at the imposing Ministry of Finance. They continued on past the Reichskanzlei, the new chancellery built by Albert Speer, and briefly joined a crowd that was staring at the balcony from which Hitler made some of his speeches. They thought it looked like a stage prop from *Romeo and Juliet.* After this they walked along Unter den Linden and marvelled at the enormously long Swastika banners draped down the buildings. They ended up at the giant Doric columns of the Brandenburg Gate and took lunch sitting outside a small restaurant in the sunshine. William, still feeling perturbed by Bauer's apparent indifference, distracted himself by writing postcards to Miss Scrimgeour and Macnab.

That evening, Bauer and his fiancée arrived at their hotel in a car. They drove to a restaurant in Savignyplatz and sat out in the garden there drinking wine. The awkward topic which was pressing on their minds was not mentioned until after dinner. 'What are you thinking of doing now that you are in Germany?' Bauer asked.

'I don't know,' Joyce said. 'I was rather hoping that you might be able to suggest something.'

'Oh, there will be something for you to do, I imagine,' Bauer said. 'So long as war doesn't start.'

Joyce stared at him. 'And if there is a war?'

Bauer looked away, embarrassed. 'Then you will be interned, of course.'

The Joyces exchanged glances. 'Together?'

'Good heavens, no,' the young man said.

As she later recalled, Margaret felt sick. She was beginning to suspect that their only contact in Berlin was not as important an official as he had led them to believe: he seemed to hold only a junior position in the Propaganda Ministry. He wasn't even important enough to have a special petrol allowance, as he went on to reveal. Joyce felt let down and angry – the question of internment hadn't even been hinted at when Bauer had spoken to Macnab – but he was polite, in part because Bauer's fiancée was present.

The Joyces felt humiliated, having fled England to avoid internment only to discover that they were to be interned instead by the very country they had come to help.

Bauer, relieved that William wasn't making a scene, insisted on driving them around to see Berlin's architectural jewels at night, dramatically floodlit. They drove under the Brandenburg Gate, past the Reichstag, through the Tiergarten, round the Siegessäule and on to the wide avenues of Charlottenburg.

After they said *auf wiedersehen*, with protestations of friendship, the Joyces walked back to their room in silence. As Margaret recalled, as soon as they got through the door, she sat on the bed and had a 'good cry'. 'Darling, I'm frightened,' she said. 'If I have to be imprisoned, at least let me be imprisoned somewhere I can understand the language.'

Joyce decided that rather than risk being interned separately they should return to London the next day, before war broke out.

The next morning the dining room was crowded with uniformed men. Whenever a new officer came through the door everyone barked: 'Heil Hitler!' and gave the Nazi salute, while remaining seated. Being a stickler for military etiquette, Joyce kept jumping to his feet and greeting each officer with a vigorous salute. He soon realized, with a self-deprecating grin, that if he didn't join in the seated saluting he wasn't going to finish his breakfast. It was the British army barracks all over again.

Back in his room, Joyce rang his only contact once more. He spoke in German to Bauer's fiancée, who tearfully told him that her betrothed had just had his call-up papers and had left the house. Joyce lit a cigarette and sat on the bed. They were on their own now, it seemed.

Outside, the streets were busy with removal vans and grocery trucks commandeered by the government and filled with troops heading east to the Polish frontier. Reckoning that sterling might soon become unchangeable, Joyce found a bureau de change and swapped his pounds for Reichsmarks. As they had not brought any soap with them they now set out to buy some, but they discovered that without rationing coupons they couldn't purchase any. With mounting panic, they tried other shops until, at last, a shopkeeper took pity and sold them a bar. Mission accomplished, they strolled along the leafy boulevards, reminiscing. They suddenly remembered that Dorothy Eckersley, an old acquaintance, was supposed to be in Berlin. Dorothy was a friend of Unity Mitford, as well as a cousin of Virginia Woolf, and – most significantly for the Joyces – the wife of a former chief engineer of the BBC. Joyce thought he remembered her saying she would be staying at the Continental. They found the hotel and decided to have lunch there. Sitting at a table in the restaurant was Dorothy Eckersley.*

The Joyces were delighted to see a friendly face. Mrs Eckersley congratulated them on leaving London and waved away the prospect of internment with a dismissive hand. It seemed their fortunes had changed because Dorothy had a friend in Berlin, a Dr Schirmer, whose brother was a senior figure in the German Foreign Office. She was meeting the doctor that afternoon at a tea party and the Joyces should come along, too. The doctor proved affable. He listened to Joyce's story and said he would see what he could do in terms of finding him work. It was vague but it was all they had to go on.

All day there had been frenetic activity at the British Embassy. A stream of offers and counter-offers were passing between diplomats in a frantic endeavour to stay Hitler's hand. That evening, the British Ambassador handed a note to the Führer stating that the British intended to honour their obligation to Poland in the event of a German invasion.

The Joyces could not have known that Hitler's invasion order was just three days away, but, like everyone in Berlin, they did sense that war was imminent. And they knew that if the stranger they had just met was unable to help them they would soon be interned. Feeling protective toward Margaret, William decided they should try and get back to London. The next morning (the 29th) they set off for the travel office in Unter den Linden. They asked for two single tickets. The assistant extracted a leaflet from a clip of papers, ran his pencil down the paragraphs, stopped and asked how they were planning to pay.

'Reichsmarks.'

'I am sorry,' he said. 'We are not allowed to accept German currency for a journey outside Germany. All I can offer are tickets to the border.'

Joyce hesitated. He felt foolish for having changed his money so impetuously. Now he worried that they might end up stranded on the border. He had just had his first encounter with petty German bureaucracy, a phenomenon that was to drive him to distraction over the coming years.

'You could try asking for help at the British Embassy,' the assistant said. 'It's just round the corner.'

---

* According to some accounts she was with her son James Clark, but he has no recollection of this.

The couple walked at a brisk pace to the embassy, an imposing building with a prime location on Wilhelmstrasse, Berlin's Whitehall. It was over-shadowed by the famous Adlon Hotel, built in the embassy gardens, and was, according to Sir Nevile Henderson, the British Ambassador to Germany, a 'cramped, dirty and dark' place. The Joyces arrived hot and panting to find the entrance all but blocked by packing cases and crates. They navigated their way past them only to be told that it was not the embassy they needed but the consulate, the building a couple of streets away in Tiergartenstrasse. When they reached it they were told their best chance was to try the consulate in Cologne. They went to a cafe and ordered beer and vodka.

'If only I hadn't changed our money,' William said.

'If only we had bought return tickets,' Margaret said.

'What do you want to do, Meg?'

Margaret thought for a moment then shrugged her shoulders. 'Oh, let's stop messing about and just stay here. They'll be just as unhelpful in Cologne. At least there is plenty to drink in Berlin.'

On Wednesday 30 August, William and Margaret went looking for cheap furnished lodgings, on foot, to avoid taxi fares. Most of the apart-ments they saw were malodorous and neglected. Those that were clean and well maintained were suddenly withdrawn when the couple explained that they were British citizens newly arrived in Berlin. Back at their hotel, feeling exhausted, they were presented with a hand-delivered note from Dr Schirmer. There was a number on it which Joyce was to telephone the following day.

On Thursday 31 August, Joyce rang the number. A secretary answered and instructed him to turn up that afternoon at a villa occupied by a Foreign Office department. Buoyed by this development, the couple continued their search for lodging with renewed vigour. They found a large room just off the Friedrichstrasse, a short walk from the Tiergarten. It contained huge twin beds. They were told by the genial landlord that the room was available and that he accepted foreigners. When his children heard Margaret speaking English they stared at her with their mouths open.

Joyce arrived early for his appointment that afternoon and was surprised to see others apparently waiting to be interviewed. All were ushered into a hall and handed writing paper. They were then given a transcript of the speech Hitler had just delivered. Joyce was told to translate it into English. He got to work and finished his translation before the others, handed it in and was paid in cash. He then realized why the others were taking so long over their translation work: they were paid by the hour. It was freelance work, but at least his name was now on a list of part-time translators.

Next morning, Friday 1 September, the Joyces packed their suitcase again for the move to their new lodgings and headed downstairs for breakfast. Martial music was playing at full volume on the radio. Most of the hotel guests were carrying gas-mask tins. As they sat down, a fanfare interrupted the music and a sombre voice said that an important announcement was to be made shortly. The music resumed. This went on for half an hour, and the listeners in the dining room became more tense every time the trumpets sounded. Finally there was a silence. Hotel guests stopped talking. A statement was read out: 'On the order of the Führer and the High Command, the armed forces have taken over the active protection of the Reich. In fulfilment of this order to put a stop to Polish violence, early this morning German troops crossed the German–Polish border and counter-attacked.'

When the announcement was over, the guests began to gabble excitedly, everyone agreed that this was only a punitive expedition against the aggressive Poles and so it wouldn't last long. Joyce did not share their optimism. He knew the invasion meant a declaration of war from the British – and that this, in turn, would make their presence in Berlin tantamount to treason. He decided he and Margaret should register with the Berlin police straight away, so that they could then start the process of acquiring German citizenship.

Outside, Berliners were tense and excited, standing around shop fronts, listening to a speech Hitler was making on the radio. The Joyces thought that as they were in Berlin they might as well go and join the crowds at the Chancellery to hear it at source. Anti-aircraft batteries were being installed on the main road leading up to it. The crowd listened to the speech in grim silence. Though Margaret did not know enough German to understand what Hitler was saying, she could tell from his tone that he was not looking for a peaceful solution to the Poland crisis. Feeling suddenly nervous, she felt for William's hand. He held it firmly as he stared up at the figure on the balcony. He could understand what Hitler was saying and it filled his heart with a mixture of trepidation and excitement.

At the police station the Joyces' passports aroused much curiosity. The police gathered around to look at them. They quizzed the Joyces about whether they thought Britain would declare war, and they smiled indulgently when warned it probably would. As if on cue, the ugly shrill of an air-raid siren sounded. It was one of several practice warnings planned for that afternoon.

Unknown to Joyce, back in London the men in trilbies and macs had come to arrest him, almost a week after Maxwell Knight had told him they would. They found Joyce's mother, his sister Joan and her friend Mercedes Barrington tidying up in his old flat. An MI5 report noted: 'When Special Branch came to arrest Joyce his mother informed them that she, along with Macnab, had seen William and his wife off from Victoria on Saturday 26 August by the 10.30 train from Dover en route to Ostend.' Among the possessions Special Branch confiscated was a file Joyce had written on the novelist Dennis Wheatley. Joyce had been to one of Wheatley's parties and the two men had talked about Germany. Joyce had expressed his disappointment that Wheatley's books were not published there. In his file, Joyce suggested that, in the event of a fascist coup in Britain, Wheatley would make a 'first class' gauleiter for North West London.

Special Branch then called on Ethel Scrimgeour at Stedham Hall, near Midhurst, and were told by her that: 'Joyce is now abroad.' When Major General Vernon Kell, the Director-General of MI5, quizzed Knight about the missing fascist he was told that 'Joyce is not a danger'. Reassured by this, Kell wrote a brief report on the matter in which he noted: 'I should not think anything could occur to shake his [Joyce's] basic patriotism. His code of personal honour is probably peculiar, but very rigid.'

That night in Berlin there was a blackout, but the cafes, restaurants and beer halls were packed. The entrances to air-raid shelters were candlelit. Using the whitewashed kerbstones to navigate, the Joyces made their way to their new lodging and guided themselves in by a chink of light from an ill-fitting curtain. Their landlord informed them that telephone links to England, France and Poland had just been cut.

At nine o'clock on 3 September, Sir Nevile Henderson arrived at the

German Foreign Office, a yellow palace with sculpted snakes wrapped symbolically round globes on its front pillars. He handed Hitler's interpreter a note giving Germany until eleven o'clock that morning to accept the British demand that Germany withdraw its troops from Poland. When the deadline passed, Unity Mitford walked into the English Garden in Munich, held a pistol to her head and pulled the trigger. Hitler was told and he anxiously telephoned the hospital where she was taken.★

News of the reaction of the British to the invasion of Poland was piped out to Berliners on loudspeakers over the Wilhelmstrasse, the government street where Goebbels' Ministry of Propaganda was. On the faces of Berliners, Joyce saw bewilderment, shock and depression. There was no war fever. He later described how he came to hear the news: 'At twenty minutes past twelve Central European time, my landlady rushed into my room and told me: "*Jetzt ist es Krieg mit England!*" ("It's war now, with England!") Her husband at once came in and shook hands with my wife and myself, saying: "Whatever happens, we remain friends." We had known these simple people only since the previous day: they had no proof that I, too, was not an enemy: but their action was typical of the whole attitude of the German people. At about three in the afternoon, the first newspapers announcing England's declaration of war were on the streets. They were given away free. Under the bridge outside the Friedrichstrasse Station, we all scrambled for newspapers. There was no sign of anger or hatred: people looked at each other as if the incredible had happened. We went to tea with some friends whose name is famous in German history [the von Bülows, whom they knew from London]. They too felt no emotion except surprise and regret. We talked of England: and my host was so inspiring in his eloquence on the subject of what England might have achieved in friendship with Germany that, as I looked out on the twilight enshrouding the Kurfürstendamm, I could think of nothing to say but Marlowe's famous lines [from *Dr Faustus*]: "Cut is the branch that might have grown full strait / And burned is Apollo's laurel bough." '

The next day, back in London, Special Branch officers paid a visit to

---

★ A couple of months later, when she regained consciousness, Hitler went to see her and asked her if she wanted to be in England or Germany. She said England and Hitler arranged for a doctor and an ambulance train to take her to Switzerland.

Macnab. They searched his flat, then they began asking questions. Macnab made a note of the dialogue that followed.

> Policeman: Is William Joyce here?
> Macnab: No.
> Has he been here?
> No.
> When did you last see him?
> 26 August.
> Where?
> Victoria Station.
> What was he doing?
> Leaving for the Continent.
> Where is he now?
> I haven't his actual address.
> Do you know what country?
> Germany, I believe.
> How do you know that?
> He wrote and told me so from Berlin.
> Did he, by Jove. Of course you destroyed the letter?
> No, I've got it here somewhere.
> When did you get it?
> About 1 September.
> If you don't mind, we'd very much like to have that letter.
> It was a picture postcard. Didn't you come across it in your search?
> No. Have you hidden it?
> No. It's here somewhere. Ah, here it is.
> Thanks very much. We could oblige you to give it up if you don't object. It's more pleasant this way.
> Certainly, by all means have it.
> Oh dear, what language is it in? I can't understand it.
> Oh, sorry, of course it's in Latin. We always use that for postcards.
> Coo! You professors!

William and Margaret were walking in the Tiergarten when they heard an air-raid siren. They wondered whether the war was to start with a massive air raid on Berlin. They thought they heard the drone of a distant aircraft engine, but it proved a false alarm. They were both beginning to suffer from war nerves and both were coming down with colds.

For the next few days, Joyce continued to turn up for his translation work, having learned now to drag each assignment out for as long as possible. The pay was not really enough to live on and their savings were disappearing at an alarming rate. In fact they were down to their last twenty Reichsmarks. William was again beginning to feel anxious when Dr Schirmer rang him and told him to report to the Foreign Office for an interview. The official who interviewed him was polite but suspicious. When asked what he wanted to do, Joyce answered that he wasn't sure, but perhaps something that could draw upon his experience as the Propaganda Director of the British Union of Fascists. He was told there was no suitable vacancy. Part of the problem – perhaps unsurprisingly – was that they assumed he was a British plant.

Eventually the official decided to refer Joyce to Dr Erich Hetzler, in Ribbentrop's private office – he was an Anglophile who had studied briefly at the London School of Economics and so would be better able to establish Joyce's bona fides. Hetzler, Sammy to his friends, listened to Joyce's account of his background and noted down his National Socialist sympathies. He asked Joyce if he had thought of working for the radio. Joyce had not but he said he would give it a go. Hetzler telephoned Dr Fritz Hesse, a former pupil of his who was now head of the English Department in the German Foreign Office. The conversation was brief. When Hetzler put the phone down he looked at Joyce and said simply: 'You are to report to the Reichsrundfunkhaus for an audition.'

TEN

'Germany calling. Germany calling. Germany calling.'

The Reichsrundfunkhaus, in the leafy and affluent Berlin district of Charlottenburg, was the German equivalent of the BBC's Broadcasting House. It was usually known as the Funkhaus. To amuse Margaret, William called it the Skunk House. Built by the architect Hans Poelzig in 1927, it had a triangular outer building, and four smaller triangular buildings and courtyards within. Like the nearby Olympiastadion, it was considered a fine example of Third Reich architecture: modern, angular, Teutonic.* Throughout the 1930s, its roof had been painted a stark white but, as the war approached, this was changed to the same dark brown as the glazed tiles which covered the building's exterior walls.

When Joyce arrived for his audition, camouflage netting was going up around the building. This was a rather futile exercise given that an enormous transmitter stood alongside it. Above the entrance, there was a large sign which read: Haus des Rundfunks. Either side of it there were black-uniformed SS guards. All wore special brass gorgets around their necks. The lifts at the Funkhaus were considered fashionable at the time – 'continuation chambers' that people hopped on and off as they trundled slowly up and down without stopping. Joyce was directed up these and to a dimly lit studio, empty except for a desk with a sausage-shaped microphone on it and a copy of *Rundvolk*, the in-house magazine. On the wall there was

* Curiously, the Rundfunk was the same triangular shape as a coroneted devil's head which Joyce used to doodle constantly in London. Examples of this are in the National Archives in London.

a framed picture of Hitler surrounded by a circle of small photographs of the main speakers at the Funkhaus.

There is some uncertainty as to the exact date of Joyce's audition but, in all probability, it was 11 September 1939.* What is known is that it didn't go that well. Joyce's cold had grown worse, he was tired – the air raid siren had gone off at four o'clock that morning – and he went over the time he was allocated to read the script. But a radio engineer reckoned he had potential. He was given his first live bulletin to read later that day. It was about the British blockade of Germany.†

Part of the confusion surrounding his first broadcast, and indeed all the broadcasts he was thought to have made in the first two months of the war, was that he had a rival at the Funkhaus. A week before Joyce's audition, the BBC's monitors in London had made a note that one of the Reichsrundfunkhaus speakers spoke such good English that it was clearly his mother tongue. 'In all references to England,' they wrote, 'his intonation is extremely sarcastic'. They noted, too, a 'slight Scottish accent' and christened this speaker Sinister Sam, 'owing to the sinister fascination which he breeds. Humour, it may be mentioned, is lacking in the range of his histrionic resources.' This was Norman Baillie-Stewart, a former officer of the Seaforth Highlanders who had renounced his British citizenship before the war. In 1933 he had been arrested, held in the Tower of London, court-martialled for selling military secrets to the Germans and sentenced to five years in prison.

---

* Margaret confirms in her diaries that this was the date. For several years she marked it as an anniversary. The date had a great significance at William's trial. According to MI5, a source in Berlin said that in his first broadcast on 10 September, Joyce introduced himself as 'William Joyce of the National Socialist League speaking to his English friends'. This seems unlikely, though from 1941 onwards he did introduce himself by his own name. He never denied that he was Lord Haw-Haw later in the war, but his defence argued that it could not be proven that he was Lord Haw-Haw – that is, a propagandist rather than a mere newsreader – in the *first* month of the war, which was the time the prosecution's only witness claimed to have recognized Joyce's voice. It was a fairly academic point because, had he been called to the witness stand, Joyce would almost certainly have admitted he was Lord Haw-Haw after the first couple of months, while his illegally obtained British passport was still valid.
† It has been suggested that Joyce's first broadcast included a line about 'Britain being ready to fight to the last Frenchman'. This, too, is unlikely. He would have been reading a straightforward report of the news, as opposed to an opinion piece. As such, his defence argued at his trial, it is debatable whether it would have constituted 'giving comfort to the King's enemy'.

After reading the news that day, Joyce was formally offered a job on the English broadcasting team. He was then introduced to the other British broadcasters. They struck him as being a bunch of misfits. There was an elderly woman called Miss Margaret Bothamley, who had a picture of the King and Queen on her desk. She was convinced she had had an affair with Hitler when she was young. Another dysfunctional member of staff was a British army colonel's daughter who sat at her desk all day knitting. Joyce and Baillie-Stewart, who was at the time considered the star turn of the English station, took an instant dislike to each other. When introduced, Baillie-Stewart said sniffily: 'I suppose you've come to take our jobs away.'

Back at their flat, Margaret was waiting to hear how the interview had gone. When she heard her husband running up the stairs she concluded it had gone well. He flung off his coat, kissed her and excitedly announced that he had landed a job at the 'Skunk House'.

The next day an order was given to arrest all adult British males living in Germany. Two nights later, when William was working a night shift, Margaret was awoken by her landlady. 'The Gestapo have come to arrest Herr Joyce,' she said. A policeman looked in to Margaret's room and, seeing her in her nightgown, waited outside until she had dressed. The landlady explained that Joyce was at the Funkhaus and the policeman said he would call back the following day. He never did because Dr Hetzler intervened to make sure Joyce was exempt from arrest. It was a close call. So far he had made only a couple of broadcasts for the enemy, which wasn't quite the point of no return. It was unpatriotic, but it wasn't exactly high treason. That would come. But the threat of arrest made William worry about Margaret. What if they introduced a similar rule for British women? After all, another new law had been introduced: anyone endangering the defensive power of the German people would automatically be sentenced to death. Already a Berlin man had been shot for refusing to take part in defence work.

In London, meanwhile, Cyril Carr Dalmain, writing under the pseudonym Jonah Barrington, was dipping his pen in the ink of history. 'A gent I'd like to meet is moaning periodically from Zeesen,' he wrote in his *Daily Express* column on 14 September. 'He speaks English of the haw-haw, dammit-get-out-of-my-way variety, and his strong suit is gentlemanly indignation.' Almost certainly he had been listening not to Joyce but to either Baillie-Stewart or Wolff Mittler, a German who spoke fluent

'Old Etonian' English and had a habit of ending his talks with what he thought was a typically English upper-class expression: 'Hearty cheerios.'

Either way, Barrington's report tapped the nation's funny bone. More people tuned in that night and, the next day, a question was asked in the House of Commons whether the Home Secretary would make it known to British subjects broadcasting propaganda for the enemy that they risked prosecution for treason. Two days later, in a burst of enthusiastic inexactitude, the French newspaper *Paris-Midi* reported that there was a new radio traitor called 'Lord Ah! Oh!' whose real name was Jonah Barrington.

The following day, 18 September, the *Daily Express* sought to clarify matters: 'Jonah Barrington, listening at the *Daily Express* short wave station in Surrey to the war on the radio, introduces "Lord Haw-Haw".' Barrington had already written about a woman speaker whom he had named Winnie of Warsaw. Now he wrote: 'Winnie of Warsaw (who really works for the Nazi station at Breslau) has a follower – Lord Haw-Haw of Zeesen. From his accent and personality I imagine him with a receding chin, a questing nose, thin, yellow hair brushed back, a monocle, a vacant eye, a gardenia in his button-hole. Rather like P. G. Wodehouse's Bertie Wooster.'

He had formally coined the sobriquet Lord Haw-Haw. It was to become a household nickname to millions.

Charles Graves of the *Daily Mail* realized that his rival on the *Express* was on to something. 'Many of you must have heard this particular German announcer and perhaps formed your own impression of him,' Graves wrote in his column the next day. 'Some people suggest that he is a monocled ass, like one of P. G. Wodehouse's titled creations. This I regard as an insult both to P. G. Wodehouse and the peerage. I am willing to have a small bet that he is a fat, elderly Shakespearian actor, probably deported from England and until war broke out a professor of elocution at some small German institute.'

Not to be outdone, Barrington replied to Graves in his column the following day. His implication was that Graves was a killjoy: 'The more people who tune in to the foreign radio impropaganda experts, the greater the joy and laughter.'

'Cassandra' in the *Daily Mirror* joined in the fun, playing up the entertainment value of the broadcasts: 'I earnestly ask all of you who are able to listen to broadcasts from Germany to this country to do so.'

One of those English listeners was Albert Hunt, a Special Branch officer who in the early 1930s had been assigned off and on to monitor Blackshirt rallies. Although he had never spoken to Joyce he claimed to have heard him speak in public on several occasions and now, so he thought, he recognized that Lord Haw-Haw was in fact William Joyce. He made no note of the date, time or frequency on the radio dial. But he did recall at Joyce's trial that he heard the announcer say that Folkestone and Dover had been destroyed in a Luftwaffe bombing raid. As this was the start of the Phoney War it would be many months before the first German bombs rained on Britain. There hadn't even been a bullet fired in France. The idea that a news station would broadcast such a report, even as propaganda, was preposterous. It would have been counter-productive, apart from anything else, because the report would have so easily been disproved and the station that broadcast it discredited. Neither the BBC monitors nor their German counterparts had any record of this report being made.

At this time, responsibility for foreign radio broadcasts fell between two rival departments: the Propaganda Ministry, run by Goebbels, and the Foreign Ministry, run by Ribbentrop, whom Joyce had now taken to calling Ribbontripe (but only in private). Neither had implemented a proper vetting procedure so, even though he was a foreigner, Joyce required no security clearance. However, Admiral Canaris, head of the Abwehr (the German military intelligence service), suspected Joyce might be a British agent, not least because his professed devotion to National Socialism seemed suspiciously fanatical. Canaris may have known, through Christian Bauer, of Joyce's association with Maxwell Knight – but, in the end, he decided not to interfere in Joyce's appointment, having no wish to challenge the authority of either Ribbentrop or Goebbels.

So it was that, on 19 September, a fortnight after war was declared, Joyce was officially appointed 'editor and speaker' at the Funkhaus. In his contract he lied, for the fourth time in official documents, that he had been born in Galway. He told Margaret that he wanted to be consistent in order to avoid bureaucratic suspicion.

The British public was already becoming obsessed with trying to work out who the mysterious Lord Haw-Haw was. Lord Donegall, who wrote a *Daily Mail* column, looked into possible suspects: 'Best known to English listeners and very dear to my heart is Lord Haw-Haw, as Barrington has christened him. Anyone can have the joy of meeting him, for he makes lengthy appearances on the short-wave band from Berlin. Whoever writes Lord Haw-Haw's stuff is a genius in the art of being unconsciously funny. At times he drops his monocle (I'm sure he has one) and becomes endearing.'

The name William Joyce was circulating in the media and Donegall contacted Macnab, with whom he had been at Oxford, to see if he could verify it was him. He asked Macnab to listen to a broadcast. They tuned in on an unearthed short-wave wireless set and, behind the static, Macnab recognized his friend's voice. He nodded. 'That's Will all right.' But Donegall said that wasn't the voice he had in mind, so he asked Macnab to come to his country house the following day to hear a clearer set. Macnab listened to the broadcaster who Donegall identified as Haw-Haw and was able to answer truthfully: 'No, that's not him.'

Macnab didn't seem to be unduly concerned that his association with Joyce might land him in prison. Perhaps he didn't know then that Joyce's brother Quentin had already been arrested as a potential fifth columnist under Emergency Defence Regulation 18B. This rule allowed the Home Secretary to order the detention of anyone suspected of presenting a possible security risk and, largely because of his connection with Christian Bauer, Quentin Joyce had been one of just fourteen rounded up (many more were to follow once the Phoney War ended). When asked his brother's whereabouts Quentin had told the police: 'I imagine William has done one of his usual mental flips.' Joyce's parents later wrote to the Home Secretary asking for leniency: 'Don't blame twenty-two-year-old Quentin for what his thirty-four-year-old brother does.'

MI5 chiefs were shocked when they now inadvertently found out from Joan Joyce that her brother William had escaped arrest thanks to an MI5 tip-off. According to a Special Branch report on 25 September: 'Miss Joan Joyce said that her brother Quentin had been greatly encouraged by an officer in the Secret Service who had visited him in prison on the morning of 19 September, as he was the individual who had advised William to leave England to avoid being arrested.'

Maxwell Knight had some explaining to do. 'You will recollect that I had a telephone conversation with William Joyce a few days before war broke out and I had every reason to think that he would have informed his brother or some member of his family of this conversation,' he wrote in an MI5 memo to Guy Liddell, the director of B Division, of which department B5(b) was a part.* 'Therefore it seemed to me that it would help break the ice with Quentin Joyce and would also show him that I was speaking the truth about my having known his brother for many years if I told him that I had actually had a telephone conversation with William as recently as a few days before. The SB [Special Branch] report of course speaks for itself but Mr White [Dick White, a future head of MI5] and Mr Sneath [Brian Aikin-Sneath, in charge of B7, a surveillance section] were a little alarmed lest SB should get the idea from the statement made by Miss Joyce that there had actually been an indiscretion on the part of an officer of MI5. I pointed out that with re to the telephone conversation with William Joyce this had been immediately reported verbally to yourself and to Mr Sneath and, of course, it is hardly necessary to state that there was no question of Joyce having been warned or given any improper information.'

There is no record to indicate whether Knight's superiors believed this version of events. But no disciplinary action was taken. And within a few months, Knight had hatched a plan that would apparently prove he was not compromised by his friendship with the treacherous Joyce.

Back in Berlin, excited men and women gathered in front of the windows of the newsagents and gazed approvingly at the maps in which red pins showed the victorious advance of the German troops in Poland. In just under a month, Warsaw capitulated, with the official surrender taking place on 27 September. In cafes, as the news came in, Berliners stood to sing the national anthem and toast Hitler.

Up to this point, German propaganda had been aimed at demoralizing the British by arguing that it was futile to help Poland and that America would stay neutral. Well-known figures such as the Countess von Zeppelin, an Englishwoman married to a German, were brought to the microphone to appeal for Anglo-German friendship. Now the mysterious Lord Haw-Haw shifted the news agenda to the British theatre of war. On 28 September he asked: 'We have an important communication for listeners. Where is the *Ark Royal*? The aircraft carrier was hit in a German attack on

---

* Liddell was a homosexual who found Knight's professed homophobia irksome – Knight would refer to 'that bugger Blunt' – especially as it was obvious that Knight was homosexual himself.

26 September at 3pm. There was a terrific explosion. Where is the *Ark Royal*? Britain, ask your Admiralty.' If this was Joyce who asked these questions then it marked a change in his remit. This was propaganda designed to lower morale and force the Admiralty to make a revealing statement of the aircraft carrier's whereabouts. The next day, whoever was making the Haw-Haw broadcasts repeated his question: 'No responsible British or foreign journalist has been invited to inspect the *Ark Royal*. Where is the *Ark Royal*?'

Night shifts made it difficult for Joyce to get home after work so he and Margaret looked for an apartment that was closer to the Funkhaus. They moved from Friedrichstrasse to an apartment on the Steifensand-strasse. They immediately struck up a rapport with their landlady, a Viennese woman called Maria Chalupa, and they nicknamed her the Sloop, because she seemed to sail rather than walk. Their room was small, with only a wide single bed, and their requests for a daily bath were politely declined.

Margaret still barely spoke any German so the Sloop helped teach her by enunciating words slowly and clearly. Food rationing made shopping difficult and they had to rely on the pity of a *blockleiter* (a lowly Nazi official in charge of a block of flats), who secured a ration card for them. At the end of the month, new restrictions on clothing were introduced. If Joyce wanted a new suit it would have to be made out of a piece of cloth exactly 310 by 144 centimetres. A shortage of leather meant people could no longer get their shoes half soled. Grocers now opened tins of sardines before selling them, so that customers couldn't hoard. By October, when the weather was turning cold and rainy, the government decreed that only 5 per cent of the population was entitled to buy new gumboots. Available stocks would be rationed to postmen, newsboys and street-sweepers.

Joyce soon became frustrated about the quality of the comment scripts he was being asked to read. Often he would be handed a new sheet of paper while talking on air and he would have to improvise because the translations were so amateurish. He knew that English audiences would find the scripts derisory, not least because German attempts at capturing English colloquialisms were pitiful. He was, for example, supposed to read out that a torpedo 'struck in the machines and kettles of the boat'. Joyce saw an opportunity to bring Margaret into the Funkhaus fold. He proposed that the Propaganda Ministry should employ her to correct his scripts.

Apart from anything else, she was growing bored and restless sitting at home all day, as was her habit. She was also feeling a little lonely and homesick. Like William, she was missing the genial company of Macnab, the Master. She needed a distraction. The station readily agreed and went further, giving Margaret an audition as a speaker. Her voice was stilted and clipped but deemed good enough. However, if she were on the radio station payroll it might save her from internment in Germany, but it would also implicate her in her husband's treasonous activities, if that is what they were. The phlegmatic Margaret took this in her stride: whatever will be, will be, she said.

So it was that, on Tuesday 3 October 1939, Margaret Joyce began broadcasting a weekly talk aimed at lowering the morale of British women by comparing their lot unfavourably with their German counterparts. 'The other day a friend, who takes an interest in these things, said to me: "Look here, the BBC and the press have been saying recently that women are unable to buy any clothes in Berlin, and that although the windows are full of nice things, if you go into the shops one can't buy anything. You ought to write a talk about that." I said: "Thanks for the tip."' She went on to list the pretty things she had seen in Berlin shop windows. 'Washable silk frocks are remarkably cheap,' she reported, 'and bright and gay cyclamen stockings are readily available.' She added that 'rationing provides generous proportions: its aim is to make injustice impossible. There is certainly no need for the BBC to sympathise with the Berlin woman because she can't get clothes – the great trouble is not to want to acquire too many – and too many bills.' Britain, of course, was considering introducing clothes rationing. She concluded her talk with the observation that, unlike London, Berlin was not being evacuated because 'air defences here are marvellous and have the complete confidence of the population.' Within days Margaret was being dubbed Lady Haw-Haw by British listeners.

Joyce took his turn on the daily news readers' rota, alternating with Baillie-Stewart, Wolff Mittler and the various other English-speaking Germans on the staff. No wonder the British were puzzled about Lord Haw-Haw's identity. And they were not alone. Because there were so many broadcasters making these programmes, the Germans, too, were at first confused as to whom their celebrated Lord Haw-Haw actually was.

By mid-October they realized that, whoever it was to begin with, it ought to be Joyce now. He was proving to be a natural behind the microphone and was soon allowed to broadcast more opinion pieces, in addition to news. The commentary scripts were written for him by officials in the Ministry of Propaganda and so tended to be flat-footed and humourless. But he made of them what he could. Only news was broadcast live. The commentaries were recorded and sent down the wire to transmitters at Hamburg, Bremen, Cologne and Zeesen. These began with the famous call sign: 'Germany calling. Germany calling.' It was usually said three times, though music-hall parodists tended to say it twice, and it became as familiar to British audiences as an air-raid siren. Because the announcer stressed the first syllable of 'Germany' in a way that sounded funny, sinister and unfamiliar to English ears, it was mimicked as 'Jairminny'. This call sign was followed by a list of the stations, the meter band, and the words 'You are about to hear our news in English.'

One of the myths about Joyce's voice is that it was sneery and drawling in tone. It was a little nasal, because of his broken nose, but it was actually quite neutral, his diction clear. A more accurate description of it would include the words 'dark', 'cold' and 'virile'. It arrested attention and stayed in the memory. At times it was monotonal. There is some anecdotal evidence to suggest that women especially found it hypnotic and even seductive. Perhaps this was because the voice sounded like it came from a man with a 'brute heart' – and, as the poetess observed so sardonically, 'every woman adores a fascist'.

Another myth is that Joyce would rant hysterically. Actually his broadcasts were measured and articulate. It was around this time that the BBC monitors identified his voice as being distinct from the others: 'There is a new announcer on these stations who speaks perfect English, but with a much less ironical tone than the other English announcer.'

The papers were still playing the guessing game as to his identity, helped by leaks from Scotland Yard. On 17 October, the *Daily Mirror* noted: 'Special Branch officers of Scotland Yard are building up evidence that the supercilious Englishman who broadcasts anti-British propaganda every day from German short-wave stations formerly held high rank in the British fascist movement. Police officers who had attended fascist meetings, acquaintances of his Blackshirt days, and a woman who used to

know him well [presumably his first wife, Hazel], are all convinced that
they have identified the speaker, whose polished manners at the microphone are very different from the violence which his wife used to suffer.'

The report stopped short of actually naming William Joyce, and if they
had been able to ask the Germans authorities outright who Lord Haw-
Haw was, the Germans would have been able to reply truthfully that it
was a man called Wilhelm Fröhlich. Although he had registered as William
Joyce with the police and had signed his employment book in his own
name, like all foreigners in Berlin at the time, Joyce was required to adopt
an assumed Germanic name for the Funkhaus payroll. He chose one which
punningly translated as 'William Joyful'.

That month the Joyces formally applied for German citizenship. For
his application William correctly stated, for the first time in an official
document, that his place of birth was New York. Keen-eyed Gestapo
officials spotted the inconsistency with his employment book and quizzed
him about it. He explained about his British passport and they accepted
this. But when they asked him to produce his passport, the Gestapo
became annoyed: he had defaced it so that it was no longer valid. He had
done this so that when he came to surrender it in return for a German
passport the Abwehr couldn't use it for one of their spies. It was a final
spark of 'British' patriotism.

Joyce now felt sufficiently confident of his position at the Funkhaus to
assert himself. He pointed out that the ten-minute topical talks were ineffectual. He could do much better himself and wrote a talk as a sample of
what he had in mind. This did the rounds at the Funkhaus for a couple of
days before returning to his desk dog-eared and out of date. But the station
bosses took his point and gave him the chance to write his own scripts. His
problem, he soon realized, was that he did not have access to up-to-date
British papers, which made it difficult to be topical. He had to make do
with more generalized comments. But these seemed to strike a chord with
the millions of Britons who were tuning in to listen to what Joyce now
dubbed, off air, 'Jerry Calling'. Listeners included David Lloyd George
who, while staying at a country house around this time, surprised his fellow
guests by interrupting a conversation to switch on Lord Haw-Haw. 'The
government ought to take notice of every word this man says,' he said.

Now that he had the freedom to write his own material, Joyce found,
for the first time in his chequered political career, a beguiling voice. He

toned down his red-blooded, street-corner style and adopted a sardonic, calm persona that mesmerized British audiences. He became a radio character, a dark Tommy Handley, a less cosy Roosevelt (who for several years had been broadcasting his popular 'fireside chats' on the wireless in America).

Yet this is not to say that William Joyce was proving effective as a propagandist. In fact he was failing. By caricaturing him as Lord Haw-Haw, the British had found a way to laugh at him and thereby neutralize him, just as they had found a way to poke fun at Mosley – Spode – and his black shirts/shorts.

It would be fair to say that at this point in the war, British audiences even felt something close to affection for Lord Haw-Haw, which would have infuriated the socially insecure Joyce. He hated being patronized. *US*, Mass Observation's weekly intelligence service newsletter, quoted one listener as saying: 'I love him and his clever tricky sayings. I love his voice and manner and would love to meet him. I feel he is a gentleman and would be a nice friend – all my intuition and his voice . . . His talk on "Soon" was great and made me chuckle – true or not true. He is a great psychologist. Always he makes me happy.' It seems the English audiences found him amusing partly because they had become addicted to the idea of Haw-Haw as a Woosterish upper-class fathead. Smith's Clocks brought out an advertisement, depicting a monocled donkey at a microphone, with the caption: 'Don't risk missing Haw-Haw – Get a clock that shows the right time always, unquestionably.' Not to be outdone, Philips ran a series of advertisements for wireless sets featuring the *Germany Calling* radio schedule. The Western Brothers, a popular music-hall double act, per-formed a fey comic review on radio which included a song called 'Lord Haw-Haw the Humbug of Hamburg'. It became so popular with their audiences they had to move it to the end of the show so as not to interrupt the flow. When Columbia released it as a record it became an instant hit. Though not especially funny, it did include one couplet that is worth quoting: 'Lord Haw-Haw of Zeesen, he wears woolly camisoles in the cold season.' Other comedians complacently joined in the good-natured mockery – all that was needed to bring the house down, they realized, was a nasal cry of 'Jairminny Calling! Jairminny Calling!' Max Miller cashed in on the image of the toffee-nosed traitor with *Haw-Haw*, a new variety show at the Holborn Empire, and Arthur Askey featured a Baron

Hee-Haw in the BBC's *Band Waggon*. In a curious way the Haw-Haw craze was helping the English to define themselves. They were becoming a nation of people who laughed in the face of mad and bad but ultimately ridiculous 'foreigners' – even those foreigners who sounded as if they belonged to the Drones Club and spent their weekends in draughty castles in Shropshire. One family from Sheffield told the *Picture Post* that they sat and listened to Haw-Haw's broadcast every night just so they could blow a raspberry in unison at the end of it.

Once the British press had created this radio personality, the Germans sought to exploit his popularity, with the emphasis more on amiable buffoonery than hard political commentary. Though Joyce had always loathed Bertie Wooster types, he played along with the role he had been allotted. Hearing about the spoofs in London, he sought to counter them by helping to write a music-hall-style sketch involving two characters: Schmidt, an urbane, politically literate German, and Smith, a monocled British ass. Smith had invested his money in 'Neverfly Aircraft' and believed that Britain was flooded with Gestapo agents disguised as Chinese. The two men had been friends before the war and were meeting in the neutral surroundings of a Swiss hotel.

> Smith: Well now, old man, tell me about this war of yours.
>
> Schmidt: My dear Smith, I don't know all about it and it isn't ours.
>
> Smith: Don't get cross. I mean, after all, Hitler started it, didn't he?
>
> Schmidt: Who declared war on Germany?
>
> Smith: Well, of course, actually we did. But you see we were solemnly pledged to defend the independence of Poland. We couldn't back out, you know.
>
> Schmidt: I see. And if I'm not mistaken you promised to give the Poles full military support, should they become involved in a military conflict with Germany?
>
> Smith: Yes, old chap. I'm glad to find one German who really understands.
>
> Schmidt: I'm sorry but I just don't understand. I want to know how many troops and how many planes you sent to the assistance of Poland before she completely collapsed. I mean, what did you actually do to save your gallant little ally?

Smith: I don't know about that. But I do know that my income tax has gone up to 7s 6d in the pound, and I suppose we aren't making all these sacrifices for nothing.

Schmidt: My good old John Bull, let us stick to the point if we can. Do you know that on the second day of the war in Poland, Smigly-Rysz wanted to surrender, but the British Ambassador in Warsaw told him that hundreds of your planes were on their way to help him, laying Germany in ruins en route?

As the first Christmas of the war approached, Joyce was offered a salary of 4,000 Reichsmarks, ten times more than Baillie-Stewart and the others at the station were earning. Not that there was much to spend his extra money on. Rationing cards for clothing were introduced in Berlin that December. There were separate cards for men, women, boys, girls and babies. Except for the babies, everyone got a hundred points on his or her card. Socks or stockings took five points, but Berliners were only allowed to buy five pairs per year. A pair of pyjamas cost thirty points, almost a third of a card, but people could save five points if they bought a night-gown instead.

Despite this, Berliners felt so confident that the war was going their way they made plans, as best they could, to celebrate a traditional Christmas. Shops were decorated with bright tinsel and red paper bells, though expensive gifts in the windows were not for sale, only for show. And a record could only be bought if the customer was able to hand over an old record as part of the transaction – an economy drive. But Germans usually gave soap, perfume, books and sweets anyway, and there were plenty of these in the shops. By 13 December, the first Christmas trees were appearing in market places and were being snapped up. As a con-cession, the government relaxed rationing in the week before Christmas. Everyone was to be allowed an extra quarter of a pound of butter and a hundred grams of meat, and four eggs instead of one.

In England that December, the Director-General of the BBC noted: 'Haw-Haw is not a person, but a well-informed syndicate.' He was right at that stage. Even so, a week before Christmas, William Joyce was named as Lord Haw-Haw in the British press for the first time. His ex-wife Hazel, now living in the village of Waldron, Sussex, told the *Sunday*

Pictorial: 'I knew it was William Joyce – my former husband – the moment I listened to his voice. My mother and sister, who knew Joyce well, have written to me. They, too, have recognised his voice. Joyce is the father of two of my children. They are eight and eleven years old. One night I turned on the wireless while they were in the room. Joyce was speaking. My eldest daughter turned pale and, when I asked her what was the matter, she said: "That's WJ isn't it?" – she always called her father WJ. I am positive he is the man. He even tells the same stories that he used to tell me. He is a brilliant linguist who speaks four languages. [She was forgetting his Old Norse and Icelandic.] His friends prophesied a great career for him when he was a private tutor, but I'm afraid he had a queer twist in his make up.'

The superintendent at Chapel-en-le-Frith, Derbyshire, who had met Joyce and his family shortly after they arrived from Ireland, also identified the voice. When interviewed by Special Branch he said: 'I have listened to his [Haw-Haw's] voice many times and he uses short vowels and his over-accented pronunciation of cultural is usually keltcheral. This voice has a slight nasal resonance and the audibility of his intake of breath suggesting catarrhal problems is no less conspicuous.'

Despite these positive identifications, the national guessing game about the true identity of Haw-Haw continued, especially in the letters pages. The theatre critic Harold Hobson wrote to *The Times*: 'That ineffable voice of his, by Cholmondeley-Plantagenet out of Christ Church, has an irresistible fascination.' The writer Rose Macaulay had a letter published the following day: 'What is this curious popular legend about Lord Haw-Haw's voice being aristocratic, upper class, haw haw, and so forth based on? Lord Haw-Haw speaks excellent English but surely not "Cholmondeley-Plantagenet out of Christ Church". He seems to have a slight provincial accent (Manchester?) and to commit such solecisms as accenting the second syllable of "comment". I should not call it public school English. Do any listeners really think it is, or is the legend merely derived from music-hall parodies, composed and sung by those who are not experts in the niceties of accent themselves?'

Lady Cynthia Colville joined in the debate and was truer than she knew. 'I have never doubted but that Lord Haw-Haw's education in the English tongue has been conditioned by residence overseas. I am never quite sure what an Oxford accent is like, but I am entirely sure that it is not his. His "wah" for "war" is as transatlantic as his nasal intonation, and I should place Chicago high among the probable influences that have produced his now famous, but hardly golden, voice.'

The *People*, meanwhile, ran a story under the headline 'WE SHOULD ALL HEIL THIS TICKLER'. It congratulated Haw-Haw on being 'a greater mirth-producer than half a dozen of our home grown comedians rolled into one.' It concluded that 'to remove him from the air and our nightly black-out will be intolerable.'

On Christmas Eve, after an early dinner at the elegant sandstone Kaiserhof Hotel, chosen because Hitler had made it his headquarters in the 1920s, the Joyces went back to the Funkhaus for the Christmas staff party. Coming from the main studio, as usual, could be heard the jaunty strains of Charlie and his Orchestra. In his thick German accent, 'Charlie' – real name Karl Schwedler – would sing, in English, dire anti-Jewish parodies of Fred Astaire hits. He was also allowed to play American jazz and swing because, although both were banned from German broadcasting, they were core components of the Funkhaus's English-language schedule. The main function of the rambling Funkhaus building was to broadcast German state radio programmes, including music (there was a full orchestra there), light entertainment and spoken word. But it also broadcast in thirty other languages and employed about five hundred people in its foreign-language service. Thanks to this division, the Funkhaus was a cosmopolitan place. In the staff canteen, renegade Englishmen would be seen drinking coffee with Frenchmen, Poles and Czechs. At this stage of the war, not all the foreigners working there were being treasonous. There were announcers from neutral countries such as America and Ireland, and from countries which had yet to be invaded, such as Holland and Norway.

That night, a large Christmas tree with electric candles shone in the hall, but it was the Joyces who were the centre of attention, the celebrity couple, the media stars. Among the personally addressed presents waiting for Joyce were boxes of cigars from Goebbels and Hermann Göring. Colleagues were impressed. Margaret especially seemed to impress the men present. One, John O'Reilly, an Irishman working for the radio station Ireland-Redaktion, swooningly noted that she was 'a tall, good-looking woman with flaming red hair. She was gay, irrepressible and vivacious, and was ever ready to welcome congenial company.' An embittered Baillie-Stewart was less impressed. He looked on Joyce as a usurper.

Talk at the party was of how the German pocket battleship *Graf Spee* had scuttled itself off Montevideo a few days earlier, the first disaster of the war for Germany. William Shirer, the Berlin correspondent for the American radio network CBS, wrote in his diary that night: 'People were dancing and making merry with champagne. Lord Haw-Haw, the British traitor who goes here by the name of Fröhlich, but whose real name is William Joyce and whose voice millions of English listen to on the radio every night, and his English wife, were at the party, but I avoided them.'

The Joyces felt happy that Christmas. As the Haw-Haw myth grew, the man behind the character began to enjoy his new celebrity status. He was especially taken by an article he was sent from *Life* magazine in America. 'On this new psychological front,' it began, 'first blood now goes to Germany, which, like other belligerents, hires renegades and traitors to undermine their countrymen's morale. A smash hit is a mysterious nightly voice on the Hamburg short wave length, the favourite star of 50% of all English listeners. Lord Haw-Haw of Zeesen has an impeccable Oxford accent, and cloaks his news and opinions with clever humor that Englishmen find irresistible.'

He was soon giving three talks a week for American listeners, broadcast on short wave via Radio City in New York. He, or rather Lord Haw-Haw, had become a worldwide phenomenon, it seemed, with large audiences tuning in on short wave not only in the neutral United States but also Canada, South Africa, New Zealand and Australia. Even Hitler now knew his name, thanks to Goebbels' enthusiastic endorsements. 'Lord Haw-Haw's name is on everybody's lips,' Goebbels wrote in his diary. 'He has become a sort of world-wide celebrity and does us incalculable service . . . Our broadcasts to England are having a great effect, according to all reports. We operate in tune with the principle: constant dripping wears away the stone.'

Margaret, too, was beginning to enjoy her husband's new celebrity and was settling into life in Berlin. In fact she was now finding living abroad exhilarating and romantic. Although there were air-raid warnings most days and blackouts every night, no bombs, as yet, had fallen on Berlin. And the time in the shelters was spent chatting, playing dice and rummy or reading – Margaret was immersed in *Gone With the Wind* that Christmas. And the social life was heady. They were treated as A-list celebrities, regularly being invited for cocktails and to dinner parties. The Joyces tended to eat in restaurants most nights and became regulars at Haffner's, a lively and fashionable bar-restaurant near their apartment. Here they would drink, smoke and talk into the small hours with staff from the Funkhaus, foreign journalists and German soldiers home on leave. The Joyces' views on the war were at a premium, because of their British perspective. Afterwards they would laugh as they groped their way back in the blackout, drunkenly colliding with lampposts and fire hydrants. As well as the parties there was the Kroll Opera House, where they saw *Tosca* and *Rosenkavalier*. There were also concerts to attend (William's preference) and clubs to go dancing in (Margaret's). There were trips to the 'Palast' cinemas on Kurfürstendamm as well, but as William wasn't keen on the movies, Margaret would usually go on these with her female friends, Helene Trübner, Dorothy Eckersley and Susan Hilton, a hard-drinking Irish lesbian. The film packing Berliners in that winter was a dubbed version of *China Seas*, starring Clark Gable and Jean Harlow. It was pure escapism: the romantic story of a rugged American sea captain who tried to turn over a new leaf after becoming attached to a refined, upper-class Englishwoman (Rosalind Russell). Margaret, no doubt, would have been first in the queue to see it.

Berlin had brought the Joyces closer together, perhaps closer than they had ever been. When they married in 1937, Margaret may have been hoping that William was destined for greatness and power within the Blackshirt movement – and she must have been stunned when he was made redundant just weeks later. The National Socialist League had briefly seemed an even more exiting prospect, but that too ended in disappointment, and their subsequent poverty put a great strain on their relationship. Above all, in London, they had always been a threesome with Macnab: they had never had a proper opportunity to find out how they were matched as a couple, and perhaps this was why they had put off having children. Margaret, then, had reason to feel disillusioned with the early years of her marriage, but in snowy Berlin that Christmas her faith in William seemed to be paying off. They were experiencing social and material success for the first time. Indeed, in a matter of a few months, William had become world-famous. And Margaret was enjoying the prestige and influence that came with her job, too. Together they had become a fascist power couple. They were a team, a double act.

In many ways it was obvious what attracted William to Margaret. He was, as she once put it, sexually enslaved. What attracted Margaret to William may seem less obvious. With his scarred face and his diminutive stature, he wasn't that prepossessing. Yet he was a manly man, physically strong and brave. And he seemed to Margaret to have an encyclopaedic knowledge of any subject she raised. He may even have been a father figure to her, as her own father was a weak and ineffectual character who never rose above assistant manager and was eventually made redundant. William liked to teach, Margaret liked to learn – indeed she treated him as her mentor, playing along even when his more esoteric theorizing went over her head. They complemented each other by their differences. Moreover, while he could be stiff and awkward socially, she was easy company, the trophy wife other men doted on.

More than anything else, William made her laugh. He was a romantic, too. In Berlin they would promenade together arm in arm through the Tiergarten. On their days off they would go on longer walks through the wooded Grunewald on the outskirts of Berlin. That Christmas Margaret wrote in her diary that on one occasion as they walked under a sublime moon, they had seen a shooting star. On these walks Margaret would listen affectionately as William fantasized about what might be and reminisced about what had been. Sometimes they would take the S Bahn to Potsdam for lunch and then catch the steamer back up the River Havel. By day they would play chess sitting under the awning of a Tiergarten cafe, by night billiards at 'their club', the Foreign Press Club in Leipziger Platz, a grand nineteenth-century building with leather armchairs, well-stocked cellars and an ornate restaurant with loudspeakers built in the walls to page patrons. There they had access to neatly pressed newspapers from all over the world. They had come a long way together, emotionally and geographically. Each felt responsible for the other's presence in Berlin. Each had helped the other through their initial feelings of homesickness and loneliness. In war-time Berlin, their *grand amour* was taking on an heroic complexion: they were, as William often said, 'lovers and comrades'. More than that, they were both committed fascists who saw themselves engaged in 'the great struggle'.

As the new year arrived, so did a front of bitterly cold weather (temperatures in Berlin dropped to −15 degrees), and under several feet of thick snow, Berlin looked enchanting to the two foreigners. In the Tiergarten, the former deer reserve of Prussian kings, drifts towered softly, and the Joyces were impressed by the Berliners who were feeding the squirrels and ducks with their rationed bread. Thousands of people skated on the ponds, while children went tobogganing on any slopes they could find. The sight of women pushing prams filled with coal struck the Joyces as quaint, too, until they realized the chronic coal shortage meant that even the Funkhaus had to go unheated. Another inconvenience: the shortage of lavatory paper was becoming so acute in Berlin, large organizations such as the Reichsrundfunk began issuing only enough for daily needs of staff so that none would be stolen.

When the central heating in their lodging broke down at two in the morning, they became seriously worried they would freeze, and so, for the sixth time since they married, they moved again. They found two rooms in the Amtsgerichtsplatz, owned by the cook at Haffner's. Here they were warmed by a 'Berlin stove', a white briquette-burning oddity which reached to the ceiling. Margaret named it 'the thug'. It provided hot water, but a new government decree meant no baths were allowed except at weekends. Joyce felt at home in the new flat and began work on a book, part political credo, part autobiography. Margaret would pour him drinks and hand him cigarettes as he clacked away at his typewriter into the small hours.

During the day he would be busy typing in the office. William Shirer noted in his Berlin diary that whenever he visited the Funkhaus he could hear 'Lord Haw-Haw attacking his typewriter with gusto or shouting in his nasal voice about "that plutocrat Chamberlain".'

Chamberlain was certainly a favourite target for Joyce at this stage of the war. He characterized him as a senile warmonger who oppressed the British working classes: 'I am well acquainted with the bankrupt mentality of British politicians, but unless I had heard it with my own ears I should never have believed it possible that any of them, however lacking in imagination, would dare to come before the British people once again and tell them that they were engaged in a war to end war. What reaction must this hypocritical claim arouse in the minds of heroes of Mons or the Marne who have for so many years been waiting for justice outside your labour exchanges.'

In London, Lord Haw-Haw's *Germany Calling* broadcasts were still being regarded as comic relief. Barrington was doing his best to perpetuate his image of Haw-Haw as an affected fop with a superior manner. He even published a spoof biography – *Lord Haw-Haw of Zeesen* – illustrated with cartoons by Fenwick. At its launch at Foyle's bookshop on 18 January 1940, he made a speech charting Lord Haw-Haw's progress from a hack Nazi announcer to a national clown and an international buffoon. He was still arguing that laughter was the appropriate response to 'the humourless Hun' and their silly propaganda. 'Heil Haw-Haw,' concluded Barrington, 'and long may he continue to keep us in fits of healthy British laughter.' In the *Daily Express*, Barrington wrote 'a fan letter to Dr Goebbels' asking the German Propaganda Minister to take a look at one of the illustrations in his new book. 'Haw-Haw, you will observe, is pleading (as usual): "Rehly, you British, it isn't done – it isn't manlah."'

Not everyone responded well to Barrington's idea of the traitor as decadent, aristocratic fop. A letter by Raymond Burns in the *World's Press News* asked: 'Was ever such a fatuous label given prominence in Fleet Street? Moreover, historians of this country may well have something to say about the mistake that has been made, by reason of extravagant publicity for this dreary name, in directing national attention to the only potentially dangerous system of enemy propaganda against this country's morale.'

Goebbels could hardly believe his luck. 'Everyone is talking about Lord Haw-Haw, and that's half the battle. They want to put somebody up to talk against him. This would be the best thing that could happen for us. We'd have him for breakfast.' In February that year he noted that 'The English are lying to the heavens again but our Lord Haw-Haw is always ready with an answer for them.' A month later, he noted: 'I tell the Führer about Lord Haw-Haw's success, which is really astonishing. He praises our foreign propaganda.'

The authorities in Britain looked on with detached interest, wary of what the Haw-Haw phenomenon might signify, and that spring the Ministry of Information made a request to the BBC to undertake a comprehensive survey to find out how many people were actually listening to Lord Haw-Haw. The BBC was happy to oblige and got to work on its survey. It also wondered whether to counter the *Germany Calling* talks with rebuttals. The problem was that if they did it might only make

Haw-Haw seem more credible. Perhaps, it was thought, it would be better to ignore them, or treat them as a joke. Besides, tolerance was considered a British characteristic. Certainly the newspapers were at pains to maintain a veneer of it. *The Times* even carried German reports at length, for balance – they were criticized in the paper's leading articles the same day, but included nevertheless. The view was that even if it was enemy propaganda it might contain shards of truth which ought to be publicly acknowledged.

In its confidential report, the BBC astutely noted that the Lord Haw-Haw of the early days of the war was probably a German. The main speaker now, though, 'has a firm grip on his audience with his sardonic almost Mephistophelean voice.' The report tried to explain the attraction of Haw-Haw: 'The blackout, the novelty of hearing the enemy, the desire to hear both sides, the insatiable appetite for news and the desire to be in the swim have all played their part in building up Hamburg's audience and in holding it. The entertainment value of the broadcasts, their concentration on undeniable evils in this country, their news sense, their presentation, and the publicity they have received in this country, together with the momentum of the habit of listening to them, have all contributed towards their establishment as a familiar feature of the social landscape.'

One factor which the BBC did not mention was that its own programming was so boring people were desperate to hear something – anything – else that was even remotely entertaining. Anyone, in fact, but Sandy Macpherson. The BBC was in the habit of broadcasting ten hours of recorded music a day, mostly of Sandy Macpherson at the BBC Theatre Organ – and listeners would write in to say they would 'rather face German guns than any more of Sandy Macpherson on his organ'. 'Cassandra' captured the mood in his *Daily Mirror* column: 'To hear Lord Haw-Haw's diatribes shouted from Hamburg in guttural English is a lot more entertaining than listening to the canned café music which is almost the sole fare offered by the BBC.' The BBC also had an unofficial ban on mocking politicians. Haw-Haw, by contrast, seemed irreverent. He provided satire and enjoyable political slapstick.

The report included the results of a survey in which a quarter of thirty-four thousand people questioned said they had listened to Haw-Haw the previous night. They were allowed to give more than one answer: 58 per cent said they liked Haw-Haw's show because they thought his version of the news so fantastic as to be funny; 50 per cent heard so many other people talking about his views that they liked to keep up with them; 38 per cent found his voice and manner amusing; 29 per cent listened to him because they wanted to hear the German point of view; 26 per cent because his anecdotes made them laugh; 15 per cent thought he was a good broadcaster; and 6 per cent admired his cleverness. There was, it seemed, a certain social cachet in listening to Haw-Haw. It showed you were neither thick nor unsophisticated. Whether you thought his broadcasts 'fantastic' or 'clever', it was de rigueur to say you were amused by them. Perhaps at some basic level, then, Haw-Haw's popularity was down to peer pressure. No one would admit they were scared by broadcasts that everyone else seemed to think as harmless and funny as Tommy Handley's *It's That Man Again!*. That show, in which Handley played the Minister of Aggravation at the Office of Twerps, had been launched just before the war and had fast become a national institution. Named after the phrase newspapers commonly used to describe Hitler, its title was soon turned into the initials ITMA, as was the fashion in wartime Britain, with its LDV and its ARP.

The BBC survey included a sample of quotations from listeners. A Manchester postman was quoted as saying: 'Haw-Haw keeps the government awake with his criticising. The ordinary man benefits.' And a woman from South Shields said: 'When wanting red hot news I listen to Hamburg.' A barman in Bolton said: 'Do you hear that bloke from Hamburg they call Haw-Haw? I never tire of him. Wherever you go somebody brings him up. He has convinced thousands. I might tell you he has opened my eyes. There's no betting, he's a bloody good speaker.' A van driver from Bolton said: 'He's bloody good, he licks any one of our announcers. I hearken to him every night.' A middle aged housewife said: 'Oh he's good, you ought to have heard him the other night, skitting about Churchill. I always listen to him.' Another housewife said: 'I think he is very good. He's very nice. We aren't educated enough to understand all the words he uses, but he's very interesting, and a lot he says is true.' One of the few dissenting voices was that of a woman from Lambeth: 'I feel inclined to smash the set, saying what he does about England.' But even those who were suspicious of him found it difficult to turn him off. One RAF man said bluntly: 'He talks a lot of cock and seventy-five per cent of his statements are either lies or propaganda, but occasionally he hits the nail on the head. It's then that he makes you think. You wonder whether a lot of his statements are also true.'

The survey also revealed that the public thought there was too much censorship on the BBC, and that its news broadcasts were out of date and unreliable. Its programmes, moreover, were described as 'stupid', 'boring' and 'poor'. Part of the problem was that the BBC had formally agreed with the British press to use no information in news bulletins that had been received after 5 p.m. until 7 a.m. next day and nothing received between midnight and 5 a.m. before 4 p.m. The consequences were farcical. When Hore-Belisha resigned as War Minister on 5 January 1940, Joyce was first with the news, and on 3 April Joyce broke the news of the British Cabinet reshuffle to the British public. As R. T. Clark of the BBC bitterly noted it was a 'marvellous scoop'. 'At 11.15 he broadcast the Cabinet changes to his English listeners who were deliberately deprived of hearing it on their own news service at nine and only by the skin of their teeth were allowed to hear it there at midnight. Is it really worthwhile conducting an anti-Haw-Haw campaign if he finds such efficient allies?'

But the result that took everyone by surprise was the listener figures. Of the whole population aged over sixteen, there were around 9 million people listening to *Germany Calling* every day, and 18 million every few days. Astonishingly this was about two-thirds of the total audience for the BBC. Suddenly Lord Haw-Haw didn't seem like a joke anymore.

ELEVEN

'We thank the French for nothing. Where is their Shakespeare? Who is their Carlyle?'

In London, Maxwell Knight was about to use William Joyce in a sting operation to incriminate Anna Wolkoff, the thirty-seven-year-old daughter of a White Russian admiral who had emigrated to Britain. Wolkoff was a dressmaker by trade but had come to Knight's attention by being an active member of the Right Club – Captain Ramsay called her his 'little storm trooper'.

The club had officially disbanded once war was declared, but unofficially had continued as an umbrella organization for fifth columnists and fascist coup plotters, at least in the minds of a few of its more unstable members, including Ismay Ramsay, the wife of Captain Ramsay, and Christabel Nicholson, the wife of a British admiral. The Right Club had set itself the task of spreading defeatist rumours and sowing discontent. Wolkoff would sit on her own in cinemas and boo at Winston Churchill on newsreels. She would also run around London sticking labels printed with rude remarks about the government to lampposts. The unofficial meeting place for the remnants of the club was the Russian Tea Room opposite South Kensington tube station, a place with polished wooden furniture and panelled walls. It was owned by Wolkoff's father and, supposedly, sold the best caviar in London.

Wolkoff was also under suspicion because one of her clients was the Duchess of Windsor, for whom she made corsets and underwear, and therefore with whom she could claim an intimate connection. MI5 had

had its eye on the Duchess ever since she, as Mrs Simpson, had been described as 'dangerous' in a memo from J. C. C. Davidson, Chancellor of the Duchy of Lancaster and Baldwin's right-hand man.* They had also been tipped off by the FBI that she might be a Nazi agent, not least because she had allegedly had an affair with the German Ambassador to London, Ribbentrop. There were suspicions that she might have been handing over copies of secret documents she had had access to through the Prince of Wales.

There was another reason that Knight was interested in Wolkoff: since February 1940 she had been sleeping with Tyler Kent, a handsome twenty-nine-year-old American cipher clerk working at the US Embassy in London. Kent had been under surveillance from Knight's B5(b) department for six months, having first aroused suspicion three days after he arrived in London: he had gone to the Cumberland Hotel at Marble Arch to meet Ludwig Matthias, a suspected Abwehr agent whom MI5 happened to be tailing. Recklessly, Knight decided not to notify Joseph Kennedy, the American Ambassador to London, that a member of his staff was a major security risk. Instead Knight thought he would watch his suspect and wait. After all, he reasoned, Kent was a complex man. He would have covered his tracks well. And he had diplomatic immunity.

According to Malcolm Muggeridge, who was an intelligence officer at the time, Kent was 'one of these intensely gentlemanly Americans who wear well-cut tailor-made suits, with waistcoats and watch-chain, drink wine instead of high-balls, and easily become furiously indignant.' A descendant of Davy Crockett, the Wild West hero, Kent was born in China, where his father was an American consul. He had been educated at Princeton, the Sorbonne and George Washington University. In 1934 he joined the diplomatic service and was posted to Moscow where he was employed as a cipher clerk. In 1939 he was transferred to London. Politically, he was an isolationist who believed that America should stay out of Europe's war. While he was far from being alone, Kent took it further than most, believing that Roosevelt was secretly planning to pledge American support for Britain and France without first receiving a mandate from the American people. And he had evidence to back up this theory. He had been copying top-secret coded telegrams sent between Roosevelt

* This was discovered by the researcher John Hope in the House of Lords Record Office.

and Churchill (who was then still First Lord of the Admiralty), smuggling them out of the US Embassy and taking them home to his flat.

Improbably, it was a charlady called Kitty Welberry who caught Kent out. In March, Kitty was given a sealed envelope for safekeeping by her employer Mrs Nicholson, the admiral's wife. She was told it was the admiral's will. The next morning Kitty was late for work and was met at the door by an anxious Mrs Nicholson who said: 'You made me sweat, Kitty! I thought you had been seized by the police with those papers. For goodness sake, stick them in your corsets or bury them in the garden.' This made Kitty suspicious. She opened the envelope but could not understand the contents, which was not surprising given that they were pencilled copies of the Roosevelt–Churchill telegrams. She took the papers to the police who, equally baffled, handed them to MI5. They ended up on Knight's desk. He realized straight away that they must have come from the US Embassy. The finger of suspicion pointed at Tyler Kent.

Knight discovered from Kitty that Anna Wolkoff had visited Mrs Nicholson's house a few days earlier. Clearly the two Right Club members were wondering what use to make of the secret papers Kent had shown them. Knight believed that Wolkoff had a contact in the Italian Embassy in London – the assistant military attaché, Don Francesco Marigliano, the Duca del Monte – through whom she could smuggle classified documents out of the country to Germany. Italy was still neutral at this stage of the war but its sympathies were clearly with the Germans and Knight believed that the German Ambassador to Rome might have seen some of the Churchill–Roosevelt correspondence via the Italian diplomatic pouch. Knight decided to lay a trap for Wolkoff and Kent involving his old friend and occasional agent of influence, William Joyce. He would make it look as if MI5 had intercepted a coded letter which Wolkoff had written and sent to Joyce in Berlin.

This letter was almost certainly written by Knight himself. In fact, it seems likely that, during the Phoney War, Knight had communicated with Joyce in Berlin several times, with the correspondence between the two being written in code. The evidence for this is circumstantial but compelling. The code used in 'the Joyce letter' is sophisticated, for one thing. It employed a normal alphabet enciphered through what is known as a 'vigenere slide'. The encipherer takes this and finds each letter of the keyword Hackenschmidt* on the moving alphabet and places it above the letter A on a fixed alphabet. Each successive letter of the clear text is found on the fixed slide and the letter immediately above it (i.e. on the moving alphabet) on its cipher equivalent. When each letter of the keyword has been found in this way, thirteen letters of the clear text will have been enciphered. The process is repeated for the next thirteen letters, then again for each successive thirteen letters of clear text until the end of the message.†

Another factor which points to Knight having written the letter is that it is obvious from the way that it is worded that it is part of an on-going correspondence, not a one-off. Also he refers to Meg. Only a close friend of the Joyces would have known that William sometimes called Margaret Meg. There is no record of Joyce even having met Wolkoff in the months between joining the Right Club and leaving England for Germany, let alone forging a friendship with her. The letter contained advice to Joyce about the *Germany Calling* broadcasts (the square brackets are mine):

> *Talks effect splendid but news bulletins less so. Palestine good but IRA etc defeats object. Stick to plutocracy. Avoid King. Reception on Medium fair but BBC 376 tends to swamp, while BBC 391 and Toulouse try to squeeze Bremen and Hamburg off air at times. Why not try Bremen at 500? Bremen 2 on Long's very weak. Needs powerful set to get. Here Krieghetze [war fever] only among Blimps. Workers fed up, wives more so. Troops not keen. Anti-Semitism spreading like flame everywhere – all classes. Note refujews in so-called Pioneer Corps guaranteed in writing [not] to be sent into firing line. Churchill not popular – keep on at him as Baruch [Bernard Baruch, a Jewish financier and friend of Churchill] tool and war-theatre-extender, sacrificer Gallipoli, etc. Stress his conceit and repeated failures with expense lives and prestige. Altmark [a vessel on which British prisoners taken from merchant vessels had been held by the Germans, before being rescued by a British destroyer] atrocities debunked by Truth [a right-wing paper]. This is only free paper,*

---

* George Hackenschmidt was a world heavyweight wrestling champion who famously lost his title in 1908 having cut a deal with his opponent, Frank Gotch.

† It is possible that Kent, as a cipher clerk, could have taught Wolkoff this code, but the two did not meet until Joyce had been in Germany for several months. Wolkoff would have had to write the code down for Joyce and send it to him, which would have defeated the object.

circulation bounding. Big man behind paper, no fear ruin. Nearly all your friends still sound, eg pay gay oo hundred percent, though Lewis wants murder you. [Kid Lewis, the boxer] All league sound. Family not persecuted by public but only by Anderson who keep Q [Quentin] imprisoned and gets F [Frank] and R [Robert] sacked BBC [Joyce's brothers had worked as engineers for the BBC] Still, family not in distress. Master [Macnab] teaching school again. Butter ration doubled because poor can't buy — admitted by Telegraph — bacon same. Cost living steeply mounting. Shopkeepers suffering. Suits PEP [Political and Economic Planning]. Regret must state Meg's Tuesday talks unpopular with women. Advise alter radically or drop. God bless and salute all Leaguers and CB [Christian Bauer]. Acknowledge this by Carlyle reference radio not Thurs. or Sun. Reply same channel same cipher.

Knight had become adept at leaving false trails. There are, then, two versions of what happened next: Knight's, as recorded in his MI5 memos at the time, and Special Branch's, as based on the subsequent testimony of Anna Wolkoff.* On 10 April, Wolkoff was approached by a man who was known to her as a fascist sympathizer and asked if she knew a way of getting a letter to William Joyce in Berlin. She said she did not. By happy coincidence, later that day, a female Right Club member of her acquaintance bumped into her and mentioned that she had a friend who was able to get letters to Germany via the diplomatic bag at the Rumanian Legation in London.

Confusingly, in one memo, Knight seems to imply that Macnab, not Wolkoff, wrote the letter.† 'The story starts when Macnab approached a certain individual known to him as a sympathiser and asked this person if he knew of any means by which a letter could be got through to Germany to William Joyce.' The sympathizer was Captain James Hughes, one of Knight's agents, who was well known to Mosley as Captain P. G. Taylor,

---

* Even after sixty-five years MI5 has no plans to declassify all its files relating to the Wolkoff–Kent affair.

† This does not stand up because if Macnab really had written it he would have been arrested and charged with espionage alongside Wolkoff and Kent, and he wasn't. Also, whoever wrote it had clearly sent letters to Joyce in Berlin before and so would not have been asking around to see if anyone knew how to get a letter to Germany. Finally, the line 'Master teaching school again' suggests it was not 'the master' himself who wrote it.

the industrial adviser to the BUF. Mosley had nonchalantly said he believed Hughes to be 'a spy for some Government department'. 'The next stage', Knight continued, 'is when, through means of their own, Special Branch obtained temporary possession of this communication which was copied and forwarded to us. It is understood that the original then found its way back to the person into whose care Macnab had originally confided it and who it seems volunteered to Macnab that an attempt was going to be made to get it to Germany via the Spanish diplomatic bag through the good office of the Duke of Alba. [Knight may have been leaving another of his false trails here, pretending the Italian link was a Spanish one.] Enquiries made by us disclosed the fact that Lord Ronald Graham was to be the person who would get the letter to the Duke of Alba and when the letter reached Lord Ronald Graham he thought better of this idea owing to the fact that he is on the point of obtaining a commission in the RNVR (this should be stopped). The letter was then handed to Anna Wolkoff for transmission. At first Wolkoff favoured using the Right Club contact in the American Embassy, Kent. This was later abandoned in favour of a channel through the Balkan Legation. It contained, it is said, some form of instruction to William Joyce regarding material for his future broadcasts and also referred to various facts about Jews in England.'

When interviewed by Special Branch, Wolkoff confirmed it was Hughes who approached her with the letter. 'In regard to the sending of the code letter to Joyce, Wolkoff said it was given to her by a man named Hughes on the occasion of his being introduced to her by Lord Ronald Graham early in April 1940. She alleged that when the latter's back was turned, Hughes asked her if she would like to do something against the Jews, and on her replying that she would, he asked her to send the letter to Joyce.'

Later that day Wolkoff was approached by Joan Miller, a glamorous twenty-two-year-old whom she knew from the Right Club. Miller mentioned to Wolkoff that, should she ever want to send a letter to Germany, she had a friend in the Rumanian Legation who could smuggle it out in the diplomatic bag. Miller, of course, was another of Knight's B5(b) agents. In fact she was his secretary, and his new 'mistress', and had infiltrated the Right Club on his orders. Miller later admitted she had been looking for a father figure when she embarked upon her (again

unconsummated) affair with him. She found his anti–Semitism and interest
in the occult 'disquieting' and was unnerved one day when he made her
watch him shoot a sick kitten with a revolver. But she was impressed by
his savoir faire and his unconventional wooing methods: on their first date
he presented her with a Himalayan monkey.

Whether Wolkoff was suspicious about this coincidence of timing with
Miller is a moot point. She claims she was. Either way, she gave Miller the
letter. The following morning, according to both women, Wolkoff rang
Miller and asked for the letter back. Miller took it round to Wolkoff's flat.
According to Miller: 'Anna had a careful look at the envelope before
opening it. It was all in code. Anna said: "This letter doesn't mean anything
to me, either."' She then typed a postscript at the bottom of the page, and
drew a picture of an eagle and a snake, the sign of the Right Club.

The message Wolkoff added was in German, but not in code. It read:
'If possible, please give again sometime in the week, the broadcast which
the German radio gave in German about three months ago, namely: The
Freemasons' meeting in the Grand Orient in Paris, 1931 (?) where Lord
Amptill [sic] was also present. It is now more important that we hear more
about the Jews and Freemasons. PJ [Perish Judah]'.

She handed the letter back to Miller, Miller gave it to Knight and
Knight may or may not have arranged for it to be sent to Joyce by an MI5
channel. A few days later, according to MI5, Joyce acknowledged receipt
of this letter by broadcasting the word 'Carlyle', as instructed. Specifically
he is alleged to have said: 'We thank the French for nothing. Where is
their Shakespeare? Who is their Carlyle?'

In the course of giving evidence, Wolkoff swore that she never wrote
the letter. When asked by Special Branch why if she was suspicious about
the letter she had not handed it to the police, she claimed that she had
guessed Miller's true identity and was using the letter as a ploy to trap her.
She asserted that the postscript she wrote on the letter 'referred to a
meeting in Paris that never took place, and that she wrote it as part of a
game of bluff.'

But combined with the top–secret telegrams which Wolkoff had shown
to Mrs Nicholson, this letter, to an enemy propagandist in Berlin, was
deemed evidence enough to arrest Kent and Wolkoff on suspicion of
espionage. But Knight's motives for writing 'the Joyce letter' are more
complicated even than that. He was involved in a game of office politics.

As an anti-Semite in favour of a negotiated peace with the Germans,* Knight was not a natural ally of Churchill, but he was ambitious – and by April 1940 it was beginning to look as though Churchill might take over from Chamberlain as Prime Minister. It would also have been clear to Knight – who had a friend, Desmond Morton, on Churchill's staff – that Churchill intended to sack Major General Vernon Kell, the director-general of MI5, as soon as he moved into Downing Street. Kell's headquarters at Wormwood Scrubs were considered to be an organizational shambles at best, a national laughing stock at worst. As Knight's department was based at Dolphin Square he wasn't directly implicated in the administrative chaos, but he was, nevertheless, regarded as one of 'Kell's men'. Kell, after all, had recruited Knight and indulged him by giving him his own semi-autonomous department. Knight's position had recently been rendered even more fragile by what was known as 'the Ben Greene scandal'. Knight had clumsily framed Ben Greene, a cousin of the novelist Graham Greene, whom he suspected of being a German spy. Greene was a pacifist. He was also a magistrate, a married one at that, and Knight used a prostitute to compromise and entrap him. Knight then asked one of his agents, who was little more than a stool pigeon, to provide false evidence against Greene. Greene had been able to prove his innocence and Knight's credibility within MI5 had been badly damaged. He needed to impress Churchill with a high-profile success: the arrest of Tyler Kent. Not only would it justify the subsequent arrest of Mosley – Churchill considered this a priority, convinced as he was that Mosley was planning a fascist coup – but it would also spare Churchill the potentially ruinous consequences of having his correspondence with Roosevelt made public, perhaps by having it broadcast to the world by Lord Haw-Haw.

The coded telegrams between Roosevelt and Churchill were highly compromising. One from Churchill was alleged to have read: 'I am half American and the natural person to work with you. If I were to become PM of GB we could control the world.' Another message referred to the preferential treatment which America would be given in terms of trade with Britain – with allies and other neutral countries being excluded from trade deals. Another was on the subject of neutral America supplying

* The following year Knight was almost certainly involved in setting up Rudolf Hess's 'peace' flight to Scotland, of which more later.

Britain with fifty destroyers – nearly six months before Congress was told about this and a year before Churchill made the historic broadcast in which he said: 'Here is the answer which I will give to President Roosevelt . . . Give us the tools and we will finish the job.'

In dealing directly with Roosevelt, Churchill was going behind the back of the Prime Minister, and indeed the whole War Cabinet. And on the other side of the Atlantic, Roosevelt was effectively drawing America into a European war without consulting either Congress or the American electorate. In many ways the telegrams were a more sensitive issue for Roosevelt than for Churchill because it was an election year in America and on the hustings Roosevelt was making isolationist noises, notably: 'I've said it before and I will it again, I will not send American boys to die in a foreign war.'

So far, that foreign war had been a Phoney War. The real war was about to start. On 7 May Josiah Wedgwood MP asked in the House whether the Royal Navy was capable of preventing invasion. 'If it could not stop a landing in Norway what chance Lincolnshire?' On 10 May, Ribbentrop arrived at the Foreign Office to read out a memorandum to the 8 a.m. foreign press conference. It argued that Britain and France were about to attack Germany through the Low Countries and that the Reich therefore deemed it necessary to send in its own troops to safeguard the neutrality of Belgium, Holland and Luxembourg. That day, as the German Panzer divisions ploughed through Western Europe almost unchallenged, Chamberlain resigned and Churchill became prime minister. 'I have nothing to offer but blood, toil, tears and sweat,' he said. Ten days later, Knight knocked on the front door of 47 Gloucester Place, the home of Tyler Kent.★ Kent was in bed with a Mrs Irene Danischewsky, his other mistress. Hidden in a suitcase, Knight found keys to the US Embassy's codes and file rooms, as well as some 1,500 top-secret documents, including copies of the telegrams from Churchill to Roosevelt. He also found the 'Red Book' containing the names of 235 Right Club members. Captain Ramsay had handed it to Kent for safekeeping on the assumption that his flat would have diplomatic immunity. Knight drove

---

★ He had asked permission from Joseph Kennedy to waive Kent's diplomatic immunity. Kennedy had agreed only after making it clear that he was furious with Knight for not telling him until then that Kent had been under surveillance for seven months.

with Kent to the US Embassy and asked Ambassador Kennedy for permission to break the lock of the ledger. He then interrogated Kent in Kennedy's presence. Minutes were taken by the only secretary available who could be trusted. When he came to read them afterwards Knight noted drily: 'Her shorthand is not quite equal to her discretion.'

During the interrogation, Knight told Kent that he knew of his association with Wolkoff. Kent did not deny it. Encouraged, Knight said: 'I am in a position to prove that Anna Wolkoff has a channel of communication with Germany; that she has used that channel of communication with Germany; that she is a person of hostile associations; that she is involved in pro-German propaganda, to say the least.' Kent seemed unflustered. But when asked if he knew any other members of the Right Club he became evasive. 'I am going to speak now extremely bluntly,' Knight continued. 'I am afraid I must take the view that you are either a fool or a rogue, because you cannot possibly be in any position except that of a man who has either been made use of or who has known all these people. I propose to show you how.' Kent admitted that he knew Ramsay through Wolkoff but that he hadn't asked what the Red Book contained. He added that he had only taken the documents from the US Embassy for his own interest. When asked if he knew William Joyce he denied all knowledge of him except that he had heard he was 'supposed to be some sort of Irishman.'

With the arrest of Wolkoff and Kent, Churchill had the proof of an active fifth column he needed; he also had his excuse to order Mosley's arrest. The Home Secretary, Sir John Anderson, had been defending Mosley in the War Cabinet up to this point, claiming he was 'A patriot who would never betray his country personally.' When Knight sent Anderson a report in which he claimed that Mosley was 'in relations' with Ramsay, Anderson had to back down.* Churchill was delighted, especially as Knight's report went on to outline the prospect of a fascist coup led by Mosley, using the Link, Right Club and Nordic League.

It is true that Mosley had vaguely positioned himself as the heir apparent in the event of a German invasion. But in his report, Knight exaggerated the case against Mosley, claiming that a fascist coup was at a far more

---

* Knight's evidence for this seems to have come from Hughes. When Mosley decided to initiate closer contact and collaboration with Ramsay and the Right Club in 1939 he chose Hughes to conduct the negotiations and to be his personal liaison with Ramsay.

developed and coherent stage than it could ever have been. Joyce provided a convenient link between Hitler, Mosley, Ramsay, Wolkoff and Kent. He was a pawn in Knight's game; a chess analogy he would have appreciated. More to the point, he was a pawn who was being sacrificed. Knight had come to realize that Joyce was now too high profile a broadcaster, and traitor, to be of any further use to him as an undercover agent.

In a War Cabinet meeting two days after Kent's arrest, it was agreed that Mosley and dozens of other fascist sympathizers, including Ramsay, Beckett and Macnab, would be interned without trial. They were the first of 750 alleged British fascists, or fascist sympathizers, detained under Defence Regulation 18B that summer. According to some accounts, Churchill ordered this round-up as a way of keeping recalcitrant peace-party Conservatives under control, sending 'a very clear warning to any groups favouring a negotiated peace that they risked being locked up.'* He even, it is said, threatened to arrest his appeasing Foreign Secretary Lord Halifax and Halifax's defeatist under-secretary Rab Butler.†

Churchill despatched Norman Birkett, a King's Counsel, to interrogate Mosley in Brixton prison – and he made it clear to Birkett that his task was to ensure, by whatever means necessary, that Mosley stayed in prison for the duration of the war. In a Cabinet meeting, Churchill argued that if peace were made with Germany, 'the British government would become Hitler's puppet, set up under Mosley or some such person.' He later acknowledged in a speech to the House of Commons that many of the internees were passionate enemies of Hitler. But things were so critical, he argued, that distinctions between friends and enemies could not be drawn. No sympathy should be extended to fifth columnists and 'the malignancy in our midst should be stamped out.'

Three days after he had Mosley arrested, Churchill sacked Kell. Not only was Knight not sacked, he was promoted from honorary captain to honorary major.

With the Wolkoff-Kent affair, Knight seems to have gone from being a maverick spymaster to a rogue one: obsessive, paranoid, uncontrollable. Even his colleagues commented on it. 'It infuriated M when people

---

* According to John Costello, a *Guardian* writer who saw a file on this subject in 1981 before it was removed from the Public Record Office by MI5.
† According to *BBC History Magazine* in 2001.

dismissed his assessments of a situation. One of his papers, entitled "The Comintern is Not Dead", predicted the development in Russia's policy with regard to Britain after the war. He sent it to Roger Hollis and Guy Liddell [his immediate boss] who expressed the opinion that M was allowing his personal distaste for communism to swamp his judgement.'

Not only did Knight bug Mosley's cell at Brixton – he recorded Mosley's private conversations with his defence lawyer and then handed the transcripts of them to Lord Birkett, as he by then was, who was preparing the case for the prosecution – he even had Ambassador Kennedy under surveillance. In fact he managed to collect evidence which suggested that Kennedy was anti-British. After a meeting with Lord Halifax, for example, in which the British Foreign Secretary had blamed the disastrous British military campaign in Norway on dense fog, Kennedy had said: 'Why didn't the fog impede the Germans as well?' When Kennedy returned to the US Embassy he had, according to MI5 files, said: 'How can England hope to win the war with a daft fool like that as Foreign Secretary?' Also, in reports he sent to Roosevelt, Kennedy had said: 'Conditions in the UK are now so bad, serious internal trouble might be expected at any time.' He added that: 'England is in an appalling muddle due to the losses in Norway.' He also characterized Churchill as a dangerous fantasist and described a Cabinet meeting at which a drunken Churchill had 'behaved appallingly'.

Wolkoff and Kent were held on remand while preparations were made for their trial, to be held at the Old Bailey in the autumn. Although the trial was to be in camera to avoid any damaging leaks about the contents of the Churchill–Roosevelt telegrams, it was, nevertheless, decided that the verdicts would not be delivered until after the US elections on 5 November, to spare Roosevelt any awkward questions about the case during his election campaign. No jury was to hear the legal arguments: the court was to be empty except for the judge, five counsel, their solicitors, warders and the accused. Even the police were to be barred from the Old Bailey. The prosecutor was to be Sir William Jowitt, the Solicitor-General, who, as Lord Jowitt, dismissed William Joyce's appeal against execution when it went before the Lords five years later.

At his trial, Kent claimed that he was a patriot and an isolationist and that it was never his intention to give the documents he stole to the Germans, but rather to American senators. In order to prosecute him successfully, it was necessary to prove that he was in league with Wolkoff, and that she was an enemy agent. There was a problem. Although the Official Secrets Act covered both the acquisition and communication of secret documents, the defendant could be convicted only if the documents could be of use to an enemy, and were communicated for a purpose that was prejudicial to the state. But there was no evidence that Wolkoff had ever sent classified material out of the country by the diplomatic bag at the Italian Embassy in London. That was just hearsay. So, when one undercover MI5 agent asked Wolkoff to post a letter to William Joyce in Berlin, and a second undercover MI5 agent conveniently offered her the means of posting it, Wolkoff was neatly made to fit the description of 'enemy agent'. For Wolkoff and Kent to be convicted it only remained for Joyce to be defined as a traitor. This the judge at the Old Bailey duly did.

The press were allowed into court only for the reading of the verdicts. Many commented upon a black-coated, bespatted and bespectacled figure who sat head bowed in the courtroom clasping and unclasping his hands. It was Admiral Wolkoff, Anna's father, and reporters were intrigued with the way his beard was trimmed into the same shape as the last Tsar's. Judge Tucker glowered at Anna Wolkoff as he passed sentence: 'You, a Russian subject who in 1939 became a naturalized British subject, at a time when this country was fighting for her very life and existence, sent a document *to a traitor* who broadcasts from Germany for the purpose of weakening the war effort of this country.' Tucker concluded that he found both defendants guilty under the Official Secrets Act, Kent on five counts, for which he would receive a seven-year sentence, Wolkoff on two charges for which she would go to prison for ten years.★

By inevitable coincidence, the same judge would preside over the Joyce high-treason trial at the Old Bailey five years later – a trial at which the judge and the jury would have to decide whether Joyce was, by definition, a traitor.

★ Kent served five years of his sentence before being deported back to the United States. Wolkoff served her whole sentence and was killed in a car crash in Spain in 1969.

TWELVE

'We know all about Banstead, even that the clock is a quarter of an hour slow today.'

The Lord Haw-Haw of the Phoney War was the equivalent of the game of football in no-man's-land in 1914: he was a strange bond between the British and the Germans; common ground; a piece of whimsy, almost. The Phoney War had been about throwing insults not dropping bombs. It had held out the vain hope of a face-saving peace deal between Britain and Germany. Its end more or less marked the end of British amusement with Lord Haw-Haw.

As a spoiler to *Germany Calling*, the BBC considered running performances by popular entertainers such as George Formby, Vera Lynn and Gracie Fields immediately after the nine o'clock evening news, to keep listeners' fingers away from their wireless dials. As was admitted by the Director-General of the BBC: 'Haw-Haw is now an important factor in the planning of both the Home and Forces programmes.'

The talk Haw-Haw gave on 16 May introduced what became a recurring theme that summer. 'Within six weeks of the British government declaring war on Germany, Hitler offered peace,' he began. 'His terms could have easily been accepted, and they would have left Germany far weaker than she is today. He did not make his offer abruptly and withdraw it before there was time for consideration. Night after night we broadcast his proposals until the whole world knew them by heart. When the warmongers of Downing Street intimated that there could be no terms of peace with the present German government, we knew that the war must be fought out to the bitter end. Britain appealed from negotiation to force. Force then it had to be, and force it shall be until German victory is total.'

On 28 May, as the 'little boats of England' evacuated troops from Dunkirk, the deadpan announcers at the Funkhaus began introducing the presenter of *Germany Calling* as 'Lord Haw-Haw'. It was a clever tactic. The Germans were supposed to be the humourless ones, so easily mocked by the wry British. They weren't playing fair, it was felt: the name Haw-Haw was our joke, not theirs. And it wasn't even much of a joke anymore. In the desperate days that followed the evacuation, people no longer listened just for entertainment value. Lists of prisoners of war were being read out as part of the *Germany Calling* programme, an obvious way to lure listeners. The Germans were also playing a shrewd game with their fairly reliable news reporting. Reuters, so the jibe went, was the greatest institution for aircraft destruction known to the world, because Churchill decided from his desk how many planes had been destroyed. Germany had made an effort to give more or less accurate numbers in Poland, Norway and France and so had built up a reputation for honest reporting, even if its commentaries on the news facts were pure propaganda. They were now trying to do the same with shipping figures as they had with aircraft. As Goebbels noted in his diary: 'I have Haw-Haw flay Churchill over the wireless about the as yet unacknowledged English shipping losses. London, however, refuses to make any statement. An admission!'

Lieutenant General Sir Frederick Pile, head of Anti-Aircraft Command, was worried about this mixture of truth and propaganda. He wrote to the BBC with the view that while the Haw-Haw broadcast wouldn't sway educated people, the working classes might be more gullible. 'Many of the statements one hears regarding the knowledge evinced in these broadcasts are untrue, or, at any rate, I personally have never heard anything startling. But the broadcasts are undoubtedly very clever. For the most part, the statements made are true; or half-true. But the man in the street, who has only a limited knowledge, believes them.' General Pile was worried his men would be affected. 'For we are pretty bored in the evenings. The BBC news bulletins are extremely dull and when someone tunes in to Lord Haw-Haw, the whole room gets up and gathers round the wireless. After it is over, they go back to their games without comment.'

To combat Haw-Haw, the BBC settled on a programme called *Post-script*, written and presented by the novelist J. B. Priestley. It was a success:

uncompromising, lyrical, reflective monologues delivered in a reassuring Yorkshire brogue. It caught the public mood perfectly. 'For this is total war,' Priestley said in one talk, 'and total war is war right inside the home itself. Emptying the clothes cupboards and the larder, screaming its threats through the radio at the hearth – burning and bombing its way from roof to cellar.' *Postscript* was broadcast at 9.15 on Sunday evenings, which was when *Germany Calling* started (10.15 German time). The trouble was, though Joyce's talks only lasted about twenty minutes, the *Germany Calling* programme ran for two hours and was on every night. There were news updates and jazz interludes. They even – the fiends – introduced a regular item directed at the British armed forces called 'From the Enemy to the Enemy', which used as its opening melody Vera Lynn's 'We'll meet again'. They then repeated the Haw-Haw broadcast at the end of the show.

The BBC, meanwhile, was taken aback by the number of requests for copies of transcripts of the Haw-Haw broadcasts. Not surprisingly, it declined to send any out. There was no penalty for listening to enemy broadcasts in Britain: in Germany, by contrast, a new rule was introduced that month which made listening to a foreign radio station an offence punishable by imprisonment. The Joyces were having to get used to the introduction of such rules on an almost daily basis. They were ordered to give up their copper, bronze, brass, tin, lead and nickel for the war effort, not that they had much. Margaret, in common with all the women and schoolgirls of Berlin, was asked to collect the combings from her hairbrush – so that they could be made into felt. Although Berlin had not been bombed yet, there was a new tension in the air. Margaret had grown afraid of walking alone after dark in the blackouts, especially after she witnessed a woman being dragged struggling and shouting into a car. She ran home to tell William but he, now accustomed to the harsh realities of a totalitarian state, argued that it was best not to report the incident. They agreed that it was probably the Gestapo that had carried out the abduction. There was, however, another reason for their reticence. They did not want to cause trouble with the authorities because, worryingly for them, they still had not been granted their German citizenship. There were bureaucratic hold-ups, or so they were told whenever they asked why there was a delay. There may have been another reason: Goebbels may have considered that, as a propaganda tool, it was more useful for Lord Haw-Haw to be an Englishman.

However, Haw-Haw soon had a more formidable rival even than Priestley. That summer, Churchill began giving occasional radio talks. In these he deployed his effortless felicity to devastating effect, stiffening sinews, waxing poetic, seemingly taking the British people into his confidence. Lord Haw-Haw never stood a chance.

Two days later, the church bells rang in Berlin and lines of swastika flags were hung from lampposts by order of Hitler. The city was to celebrate the victory in Flanders. The cafes on the broad, tree-lined avenues filled with thousands of Berliners chattering excitedly as they drank their coffee and ate their ice cream. It was a hot day and many celebrated by taking the afternoon off and heading for the woods and lakes on the outskirts of the city.

On 9 June, another eminent English novelist stepped inadvertently forward for a cameo in the Joyces' story. P. G. Wodehouse was taken prisoner at his villa in Le Touquet. He was registered as prisoner Widhorse (crime: 'Anglais'). He and his wife Edith had tried to escape by car but engine trouble had forced them to return to their house and await internment. The following day, Italy declared war on Britain and France and a second literary figure found himself facing some tough choices. Ezra Pound, the American poet, had been living in Italy since 1908 – and America's sympathies were with Britain and France.

On 14 June, as the German army marched on Paris, Lord Haw-Haw said in a broadcast: 'It is surely time for the English people to reflect that if it is Paris today, it can be London in the very near future . . . The day cannot be distant when the full force of Germany triumphant will be turned against Britain herself . . . To any Englishman who still follows those politicians who have led him to the tragedy in which he finds himself, I can only say, "Look thy last on all things lovely, every hour."'

Churchill did not need to quote Walter de la Mare to achieve his poetic resonance. On 18 June he gravely told the House: 'The Battle of France is over. I expect that the battle of Britain is about to begin . . . Let us therefore brace ourselves to our duties and so bear ourselves that if the British Empire and its Commonwealth last for a thousand years, men will still say, "This was their finest hour."'

With the fall of France, the British assumed a German invasion was imminent. The occupation by German forces of the whole of the European seaboard facing Britain threatened an even greater weight of air attack than had at first been feared. However, the Luftwaffe had to win control of the skies over southern England long enough for German naval and land forces to make landings on the south coast. This would be achieved by destroying the RAF's fighter force. Without supporting air cover, the Germans reasoned, the Royal Navy would be neutralized, unable to oppose their invasion forces.

That was to come. First, in Berlin, there was some celebrating to be done. After all, in just five weeks, Hitler had conquered most of Western Europe. With the fall of Paris, there was dancing in the Tiergarten, impromptu parties in the government quarter and marching songs sung along Unter den Linden. A crowd gathered spontaneously outside the Ministry of Propaganda calling for Goebbels to appear. Members of staff at the Funkhaus, meanwhile, celebrated with champagne. Margaret charged everyone's glasses and William proposed a toast to his colleague, the news reader of the French Service. 'We realize that it must be a difficult time for you,' he said. 'But we wish your brave country well.' The Frenchman may have been betraying his fellow-countrymen by broadcasting Nazi propaganda to them, but part of him still felt patriotic, or at least sentimental about his homeland. He tried to make a speech in reply but became too tearful to finish it. The celebration was cut short by an air-raid siren and an evacuation to the Funkhaus shelter.

Those still listening to Lord Haw-Haw now noted a cold menace in his voice. Tellingly, a transcript monitor at the BBC wrote down the *Germany Calling* speech which Joyce made that night, 22 June, and under-lined the words he emphasized, and described in parenthesis his manner of delivery. 'In this matter [of Allied bombing raids on Germany], as in all others, the Führer has been very patient. But it would be absurd to assume that nothing would be done to protect ordinary non-combatant people of Germany. *All resources of warning have now been exhausted.* You will agree that these warnings have been numerous and now [sinister pause] unfor-tunately [this word was laughed], you will see the result of disregarding them. The British people have taken no action to restrain their govern-ment from attacking our non-combatants, and *deeply as we regret the necessity* for departing from a principle which we honoured long after England had abandoned it, it will be shown once again that the Germany of today *cannot be provoked with impunity.* Her women and children are entitled to be protected in the *most effective fashion.* We wanted, and tried, to keep the war as clean as possible. Churchill wanted to make it dirty, and he has succeeded. To the British people we would say: Do not waste your time abusing us for *repaying like with like*. Take your complaints to Churchill, who must bear full responsibility for this terrible development in a war that we tried to wage against combatants only. *He is the culprit.*'

There were wild scenes at Berlin's main station when Hitler's train arrived back from Paris at 3 p.m. on 6 July. Crowds waved flags, raised their arms and cheered his motorcade all the way to the chancellery. The shame of defeat in the First World War had been expunged. Four days later, the Luftwaffe embarked upon its first mass raid on the south of England. In London on that day, John Beckett, the man with whom Joyce had founded the National Socialist League, was questioned by an internment committee led by Norman Birkett KC. He was asked about Joyce.

> Birkett: Joyce is Lord Haw-Haw, I am told. Have you listened to Lord Haw-Haw?
> Beckett: Very often.
> Do you confirm it?
> I cannot confirm it, but think it is very likely.
> Not that it matters, but we are told that it is so. We know Joyce has gone to Germany.
> He is in Germany. Of course, he was never a British subject.
> *Was he not?*
> No. He was an American subject, he was born in America, but I did not find that out until after we had parted.

This was the first time the establishment learned about Joyce's true nationality. He may never have been a British subject, but, finally, he was about to become a German one. Margaret, too. As she noted in her diary on 15 July, she went for a health check that morning, as part of her naturalization process. She cursed about this indignity, but, in her droll way, noted that her lung had aroused much curiosity among the medical staff.

On 16 July, Hitler gave his generals orders for Operation Sea Lion, the invasion of England. Two days later, for the first time since 1871, hard-faced, steel-helmeted troops staged a victory parade through the Brandenburg Gate and were greeted by military bands, showers of confetti and children holding flowers. Stores and factories were closed, by order, and Berliners turned out in their thousands to cheer. They were twenty deep and were dangling from lampposts, trees and statues for a better view. Although the Funkhaus remained opened, William and Margaret managed to slip out to watch the goose-stepping. The weather was so sultry, scores of women along Unter den Linden fainted. Red Cross personnel hauled them from the pavement on stretchers to a nearby first-aid station. One officer's horse, unused to victory parades, kicked wildly and backed into the reviewing stand, narrowly missing Goebbels.

Hitler spoke to the Reichstag the next day but Haw-Haw was not allowed to broadcast advance notice of this in case the British bombers came over. Hitler, standing astride the continent as its conqueror, was in a magnanimous mood. 'In this hour,' he said, 'I feel it my duty before my own conscience to appeal once more to reason and common sense in Great Britain as much as elsewhere. I consider myself in a position to make this appeal since I am not the vanquished begging favours, but the victor speaking in the name of reason. I can see no reason why this war must go on.' There was no applause, no cheering, no stamping of heavy boots – just awed silence and tension. 'I am grieved to think of the sacrifices which it will claim. I should like to avert them, also for my own people.'

Gold-braided generals, their chests heavy with crosses and decorations, filled a third of the balcony. Vidkun Quisling, the Norwegian collaborator, was also there in a corner seat in the first balcony. Throughout the speech Göring leaned over his desk making notes. He chewed on his pencil and scribbled, stopping to applaud every few minutes. At the end of his speech Hitler made Göring a Reichsmarshall, handing him a box with the insignia of his new rank. Göring beamed and took a peak under the lid before continuing with his scribbling.

As Lord Haw-Haw, Joyce made a broadcast that evening in which he said: 'There is at this time a real possibility, I might say a probability, of a negotiated peace.' But he now had another 'voice' at his disposal as well. He had begun dividing his time between writing and performing his regular *Germany Calling* broadcasts – known as 'white propaganda' – and writing scripts for a secret project called the New British Broadcasting Station, which was engaged in 'black propaganda'. Based in the Büro Concordia, a heavily guarded villa near the Funkhaus,* the NBBS was set

---

* The secret station later moved to the Berlin Olympiastadion.

up to sound as if it was broadcasting from Britain. It opened with the reassuring refrain of 'Loch Lomond', went out for half an hour a day on short wave, and closed to the strains of 'God Save The King'. The programme was even listed alongside those of the BBC in British newspapers. Joyce could not do the broadcasting himself – his voice by now was far too recognizable – and so British soldiers with regional accents were lured away from prisoner-of-war camps to read out the scripts instead. Joyce recruited some of the candidates personally. The incentive for the soldiers was that they would be moved to Berlin where they would be accommodated in a house, allowed to wear civilian clothes and paid a salary. No pressure was to be applied, so that a speaker wouldn't seem resentful. Joyce tried to hide his identity so that prisoners wouldn't think they were collaborating with a traitor. But it was pointless. The third man he interviewed ran out shouting: 'I've just been talking to Lord Haw-Haw! I've just been talking to Lord Haw-Haw!' Another, quartermaster sergeant John Brown, later described his meeting: 'Joyce asked me if I had ever heard Lord Haw-Haw and I told him I had in England. He asked me why I had listened and I told him that lots of people listened as they found it very amusing. He appeared surprised and annoyed.' There were some forty British subjects who broadcast propaganda for the Nazis during the war, and about eight of these were servicemen recruited in this way.★

The British were developing their own black-propaganda stations using German prisoners of war. Their programmes would concentrate on casting aspersions about the sexual deviances of the Nazi leaders. Typically the speakers would pretend to be German workers complaining about how the top Nazis were indulging in homosexual orgies, or visiting Jewish prostitutes.

The Germans weren't quite so imaginative at this stage of the war. The scripts Joyce wrote were clunky, the performances by the soldiers wooden. They weren't deemed a great success and the listener figures never amounted to much, certainly not compared to the success of the *Germany Calling* broadcasts. The idea behind them was to persuade the British that they were fighting the wrong enemy. Joyce ran the station with almost complete autonomy, but refused to take a salary increase. He said his salary

---

★ Several of these were tried for treason at the end of the war but only two, Joyce and John Amery, of whom more later, were executed.

was enough to live on and that it was his patriotic duty to Britain to warn them about the Soviets. All he could be persuaded to accept were bonuses for working holidays. Goebbels seems to have been perplexed, amused and intrigued in like measure. In his diary he noted of Joyce: 'That boy's all right! And besides totally incorruptible. He genuinely wants to serve England.'

Joyce tried to make his scripts for both *Germany Calling* and *Workers' Challenge*, the main programme on NBBS, topical, even though the British papers arrived a day late. They were delivered by plane to airports in neutral Spain and Sweden, from where they were flown to Berlin. A good example of his technique was when he took an item he spotted in the *Daily Mirror* about the Duke of Westminster shipping his prize collection of orchids out to Florida for safety. Haw-Haw reported this and added without comment that 643 children had been killed in air raids that month. He also took delivery of *The Economist*, the *New Statesman and Nation* and *Punch*, a magazine which ran regular cartoons about Lord Haw-Haw. His only restriction on NBBS was that he wasn't allowed to criticize the Führer, which he felt undermined his credibility as the supposed radio voice of patriotic Britain.

Workers' Challenge was aimed at the working classes, and Joyce wrote in the colloquial, if patronizing, guise of a labourer. On the day of Hitler's Reichstag 'peace speech', his working man opined: 'This is a day which will go down in history. Now at the eleventh hour, when Churchill and his gang are urging us to pursue the war until London is in ashes, Hitler gives us another alternative. He offers us peace instead of annihilation.' He argued that an understanding with Germany did not mean that Britain must go Nazi. 'The workers of Britain don't want to fight their fellow workers of Germany. And if the Germans have a Nazi system, that's their look out, not ours. If we make peace we're not going to have a Nazi system here. We're going to have a state of workers, run by and for the workers . . . We know bloody well one reason why Churchill wants the war to go on. He's afraid that if he isn't kicked out by the Germans he'll be kicked out by us.'

With his socialist tendencies – Joyce's version of National Socialism had placed great store on social equality and had always attacked inherited privileges, the public school system and the excesses of capitalism – it is tempting to believe that he meant every word he said that night.

On 22 July Lord Halifax, the British Foreign Secretary, broadcast Britain's answer to Hitler's peace proposal. It was a resounding 'no'. There were angry Nazi faces at the noon press conference that day. The spokesman said to the foreign press corps: 'Halifax has refused to accept the peace offer of the Führer. Gentlemen, there will be an invasion.'

Judging by his *Germany Calling* talk that evening, Joyce had been jolted out of his complacency, too: 'Lord Halifax', he said, 'has spoken in the smug language of a sanctimonious churchwarden, and with snivelling hypocrisy.' A few days later he continued his theme, this time directing his invective at Churchill: 'It is unnecessary to say that a terrible retribution will come to the people who tolerate as their Prime Minister the cowardly murderer who issues these instructions. Sufficient warnings have already been given. Bombs will speak for themselves . . . The people of England will curse themselves for having preferred ruin from Churchill to peace from Hitler.'

This made for chilling listening. A line had been crossed. A new phase of psychological warfare had been entered. These broadcasts were no longer aimed at encouraging Britain to make peace but in breaking the morale of the enemy, trying to make them panic in the face of an imminent invasion. *Germany Calling* was now mocking and scolding in tone. There was an end to comic dialogues and innuendo, and instead monologues presented the English as bovine, snobbish and cowardly. It was a propaganda blitzkrieg in advance of the London Blitz. And this had been the plan all along. As early as 1933 Hitler had said that in a future war psychological dislocation through propaganda would replace artillery before an attack: 'The enemy must be demoralized and driven to passivity . . . Our strategy is to destroy the enemy from within, to conquer him through himself. Mental confusion, contradictions of feeling, indecision, panic – these are our weapons.'

In his other guise as the writer of scripts for NBBS, Joyce sowed discontent by starting rumours about foot-and-mouth plagues on farms and about tinned meat imported by Britain from Argentina which had been poisoned by German agents and fifth columnists. He also urged his listeners to rise up against Churchill and hiss him when he appeared in public. He hinted that there was a brave resistance movement in Britain that was always just staying one step ahead of its trackers, moving its transmitters around the country. 'You'll probably 'ear us again tomorrow night,' said the announcer, hamming up his cockney accent. 'But it's getting 'ard. The police are always on our 'eels nowadays.' The Home Guard became so jumpy that month that on one night alone they shot dead four innocent people at checkpoints.

On 25 July, Lord Haw-Haw had a dark message to convey to his listeners. 'Londoners will now know the taste of monkey or alligator, and the Zoo will continue to be one of the few institutions to keep to the old slogan "Business as usual". Starvation now threatens England. Who is to blame for this? No one but the small circle of rich people which is indifferent as to whether the people starve or not. These people have already got their children to safety. When things get bad enough they will make a getaway as well. The British people will, in the meantime, starve. Is this the wish of the British people?'

With this change in tone, not surprisingly, Haw-Haw's popularity began to wane. His broadcasts were now inspiring more fear, less amusement. One listener confessed to Mass Observation's newsletter: 'I think that, secretly, we are rather terrified by the appalling things he says. The cool way he tells us of the decline of democracy and so on. I hate it: it frightens me. Am I alone in this?' It took a certain amount of masochism to continue listening. The trouble was, the more people stopped listening, the more they talked about what Haw-Haw was saying, or at least what other people had told them he was saying. Britain became a basket case of rumour, almost reverting to levels of dumb superstition and folklore not seen in England since the Middle Ages. In many ways the urban myth-making was an understandable symptom of the stress and anxiety people felt; a case of pre-invasion nerves that bordered on mass hysteria.

In the summer of 1940 – 'invasion summer' as it became known – people were twitchy. They were paranoid about the smell of pear drops, geraniums and musty hay – signs, supposedly, that Hitler was trying out his poison gases. According to some gossips, certain lampposts had been marked with coded directions so that it wouldn't matter if the British removed all the road signs to confuse the enemy. Others were convinced the invasion had already been attempted and hundreds of German bodies were now floating in the English Channel. There was a particularly fevered belief that the Germans were infiltrating cities with spies, and to fuel this paranoia the Luftwaffe dropped maps, equipment and empty parachutes. As a number of these landed on wheat fields which were undisturbed by tracks of parachutists walking away, it was soon realized, by the authorities at least, that the German paratrooper spies were mere phantoms. But as far as the general public was concerned, German spies were so widespread they knew what was going on in every factory in every town – and always the proof for suspicion was something someone had heard Lord Haw-Haw say. Even the newspapers repeated some of these wild rumours. A common one was that Haw-Haw had announced which cities and towns were to be bombed the next night, even which individual buildings. People's imaginations ran away with them. In fact some seem to have imagined that Haw-Haw was able to go over Göring's head to direct the Luftwaffe to bomb certain streets out of personal revenge. One in Shoreditch was bombed, supposedly, because Joyce had been involved in a brawl there in 1937.

Village pubs hummed with Haw-Haw rumours about where the next bombs would be targeted, not least because they usually applied to the particular village, and sometimes even the particular pub where the humming was going on. Newspapers were deluged with letters from readers claiming to have heard about the Luftwaffe's bombing plans from Lord Haw-Haw. Again and again, the Ministry of Information was compelled to issue a standard statement: 'It cannot be too often repeated that Haw-Haw has made no such threats.' Bill Greig, a columnist on the *Daily Mirror*, wrote: 'In six months Lord Haw-Haw has gone from being England's biggest joke to the biggest danger to the nation.'

What seemed to spook people most was the town-hall clocks. Lord Haw-Haw was uncannily well informed about which were running slow, according to the rumour-mongers. 'We know all about Banstead, even that the clock is a quarter of an hour slow today,' was the most often repeated phrase. But there were many, many variations on it, with Banstead replaced by Gosport, or Guildford, or East Ham. To the people of Cambridge he was alleged to have said: 'Don't bother about your new Guildhall clock. We shall put that right for you.' And listeners in Wolverhampton were convinced that their town clock stopped one night at 8.55 and that this fact was reported that same night at 9.15 by Lord Haw-Haw. (It would have been impressive if it had been, given that the *Germany Calling* programmes were pre-recorded.)

Readers were particularly astonished by Haw-Haw's inside knowledge about specific factories: he was said to have expressed regret that when a factory in Ipswich (or Northallerton, or Kidderminster, or wherever) was blown up it would mean the pontoon card school in the canteen would have to be disbanded. A drop in production was recorded at a munitions factory in the Midlands – one which employed five thousand workers – because Haw-Haw had supposedly threatened that it would be bombed. Apparently he had added: 'Don't trouble to finish the new paint shed, you won't need it.'

According to another famous rumour, he had said that Orpington High Street (or Carshalton, or Dudley) needed widening and then he had added, with a sneer of course, 'Don't worry, we'll do that for you.' He had also said that the town's bakery was a good landmark for German bombers. A reader in Portsmouth, meanwhile, reported that a friend of his had heard Haw-Haw say: 'There is no need to take the old tramlines up in Commercial Road. German bombers will do it for you.'

Troop movements were another recurring theme of the Haw-Haw rumours. The wife of a company sergeant-major at Paignton was in tears when met by a *Daily Mirror* reader because Haw-Haw had said that a local territorial battalion was leaving the town for Devonport en route for Egypt and had voiced the threat: 'It is reasonably certain that German U-boats will see that none of the men arrives at his destination.'

If there had been the odd genuine report among these it could have been explained as guess-work, combined with a little pre-war knowledge of English geography and a scan of the British papers. But there weren't. Lord Haw-Haw commented on major news events only – village bakeries, roadworks and town clocks were not part of his remit. As the historian A. J. P. Taylor put it: 'Most of the broadcasts attributed to Joyce were not in fact made, either by him or by anyone else. No German broadcaster, for instance, ever gave the names of British towns which the Luftwaffe would bomb the next night, nor stated that the clock at Banstead was ten minutes slow.'

Realizing that nerves needed to be steadied, the British authorities tried to clamp down on this proliferation of nonsense. Two people were prosecuted for spreading Haw-Haw rumours. The *Daily Mirror* formed the 'Anti-Haw-Haw League of Loyal Britons' aimed at stopping the scatter-brained spreading rumours. Members had to sign a form which stated: 'And may heaven help the rumour mongers I meet.' As a reminder of the pledge not to listen to *Germany Calling*, members were supposed to cut out a notice and stick it on the side of their Bakelite wireless sets: 'This set is Anti-Haw-Haw. It hears no evil, speaks no evil.' Membership totalled many thousands. The *Daily Mirror* reported: 'Haw-Haw used to be a joke. Not much of a joke, but good enough for some apparently. These dolts went on boosting him as if he were Arthur Askey.' A chalked notice in an Islington cafe also captured the new mood: 'Don't go home and listen to that traitor Lord Haw-Haw. Ignore the bastard.' In a newspaper advertisement, the government posed the question: 'What do I do if I come across German broadcasts when tuning my wireless?' The answer was 'Switch 'em off or tune 'em out. These broadcasts are just part of a plan to get us down.'

Perhaps prompted by Joyce's line that 'when things get bad enough they will make a getaway', a rumour began to circulate that Churchill and the Royal family were preparing to leave for Canada. Mrs J. E. Smith wrote to her MP: 'It is surely time some assurance be given the general public that there never has been the faintest idea for the government to leave England for Canada. Lord Haw-Haw's lies to this effect are being repeated so endlessly, and although his vile propaganda is generally laughed at and despised, there is a certain section of poorly educated folk who are being alarmed. I am a Sussex farmer's wife and find that many of the farm labourers and other working folk do still listen to these German broadcasts and are being disturbed.'

A nationwide campaign was also launched that warned the general public against loose talk and the dangers of unwittingly giving information to enemy sympathizers. The slogan 'Careless Talk Costs Lives' was born and the Ministry of Information distributed two and a half million posters to offices, shops and pubs. Most were drawn by the *Punch* cartoonist 'Fougasse' (Kenneth Bird). He created a comical series showing Hitler and Göring listening in on unsuspecting gossipers on buses, in tubes and in cafes. Duff Cooper, the Minister of Information, proposed that there should even be a silent army of Englishmen who reported gossips. 'Cooper's Snoopers' didn't prove popular and the idea was soon dropped.

But this doesn't give the whole picture. Countryfolk seem to have been more susceptible to Haw-Haw rumours than their more sophisticated metropolitan counterparts. And it may have been that people secretly guessed that the friend of a friend who heard a particular broadcast probably hadn't really heard it, but they enjoyed repeating it all the same.

As the author E. S. Turner put it: 'It was an exciting, bracing time. The exchange of daft rumours even helped to keep up morale'. Perhaps this was part of the true Dunkirk spirit. As U-boats threatened to starve the nation, and the Luftwaffe threatened to level the cities, the British public took comfort in regarding the leaders of Nazi Germany as essentially comic figures. A. J. P. Taylor when asked to describe what the summer of 1940 was like said: 'Wonderful, wonderful. People weren't at all worried that Britain was on its own, in fact they said Britain was better off without the foreigners. We could manage by ourselves.'

Perhaps those who weren't at all worried hadn't listened to Lord Haw-Haw on 6 August. 'I make no apology for saying again that invasion is certainly coming soon,' he said. 'But what I want to impress upon you is that while you must feverishly take every conceivable precaution, nothing that you or the government can do is really of the slightest use. Don't be deceived by this lull before the storm, because, although there is still the chance of peace, Hitler is aware of the political and economic confusion in England, and is only waiting for the right moment. Then, when his moment comes, he will strike, and strike hard.'

Goebbels was so pleased with Lord Haw-Haw's efforts he sent, as Margaret put it in her diary, 'some cigars and congratulations to Will on his work and what not.' The Joyces, in turn, were feeling as if their gamble had paid off. They had backed the winning side and they were now comfortable with their new lives in Berlin and at ease with each other, enjoying feeding the squirrels together on their daily walks in the Tiergarten. They were appreciating the spoils that came with victory: food from Poland, furs from Norway, wine, champagne and brandy from France. Plentiful supplies of silk stockings and perfumes also began appearing in the shops and Margaret for once did not have to exaggerate in her talks when she said how good life was in Berlin.

By mid-August, Hitler was so confident of victory, either by conquest of Britain or by a negotiated peace, he ordered stands to be made ready for another big parade through the Brandenburg Gate. On their way to lunch one day, William and Margaret watched workmen erecting them in the Pariser Platz. Two huge golden eagles were being installed at each end of the stands, along with giant replicas of the Iron Cross.

But the celebrations were premature. On 20 August, in response to Churchill's 'Never in the field of human conflict was so much owed by so many to so few' speech that day, Joyce said: 'Winston Churchill was one of those who did most to procure England's declaration of war last September. And we now have his admission that nearly a year later his country is neither properly equipped nor has it properly started. Surely the time to think of proper equipment was before the war was launched! One day the British people will have cause to remember this confession of the chief warmonger – that he drove them into this disastrous conflict well knowing, as he did, that they were not prepared to wage it. Out of his mouth, Churchill stands convicted as a traitor to England. But this much the people have failed to realize. It was, until very recently, that their battle was fought by proxy. They had not heard the roar of those engines of destruction, which, thanks to Churchill, descended on their cities, towns, factories, docks and railways. It will not be long before Britain has to yield to the invincible might of German arms, for Germany started when the war began, and was equipped before that. But this also I feel, that short as the time may be, every day will have the length of a year for the people whom Churchill has condemned to ruin . . . in his crazy and fantastic plan to blockade Europe, the dictator of this little island showed the depths of his immoral malice.'

It was now one year since the Joyces' arrival in Berlin, and they now had a fairly fixed daily routine. They would take the tram to the Funkhaus together most mornings. William would then attend a meeting with an official from the Ministry of Propaganda who would hand him a green sheet of paper with a list of the important subjects of the day, as determined by Goebbels. He would read the previous day's British papers and dictate a NBBS script to one of the station's secretary for an hour, or perhaps to Margaret if she wasn't working on one of her Lady Haw-Haw scripts. In the afternoon he would check over his scripts and have them delivered to the NBBS. He would then write and pre-record his evening Haw–Haw commentary before going to the Press Club to meet Margaret for dinner, and if it was still light this might be followed by an evening stroll in the Tiergarten. Over the months, whenever they had felt like strangers in a foreign city, they had turned to each other for comfort. When their spirits were high, or when they had been drinking, they would invent games, do impersonations or tease each other with ever more pet names. By night now they would sometimes be kept awake until two or three by distant British bomber raids. Sometimes they would stand at their window mesmerized by the green and red flares that were marking out targets for British bombers, wondering whether they should go down to the shelters, with their steel doors and phosphorescent signs pointing the way to the Gassleusse (the gas-proof room).

Most of the noise came from the north, where the armaments factories were, but sometimes flashes of light would fill their flat and they would hear the hum of a bomber engine overhead. In the morning they would find shrapnel on the walk to the Funkhaus. They would also find leaflets which the British bombers had dropped. They read: 'The war which Hitler started will go on, and it will last as long as Hitler does.'

Bombing was still considered a novelty and crowds would gather to survey the damage done to prominent buildings such as the Opera House. But on 26 August, Berlin had its first fairly big bomber raid of the war. The anti-aircraft guns pounded away into a low ceiling of cloud, following the noise of the engines, but no planes were brought down. The searchlights which flashed back and forth across the skies were unable even to pick them out. Joyce happened to be in the Funkhaus that night. He had returned to read the evening news, something he occasionally did as part of a rota of English-speaking news readers. The windows rattled each time a battery fired or a bomb exploded. To add to the confusion, the air-raid wardens in their fire-fighting overalls kept racing through the building ordering everyone – mostly porters and office boys because it was night-time – to the shelters. Outside there was the sound of shrapnel from the anti-aircraft guns dropping through the trees like hailstones.

In his diary that night the CBS correspondent William Shirer wrote: 'Lord Haw-Haw, I notice, is the only other person around here except the very plucky girl secretaries who does not rush to the shelter as the siren sounds. I have avoided him for a year, but have been thinking lately it might be wise to get acquainted with the traitor. In the air raids he has shown guts.'

The next morning, on their way to work, the Joyces surveyed the damage. The Tiergarten was roped off and several bomb craters could be seen. There was a film of dust and rubble on everything. There was also a smell of gas in the air. Glass, bedding and fragments of furniture littered the roads. Berliners were in shock, standing around staring, open-mouthed, confused, aimless. They had been assured by Göring that a big raid on Berlin couldn't happen. Three days earlier he had said that Berlin's

population of five million need not go to their bunkers when the air raids
sounded, unless they could hear flak in their immediate vicinity. The day
after the big raid, the papers were allowed to report that enemy planes had
flown over the suburbs and had dropped incendiary bombs destroying one
wooden hut in a garden. There was no mention of the three streets roped
off to prevent Berliners seeing the destroyed houses. There was an item
about the Ministry of Education, though. It had decreed that in case of air
raids lasting after midnight, schools would remain closed the following
morning in order to allow the children to catch up on their sleep.

With this first big raid the authorities realized that the city's triumphant
'East–West Axis' street, five miles long and a hundred yards wide, looked
like an arrow pointing to the government quarter and so Berliners erected
a two-mile decoy of scaffolding covered with netting. Open spaces such as
the Adolf-Hitler-Platz were filled with false buildings. Berlin was changing. Seventy huge gun batteries and eighteen searchlight batteries had gone
up. Three green-painted 130-foot-high cement flak towers were erected
in the parks. There were posters everywhere about tackling incendiaries;
one had a skeleton of Death riding a plane and tossing a bomb at a building
which had ignored the blackout. The Gestapo announced that anyone
caught committing a crime at night would be beheaded. Two looters were
executed within days.

On 29 August, Berliners were killed by British bombs for the first time:
ten dead, twenty-nine wounded. The papers could no longer pretend the
bombing was minor and distant. Goebbels changed his tactics. He ordered
the newspapers to complain about the brutality of the British who
'attacked defenceless woman and children'. The headlines read COW-
ARDLY BRITISH ATTACK. They added that German planes only attacked
military objectives in Britain. Berliners spread rumours about why the
searchlights seemed unable to pick out British bombers in the night sky:
the planes were coated with an invisible paint. The Reichsrundfunk came
up with a devious ploy of its own. It installed a lip microphone for
William and Margaret Joyce and the other broadcasters to speak into, so
the thunder of the anti-aircraft guns outside did not register. Perhaps this
accounted for the tone of subdued menace in William Joyce's voice as he
uttered the words: 'For every microscopic part of enamel England rubs off
a German tooth, England will lose a complete set of her own.' He also
tried a new tack: divide and conquer: 'We have learned with horror and

disgust that while London was suffering all the nightmares of aerial bombardment a few nights ago, there was a contrast between the situation of the rich and the poor which we hardly know how to describe. There were two Londons that night. Down by the docks and in the poor districts and the suburbs, people lay dead, or dying in agony from their wounds; but, while their counterparts were suffering only a little distance away, the plutocrats and the favoured lords of creation were making the raid an excuse for their drunken orgies and debaucheries in the saloons of Piccadilly and in the Café de Paris. Spending on champagne in one night what they would consider enough for a soldier's wife for a month, these moneyed fools shouted and sang in the streets, crying, as the son of a profiteer baron put it, "They won't bomb this part of the town! They want the docks! Fill up, boys!" '

On 4 September, Hitler made a speech in which he taunted the British. 'In England they're filled with curiosity and keep asking "Why doesn't he come?" Be calm. Be calm. He's coming! He's coming!' The same day Joyce fuelled British anxieties about the imminent invasion with his *Workers' Challenge* script. He latched on to a story about how the Commons had had to be evacuated for two hours during a debate. 'Well, workers,' a cockney character supposedly sitting in a pub said, 'Mr Bleeding Churchill made a nice fool of himself in the House of Commons yesterday.'

On 9 September, as Lord Haw-Haw, Joyce broadcast: 'Must we remind them of the fact that it was Britain who declared war on Germany, who started to wage it on women and children by preparing the hunger blockade? Must we recall to their memories the air raid in Freiburg when children were killed in an attack on an undefended town in broad daylight, with no military objective even in the vicinity? For months the German people and their Führer have suffered indiscriminate bombing of non-military objectives. Time and again the Führer has offered the hand of understanding and even friendship to the very nation which starved the German people after the peace was concluded in 1919. Time and again the Führer has warned Britain of the necessary consequences that these brutal attacks might have. Last week he uttered what was his last warning in no uncertain terms. Now just retribution has befallen Britain. If there are civilian casualties and destruction of homes in London, then these are such as cannot be avoided in any really large-scale attack on the main objectives of military and economic importance in the East of London. Misery thus caused is not to be laid at Germany's door. Those who refuse to listen to reason – those who drove their nation into senseless war in order to perpetuate an injustice, just in order to save the interests of a small group of Jewish financiers and inveterate warmongers with Winston Churchill at their head – these men are responsible, not Germany.'

Goebbels must have had this aggressive speech in mind when he wrote in his diary two days later: 'We're re-orienting our radio service. The English-language and the Freedom station to produce terror and panic. We're really stepping up the pressure. Lord Haw-Haw is brilliant.'

Goebbels did not mention in his diary that day the bombs which dropped on the Reichstag and then fell in a direct line towards the Potsdamer station and the Brandenburg Gate. Nor did he mention the long Red Cross train that stretched from the main station in Berlin for half a mile to beyond the bridge over the Landwehr Canal. The wounded were unloaded under cover of darkness because Berliners were still trying to pretend that they were living in a fortress. Londoners, by contrast, recognized the value of being more open about bomb damage. When Buckingham Palace was hit by a bomb on 13 September the Queen declared: 'I'm glad we've been bombed. It makes me feel I can look the East End in the face.' This sentiment worked wonders for public morale and came to epitomize the Blitz spirit. Fear was turning to anger and iron will. Over in Dulwich, south-east London, another regal figure, Joyce's mother Queenie, was, in her own way, showing similar poise. Standing in the fish queue she heard a woman complaining about the Blitz and 'that blasted Lord Haw-Haw!' Another woman said: 'Hush, that's his mother right beside you.' In her thick Irish voice, Queenie said: 'Never mind, my dear, I'm sure you didn't mean it unkindly.'

Twilight Over England was published at the end of that month. Joyce had written it in just three weeks, back in January, dictating most of it to his secretary at the Funkhaus. The style of the prose owed much to his oratorical skills and to the learning that he wore so heavily. Invariably, he sounded portentous, but said little. The book was 50,000 words long and the German Foreign Office paid him 10,000 Reichsmarks – the equivalent of £500, more than an MP's salary at the time – for it. It was published in English with a print run of 100,000 and was intended for sale in the

United States and India. In the end it was distributed mostly through the prisoner-of-war camps.

With a mixture of dark flippancy and prescience, Joyce began by predicting his future. 'The preface is usually that part of a book which can most safely be omitted,' he wrote. 'It usually represented that efflorescent manifestation of egotism which an author, after working hard, cannot spare either himself or the readers. More often than not, the readers spare themselves. When, however, the writer is a daily perpetrator of high treason, his introductory remarks may command from the English public that kind of awful veneration with which £5,000 confessions are perused in the Sunday newspapers, quite frequently after the narrator has taken his last leap in the dark.'

He justified his decision to leave England: 'If an Englishman cannot fight in his own streets against the domination of international finance, it were better for him to go elsewhere and impede by every means in his power the victory of his Government: for the victory of such a Government would be an everlasting defeat of his race. It would put an end to all prospects forever of social justice and economic reform . . . I hope and believe that when the flames of war have been traversed, the ordinary people of England will know their soul again and will seek, in National Socialism, to advance along the way of human progress in friendship with their brothers of German blood.'

The second chapter began: 'The reader may have innocently hoped at the close of the last chapter that the historical discussion had come to an end. In this life, the innocent are often maltreated and the hopeful disappointed.' The book amounted to a random and bigoted history of Britain from Cromwell through Victorian England to the Treaty of Versailles, the return of the Gold Standard, the General Strike, the abdication of Edward VIII and British policy on India and Abyssinia. Stanley Baldwin was 'the pompous hardware monger from Ipswich, always trying to ape the ways of a country gentleman, with a canting Puritan whine in his voice.' Churchill was referred to as 'the thing that Mr Chamberlain picked out of the political gutter to make First Lord of the Admiralty.' Chamberlain's declaration of war was unconstitutional, because governments held mandates only to execute the policy they had submitted to the electorate. There should, Joyce opined, have been a referendum on the declaration of war in 1914. 'The system of Government in Britain today deserves one description only: it is plutocratic oligarchy, materialist in philosophy, Jewish in purpose, and tyrannous in effect.'

As well as attacking Jews he attacked capitalism and communism, and the decadence of the British aristocracy. He railed against the betrayal of British agriculture and the exploitation of the British working classes. He also revealed that he had a moral dimension of sorts. He attacked pornography, seeing it as degeneracy that British newspapers carried pictures of bathing women. 'Each issue tried to surpass the former in exhibiting the pectoral and fundamental aspects of women.'

According to Joyce, 'The poor Conservative Party wandered about from pillar to post, never quite knowing what it was trying to conserve.' The Liberals were 'Victorian Pharisees, whited sepulchres, dead men's bones who talked glibly about the Parliament of Man and the Federation of the World because their interest lay not in the building of an empire but in the acquisition of a larger area for their financial depredation.' The Labour Party's 'endocrine glands were poisoned by Liberal politics, Marxist materialism, and the crazy doctrines of Rousseau and the French Revolution. Its MPs were corrupted by sherry, champagne, becoming Duchesses, stock exchange tips, the Order of the British Empire and Freemasonry, and they failed to see that while being won over they were being laughed at.'

The book contained colourful flourishes and tirades of anti-Semitism that bordered on stream of consciousness. 'Just as in Freudian psychology, jazz and Surrealism, the Jew loves to see the poor Goy making a thorough ass of himself, crawling downstairs on all fours, as it were, with top-hat on his head and a piece of soap in his mouth, so there was something delightful to the Jewish mind in all the gabble that went on, all the mummery, and the thousand possibilities of shady intrigue that arose every day.'

Oddly, the unwritten target of this book was German bureaucracy. Joyce clearly felt that some Germans, the niggling officials at the Foreign Office who had driven him to distraction when he was writing it, were unworthy of National Socialism. They had edited the book again and again, changing the sense of certain passages and striking out his attacks on the Soviet Union and communism (the Soviets were still German allies at this stage). He blamed this on 'Ribbontripe', who for Joyce typified

German literal-mindedness, humourlessness and obsession with petty bureaucracy. He could not resist a sarcastic dig at his new masters in his preface: 'That I have been permitted to write freely what I would is due to the respect for freedom of honest expression which I have found everywhere in Germany since my arrival.'

He was more blunt in private, describing Ribbentrop as a hellhound from the infernal regions. Vanity, ignorance and humourlessness, he added, were among the Foreign Minister's best features.

Fortunately, as far as Joyce was concerned, the Foreign Office under Ribbentrop no longer had any control over the Funkhaus. Goebbels was in sole charge and he had appointed a new controller for the English section, thirty-one-year-old Eduard Dietze. Dietze was an urbane, bespectacled teetotaller with dual British and German nationality, having been born in Glasgow to a Scottish mother and a German father. His father returned to Germany in 1914 to join the army, and Dietze and his mother followed in 1916. He read philosophy at Hamburg University, and in the 1930s was by turns Berlin correspondent for the BBC and NBC. He specialized in covering events in the capital with simultaneous translations and commentaries in faultless English. Dietze and Joyce sounded remarkably similar, indeed Dietze deputized as Lord Haw-Haw on Wednesday nights and no BBC monitor ever commented on the difference. With his considerable experience as a radio producer and broadcaster, he became something of a mentor to Joyce. The two also became friends, after some initial mutual suspicion. 'Joyce was a man of great ability and great gifts and I felt at the end that he was definitely a personality. He did nothing for personal ambition but always because of inner conviction,' Dietze said in a statement after Joyce's capture. His wife Edith was more reserved: 'William was gifted but difficult. It was Margaret we all loved.'

Joyce presented Dietze with a signed copy of *Twilight Over England*: from Faust to Mephistopheles, he wrote in it. Already he had cast himself as the tragic hero. He gave his secretary Vera a signed copy, too. In that he wrote that she wouldn't understand it, but that she might get tobacco for it later. Joyce realized that in years to come, on the black market, notoriety would be just as tradable a commodity as fame.

THIRTEEN

'Haw-Haw can drink as straight as any man.'

A year and a month after arriving in Berlin, William and Margaret Joyce handed their defaced passports in at the Berlin Police Headquarters on Burgstrasse and were issued with certificates proving they were citizens of Prussia. In both their new German passports, under 'profession' was the incriminating word 'commentator'. In her diary entry for 26 September 1940 Margaret wrote: 'We got a letter to go to Burg St and then on to see Hesse [Dr Fritz Hesse, radio adviser to Ribbentrop]. We have now become Germans and had lunch at the Kaiserhof to celebrate.'

That night, during the punctual British bombing raid, William and Margaret were still in celebratory mood. With the Funkhaus vibrating from the distant blasts, they decided to go downstairs to the bomb shelter. William Shirer was already there, trying to read a book in the poor light. Margaret produced a litre bottle of schnapps and invited 'Bill', as she called him, to share it with them. William then suggested they steal out. They dodged past the guards and found an unfrequented underground tunnel where they continued drinking. 'When the bottle was finished we felt too free to go back to the cellar,' Shirer recalled in his diary. 'Haw-Haw can drink as straight as any man. And, if you can get over your initial revulsion at his being a traitor, you find him an amusing and even intelligent fellow.' Emboldened by drink the threesome then found a back stairwell that led to Joyce's office. Here they opened the blinds and contemplated the flashes from the anti-aircraft guns. Shirer was the first to break the companionable silence. He asked William if he saw himself as a traitor. 'I have renounced my British nationality and taken German citizenship,' he replied. 'I am no more a traitor than the thousands of British and Americans who had become comrades in the Soviet Union or the Germans who renounced their nationality after 1848 and fled to the United States.' Joyce continued in this vain, referring several times to 'we'; Shirer asked who he meant by this. 'We Germans, of course.'

Joyce must have struck Shirer as a man of stature, as he added two and a half inches to his height when he described him as 'a heavily built man of about five feet nine inches, with Irish eyes that twinkle and a face scarred not by duelling in a German university but in fascist brawls on the pavements of English towns.' Shirer noted that Joyce spoke fair German and had two complexes: a hatred of Jews and of capitalists. 'Strange as it may seem, he thinks the Nazi movement is a proletarian one which will free the world from the bonds of the "plutocratic capitalists". He sees himself primarily as a liberator of the working class. On the radio this hard-fisted, scar-faced young fascist rabble-rouser sounds like a decadent old English blue-blood aristocrat of the type familiar on our stage.'* Joyce presented Shirer with a copy of *Twilight Over England*, which he had on his desk. Shirer reciprocated the gesture by presenting William with a copy of *The Death of Lord Haw-Haw*, a novel by Brett Rutledge (a pseudonym of Elliot Paul), which had just been published in America and which he happened to have with him in his bag. The blurb on the jacket described Haw-Haw as 'No 1 Personality of World War No 2.' Joyce nodded with satisfaction as he read this, seemingly pleased that his fame had spread across the Atlantic. The story concerned the hunt for, and eventual assassination of, 'the real Lord Haw-Haw', a homosexual communist sympathizer broadcasting from New York.

One of the characters in the novel says: 'Clever Lord Haw-Haw. I must say he hits it on the nail now and then. I haven't missed his broadcast in a fortnight.' Another adds: 'There is something sporting about listening to unpleasant truths from an enemy announcer, and the fact that the voice is a traitor's does not offend your Englishman as much as a foreign accent.'

The novel compared Lord Haw-Haw to Bertie Wooster, P. G. Wodehouse's endearing comic creation, and shrewdly noted that this was

---

* Shirer gave a fuller account of this meeting the following year in an American newspaper article.

an unfortunate comparison because it meant the English came to like Haw-Haw. 'He personified ease and contentment. One could easily picture Bertie Wooster at the Drones Club giving a rollicking imitation of a German radio announcer or news interpreter, after several rather stiffish Scotch and sodas. Not only did the British public begin to listen in each time Haw-Haw's voice sailed out on the air, but secretly the English began to like the fellow.'

Of course, the book made mention of Joyce – as only a stand-in for the real Haw-Haw – and he seemed rather amused by the portrait of him as a brutal-looking, sexually abnormal 'low and surly fellow'.

The novel was remarkably well informed about Joyce's American birth, given that this was the late summer of 1940 and the British establishment had only just discovered this truth from John Beckett a few weeks earlier. 'Now William Joyce, American born, and one of Mosley's Fascists, with his brutal degenerate countenance, was not an attractive personality to be pinned on Lord Haw-Haw, from the German point of view. It was not likely to increase his audience or the faith of the British public in his words . . . Yet what did the Germans do but encourage the idea of Joyce as Haw-Haw by putting on the same radio programmes, just after the Peer of Zeesen, Joyce's second wife, a ballet dancer who performed a lamentable vaudeville act.' Shirer does not mention whether Margaret laughed when she heard this description of herself.

A few days later, the novel turned out to be more prescient than its author knew. A Gestapo officer warned Joyce that he had been given a tip-off about a plot to assassinate him. For the next six weeks, until the threat was deemed to have passed, policemen took it in turns to stand guard outside his flat and escort him to and from work. Joyce was also issued with a pistol, for self-protection.

Contemplating this threat put Joyce in a philosophical state of mind. Perhaps having so narrowly escaped the assassin's bullet in Ireland, he seems to have been fairly resigned to such a prospect. With Margaret he even mused that assassination might not be such a bad outcome. He had, it seemed, convinced himself that he would not survive the war, whichever side won it (and after 12 October, when Hitler formally postponed his plans for Operation Sea Lion, the outcome no longer looked certain). He took a decision to live for the day and not brood upon the future. He had, after all, reason to be content with the present. He was now a man of power and influence around the Funkhaus. The walls of the green room there were decorated with caricatures of the star speakers and those of William and Margaret were now the most prominently displayed. There was an aura around them. They would receive fan letters from Germans, one to William being unironically addressed to 'His Lordship'. The young English broadcaster James Clark recalled walking into the office one day to see William sitting on the edge of a desk giving an impromptu reading from James Joyce's *Finnegans Wake*. There was a semicircle of Reichsrundfunk staff sitting around him, gazing up at him. He was reading in a thick Irish accent and this had 'a stunning effect, even though the audience didn't know what language he was talking.'

Margaret at this time had aspirations to write a literary masterpiece of her own, a novel. But she never got round to it. Instead she left a fascinating record of her time in Berlin. Since arriving in the city, she had been writing daily entries in a set of small ring-bound diaries. She wrote in pencil in a neat, right-sloping hand that became so pinched at times it needed a magnifying glass to read it, as if she were hoping her own daily acts of treachery could be kept secret. Sometimes, when information seemed particularly sensitive, she would write in shorthand, as, for instance, when she stayed the night at her friend Susan's house and discovered that 'Susan is a Lesbian! And Jerry is frightened of her!' Occasionally she doodled in the margins: swastikas, pigs, a centipede she whimsically named Arthur.

From these diary entries it is possible to build up a picture of her typical day. After making breakfast for her husband, she would, if not needed in the office, have a 'lazy' morning. This might involve sunbathing, having her perm done at the hairdresser's, or 'doing a round of the shops' with her friend Inge. Officially she was doing research for her talks on Berlin life, unofficially she shopped because she liked shopping. Indeed, she recorded certain purchases with obvious relish: garnet earrings, frocks, blue shoes and, deserving three exclamation marks, 'my fur coat!!!' She and William ate in restaurants every lunchtime and afterwards would go back to their flat for a siesta before returning to work in the mid-afternoon. Margaret sometimes recorded that she was in one of her 'drinking moods'. Most evenings ended with her being 'very tight'. Their friends often stayed the night when they were too drunk to go home. Perhaps not surprisingly, the Joyces were often feeling ill: they regularly

caught colds and had food poisoning. William got toothaches which he
cured with whisky, Margaret would sometimes faint. Periodically she
would try to stop smoking because the putrid cigarettes were affecting her
heart. In the summer of 1940 she calmly noted that she had contracted TB
and that the doctors were keeping an eye on it. It proved to be a false
alarm. She worried about her tax bills, presumably because she was
enjoying the night life of Berlin too much to bother saving her money.
They drank champagne and brandy regularly and celebrated their anniver-
saries with expensive dinners at the Kaiserhof Hotel where foie gras,
oysters and lobster were always on the menu.

She would often 'fool around', by which she usually meant gossiping,
flirting, playing cards or, a particular pleasure of hers, sewing. Self-
deprecatingly she would refer to her sulks, her laziness and her low
boredom threshold, but she was not introspective. She recorded major
events in the war with almost complete indifference. Dunkirk was mentioned in passing: in the next line she gave details of a birthday party she
attended. It is clear where her loyalties lay. In the summer of 1940 she
wrote in her diary that her side had lost only ten thousand men since the
main fighting started. That was the official number of German casualties at
the time. When she saw two planes shot down over Berlin, British planes
presumably, she merely records that it was 'very exciting'.

The Joyces were enjoying living in Berlin, the glittering showcase of
the Third Reich; the war was elsewhere and, the Battle of Britain apart,
the Germans seemed to be winning. Rommel had yet to encounter
Montgomery, and world leaders would still have had difficulty locating
Stalingrad on the map. For two fascists in love, Berlin was a more Byronic
and glamorous city than either Paris or Venice. The glitzy, swaggering
capital had energy and confidence. There were Mercedes sports cars,
risqué reviews at the Metropol, and naked women dancers at the Scala
(they were permitted because they were considered a distraction for
soldiers home on leave). And 'banned' jazz and swing was being played in
certain clubs, if you knew where to go. There were celebrities to spot,
too. Margaret felt star-struck one night when she met a film actor who
she thought would not look out of place in Chelsea. Political grandees
could be glimpsed as well. When her husband saw and heard Hitler,
Goebbels and Himmler at a public meeting one day she recorded enviously
that he was a 'lucky bugger'. On days that they were working at the Büro

Concordia, the Joyces would sometimes sneak off to watch German championship football matches at the Olympic stadium, as it was on their doorstep. Margaret was especially excited by a Germany versus Spain match she watched there.

Hitler may have had thousands of his own people tortured and murdered, but many Berliners were enjoying prosperity and so were loyal to their Führer. In the 'golden thirties' Hitler had lavished attention on the capital. Cinemas, theatres and luxury hotels had been built. The most opulent hotel, though, was still the Adlon. With its frescoes, marble floors and gilded ballrooms, it epitomized this arrogant and pompous city – and the Joyces would never pass up an invitation to go there.

As far as William Joyce was concerned, his German adventure had brought him fame, the admiration of his hero Goebbels and a much better income than he had enjoyed as a tutor in London; and, perhaps most importantly of all, it had made him appreciate how lucky he was to be married to Margaret. In bringing her with him to Germany, he had separated her from her friends, her previous life, and all her sources of social and psychological support, and she, as a consequence, had become dependent on him. After all, she didn't even speak German at first. The two had become inseparable, codependent, allies against the world.

Or so William thought. For her part, Margaret was beginning to feel neglected and claustrophobic. William seemed to care more about his work than he did about her. That year, as she peevishly noted in her diary, William had even forgotten their wedding anniversary. At the end of October, she confronted him about this general neglect. William tried to make amends, taking her on a four-day holiday to Dresden. They stayed at the smart Park Hotel, attended a performance of *Il Trovatore* at the opera and strolled around in the sunshine in good spirits. The only reminder of the war for them was the art gallery, which was closed, the pictures having been removed for safety. On the last day, however, a pall of fatalism returned and William said: 'A beautiful place this, but I shall never come back.'

Until now Margaret had been giving her weekly talks for women anonymously. As with Lord Haw-Haw, there were in the early months of the war other contenders for the title Lady Haw-Haw, Margaret Botham-ley being one of them. But in March 1940, the *Daily Mirror* had identified Lady Haw-Haw as Margaret Joyce – and in her diary that day she had written that she was furious – and from 10 November that year it was Margaret who was announced as Lady Haw-Haw. Her programme – which was rather unimaginatively called *Weekly Talks for Women* – dealt with economic problems, contrasting the British system unfavourably with that of Germany. She wrote the scripts for it herself.

In one talk she said: 'Doubtless there will have to be a nine o'clock curfew for [British] land army girls – as though it were possible to ascertain whether these girls were really in bed or making fools of themselves with soldiers and air crew in nearby camps. Isn't it all a little bit disgusting? As if, in their heart of hearts, any of the women who are listening to me wanted this war. Even if England is so terribly in the wrong, as England is, things should be in different spirits. Local ARP women are being accused of drinking and gambling. What a spirit on which to enter a war against Germans. I am English and I used to be proud of my country. German women help their neighbours, do shopping or look after children for neighbours going out to work or doing war work.' As a way of lowering morale on the Home Front, she described the supposed conditions a woman evacuated from Willesden with seven children had to endure. This woman was forced to share a house with another mother who had five children. They had no lighting or heating and were forced to live off canned beef and tinned milk. They had four mattresses between fourteen of then, and seven blankets, four of which had to be used to black out windows. 'No light, but still had to black out windows!'

In her broadcasts the lot of the British housewife was always compared unfavourably with that of the German. 'Women in England are so frightened by war propaganda from the British Misinformation Ministry that they are too frightened to remain in London. No mother here in Berlin is separated from her children and there has been no evacuation of German cities. Why? Because the state provides adequate provision for air-raid shelters and has no desire to create chaos by moving large masses of the population . . . In London the government does not really care whether mothers and children are safe or not. There are chaotic and miserable conditions of poor people. And there is an almost complete lack of feeling among the idle rich.'

It was hypocritical of Margaret to take the moral high ground about women drinking, gambling and 'making fools of themselves with soldiers'.

She had been busy making a fool of herself with a soldier for several months, a German one at that. Actually, it was more than fooling around. It was a full-blown affair in which each declared their love for the other. And it wasn't with a mere soldier, either. Nikolaus von Besack was an officer who worked for Wehrmacht intelligence. He was a handsome aristocrat and, born on 27 May 1904, seven years older than Margaret. A married man, he nevertheless had a reputation as a womanizer, being described by James Clark as a 'cheerful and utterly unreliable rogue'. Howard K. Smith, a CBS war correspondent who wrote a contemporaneous account of his time in Berlin, recalled a drinks party he hosted at which a Prussian officer fitting Besack's description drank to the health of a female guest, drained the glass dry, then turned on his heels, raised the glass high in the air and smashed it on the floor. 'Unruffled by the awed silence which followed the crash, he marched a couple of steps to me, snapped his heels together, bowed stiffly and apologised. I was overwhelmed by the grace of it all.' Not long afterwards he drank to the woman again and crashed a second glass to the floor and then apologized in the same way. 'I should have been angry,' Smith wrote, 'but his manner was so irresistible that I almost felt he was doing me a favour.'

Besack also, like William, had a gift for languages – indeed he spoke perfect English, which was how Margaret came to meet him. He had been called back to Berlin in November 1939 on secondment to work as an editor at the English-language station at the Funkhaus, which is how Smith would have met him, too. On his first day at work, Margaret noted in her diary how dashing he was. A few months later she and Nicky, as she called him, were moved to a new office at Kochstrasse in downtown Berlin, some distance from the Funkhaus in western Berlin, and so from William. Here she worked on *Back Numbers*, a programme aimed at demonstrating 'British propaganda lies' by the use of selective quotation from the British press. Here, too, she had the freedom to see as much of Nicky as she liked. As she recorded in her diary one day, he tended to drift in and out of her office a great deal.

The affair began, as office affairs invariably do, with a quick drink after work. The drinks became a regular fixture and turned into early suppers. William didn't seem to notice Margaret's absences – he was buried in his work. It was another harsh winter in Berlin and, one night, when Nicky walked Margaret home in the blackout, their hands in front of them to feel the way, they found themselves in a snow drift. They thought it funny. That night she didn't get home until two in the morning.

Whether or not William knew he was being cuckolded in his second marriage, as he had been in his first, he affected not to notice. It would have been understandable if he had suffered from a mild inferiority complex – he was, after all, a short 'Irishman' who had reinvented himself as a languid English aristocrat – although there is little evidence to suggest he did. To Margaret he seemed preoccupied and distant. And perhaps he was deliberately immersing himself in the political world in order to escape Margaret's sexual politics at home. In early January he left Berlin for a few days on another recruitment drive around the prisoner-of-war camps. When he returned, with among others, Walter Purdy,★ he joked that it was the promise of cakes and ale that swung it for the PoWs. He was in a good mood because he had managed to get his hands on a supply of British Red Cross soap, having bought it in the prison camps with much-needed German hard currency.

His jovial air was soon dropped as he began to find Margaret's behaviour suspicious. Things came to a head on 18 January 1941. Nicky had told Margaret that he was getting divorced. In her diary she wrote: 'Talk 8.30 [her broadcast]. Dinner Funk-Eck. Gilbert came in. He took me home. Nick came in for a drink. He stopped rather late and as he went Will came in. I was frightened because I thought he would be angry – he was.'

For the next five days, the tension between the couple mounted, with William swinging from denial to indignation. Finally he lost his temper and struck Margaret. 'Left town to be out for W,' Margaret wrote in her diary that night. 'Lunch at Wilhelmshallen, then home. Will slept and I sorted out stuff. Then he beat me, because of Saturday, until I could hardly stand, and then we went to dinner at the Club. Gilbert came in and came back with us for a drink.'

It was typical of Margaret that she was able to record such an ordeal in so insouciant a manner. Perhaps she was feeling guilty about her infidelity. Maybe she felt that with her fiery temper she provoked William into hitting her. According to her diary, it wasn't the first time it had happened.

★ Purdy was sentenced to death at the Old Bailey in 1945 for treason.

In an earlier entry she had written simply that William had come home and 'bang, bang, bang'. She could have been referring to bombs falling, or using 'bang' in its colloquial sense (since the mid-1930s it had been a euphemism for sex; and three days later she did write that she was suffering from unrequited affection). But in all probability she was referring to being hit. Whatever her reasons, like so many abused women she did not walk out on the man who abused her, yet. She would threaten to, of course. And then William would turn on the charm. Not only would he apologize and swear never to repeat the episode but he would become attentiveness itself. This may even have been what she was wanting, in that she may have had what psychologists call a passive-aggressive personality. Traits associated with this condition include wilful laziness, scorn of authority, a tendency to be sullen and argumentative, and a habit of alternating between hostile defiance and contrition. Sexually, passive-aggressive types veer between submissiveness and dominance. Above all they tend to be subtle in the way they manipulate others. Each time William lost his temper it was a little victory for Margaret. She enjoyed provoking and tormenting men, especially William whom she liked to call 'Fat Will' because she knew it annoyed him. In one diary entry she described with cool detachment and some satisfaction how she baited her husband until he 'lost his temper and nearly had a stroke.' She was also aware that in this particular battle she had the decisive weapon: her narcotic sex appeal. After an earlier quarrel, Margaret had written in her diary: 'Grand union scene with Will who, at last, showed faint glimmerings of jealousy.'

It is possible that William, too, had a sadomasochistic side to his character and that, in this connection, his sexual tastes inclined towards the exotic. According to A. K. Chesterton's unpublished notes on Joyce: 'A woman typist at the Black House once saw him using his arm as a pin cushion, sticking pins in with his sleeve rolled up.' It may, then, have been that William quite enjoyed watching his wife flirt. As she recorded in her diary one night in Berlin, 'Terribly drunk. W made me flirt with a Bavarian!' Not that she needed much encouragement. On another night she records that she was 'flirting violently' with Sammy, her boss, who 'permitted himself a little heavy pleasantry with me.'

Whether William felt guilty about his particular act of violence in January 1941 is not recorded, though in his prison letters he returned repeatedly to his feelings of guilt about the way he had treated Margaret generally. Perhaps he thought of his actions as crimes of passion. Either way, theirs was an extraordinary love affair, with dramatic highs and lows, and extremes of emotion, all played out against the backdrop of a titanic struggle, a world war.

And Joyce had another distraction at this time: the prospect of having to fight for the Fatherland. The moment he had become a German citizen he had also become eligible for conscription – radio-speakers were not exempt – and on 12 February 1941 he formally registered for military service (although he refused to join the Nazi Party, and never did). The atmosphere in Berlin had changed in subtle ways since the heady summer of 1940. People still assumed that Germany would win the war, but now there was uncertainty about when. Symbolically, the review stands that had been erected in August to celebrate the invasion of Britain were now dismantled. Berliners watched in thoughtful silence as a squad of workers knocked the planks off and carted them away. The gilt on the stand's triumphant eagles had tarnished in the snow, and winter gales had ripped the camouflage canopies from the East–West Axis and blown the gauze-and-wire trees off the lampposts, leaving them dangling on the real, leafless trees of the Tiergarten. For Joyce, the prospect of becoming a conscript at this time would have been sobering, to say the least.

But Goebbels had other plans for the man he called his 'world celebrity' – he wasn't going to squander him on military service. In his diary that month, after Göring expressed great admiration for Haw-Haw's work, Goebbels described Joyce as 'The best runner I've got in my stable.' Nevertheless, this being Germany, the bureaucratic hoops had to be jumped through. On the registration form, Joyce gave his religion as *Gottgläubig* ('believer in God', faith not specified). He also gave his correct place of birth as New York. But, in a moment of embarrassment at his father's humble-sounding occupation – building contractor – he lied on the form and described him as an architect. In fact, since he left for Germany, his father had been working as a door-to-door vacuum-cleaner salesman. William did not know this. Nor did he know that, just as he felt a twinge of shame about his father, so his father had come to feel ashamed of him. Indeed, neighbours said the shame of knowing his son was Lord Haw-Haw broke Michael Joyce's heart.

As he was reading the British papers on 21 February, a day late as usual, William's eye was drawn to an item under the headline FATHER OF LORD

HAW-HAW DIES. Michael Joyce had died of a heart attack, at the age of seventy-four. It was a grim way for William to find out about his father's death. He turned to Margaret for comfort and the two sat up talking into the small hours. Like his father, William had changed nationality. He had also lived an unsettled, peripatetic life that had seen him move from New York to several locations in Ireland, half a dozen addresses in London and as many in Berlin. Perhaps as a reaction to his father's death, William announced to Margaret that they were going to move house again. With the 10,000 Reichsmarks advance he had been paid for his book, as well as his 4,000 RM salary, and the 2,000 RM a year Margaret was earning, they could afford to move into more comfortable accommodation, he said. It would represent a new start for their marriage, too. They found an elegant flat on Kastanienallee, a chestnut-tree-lined street ten minutes' walk from the Funkhaus. It was well furnished, with plenty of space for Joyce to put up the books he had been collecting, and a table for his gramophone and the collection of Wagner recordings he enjoyed playing on it. The flat also had a balcony on which Joyce could sit and smoke and contemplate the street below. The landlady of the flat agreed to cook breakfast for the couple every morning, as well as looking after the heating and cleaning.

Perhaps most importantly, it was a short walk from their favourite bar, the Funk-Eck, which was at the other end of Kastanienallee from their flat. Once through the door customers negotiated a push-through curtain and then faced dozens of tables with coloured cloths and candles. Sitting at them would be grey-uniformed soldiers home on leave, civil servants from the government quarter and staff from the Funkhaus. In the corner a pianist or an accordionist would be playing. The walls were decorated with folksy woodwork, cowbells and horse brasses and, naturally, a prominent photograph of the Führer. There was also a message board where regulars pinned postcards, banknotes and signed photographs of well-known customers, the Joyces among them. They were always treated royally there. As Margaret recalled, 'they killed the fatted calf for us'.

Once they had settled into their new apartment, Margaret again felt the strain of living with her secret. She was in love with Nicky – she referred to him as her 'too charming Prussian' or, the ultimate betrayal, her honorary sheep – and she couldn't forgive William for hitting her. Their relations deteriorated. Where once they used to talk all night, now they would argue. Temperamentally they were similar in this respect; she could be just as opinionated as he was and they both enjoyed a good fight. Her diaries are full of accounts of her 'quarrels' with people, usually William and Nicky, but also with her girlfriends. 'I was rude to Willy and made her cry,' she noted one day. William constantly complained that she was unable to control her temper, and there are accounts of her kicking people who crossed her in the air-raid shelters.

William could be calculatingly hurtful in his words, too: 'I have never had such a drunken whore on my hands as you,' he said during one argument at the Club. On 23 March 1941, as they were arguing at the flat, the truth came out. 'I'm having an affair,' Margaret said, looking him in the eye.

William was speechless.

'I'm having an affair,' she repeated.

'I don't understand,' he said eventually. 'How could you? After all we have been through?'

It was Margaret's turn to be silent.

'Didn't you mean anything of what you said?' William continued. 'Is he better than me?'

Margaret told him everything. They talked all night until Joyce opened the blackout curtains and let the daylight in. Then they went to work, and that night, instead of catching up on sleep, they talked till dawn again. Margaret later recalled that William was being surprisingly kind and gentle.

'I don't want you to stay,' he said. 'But I don't want you to leave.'

Margaret had always suspected that, because of his Irish background, part of William still considered sex wicked and sinful, and this seemed to borne out by his Victorian comment that night that she was a scarlet woman. Her friend Maja Guth, a dark-haired Rumanian she knew from the Funkhaus, rang to say that she had been talking to Nicky and he had decided to marry Margaret as soon as his divorce was finalized. When Margaret then rang Nicky he seemed 'sweet and embarrassed'. After this she went to the Funk-Eck and met her husband: 'W was sweet all right,' she wrote that night. 'Poor pet, he does love me.' After a third sleepless night, Margaret moved out to stay in a flat Maja rented on Bülowstrasse in the southern Berlin district of Schöneberg. She told William it was a temporary separation, until they could decided 'what to do for the best'. Nicky came to see her: 'He was embarrassed at first but unfolded later. He said he loved me.'

Maja suggested to Margaret that she should leave Berlin for a while to gather her thoughts. In a friendly gesture she offered her the use of an 800-acre estate near the port of Danzig, in occupied Poland, where her sister-in-law lived. Margaret agreed, and so did William, not least because it would mean his wife wouldn't be seeing her lover. Dietze also agreed it would be for the best and gave Margaret a month's sabbatical from work. As she was packing her suitcase, Nicky came to say goodbye and was, according to her diary, 'the same cheeky old Nick'. Distracted by him, she forgot to take food for the train.

Tellingly, she was now able to afford a first-class ticket to Danzig, but nevertheless arrived feeling hungry, tired and cold. With her typical English understatement she described herself as being a shade tearful, too. There were no taxis available, and no hotels that would take her. Because of the blackout she couldn't even work out which direction to walk in to find help. Some soldiers saw her in distress and went to talk to her. In her pidgin German she explained that she was lost. When they asked what an Englishwoman was doing in Danzig, she said she was on holiday and that she worked at the Berlin Funkhaus, in fact, that she was Lady Haw-Haw. They must have heard of this nickname because they seemed to be impressed. They offered to help, picked up her cases and took her to a guest house where they explained to a no doubt bemused elderly woman that the young English woman was the famous Lady Haw-Haw. She was shown to a spare bed, while the soldiers waited downstairs, eager to take her out on the town. The group went to a *Bierlokal* packed with noisy, drunken soldiers and Margaret soon found her mood lightening. She was always at her happiest, and most flirtatious, when surrounded by admiring young men in uniform.

At the estate, over the following few weeks, she listened to the *Germany Calling* broadcast at 10.15 every night and translated it for her news-hungry hosts. On 2 April, she heard her husband say something so unexpected it took her a few minutes before she felt composed enough to translate it. Speaking slowly and deliberately he had said: 'I, William Joyce . . .' She had known for a while, since his father's death in fact, that William no longer wanted to be anonymous, but clearly now Goebbels or Dietze had given him permission to reveal who he was. She did not know that something else had forced William's hand. He had been annoyed by an article in the *Evening Standard* the previous day which had accused him of

PEMBROKE BRANCH TEL. 6689575

being a German spymaster who during his time in London had controlled
three hundred spies. Margaret continued listening . . . 'I, William Joyce,
left England because I would not fight for Jewry against the Führer and
National Socialism. I left England because I believed most ardently, as I
do today, that victory with a perpetuation of the old system would be an
incomparably greater evil for England than defeat coupled with a possibility of building something new, something really nationalist, something
truly socialist.'

He almost certainly meant it. From that night on, he was introduced with the words, 'You are about to hear "Views on the News" by
William Joyce, otherwise known as Lord Haw-Haw.' The station clearly
thought the nickname too valuable to drop. And Joyce must have agreed
because, around this time, he took to signing his letters 'William Joyce
(Lord Haw-Haw)'. Aware of the legend he had helped to forge, he was
now cultivating it.

Because of the fuel shortages, most of Margaret's sightseeing journeys
around the Danzig area were by pony and trap. From this she saw a U-
boat in the harbour, an event so thrilling it earned a mention in her diary.
One morning, though, she was taken on a tour in a car, and encountered
a disturbing sight: a column of shaven-headed prisoners being force-
marched. They were wearing striped prison suits and looked malnourished.
'I was glad I was in a car and moving fast,' she wrote that night.
Construction of Auschwitz had begun a year earlier, but more likely these
prisoners were from Stutthof concentration camp.

On 15 April, she received what she described in her diary as a 'an
awful letter from Nick and a nice one from Will.' Every night as she
listened to her husband's voice on the radio her affection for him returned
until she eventually wrote: 'Everything upside down.' A fortnight later she
wrote: 'W sent some money and two rather queer letters – we have to
pay an awful lot of income tax.' On 1 May she decided it was time to
return to Berlin and face the music. She called in to see William before
visiting Nicky. They were formal with each other; overly polite. William
calmly informed her that he had been to see Nicky and that they had had
a man-to-man talk. Nicky had told him that he was to be transferred out
of Berlin to rejoin his division on the Baltic. William told Margaret that
she was not to see Nicky again. He also told her that he had arranged for
her to be transferred from her office in downtown Berlin back to his at

the Funkhaus, where she would continue to work on archives, produce scripts and give her talks.

That month there was a surge in the number of people in Britain tuning in to Lord and Lady Haw-Haw. The British, having survived the Blitz, were going through another of their periodic attacks of nervousness and superstition. Some turned to astrology, others to folklore. One belief that had common currency was that the last time broad beans grew upside down was in 1918, the year the Great War ended, and the same was supposed to be happening in 1941. Those that needed more information than the local vegetable patch could provide had to go somewhere – and that was to Lord Haw-Haw. The big Luftwaffe bombing raids were now being targeted at cities other than London. Between 1 and 8 May, over seven consecutive nights, German bombers dropped 870 tonnes of high-explosive bombs and more than 112,000 incendiary bombs on Merseyside. The fires were horrific. Lord Haw-Haw is said to have addressed the people of Bootle with the words: 'The kisses on your windows won't help you', referring to the tape intended to prevent flying glass. Thousands left their homes and spent the nights in fields. The curtains flapping from the broken windows led to rumours of white flags being raised. The government in London was once more concerned about the rumour-mongering. A new rumour that Churchill's health was failing and that Beaverbrook was being groomed for Number 10 began to circulate.★ The Ministry of Information believed Haw-Haw had started the rumour, but there is no record of it having been broadcast.

There was another Englishman broadcasting from Berlin that month, a genuine Englishman. After his arrest the previous summer, P. G. Wode-house had been interned at Loos near Lille, then moved to a converted lunatic asylum in Tost, a small town in Upper Silesia thirty miles from Auschwitz (prompting him to ask, 'If this is Upper Silesia, what must Lower Silesia be like?'). There he had received many fan letters from still-neutral America. He was due to be released when he reached sixty later that year, as he would no longer be of military age. But in May a German officer asked Plum, as he was affectionately known, whether he would like to make a radio broadcast for his American fans who were worried

---

★ The rumour was premature as it wasn't until December that year that Churchill suffered a mild heart attack while staying in the White House.

about his safety. It was a cunning ruse and Wodehouse foolishly fell for it. He was put up at the Hotel Adlon in Berlin, and made a total of five broadcasts from the Funkhaus, in which he described his time in internment in typically whimsical Wodehousian style. 'Young men starting out in life have often asked me how can I become an internee?' he began drolly. 'Well, there are several methods. My own was to buy a villa in Le Touquet on the coast of France and stay there till the Germans came along. This is probably the best and simplest method. You buy the villa and the Germans do the rest.' The only vaguely controversial thing he said was: 'I'm wondering whether the kind of people, and the kind of England I write about, will live after the war – whether England wins or not, I mean.' That line went down badly in England. Some considered it defeatist. But that line was as bad as the Wodehouse broadcasts got, which wasn't very bad at all. The rest of his talks were light-hearted and mildly anti-German accounts of his time in internment. 'An Associated Press man who came down to interview me later wrote in his piece that Tost Lunatic Asylum was no Blandings Castle. Well, it wasn't, of course, but still it was roomy. If you had a cat, and had wished to swing it, you could have done so quite easily in our new surroundings.'

Nevertheless, the broadcasts caused outrage in some quarters back in Britain. William N. Connor, author of the 'Cassandra' column in the *Daily Mirror*, launched a bilious attack in a broadcast for the BBC, creating the myth that Wodehouse had treacherously bought his freedom by doing the broadcasts: 'I have come to tell you tonight of the story of a rich man trying to make his last and greatest sale – that of his own country. It is a sombre story of self-respect, of honour and of decency being pawned to the Nazis for the price of a soft bed in a luxury hotel. It is a tale of laughter growing old and of the Judas whine of treachery taking its place. It is the record of P. G. Wodehouse ending forty years of money-making fun with the worst joke he ever made in his life. The only wisecrack he ever pulled that the world received in silence. The last laugh bought for him by that prince of innocent glee – Dr Josef Goebbels.'

On 9 July, Anthony Eden stood up in the House of Commons and accused Wodehouse of having 'lent his services to the German war propaganda machine'. In the same debate Quintin Hogg charged Wodehouse with 'committing just as much an act of treason towards his country as Lord Haw-Haw', and Harold Nicolson wrote in his diary, 'I do not want to see Wodehouse shot on Tower Hill. But I resent the theory that "poor old PG is so innocent that he is not responsible". A man who has shown such ingenuity in evading British and American income tax cannot be classed as unpractical.'

Whether or not Wodehouse encountered the Joyces in Berlin is debatable, but he certainly availed himself of the Press Club, where they were regulars. And Margaret noted in her diary that she was able to listen to the recording of the first Wodehouse talk live in the studio, because she had just finished her own talk and didn't have to rush off. Afterwards she went back to Maja's flat in Bülowstrasse. She was staying there because her marriage to William was ending in a stalemate. He still loved her, in his fashion, but he thought it would be for the best if they lived apart. A few days later she noted: 'Drink with Will. Said he would never trust a woman again.' But by 12 May the couple had something other than themselves to talk about. A big news story had broken. That day Margaret wrote excitedly: 'We heard that Hess had pinched a plane and gone to England. He's gone mad. Got tight.'

The line that Rudolf Hess, the Deputy Führer of the Reich, had gone mad was the one being spun by Dr Otto Dietrich, Reich Press Chief, on Hitler's direct orders. The truth may have been more complicated and mysterious. The Nazis, especially Hess, were obsessed with the occult. Our old friend Maxwell Knight is believed to have recruited an astrologer as an MI5 agent and sent him to Germany to infiltrate the occult court of Hess. The agent is said to have briefed Hess that the Duke of Hamilton was prepared to meet him to act as a peace negotiator between the German government and the British. The deal, broadly, would be that the English could have a free hand with the British Empire, if Germany could have a free hand in the East. Hess considered Hamilton a kindred spirit, having met him and got on well with him when he came over to Germany for the 1936 Olympics. Hess also knew the Duke was one of the many British aristocrats who had been fascist sympathizers or appeasers in the 1930s and that on 6 October 1939 he had written to *The Times* saying hostilities should cease and peace with Germany should be negotiated. When the planets were aligned portentously on the night of 10 May 1941, Hess set off on his historic solo flight. Just before his Messerschmitt 110 crash-landed on a remote Scottish hillside, near the Duke of Hamilton's estate, he parachuted to safety. According to numerous accounts, a welcoming committee consisting of the Duke of Hamilton, the Duke of Kent (the King's younger brother), and various MI5 and MI6 officers had gathered at the Duke's estate alongside a makeshift runway lit with torches. Hess never made it to the meeting place and the next day was captured by a farmhand with a pitchfork.

According to a popular joke in Germany, Churchill was supposed to have summoned Hess and said, 'So you're the madman, are you?' and Hess replied: 'No, only his deputy.' The bizarre flight was dismissed in both Britain and Germany as the deranged act of a disordered mind, and because Hess never broke his silence on the subject, there has been endless speculation as to his true motives. But if, as Stalin suggested, the British government had lured Hess·under false pretences in order to stage a propaganda coup, it seems odd that they downplayed his capture. Indeed they insisted that his unexpected arrival on British soil was of no lasting consequence. In all probability, the Secret Service had wanted to give Hess the false impression than an actual coup was about to be staged in Britain, which would mean there would be no need for a German invasion.

Joyce was among those keen to downplay the Hess 'peace flight'. In an NBBS script he wrote: 'We had no intention of entering into any discussion upon the arrival in peculiar circumstances of Rudolf Hess in Scotland, but since he has created far more interest than the Loch Ness Monster, and since we believe this interest to be disproportionate to the event, we feel constrained to make some comment on what has become a matter of public opinion. Hess should be offered a seat in the House of Commons as an Independent Conservative Invasion member. Whether he is sane or insane is of no importance in this connexion for he would be working with the likes of Winston Churchill whose mental condition has long been open to doubt . . . Hess is with us but victory is as far off as ever. If we could, however, persuade Churchill to undertake a flight to Germany, there might be some cause for public rejoicing.'

Joyce was about to have a brush with another 'sane or insane' famous person, Ezra Pound, the American poet who lived in Rapallo, Italy. After hearing *Germany Calling* during the Phoney War, Pound had lobbied Italian radio officials to let him do similar broadcasts to the American people from Rome. Beginning on 23 January 1941 he was given a ten-minute slot every three days on the 'American Hour'. In these broadcasts he railed against the 'money hungry Americans' for sending aid to Britain and warned against the cost of intervention: 'For God's sake, don't send your boys over here to die for the Shell oil company and the Jewish war profiteers.'

Pound had written a fan letter to the Funkhaus asking for a schedule of Joyce's talks. His letter had been passed on to Joyce who replied on 3 June 1941 giving his schedule and promising: 'In the very near future I propose to inflict a real letter on you. Meanwhile, all the best. Heil Hitler.' Pound responded with a three-page letter full of suggestions. 'Can't remember when I first heard of yr transmissions,' he wrote, 'but have been hearing 'em ever since.' He signed off with 'Heul Hitler and nach Vladivostock.' Joyce wrote a short, polite letter back: 'I agree with you that it is not easy to make an impression of an obvious nature on the thing called the British public, but I nevertheless think that we are succeeding and that the results will be cummulative [sic] when they emerge.'

After this came the deluge. Pound became a postal stalker, regularly firing off three-page letters to Joyce full of bizarre spellings and even more bizarre ideas. 'Can't you put a proper Berlin psycopath [sic] onto the FILES of the newspaper, to see, if Roosevelt gets worse at full moon?' Another began: 'Dear Joyce, Am still feeling lack of coordination. Faint dawn of hope, or at faith in the American people, I mean IF we can hold out a few months longer, the American electorate will I think squash that unspeakable louse, that cunt of all infamy Roosevelt at the autum [sic] elections next year . . . GOD damn Roosevelt, and the brit. Gang. ANYhow what shit, what muckers!' The letters continued and Joyce, perhaps sensing that Pound was a lunatic, gave up replying to them.★

Margaret, meanwhile, was engaged in her own clandestine correspondence, regularly writing to Nicky. On 5 June, when he came back to Berlin on leave, she had a furtive lunch with him. 'He is worried,' she noted in her diary. 'He wants to keep me but thinks I ought to go back to W. Dinner with W at Irish Exchange – we talked about things and I really decided to go back, but broke down at the thought of losing Nick.'

★ It has been suggested, in Bergmeier and Lotz's *Hitler's Airwaves*, that Pound turned up in Berlin the following spring, spoke to America from the Rundfunk, and met Joyce. The two men did not 'mesh'. In his prison letters, however, Joyce refers to Pound affectionately as 'Esrapunto'.

The next day she wrote: 'Lunch at Gerald – Sammy and Will there. W forced it out of me that I'd stayed with Nick after getting his letter – left the restaurant in a passion. I had dinner at the Funk-Eck and he was there so we sat together – he told me what he thought of me and then said goodbye.'

A week later, William's 'passion' had not abated. 'I went to the Funk-Eck for dinner and met Will coming out – he cut me.' Three days after this she seems to have made up her mind to go with Nicky. 'Nick came to Funkhaus to see me – he says his business is all arranged – we can get married. Completely flattered. Will asked me to go back to him again.'

It is tempting to speculate that the emotional turmoil in Joyce's private life that summer affected the tone of his broadcasts, giving them an even more malevolent edge than usual. Certainly, on 22 June 1941, when Germany invaded the Soviet Union – 'Barbarossa' – he entered a more toxic phase in his career. He had long felt like a hypocrite about the way he had been obliged to draw a veil over the Hitler–Stalin pact. Now the unholy marriage between fascism and communism was at an end and he was allowed to express his true feelings on the subject. That night in the bar, everyone wanted to know Joyce's opinion. 'Everything will be all right so long as America doesn't enter the war,' he concluded. The next day, he said in his *Germany Calling* broadcast: 'Even in Britain, many people are praying that the Bolshevists will be beaten, for they realize that a Red victory would mean a communist dictatorship in the British Isles. In spite of the bitter war between Germany and Britain, the Führer is fighting the battle, not only of Europe, but also of the ordinary decent British people to whom communism would be worse than death.'

With the German attack Joyce regained some of his rubbery optimism and biblical self-righteousness. Indeed it put him in such a positive mood he was prepared not only to forgive and forget Margaret's adultery but also say sorry for his own behaviour. She noted in her diary: 'W saw me and apologised for his behaviour and said the whole thing his fault.' The next day, Nick told her he had extended his commission in the army. 'Awfully upset,' Margaret wrote. 'I stayed night with Nick but he would not sleep with me.' Two days later she added: 'Told Will I was quite definitely in love with Nick. Spent the night at Nick's. He softened enough to sleep with me.'

On 11 July, Lord Haw-Haw said: 'There must be in Britain very many people today – I know some – who realize that Hitler is doing a work which they have long known to be necessary. Britain was never more isolated than she is today; Germany never had so many friends. Whatever the dreary blunderer of Downing Street and the designing Hebrews of Wall Street may say, Europe as a whole will save herself from the Red Menace. Today the Red Front is being broken. Let Stalin look with his mind's eye on the blood-spattered faces of the priests and nuns whom his assassins tortured and murdered. These martyrs are being avenged, and the ideals for which they died shall live.'

The following night he became even more graphic: 'Before the Bolshevists fled from Lemberg [Lwów] they ran amok in a blood orgy. They murdered their victims wherever they could find them. Women and children were nailed to prison doors. Corpses were stuck through with bayonets. Two young Ukrainian girls had their stomachs slit open, and it was evident that they had been raped. Boiling water was poured over the bodies of men, and their skin was torn from them. This blood bath shows the methods by which the Bolshevists hoped to destroy European civilisation and culture.'

By sparing no details in his report, Joyce was clearly on a mission to turn the British against their new Soviet allies. It was also clear that his hatred of the Soviets was passionate and sincere and that he was taking a certain evangelical pride in his work. Yet on 19 July, Imperial Censorship, Bermuda, intercepted a curious piece of correspondence from 'Maurice', of Norfolk, Virginia, USA, to 'William Joyce in Berlin', which suggested that Lord Haw-Haw was becoming disillusioned with his German masters.

> *Thank you very much indeed for the remarkable photographs showing widespread damage of several sections of Berlin as the result of RAF bombing. They are far superior to some similar snapshots which I received from Ed Delaney many months ago. It is perhaps indiscreet to ask, but how in the world did you manage to get them past the censors?*
>
> *Your last letter was rather unusual in one respect: we feel that you are losing interest in your job in Germany and Martha is quite positive that you plan to leave there should you have the opportunity to do so. But for Heaven's sake man, where could you go? Martha is a genius at reading between the lines and, strangely enough, the information which she gleans there from invariably turns out to be*

*true, as you very well know. I am toying with the idea of joining up
with the British in whatever capacity they will have me. Send more
interesting pictures.*

The British Foreign Office was intrigued. What did the letter mean?
Was Joyce secretly working for the Allies? A Foreign Office memo set out
the possibilities. '1) It is a plant by Joyce to confuse our ideas about him.
2) an attempt by 'Maurice', at our instigation, to compromise Joyce with
the Germans or 3) it means that Joyce is thinking of emulating Hess. Very
odd.'*

Quite what the letter did mean is by no means clear, although the
second option seems the most likely. The Secret Service had many
divisions, some more accountable than others. It is possible that a maverick
intelligence officer was behind this particular operation to undermine Lord
Haw-Haw and he had simply neglected to brief the Foreign Office about
it.

Despite his lightened mood, William was still angry with Margaret,
though this did not stop him from seeing her on his days off for lunch at
the Funk-Eck and dinner at the Press Club. They had a new topic of
conversation, after all: their divorce. They had to be careful how they
went about it. The attitude of the Nazis to marriage and divorce was
strange. Hitler believed he was married to Germany. Goebbels had wanted
to divorce his wife Magda when he fell in love with the Czech actress
Lidia Baarova in 1936, but Hitler had forbidden him and, for a while, had
been annoyed with him for letting the Fatherland down. Martin Bormann's wife Gerda, on the other hand, believed that every German man
should have a mistress, which was why she was happy to openly share her
husband with his. A divorce was generally frowned upon. So when
William's lawyer filed for one on the grounds of Margaret's infidelity, and
Margaret's lawyers cross-petitioned on the grounds of William's alleged
mental cruelty, they tried to do so with the minimum of publicity. The
case was presented on 12 August 1941. Only eight people, including two
lawyers, were present. The judge reminded the Joyces of a Nonconformist
minister and Margaret drew a doodle of him on a page of her diary during

---

* Ed Delaney was Edward Leopold Delaney, an American broadcasting German propaganda
to America from Berlin. It is not clear who Maurice was.

the proceedings. She and William were drawn with their heads in their hands. Being something of a dreamer, her mind wandered in court and the judge had to ask her if she properly understood what she was doing. The divorce was granted, with each party being made to pay their own costs. The couple left the court accompanied by their two lawyers. They walked at an appropriate distance from each other along the corridors of the courtroom and down the steps. They then halted, turned slowly to one another, burst into tears and rushed into each other's arms. After this they had lunch, then, as was their habit, went for a long walk and ended up dining together in the evening. That night in her diary Margaret didn't write anything, she merely drew a picture of an exploding bomb. William went back to their flat, Margaret to Maja's flat.

After this, they played chess almost every afternoon, sitting outside one of the cafes in the Tiergarten. A few weeks later, the couple were strolling arm-in-arm through one of the squares in Berlin when an elderly man in a black homburg came walking towards them at a sedate pace, appearing not to notice the passers-by who stared at him. On his black overcoat was a yellow star. Joyce had never seen one of these badges before, though he had heard they were about to be introduced. The two passed within a yard of each other, the branded Jew appearing oblivious to the humiliation he was having to suffer on the order of the government. Joyce was stunned; disturbed by this confrontation with the reality of what he as an anti-Semite preached. With the sentimentality of the bully, he felt pity for the man, upset about having witnessed the unpleasant realization of his political ideal. The old man was a 'harmless' and dignified Jew, not some Fagin-like monster, or one of the plutocrats, capitalists or communists Joyce was wont to rail against. He watched him walk away, lost in his thoughts.

The debate over how much ordinary German citizens really knew about the Holocaust is academic, but Berliners were given some pretty unambiguous clues as to what was going on. After all, it took Goebbels just two years to declare Berlin *Judenfrei*, free of Jews, and this he proudly announced was his 'greatest political accomplishment'. The process began in October 1941 and, in the months that followed, some seventy thousand Jews were herded onto trains at Berlin's three stations, the Grunewald, Puttlitzstrasse and the Anhalter Bahnhof. Berliners, it was said, would turn away as the silent columns were marched through their streets to the stations. Rumours about where the Jews were really going were rife, not least because all the civil servants involved in the administration of the death camps worked in the government quarter of Berlin – from those involved in the procurement of Zyklon B to those who issued the one-way train tickets and organized the street auctions of Jewish property and goods that were 'no longer needed'. But if Berliners chose not to know what was happening, the Jews themselves did. In all, six thousand committed suicide in Berlin rather than face 'resettlement'. Some of the suicide stories made the news, so the Joyces would have heard them. One in particular shocked Berliners: when the Gestapo arrived to take away the Jewish wife and child of a famous Aryan film actor, Joachim Gottschalk, they found all three dead.

With Hitler's sudden and deep advances into Russia, meanwhile, came euphoria in Berlin. The CBS correspondent Harry Flannery noted: 'I listened to their conversation around the newsstands and on the subways. I talked with a number of them. They said: "Now we are fighting our real enemy."' The Soviet Embassy on Unter den Linden had been closed and a huge sign erected announcing that it was being fumigated. Loud-speakers were set up in squares so that Berliners could follow news of the victorious progress of the German army. Everyone would stand in silence as they listened. Waiters would stop serving. When a tinny rendition of 'Deutschland über Alles' signalled the end of the newsflash there would be a cheer. That month the papers reported 'THE GREAT HOUR HAS STRUCK!'. People hung wreaths of late-summer roses on German army vehicles that trundled through the city. Bookshops began stocking Russian dictionaries and phrase books in readiness for the occupation. The books would prove useful, but not until the end of the war.

Now that he was divorced, William could not intervene when his rival Nicky came home on leave. Margaret moved in with Nicky for a few weeks, the two of them staying in a villa which Nicky shared with a couple of his friends. William felt depressed. He missed his meals and chats with Margaret. He began drinking heavily, taking comfort especially in Steinhaeger, a Westphalian gin that came in an earthenware flask. An exotic taste in alcohol was something of a trademark for him. In London he had consumed excessive amounts of a cheap Spanish drink called Segovin. It made him more garrulous. Indeed, when guests came round and he began to hold forth on politics, Margaret would say William had become 'segovinned'. When not drowning his woes, he distracted himself by playing endless games of chess with a new friend of his, Subra Chandra Bose, the leader of Berlin's Indian community, who insisted on being addressed in public as 'Your Excellency'. The two men had treachery in common – Bose encouraged his followers to fight against the British Empire by joining a special Indian legion of the Wehrmacht.

When Nicky left for the Baltic again, Margaret wrote to him every day but never received a reply. After a few weeks she concluded that he had either been killed or found someone else. She too was now feeling depressed – and bored – and met William in a restaurant, surreptitiously, as though on a first date. Both seemed to enjoy the role-playing. Their relationship had disintegrated, yet at some level it had remained strong.

In the first months of the war, Lord Haw-Haw had repeatedly asked, 'Where is the *Ark Royal*?' It had almost become a catchphrase – the implication being that the aircraft carrier had been sunk. On 14 November, it really was sunk, leaving Joyce with a dilemma: to gloat or not to gloat? In the end he lamely said that he had never said the *Ark Royal* was sunk, he had merely asked where it was.

On 7 December 1941, the Japanese attacked Pearl Harbor. When, four days later, Germany and Italy declared war on the United States, Joyce assumed an air of studied nonchalance, but this was the news he had been privately dreading. In public, as Lord Haw-Haw, he said: 'The Japanese command has shown a splendid example of comprehensive modern strategy, and the troops have proved again that heroism for which the Japanese nation has been famed through the centuries. Roosevelt certainly wanted war with Japan, but it is very hard to believe that he wanted this kind of war. There is no doubt about the result. Germany, Italy and Japan as comrades in arms with the greatest military strength and the greatest resources in the world at their disposal fight on until victory is gained. The German advance into Russia will slow down because of the winter but the magnificent victories won by Germany and her allies have rendered the defeat of Bolshevism and its complete extermination quite inevitable. Meanwhile, the British island is being attacked both by air and by sea. The German blockade is being enforced with unremitting vigour, and the Luftwaffe is continuing its systematic bombardment of objects of military importance in Britain.' From his tone, it seemed that Joyce had succumbed to what he called 'German defeatism'. Not so much Blitzkrieg as long struggle.

It was coming up to Christmas again, the Joyces' third in Berlin, and the atmosphere, they noted, was becoming neurotic and dispirited. Rationing was beginning to take its toll. The Joyces' favourite restaurant at the Kaiserhof Hotel began the practice of issuing a menu with two meat dishes on it, when the kitchen could only serve one. In its all but empty bar, bottles of coloured water were put on display. One of the recurring themes of Margaret's talks, that Berlin housewives were spoilt for choice, was now dropped. That winter, she didn't mention that the shops in the German capital were nearly all empty apart from toy shops, where there were numerous cardboard games with names such as 'Bombs on England!'. Any tobacconist that managed to find adequate supplies had queues fifty yards long. To counter the shortage, the Propaganda Ministry began a press campaign warning Berliners about the dangers of smoking. This was followed by a decree banning *lokals*, or pubs, from selling cigarettes to women. Margaret made several references in her diaries to trying to give up, and these, tellingly, coincide with the campaigns.

When William Shirer had taken his leave of Berlin the previous year, he had told his successor Harry Flannery all about Joyce and added: 'I have a sneaking liking for the man.' Flannery soon admitted he, too, did not find Joyce 'unlikeable'. 'His broadcasts were witty at first,' he said, 'but sour later.' On New Year's Eve, Flannery found himself alone with William and Margaret, who were in mischievous mood: 'Lord and Lady Haw-Haw, when I came across them this evening at the radio station, asked me to join them in a bottle of champagne. He dodged under the roller shutters and went out on the balcony for a bottle. The radio was on. It brought the bells of Cologne Cathedral sounding the midnight hour, and then a Nazi radio band began the Horst Wessel song. Lady Haw-Haw stiffened her expression. She became tense, and her arm came up in a Nazi salute. Lord Haw-Haw came from under the shutters, noticed his wife, put down the bottle, clicked his heels together, and joined in the salute.'

They were drunk again, and about to get back together, again.

FOURTEEN

'The deed was done. 9.30'

As usual, January in Berlin brought heavy snow. The city seemed especially cold to Lord and Lady Haw-Haw because, despite their occasional drunken encounters, they were living separately, and still both feeling miserable and lonely. They no longer looked forward to their days off. William still loved Margaret and would sidle by her office to catch a glimpse of her, pretending he was looking for files. One day she wasn't at her desk and he was told she had been taken ill. He found out from the Funkhaus doctor that she had gastro-enteritis and dysentery and that she needed to take carbon tablets, if she could get them. It was a big if. The overworked doctor did not know of any supplies anywhere in Berlin and he clearly didn't think finding some should be his priority. William thought of a way of winning his ex-wife back. There were strings he could pull.

Margaret was in bed, feeling feverish. She had had no letters from Nicky and the doctor had been too busy to call. She hadn't even been able to see her girlfriends, because the nightly air raids and the blackouts had made journeys too hazardous. One afternoon she woke to find a cigar box on her bedside table. It contained carbon tablets, a red rose and a note from William. She was touched. She telephoned him. They arranged to meet. He was animated, funny and gentle. They agreed to meet again. And again. William seized the moment and, before she had chance to change her mind, asked her to marry him a second time. She accepted and wrote to Nicky to tell him the news.

Meanwhile, on 3 February 1942, Anthony Eden was asked a curious question in the House of Commons by a Conservative MP, Cmdr Locker-Lampson, on behalf of another Conservative MP, Mr Liddall. 'Is the Foreign Secretary aware that a person named William Joyce currently working for the German broadcasting authorities is in receipt of £10 a month from the British government?' Eden said he was not aware but that he did not believe this to be the case. The matter was not explored any further. It is not known whether Joyce, or Knight for that matter, heard about this question. Had a whistleblower working in a Whitehall accounts department noticed this anomaly and tipped off Mr Liddall? The question would hang in the air unanswered until it eventually faded from memory, though not from the pages of Hansard.

Whether Joyce knew about this question or not, he had more important domestic considerations on his mind. The curious second wedding ceremony of William and Margaret Joyce took place at the Charlottenburg register office on 11 February 1942, two days before the fifth anniversary of their first marriage, and six months after their divorce. 'THE DEED WAS DONE. 9.30', Margaret wrote in her diary. The capital letters were justified. It is not often a woman marries a man twice.

There was no time for a honeymoon because 14 February was the day the Japanese entered Singapore, a disaster for the British which meant the surrender of 138,000 troops. The island was considered a vital part of the British Empire and supposedly impregnable as a fortress. The British saw it as their Gibraltar in the Far East. Lord Haw-Haw was especially sarcastic that night: 'Japanese troops have entered the city of Singapore. And now we ask the British whether their government is capable of learning through experience. Of course, in England a man cannot be regarded as a serious politician until the first stages of arterial sclerosis have set in, by which time he may be described as a coming man. When senility has caused severe damage to the brain, he is a rising man, and when local mortification has begun, he is recognized as a success, fitted to receive the votes of confidence irrespective of circumstances. Under these conditions, it is not surprising that the British concept of war should be somewhat antiquated. But what must the British think when they learn that the city of Singapore has been entered by Japanese troops? In Norway, in the West, in the Balkans, Crete, North Africa, and in Russia the German Command has given proof of its mastery of a war as a science. The Japanese, too, have demonstrated their modern efficiency by the tremendous scope and rapidity of their success. Remember: they've entered Singapore.'

Three days after the wedding, Nicky telephoned Margaret and admonished her for her lack of faith. He told her he had been unable to reply to her earlier letters because he had been in action on the Eastern Front and had had to leave without giving her his new army post-office address. Nicky seems to have liked the idea of having a flame-haired Englishwoman as his Berlin mistress (there were rumours of another woman in the Baltic, and Margaret had also heard he had fathered a child, but not with his wife). Although he had claimed that he loved her, he had toyed with her affections, blowing hot and cold, and he had always been at his most amorous when drunk. As Margaret had noted in her diary one day: 'Nicky came round looking very well, but very drunk.' Her own passionate nature, meanwhile, fuelled by alcohol, had doomed the relationship almost from the start. She had quarrelled with Nicky almost as much as she had quarrelled with William. They had, as she put it, got in each other's hair.

Although Goebbels was in the habit of presenting Joyce with boxes of cigars, there was no wedding present from the Reich Minister. In fact he probably never knew that the Joyces had divorced, let alone remarried. Joyce could do little wrong in Goebbels' eyes. Indeed he said that month Joyce never made a 'single psychological error'. But this wasn't true. His talks caused as much resentment as fear or amusement. They left British audiences feeling angry and humiliated, and more willing to fight, especially when he referred to England as 'this doomed island' and the Home Guard as 'that guerrilla rabble' and to the much-loved Churchill as a 'cockney guttersnipe'. According to the Ministry of Information that spring: 'His Lordship's audience has shrunk to a fraction of its former size.' A good example of how his broadcasts backfired came that spring when Joyce may have made another of his contributions to the lexicon of the Second World War. Tobruk had been cut off by Rommel's Afrika Korps for a year and Haw-Haw, it was said, had taken to referring to the British Eighth Army troops trapped there as 'the rats of Tobruk': the legendary 7th Armoured Division adopted the name, calling themselves 'the Desert Rats'. *Germany Calling* seems to have been drawing in more listeners from the British army and perhaps that is why, in his diary on 23 May 1942, Goebbels wrote: 'Lord Haw-Haw is especially good at biting criticism,

but in my opinion the time for spicy debate is past. During the third year
of the war you must wage it quite differently from during the first year.'

After the RAF's first thousand-bomber raid, on Cologne at the end of
May 1942, listeners tuned in to *Germany Calling* gleefully hoping that 'for
once Haw-Haw would be at a loss.' Joyce's statement that the raid was
a reprisal for the big Russian defeat at Kharkov puzzled and perturbed
listeners, especially as at that stage the Red Army was winning at Kharkov. The Ministry of Information called it 'a clever twist'. A few weeks
later Rommel took Tobruk with thirty-five thousand Allied prisoners,
an event which the British Ministry of Information described as 'the
greatest single blow to public confidence since the fall of Singapore'. The
public's willingness to listen again to Haw-Haw was said to be due to
a growing readiness to consider the German news more reliable than
the BBC: 'We were told everything was all right at Tobruk, while the
enemy was announcing its fall.' According to the rumours, Haw-Haw
was once more 'promising visits'. The important industrial centres he promised a visit to that summer were Bargoed, Wellingborough, Biddington,
Penzance, Bexhill, Grimsby, Cleethorpes, Great Ashfield, Weybridge,
Somerton, Newton Poppleford, Hereford, Norwich and Torquay.

If Goebbels was having doubts about Haw-Haw's 'spicy' approach they
did not last for long because, the following month, Joyce was officially
promoted to Chief Commentator of the English Language Service, a post
he had held unofficially for some time. With the promotion came a four-
fold salary increase to 14,400 Reichsmarks a year, a Christmas bonus and
the right to three months' notice.

Margaret was also promoted to Commentator and Director of
Language (Sprachleiterin). Her daily salary was 25 Reichsmarks but she
received extra payments of 160 Reichsmarks for every talk and as she was
now sometimes broadcasting three times a week this meant she was
earning almost as much as her husband. Indeed, records show that in one
tax year, 1944, she earned 13,650 RM. For a couple of months she had
been working on a programme called *Join the Ladies*, which went out at
8.30 on Fridays. This was later changed to *Ladies First* and was brought
forward to 6.15. She also had a Saturday night talk which went out at
11 p.m. officially called *Remarks in Passing* but which she called 'Cow's
Corner'. She clearly took pride in her broadcasting career because in her
diary she always noted when Dietze had praised her talks and this would

be followed by the words 'ho ho!' or 'bloody cheerful'. When her boss told her that her programmes were 'very popular' in the United States, she made a note of this in her diary, in her own form of Pitman's shorthand, which suggests that her American broadcasts were supposed to be kept secret. The extent to which Dietze valued her contributions was shown one day when she rang to say that she had a cold and didn't think she could come in: he sent his company car to pick her up from her flat, wait for her and take her back home after her talk. A couple of her regular programmes were 'black propaganda' for the secret station, Büro Concordia, which she called Konk. One of the many ironies about the trial of Lord Haw-Haw and the non-trial of Lady Haw-Haw was that if their black-propaganda work had been known about there would have been little ambiguity about their treachery in the eyes of the law. As it was, Joyce was convicted largely on what he didn't say, that is on the white propaganda people thought he had said. His black propaganda was never mentioned at his trial.

MI5 had begun building its case against Margaret Joyce the previous summer. Two witnesses had been found to testify that hers was the voice of Lady Haw-Haw. In *Twilight over England*, it had been noted, Joyce wrote: 'It was through National Socialism that we met; and it was therefore only fitting that our decision to leave London for Germany on 25 August 1939 was a joint decision.' They had also contacted Carlisle City Police, who had questioned a number of Margaret's former colleagues and had taken a statement from Donald Nicholson, her boss at Sundour Fabrics. He had first heard her broadcasting in November 1939. 'I was amazed to hear Margot White's voice,' he said. 'She praised the German methods and suggested that the sooner Germany took over control of Britain the better for the backward Britons. I reported this to the Carlisle police. I did not then know that William Joyce was Lord Haw-Haw and I did not know that the man speaking before her was Joyce. I just thought she had worked her way on to the German radio through her own initiative. What I heard was quite sufficient to make her a traitor. If necessary I shall be only too pleased to go south or anywhere to help identify her and that speech.'

In June 1942, as a further reward for their work, Lord and Lady Haw-Haw were offered a holiday abroad and were given a choice between Turkey, Portugal or Norway. As William had long been fascinated with

Nordic sagas he argued the case for Norway and Margaret went along
with it. He was flown to Oslo on a military plane carrying occupation
officials. The plan was for Margaret to follow. But first, in keeping with
her celebrity status, she had a swimwear photo-shoot at the Olympiastadion to do. Like Eva Braun, Margaret enjoyed cavorting around in her
swimsuit for the benefit of the cameras – perhaps, in part, because both
aspired to some health and fitness ideal of German womanhood. Margaret's
poses included swinging balletically from a pole, sunbathing and sitting
coquettishly on stone steps, showing off her long legs. Lady Haw-Haw
was photogenic and she knew it. The photographs done, she travelled by
train and ferry to meet William. From Oslo they drove north to stay in a
hotel reserved for Quisling, the Minister President of the State Council of
Norway, and his guests. The food was good and plentiful, a welcome
relief after the rationing of Berlin. They spent their time walking in the
countryside, gathering wild flowers, breathing deep the clean air. One
valley proved a favourite and the Joyces befriended a young farmer they
met there every day. When Joyce revealed his identity to him the young
man said: 'You'll be hanged if they get you.'

'I know,' Joyce replied. 'It doesn't matter.'

Joyce seems to have developed a death wish around this time, or at
least he became resigned to his fate, and indifferent to danger. He seems
to have felt especially that it would be poetic justice if he were to die
during a British bombing raid. Bombardier Francis Maton of the Royal
Artillery, a colleague from the Funkhaus, recalled in a statement: 'Joyce
showed courage during some of the worst raids and when most of us were
shivering down in air-raid shelters he stood alone recording his broadcasts.'
Madeleine Stuart, a German married to the Irish writer and broadcaster
Francis Stuart, confirmed this strange habit: 'I saw what a courageous man
he was,' she wrote in her memoirs. 'When one night there was a heavy
bomber attack everybody fled to the air-raid shelter. But he had remained
in the office, gone to the window and looked out at the sky with the
bombs falling in the distance. I stayed with him, after he had assured me
that the bombers did not, as yet, drop their bombs over residential districts,
but concentrated on the industrial surroundings of Berlin.'

His indifference to death may have been linked to his chaotic feelings
for Margaret. Having sworn she would be faithful to him, she now calmly
announced that she had been writing to Nicky again. He hadn't replied

but the comment had the desired effect. It goaded William. On 8 October 1942, after yet another row, they decided to get divorced for a second time. 'We shall get divorced but be friends,' Margaret noted matter-of-factly in her diary. They seem not to have got round to it this time because of pressures at work. Every time a large number of British troops was captured, listener figures for *Germany Calling* went up. Anxious families hoped that Haw-Haw would give out the names of servicemen taken prisoner. In August 1942 the postal-censorship authorities intercepted a letter which typified the attitude: 'What do you think of Richard's name coming over the wireless from a German station last Monday? So he's a prisoner! Haw-Haw gives six names every night, quite a few heard it.'

Having partially seen off a rival at home, Joyce now found himself with one at work: John Amery, the dissolute and delinquent thirty-year-old son of the distinguished statesman Leopold Amery, the Secretary of State for India and Burma. He had been an embarrassment to his father since childhood, having been rebellious at Harrow, and a bankrupt by the age of twenty-five. He had made countless appearances in magistrates' courts and had become a reckless playboy, a bisexual one at that. When war broke out, Amery decided to throw in his cap with the Axis powers, but ended up drifting around Spain and France singing the praises of fascism to anyone who would listen. In the autumn of 1942, the Nazis finally heard him and an SS officer was despatched to bring him and a French woman, who may or may not have been his wife, to Berlin. There he was received as a glittering trophy by Dr Hesse, who had been Ribbentrop's radio adviser and was now on Hitler's personal staff. Amery soon became the most petted and best-advertised English propagandist at the Funkhaus. Great trouble was taken to draw the world's attention to his weekly broadcasts, which were repeated several times in an evening. He was given luxurious hotel accommodation and a generous expense account. He was also photographed and filmed as if he were a Hollywood star.

Joyce's nose, broken in childhood, was severely put out of joint, especially when Amery began blithely telling his station bosses that Joyce's propaganda was backfiring in England because it was too hostile. Joyce should have been trying to win the British over, he argued. The criticism stung, not least because it was so obviously reasonable. It also rankled because it came from the sort of decadent British fop Joyce had always felt contempt for. John Amery had been heir to many advantages in life and had squandered them all. As for Joyce's intellectual superiority over the dim-witted Amery, that must have really jarred.

As it turned out, it was Amery's broadcasts which backfired. He was known to every British newspaper reader as the difficult child of noble and long-suffering parents. When they heard his broadcasts, English listeners merely felt sorry for his family. They also felt vindicated in their belief that there were no depths which the caddish Germans would not plumb.*

There was another upward surge in the listening figures that autumn, but not because of Amery. Schadenfreude had became the new reason to tune in to *Germany Calling*. On 23 October, Montgomery launched the Third Battle of El Alamein with a ferocious thousand-gun artillery bombardment. Rommel, the Desert Fox, was on the run. On 10 November Churchill said: 'This is not the end. It is not even the beginning of the end. But it is, perhaps, the end of the beginning.' Two days later, as the Eighth Army re-took Tobruk, the British public listened 'for the pleasure of hearing excuses being made for Axis reverses in Russia and Africa.' These reverses, it was agreed, had 'curbed Lord Haw-Haw's arrogant, self-confident tone.' No wonder the clamour for vengeance against the traitor Lord Haw-Haw was so great at the end of the war. For those sitting at home, following the war on their wireless sets, Haw-Haw personified the enemy.

William Joyce soon reasserted his dominance of the English-language station, and Amery lost interest in his broadcasting career, having become excited by his new project: recruiting British prisoners of war for the British Legion of St George, a Waffen-SS formation that was being created. The idea was that British PoWs would join Germany in the fight against Soviet communism but would not be deployed against British forces. Amery was often booed when he went around the prison camps and only managed to recruit two or three soldiers to his cause, which didn't exactly constitute a regiment. The scheme, whilst having some

---

* Amery was arrested by Italian partisans in April 1945 while driving between Milan and Como and was handed over to Captain Alan Whicker of the Army Photographic and Film Unit – who became later a television personality.

propaganda value, eventually fizzled out and the recruits proved to be more of a burden to the German authorities than they were an asset. They were hopelessly ill-disciplined, for one thing, spending all their time either lazing around barracks, getting drunk or chasing women.

Margaret's talks were no longer making much of an impression either. In one she attempted to address the social conditions in Britain seriously, but ended up sounding trite and hyperbolic: 'The condition of the poor in England is worse than ever before . . . Can it be worse when an old woman, scarcely able to stand, must go around picking up bits of rubbish in order to make herself a meal? Can it be worse than when children can't go to school on a wet day because they have no shoes? Can it be worse when more than eighteen millions are undernourished?'

If there was any doubt remaining as to the true identity of Lady Haw-Haw it was dispelled on 9 December 1942. From that date on, Margaret was announced as 'Margaret Joyce, otherwise known as Lady Haw-Haw'. She seemed content with this and the change may even have been at her behest. Risking exposure as a traitor may have suited her reckless character. It might also have come about because – always a heavy drinker – she was now drinking far too much. As she noted in her diary on 18 January 1943: 'William has never seen me so tight.' William seems to have resigned himself to her infidelity because, two weeks later, he told her she could write to Nicky whenever she liked.

The beginning of the end followed the end of the beginning more quickly than Churchill had anticipated. On 2 February 1943, the German Sixth Army surrendered at Stalingrad, after a five-month battle that had cost the lives of more than 800,000 Germans and 1.3 million Soviets. The 91,000 Germans taken prisoner were starving, frozen and broken. Only about 4,500 survived captivity. The dread news of the defeat was heralded on German state radio by Beethoven's Fifth Symphony. It was followed by three days of solemn music. From a propaganda point of view, Hitler had put Joyce in an awkward position because he had repeatedly insisted that surrender at Stalingrad was unthinkable. The talk Lord Haw-Haw gave that night was an exercise in wishful thinking and denial. 'It would be a profound, cardinal error to suppose that the German nation does not know how to take one defeat after so many victories. Nor, if the truth must be told, am I convinced that Stalingrad was, in the worst sense of the word, in the most essential, in the psychological sense, a defeat. Let us look at the facts. I think it was Napoleon who said, "In warfare the moral is to the physical as three to one". So far as divisions, brigades and battalions are concerned, Stalingrad was a German defeat. But when a great power like the National Socialist Reich is waging a total war, divisions and battalions can be replaced. If we review the position in sober and cold calculations, all sentiment apart, we must realize that the fall of Stalingrad cannot impair the German defensive system as a whole. Whatever individuals have lost, whatever they may have sacrificed, there is nothing in the position as a whole to controvert the view that the main objectives of the enemy offensives have been frustrated. Stalingrad was a part of the price which had to be paid for the salvation of Europe from the Bolshevik hordes.'

More psychologically damaging Axis defeats were to follow, at Tunis and Kursk. In May came the Dambusters' Raid. In June the Allied Combined Bombing Offensive over Germany began, with the Americans bombing by day and the British by night. Margaret embarked on a new affair that summer with a German called Rictor. It followed the usual pattern. They met regularly for drinks. They had furtive lunches. They rowed. They broke up on 26 July 1943, after just two months.

Joyce was too distracted to notice: the fall of Mussolini was reported that day. In his Haw-Haw talk that night he waxed both nostalgic and sentimental. 'When I joined the first fascist movement in Britain on 6 December 1923, I saw that night in Battersea the mob violence, the broken heads and the broken bodies, the typical evidence of the disruption which communism can bring to a nation, and while I heard the dismal wail of the Red Flag intoned by the sub-men out for blood, I thought of Mussolini and of what he had been able to do for Italy. I was not pro-Italian, I was merely pro-human. There were many millions of people throughout the world at about that time who had the same thoughts, and when I looked back on these twenty years I can only say that Mussolini has, in that period, become one of the greatest figures in history.'

The next day, he found out about Margaret's latest affair. In her diary that night she wrote: 'Lunch alone at Raband. W spoken to R. Very miserable, damn it . . . Will said it was too late for me to become a whore!'

In August 1943, a week before 'Bomber' Harris launched his heaviest bombing raid on Berlin to date, RAF planes dropped leaflets on the city calling for all women and children to leave. Notices went up on every house ordering the evacuation of all children and non-essential women workers. A million were evacuated. Unfortunately for Margaret, she was deemed an essential worker. However, the staff of the Reichsrundfunk were also soon made to leave, relocating to Radio Luxembourg for a few weeks. Berlin was deemed the 'heart of the Nazi monster' and it became the ambition of Allied bomber crews to fly 'the Big B'. Bomber Harris told his crews: 'Tonight you go to the Big City. You have an opportunity to light a fire in the belly of the enemy and burn his black heart out.' Berlin did burn, but not as badly as Hamburg which, because of its narrower streets and wooden houses, became an inferno.

In his talks from Luxembourg, William dropped his usual tone of sarcasm in favour of a more measured and philosophical one. Perhaps it was the influence of the subtle and cultivated Eduard Dietze. That month, Dietze presented him with a *Punch* cartoon of Lord Haw-Haw. On it he wrote: 'From Mephistopheles to Faust – with best wishes Dietze.' Perhaps Dietze had been brooding upon John Amery's argument that Joyce should be more conciliatory. Whatever the reason for the change, Joyce's talks came to reflect his own psychological contours. They also became more autobiographical and spontaneous. It was noted by one of his colleagues at the Funkhaus that he was now in the habit of listening to the news and walking straight over to the microphone to record his talks without making any notes. His reminiscences on 9 September, following the Italian armistice, are a good example of his change of style. Here is his talk in full. (Just as he always referred to Angus Macnab by his first name John, so he always referred to Eduard Dietze by his middle name, Roderick.)

'It will scarcely be a surprise to you if I devote this evening's "Views on the News" almost entirely to the developments which have taken place in Italy and which have no doubt constituted a world sensation. Last night at this time a preliminary review of the situation was given by Roderick Dietze, who brought the day's events into focus and at the same time related the treachery of Badoglio★ to the broader and wider conspiracy to make a Bolshevik hell of Europe. I was especially impressed by his reminder that, after the Duce had been betrayed, red flags appeared in the streets of many Italian cities. This evening I am not pretending to review

★ Marshal Badoglio's government had surrendered unconditionally on 3 September.

the Italian situation as a whole in a purely and chronologically objective manner. It is an occasion when I may be permitted to record some personal observations and impressions. Since as long ago as 1923 I belonged to the first fascist movement in Britain, and then, as subsequently, regarded Benito Mussolini as one of the greatest men, not only of our century, but of our age. When Roderick Dietze mentioned the appearance of the red flag on the streets of Italian cities, I thought: "Yes, and it was in answer to this challenge of the bestial underworld that Mussolini first arose to save his country."

'I did not for one single moment believe that a great energising phenomenon like fascism which has breathed new life into Europe, which bears the character of a creed for the ages, could be simply snuffed out by a couple of shifty old men, surrounded by jackals and parasites, who had consistently conspired against the front-line fighters. It did not seem compatible with the nature of historical development that this successful revolution should be abruptly undone by a handful of senile intriguers who had long shown the marks of subornation and moral decrepitude, and now I am more than gratified, more than satisfied to see that the Italian people have spontaneously formed a national and fascist Government to vindicate their honour and pursue the fight for their rights.

'Perhaps some of the malevolently minded commentators in the BBC who, to judge by their remarks, listen to my broadcasts with close attention, might have expected me to show some sign today of embarrassment, or even depression. Well in that case they must be deeply disappointed. On 22 June 1941 when the Führer drew the sword [an echo of the archaic phrase Joyce used about himself in his OTC application in 1922] in Europe's defence against the Bolshevik colossus, I felt, like all National Socialists, that history was taking its rightful course and the hand of providence was guiding the German nation. Today again I know that history is taking its rightful course, now that the fascist banners have again been raised, now that patriotic Italians have taken up the torch that Badoglio and the recreant relic Savoy tried to extinguish. What matters most is that the dynamic urge of Europe to live in the light of her new faith should be strengthened and perpetuated. Like the phoenix from the ashes, Italy has risen again, and whatever she may suffer, whatever trials may beset her on the road to victory, she has now once more recovered the spirit of ancient Rome and, come weal or woe, she has inscribed on her standards the Latin word Resurgam – I shall rise again.

'Eisenhower has done all the boasting necessary and far more. Now I expect it will be left to the British to bear the brunt of the fighting. And henceforth they will be facing serried ranks of resolute soldiers, without one traitor behind the lines, without a single venal creature to sell the passes. To that extent our enemies are the poorer. Perhaps it seemed a brilliant and cunning thing to contrive the downfall of a great patriot like Mussolini and substitute for his government, for his indomitable leadership, a quivering mass of unwholesome blubber interspersed with ancient bones. But such a thing could not live. It could not survive. It has perished. And now Germany and Italy can go in to battle again, comrades in arms, to defend the sacred cause of the Europe revolution. And once more the soldiers of both nations know that they have the common purpose to wage the struggle against vested powers, Red front, and massed ranks of reaction, the fight for freedom and for bread. It is well indeed that the canker has been removed. Badoglio has surrendered, and the Axis lives again.'

It wasn't just the BBC listening in to his broadcasts 'with close attention'. That month MI5 had stepped up its operation to gather evidence against William and Margaret Joyce, having already put both their names on a passport Black List. They had by then transcribed a number of their talks but now they wanted to make sure that they had some that could be proved authentic in court. Lord Haw-Haw, of course, was the priority. MI5 was determined that he should hang, perhaps out of fear that he might talk about his association with it. There was some concern, however, that the wording of the existing Treason Act could not be stretched to include Joyce's circumstances. 'The words of the Act are somewhat limited,' E. H. Tindal Atkinson wrote in an MI5 memorandum. 'I find it difficult to apply them to the kind of propaganda put out by Joyce.' Nevertheless he would have to try, and seven Special Branch and MI5 officers were duly despatched to record solemnly examples of the Haw-Haw broadcasts at a cost of £5 a record. When a recording was completed the party adjourned to another room where the records were played back and a Special Branch officer transcribed them in his notebook. Everyone present then had to write their names with 'a sharp instrument' on a central part of the record. The records were then dated, placed in cardboard containers and fastened together with tape. The tape was sealed and an MI5 officer, T. M. Shelford, impressed his signet ring on the sealing wax.

Two years had now passed since William and Margaret had divorced, and eighteen months since they remarried. Yet still their relationship was rackety. When they drank they enjoyed each other's company, but when sober Margaret felt bored and patronized because William treated her like 'a half-wit'. She had taken a new lover, Bob. He seems to have been a friend of Nicky, because, according to Margaret's diary that month, he told Nicky that he had fallen in love with her. William seems to have known about Bob, too, because Sammy Hetzler, their boss at the Büro Concordia, told him. As Margaret noted: 'Will told me Hetzler complained about me and Bob.' Her heart wasn't in this new affair anyway, at least not since Nicky had started replying to her letters. When he came home on leave and called in on her, they resumed their affair straight away. One evening while Joyce was typing up a talk, Margaret walked into the flat and announced: 'I'm going.'

'Nicky?' William asked quietly.

Margaret nodded.

'Oh.'

As she left she heard the sound of typing.

Perhaps William felt too fatigued to care. His hair was thinning, he was pallid and, having chosen not to request the extra food rations which, given his status, he would have been granted, he was losing weight. He did accept a special allowance of cigarettes and schnapps, however, which he said he needed to work. But this didn't help his health. His only extravagances were the books he bought, a navy blue suit he had made, and the occasional use of a chauffeur-driven car. Around this time he seems to have realized what an austere life he was leading. It may have dawned on him, too, that, since his wife walked out on him for the second time, he was technically single. He was also famous, and the Funkhaus was full of impressionable young women. His first affair was with a German colleague called Mita. Margaret must have been jealous about this because, when she heard, she wrote in her diary: 'Will, the little beast, is in love with Mita.'

After truth, of course, fidelity is the second casualty of war. And adultery in the Berlin of 1943 was not about sex so much as death. With bombs falling randomly around them every night, 'carpe diem' became the abiding principle.

In early October, William went to Luxembourg for a few days with Greta, the wife of a Finnish diplomat. Greta tended to turn heads around Charlottenburg – the nineteen-year-old James Clark described her as 'the first sexually powerful female I ever saw'. Joyce went further: according to his diary she was 'a blonde goddess' and 'unforgettable'. But not that unforgettable. Back in Berlin, Margaret turned up unexpectedly at the flat and caught William with a Funkhaus secretary, Gueta-Lisa, in flagrante delicto. Margaret and Gueta-Lisa eyed each other coolly. William, for once, was tongue-tied and embarrassed.

Nicky, meanwhile, had gone back to the Eastern Front and his parting words to Margaret were that they couldn't marry because she wasn't a German. As she had taken German citizenship this seems to have been a lame excuse. Margaret moved back in with William and not only resumed her conjugal duties in the bedroom but, as she recorded in her diary, also did his washing and made his breakfast every morning.

On 12 October 1943, Italy declared war on Germany. The following month, Sir Oswald and Lady Mosley were released after three years of internment. Outside the main gate of their prison there was a crowd of reporters and photographers. Communists organized protest marches. Bernard Shaw, when asked whether he thought it dangerous to allow Mosley out, said: 'I think this Mosley panic shameful. Even if Mosley were in rude health, it was high time to release him with apologies for having let him frighten us into scrapping the Habeas Corpus Act. Mr Morrison [Herbert Morrison, the Home Secretary] has not justified the outrageous conditions – the gag in Mosley's mouth and the seven-mile leg-iron. We are still afraid to let Mosley defend himself and have produced the ridiculous situation in which we may buy Hitler's *Mein Kampf* in any bookshop in Britain, but may not buy ten lines written by Mosley.'*

Joyce made no comment on the release of his old leader. He was too

---

* Upon his release Mosley disappeared to his country retreat and kept a low profile for the rest of the war. He returned to British politics in the Sixties when he campaigned for his own 'Union Movement', whose members would later join the National Front. After that he and Diana moved to France, where they enjoyed a close friendship with the Duke and Duchess of Windsor. Sir Oswald died in 1980, Lady Mosley in 2003.

preoccupied with the magnanimity of his new one. 'In the speech which
the Führer delivered yesterday there was one characteristic which dominated: the note of calm and complete confidence in victory, based not
only on feeling and faith, but upon reason; upon the knowledge that
Germany has in her hands the means of winning this war; that the raw
materials at her disposal are sufficient for the purpose; that her food
supplies are assured; and that, as the Führer said, wherever the battle front
might be, Germany would always parry every thrust and go over to the
offensive. No doubt the press and radio, secure in the knowledge that the
vast majority of their public understand no German, have given quite a
different impression of the speech, in accordance with their established
custom. But every German who listened to the Führer yesterday must
have realized more clearly than ever what immense reserves of strength his
country possesses, and what singleness of purpose actuates its leaders.'

With his mind on such higher themes, William failed to notice that
Margaret's rekindled affair with Nicky had ended in a row. Nicky declared
that he was a fool for falling in love with her and left Berlin. This time, he
would not return – not least because, three months later, he married
another woman, a Fräulein Kutz. Margaret found out about this from an
announcement in a newspaper. 'Nikolaus von Besack – Ellen von Besack
geb kutz. Zur zeit im felde / berlin w15 Kurfürstendamm 43.' She cut it
out and stuck it in her diary.

The jilted and heartbroken Margaret seems to have spread her sexual
favours freely around Berlin as a consequence. Bombardier Francis Maton,
a British renegade working at the Funkhaus, remembered Margaret as 'a
rather fast woman who had affairs in Berlin with a large number of men.'
This was perhaps an exaggeration but there are records of liaisons with a
Spaniard, Pablo, a Frenchman, Jean, and an Englishman, Eric. Indeed Eric
Pleasants, who was a member of the British Free Corps, claimed in his
memoirs that he seduced Margaret at the Funkhaus while William was on
air.

When not being seduced or doing the seducing Margaret lunched with
Dorothy Eckersley and played pontoon with Susan Hilton. Inevitably,
though, she soon grew bored and drifted back to Joyce who, whatever his
faults, was rarely boring. Equally inevitably, he took her back. As their
colleague James Clark noted: 'They had majestic rows, majestic sulks and
even more majestic reconciliations. They were passionate people.'

The reconciliation followed a heavy raid. By this stage of the war some 300,000 German civilians had been killed in raids, compared to 45,000 in Britain.* Most of the losses had been in Cologne, Hamburg and Berlin. Howling sirens and the bark of anti-aircraft guns could be heard every night and often during the day, too, as wave after wave of Allied bombers droned over Berlin. Phosphorous bombs caused hurricane-like winds and the city was permanently enveloped in a cloud of smoke and ash. And the bombs had been falling ever closer to the Funkhaus. One wintry night an explosion rocked the very foundations of the building. Joyce, as usual, had refused to go the shelter and was standing in the control room when a second blast knocked him off his feet. Many of the windows were smashed and the building filled with choking dust. A few days later, a crowd formed around the tail of a Lancaster bomber that had crashed nearby, one of more than a thousand to be brought down during the Battle of Berlin. The body of an air-gunner was pulled out and taken away on a stretcher. After such close calls, it was decided that the netting that covered the Funkhaus should be extended several hundred yards to cover the giant transmitter, too. On top of the building a mock-up of a farm was assembled, complete with dummies of cattle and sheep to fool reconnaissance planes.

William had taken to wearing a long trench coat and carrying a walking stick, and one night, looking like a Raymond Chandler detective, he tracked Margaret down to an air-raid shelter near the Funkhaus and said: 'It's time you moved back home, Meg. I'm sick of having to come to your place to see you are safe. We can talk about Nicky after the war when there is time.'

* The final figure would be 75,000 Germans compared to 60,595 British.

FIFTEEN

'Excellent day. Plenty to drink.'

The following spring, white vapour trails from warring aircraft became a common sight in the sky over Berlin. Round-the-clock saturation bombing was making normal life in the capital almost impossible. On 6 March 1944, US Eighth Air Force bombers made their first large-scale daylight raids on the city and lost one in ten of their aircraft. Two days later they were back with 1,800 bombers escorted by 1,000 long-range fighters. In desperation, the Germans resorted to deploying training aircraft to try to stop the armada. Goebbels made matters worse for the already traumatized Berliners by exaggerating reports of the damage in the hope of convincing the Allies that there were now no longer any worthwhile targets left to bomb in Berlin.

Nevertheless, the thousand-bomber 'terror raids' on Berlin continued, with more bombs being dropped on the city than on England during the entire war. Berlin had become an eerie place, dark and twitchy, the only light at night coming from the red lamps waved by air-raid wardens. The carpet bombing had left entire areas flat. There were no Jews, few women and children, and, by that spring, one and half million homeless people. The Gestapo, meanwhile, had created a climate of suspicion, fear and paranoia which had paralysed the city and made it almost impossible to organize resistance.

In London at this time the legal advice of the Attorney-General, Sir Donald Somerville, was being sought regarding the prosecution of William and Margaret Joyce. It was not what MI5 wanted to hear: 'I am of the opinion that the act of broadcasting is not an offence under section 1 of the Treason Act,' he declared. 'I am satisfied that reading out a broadcast is an act, but am of the opinion that the words here used, although of course they might affect morale, are not likely to give assistance to the naval, military or air operations of the enemy.' MI5 would have to come up with something better, assuming, that is, that the Joyces survived the war, an outcome that with the bombing of Berlin was looking increasingly unlikely.

Although a row of buildings was destroyed near the Funkhaus, the broadcasting house itself remained unscathed and Lord and Lady Haw-Haw, both deriving courage from the schnapps bottle, continued trying to put a brave public face on the way the war was being prosecuted. Lady Haw-Haw's talks had become less feminine. One that spring compared supposed unemployment in England with full employment in Germany: 'This is one of the problems the Allied nations are facing,' she said in her crisp voice. 'The former Chancellor of the Exchequer, the late Sir Kingsley Wood, said early last year that the establishment of full employment would be one of the first tasks after the war. The *Times* of September 1938, in speaking of the German system, asked how it would be possible to keep pace with a nation which had found a way to give full employment and to maintain it, as Germany had . . . When you think this over you may realize that that is one of the reasons why so many English people who longed to see this problem of distribution and employment solved among their own people were distressed to see the situation in Germany being so misrepresented in England. They wanted to join on with a country which had shown so much wisdom and care to its own people . . . The more they realize this, the more they are saying: "What on earth is this war being fought about?" '

Dietze was concerned that she was becoming too politicized and asked her to revert to social and domestic issues. This she duly did in her new programme, *End of the Weekend*. One talk she gave on Mother's Day was, unknown to her, monitored and recorded for posterity by MI5 in London. It is possible that because she had by then decided that she wanted to have a baby, the theme of motherhood was foremost in her mind.

'Today [14 May] is Mother's Day in Germany. Mysterious little parcels prove to be presents made secretly and with difficulty. Flower shops are ransacked for bouquets, and now it has even more significance because, under National Socialism, mothers have taken their place in the national scheme, and it is not just a matter of chance whether or not they are looked after: it is recognized that the wife and mother has as much to offer the state as the skilled artisan, or the professional man, and she is treated accordingly – even now in war time. Therefore, I think, today is a good time to discuss a problem which came up recently when the BBC News Service reported that demands had been made that more consideration should be paid to mothers employed in Britain. The demands, by the way, were made by delegates of the Conference of Women Engineers. Allowances were asked for: more free time for shopping, and household duties, women welfare workers for all factories, and, for expectant mothers, a law freeing them eight weeks before the birth of their child, and six weeks' holiday afterwards. In Germany every housewife who works – and women with children under fourteen only work if they want to – gets an extra half day a week in order to do her shopping. Britain's politicians often claim they are fighting for civilization and progress, and to improve conditions. Yet, even in the fundamental social measures which they should be taking to protect their women workers, and their mothers, they have failed.'

Not surprisingly, *Germany Calling* offered only partial coverage of D-Day, highlighting the setbacks, such as the heavy American casualties on Omaha Beach, and playing down the successes. By having commentators speak against a soundtrack of explosions and bullets, the 'war correspondents' in Berlin tried to give the impression they were talking live from the scene. Joyce produced three scripts that day. 'It is no longer necessary for me to observe that restraint which was until today requisite in discussing German withdrawals in Russia and Italy, for now their underlying cause is manifest,' he bluffed. 'The place and time of the invasion could not be better from the German point of view. I beg you not to forget that this holocaust was organized at Stalin's request' – Stalin had been lobbying Churchill and Roosevelt to open a second front against the Germans to ease the pressure the Red Army was under in the East.

Joyce tried to put a positive spin on the Normandy landings but the best he could come up with was the fact that *Germany Calling* had scooped the BBC in reporting them. On 7 June, he declared: 'On the first day of the invasion, on D-Day in fact, the world, including Britain, had to accept the reports issued by the German authorities as the sole criterion of events. Not only in neutral capitals, but even in London, the dominant question was "what is the latest information by the German radio?" Naturally it must be allowed that the German Supreme Command is in a superior position with regard to the appreciation of the military situation on the Normandy coast. The defences have been systematically prepared for more than three years. The German commanders have perfected their knowledge of the country and have organized their communications with the thoroughness which the enemy sometimes likes to describe as Prussian. In dealing with the German Supreme Command, Mr Churchill is not dealing with a class of junior field officers at Camberley, or with American generals whose experience is compounded of memories from the last war and reminiscences of the exploits of Buffalo Bill . . . On the whole, I can assure you that Germany's military position is now better than it has been for some time. The enemy in the West has been so obliging as to select the very ground upon which the German Command desired the decisive battle to be fought. Not all at once, not in every skirmish, will the accumulated strength of the German reserves manifest itself. When in due course the campaign can be assessed on the basis of established fact, the optimism which Churchill nurtured amongst his people will sink into ashes and dust. Before us lies a period in which many riddles will be solved and in which much that has been obscure will become clear.'

But not that clear. Joyce had not realized that the BBC's failure to report the D-Day landings first had been deliberate. It was playing the invasion down as part of a series of deception plans to make Hitler think the real offensives were to be in the South of France, Biscay, the Balkans, Norway and the Pas de Calais. As usual Joyce's tone of lofty magnanimity masked the grubby view he held in private that, really, it was the Jews who were to blame. This sentiment manifested itself in a piece of doggerel he penned at the time.

Oh, D-Day was a great day in the history of the world,
When the Allied flags of freedom were so bloodily unfurled.
The boys who did the fighting were engulfed in Hell on earth,
While the Jews at home delighting watched their stocks increase in worth.

Oh, D-Day was a grand day on the good old Stock Exchange,
For the paratroops of pockets, well outside the German range.
Like the vultures, they descended on the battlefield of gain;
By the time the day had ended, they'd made sure 'twas not in vain.

Oh, D-Day was a great day, when they gathered up the loot,
These money-grubbing Hebrews who'd never launched a 'chute'
While England's lads were dying amidst the hellish roar
And their heroes' blood was drying on the fatal Norman shore.

For some weeks, Haw-Haw had been dropping chilling hints about a 'secret weapon'. The V-1 flying bomb, better known as the doodlebug, was launched a week later. 'London and southern England have now been under bombardment for more than a week,' he said in a broadcast to mark the occasion. 'For nine days, with very little interruption, the V-1 projectiles have been descending on the British capital. May I remind you, the name V-1 has been given to them officially. "V" is the capital letter of the German word "Vergeltung", which means "retaliation", and its use to denote the concept of victory must be familiar to nearly all of my listeners. The very term V-1 implies, of course, that Germany has other new weapons which have not as yet been employed against the enemy. That is a fact, and is a fact which even the British government is beginning to realize.

'The emergence of V-1 has provided a surprise for Germany's enemies and I believe they will have several other surprises "before the autumn leaves fall", if I may borrow a phrase which Mr Churchill used on a certain occasion. Germany's military policy in this war is based not on slogging and on squandering but upon a scientific economy and application of energy, but this is the kind of policy the details of which must never be disclosed before the right time. It can reasonably be assumed that the battle in the East against the Bolshevik foes of civilization will be hard and fierce and there is every reason to believe that the battle in the West against the capitalist agents of Jewish international finance will attain a climax of violence possibly without precedence. But in the closing rounds of this war it will be seen that Germany has conserved her strength to a degree that will confound her enemies.'

On 20 July, an attempt was made to assassinate Hitler. Joyce, on one of his rare days off, was sitting in the Press Club having lunch with Margaret when he heard the news, or rather when everyone in the room began chattering anxiously. He tried to leave the club to get to the Funkhaus to find out whether the rumours were true, but, ominously, soldiers with fixed bayonets had arrived and were ordering everyone back inside. The government quarter had been cordoned off. When he and Margaret persuaded the guards that they were needed at the Funkhaus, they returned to their flat. Joyce collected his revolver and set off alone for the radio station. It was bristling with field-grey-uniformed guards. Machine-guns were mounted in the windows. For several hours there was no confirmation that Hitler was alive.

Once news of the Führer's survival was broadcast, Joyce adopted a manner of aloof contempt for the Germans who had 'flapped'. 'They've gone nervy,' he observed to his wife. When surrounded by 'excitable foreigners', they both liked to play up to a very English image they had of themselves as being unflappable.

That evening, Joyce returned to the club and was sitting on a high stool at the bar when he was joined by Charles Bewley, an Irishman who had been a diplomat in Berlin before the war and had stayed on to work as a journalist. Bewley introduced himself.

'I'm delighted to meet an Irishman,' Joyce said warmly. 'It's a long time since I did.'

'I wonder we never met before,' Bewley said, 'either in Ireland or in Germany. I used to go to Galway when you were there, to defend Sinn Féin prisoners before British courts martial.'

As Bewley later recalled in his memoirs, Joyce looked at him with an expression half embarrassed, half amused before saying simply: 'I was on the other side.' He added: 'You see, I have always been an Empire man.'

'And now?'

'Now, and I always say so on the wireless, I believe Britain has taken the wrong side in this war. Her real enemy is international communism. She should have joined Germany to defend Europe.'

Bewley later wrote of this encounter: 'I had no doubt of his sincerity. After all, what object could he have had in lying to me? We were in Berlin with Allied bombs falling about us. Nothing that I could do was likely to affect his fate if he fell into the hands of the English; he was far too deeply compromised to have any hope of escape. It gave to his profession of faith the solemnity of a deathbed confession. It had a certain logic, but it was a logic run wild, and it had led him to tragedy. However, he fortunately did not ask for my opinion, and soon a messenger came in to say that the streets were now free and we could go home.'

In his broadcasts, Haw–Haw used the 20 July conspirators as a way of distracting attention from rumours that Paris was soon to be liberated by the Allies. The bomb plot unearthed traitors in the High Command, he suggested, the people who had deliberately held back the reinforcements in the battle for France.

After the liberation of Paris in August 1944, the British government issued orders to put P. G. Wodehouse under house arrest until a decision was made as to whether he should be sent back to England for trial. Major Cussen, the MI5 man leading the investigation against Joyce, took charge of the Wodehouse case. He despatched Malcolm Muggeridge, then a British intelligence officer, to interrogate the novelist at the Hotel Bristol, where he had been staying since the previous September. Muggeridge concluded that he had 'acted naively but had not been a traitor'. The author argued that his broadcasts were not pro-German but he did admit that he had made a 'hideous mistake'. 'It never occurred to me,' Wodehouse said, 'that there could be anything harmful in such statements as: "When in camp I read Shakespeare," or "men who had no tobacco smoked tea," or "there was an unpleasant smell at Loos prison."'

Sir Theobald Mathew, the Director of Public Prosecutions in London, agreed that the broadcasts were not pro-German and were unlikely to assist the enemy: 'Whatever view one may take of the antics of this vain and silly man, I am satisfied that, on the present material, there is no evidence upon which a prosecution can be justified.'

The same could not be said of William and Margaret Joyce, especially after 1 September that year when Hitler awarded them medals. Joyce received the War Merit Cross 1st Class, Margaret the Civil War Merit Medal. They were signed in facsimile by Hitler but, according to Margaret, 'presented by some Radio big bug, not, of course, the Old Man [Hitler] – he was too busy.'[*] The couple never met Hitler. They don't even seem to have met Goebbels, despite his many visits to the Funkhaus.[†]

Clement Attlee, meanwhile, gave a pledge in the House of Commons

---

[*] According to Joyce's letters the presentation took place on 18 October.

[†] According to MI5: 'Joyce became a personal friend of Goebbels, whom he saw three times a week.' And in a statement made on 28 May 1945 by Dr Friedrich Schoeberth, who worked at the Funkhaus under Dr Hesse, it was revealed that 'Wodehouse worked at the Foreign Office and Joyce didn't meet Goebbels until 1944'. But in his diary in 1945 Joyce wrote: 'I have not even shaken hands with Goebbels.'

that British broadcasters working for the Germans would be prosecuted. Also that month, the first V-2 rocket landed on London. The BBC did not mention it for fear that the Germans would be able to target the next one based on news of where it had landed. The attacks slowed down that autumn as the Allied advance drove the Germans back and the V-2s out of range. As the Germans retreated they tried to destroy any incriminating documentation they couldn't take with them. But sometimes the Allied momentum was too great, and with the liberation of Luxembourg came a cache of evidence against the Joyces. Since the summer of 1943 they had been working there intermittently on secondments. When Captain Skardon of British Military Intelligence searched the station he found twelve discs of recordings of 'Frau Joyce'. Her subjects included British food shortages and the break-up of British family life, a morale-sapping subject with so many soldiers abroad. They also found records of 500 other broadcasts she had made between 1941 and 1944 and payments to her totalling 33,000 Reichsmarks. This was damning evidence of treason and she duly became 'case number 9' on MI5's prosecution list.

Berlin was now a cold and grim place. It was filling with wounded troops: soldiers missing limbs, wearing eye-patches, walking on crutches. Women were now wearing mourning black as a matter of course. The theatres had closed. Dancing was now *verboten* and Berlin's prostitutes were sent to the Eastern Front to divert the troops there. Berliners were informing on their friends and calling in favours. If you knew Goebbels, or gave the impression that you knew him, it gave you much leverage. The Joyces could claim to be well known to him, but Margaret nevertheless had to repair her shoes with straw, and 'Fat Will' couldn't get any extra food. Ration cards were no longer of any value as there was nothing in the shops. The only way of avoiding starvation was to use the black market, but the penalties for this were severe. The Funk-Eck had closed the previous summer and, like all of Berlin's smart restaurants, the Joyces' new haunt, the Raband, was now also closed, on Goebbels' orders.* At least the Joyces still had 'the Club'. It became their second home.

While Lord and Lady Haw-Haw put on their determined faces in public, in private Mrs and Mrs Joyce sensed that the game would soon be

---

* Knowing that Göring would protest at the closure of his favourite restaurant, Hörcher's, the previous year, Goebbels had sent the Gestapo to put a brick through its window.

up. William especially knew he would have to pay the price for his fame. Mephistopheles had honoured his side of the bargain, now it would be Faust's turn.

Though he was not to find out for another nine months, on 15 September, Joyce's mother, Queenie, died at St Mary's Hospital in Paddington. She was sixty-six. The office which William and Margaret shared, meanwhile, was moved away from the outer windows, into the centre of the Funkhaus, to protect the radio stars from bomb blasts. William would probably have preferred it if he had been left in danger's way, if a morbid habit that he developed around this time is indicative. After a few drinks he would sit on the edge of his desk laying odds with colleagues on the most likely way he would meet his end: after the Hitler assassination attempt, and the death threat he himself had received in 1940, there was an outside chance of him being done in by a British SOE agent. But being killed in an air raid was the odds-on favourite, especially as he still didn't always bother to take cover in the air-raid shelters. One bombing raid that autumn even failed to put him off his meal. Margaret noted with 'real curiosity' how he looked unperturbed as he crunched away at the 'the undulating supper' amidst the blast.

His personal bet was that he would die on the end of a rope. Indeed he began indulging in gallows humour on this subject – he would refer to the drinks cabinet in his room as 'The Hanging Judge', his own private pub. His hope, however, was that he would die fighting the Russians on the streets of Berlin. To this end, on 22 October, he realized a life-long ambition by finally joining the army, well, an army of sorts: the Volkssturm, the German Home Guard, which was composed of teenage boys whose helmets were too big for them and gaunt old men who could barely run ten yards without recourse to a respirator. Joining up became compulsory that autumn – even hospital staff were having to negotiate with Nazi Party officials to be excused – and Goebbels, now also Reich Defence Commissar for Berlin, tried to whip up enthusiasm for it with a propaganda campaign. It included slogans such a 'The Führer's call is our sacred order!' And 'Believe! Fight! Win!' Cinemas showed newsreels of old men and teenagers marching shoulder to shoulder. Joyce did not need encouraging. He was only too glad to believe, fight and win. When the official filling in his enrolment forms asked him if he had any previous military experience he answered truthfully, if mischievously: 'Yes, British army.' According to Margaret: 'This was calmly filled in without an eyelash being batted, after nearly five years of war.' His Volkssturm detachment – the Bataillon-Wilhelmsplatz, the special unit of Propaganda Ministry staff – was sworn in with an oath of allegiance to the Führer. They then spent hours practising the Nazi salute rather than learning how to defend themselves. Joyce, for all his enthusiasm, proved a clumsy recruit. He was hopeless at drill and a danger to his fellow home guards, nearly killing one comrade when he accidentally set off a Panzerfaust anti-tank rocket.

His hunch about the hangman's rope was right. That month, a meeting was held in London to discuss the case of high treason against Joyce. Preparations for a trial were well underway. Theobald Mathew, the DPP, told senior MI5 and Special Branch officers: 'The case is one which will be a leading state trial. Its importance cannot be exaggerated.'

By December, the tone of Haw-Haw's broadcasts was resigned and gloomy. They were aimed at Allied troops storming across Europe: 'What the dollar imperialists succeeded in acquiring during this war they will certainly not yield up to their British cousins after the ceasefire has sounded,' he said. 'The bases and other territorial acquisitions, the markets, the capital values and the commercial opportunities which the USA have gained will be set off against the services, real or imaginary, rendered by Roosevelt to Churchill.' Trying to turn the British against the Americans was his main strategy by this time, or rather his last resort. 'Your half-American leader Churchill sold the British Empire to Wall Street financiers in 1940 for fifty-eight tubs, misnamed destroyers.'

Joyce began keeping a diary, written in pencil in an erratic, right-sloping hand. He used a cheap notebook and filled 112 pages of it. 'I regret having kept no diaries in the past fifteen years', he wrote. 'They would have been full of interest today, however conceited their tone. Just now and then I realise how full my life has been.' One of his earliest entries, for 22 November 1944, records a casual fling with a woman identified only by her initials. 'Take MT [Mita, presumably] out to dinner and sleep with her.' The abrupt style is repeated in the entry for 24 December. It reads simply: 'None too happy.' By 4 January 1945 he had perked up. 'Excellent day. Plenty to drink.'

Like all Berliners at this time the Joyces became almost demented with lack of food, alcohol and sleep. Of the three, lack of sleep seems to have

affected the health of Berliners the most. The constant sound of exploding
bombs and 'wailing winnies' (air-raid sirens), combined with nights spent
in uncomfortable bunkers, had left nerves shattered. There was a mood of
quiet hysteria and defeatism. The German Red Cross predicted a typhoid
epidemic in the capital and, not surprisingly, cases of hypochondria rose,
as did the number of suicides. The atmosphere of terror about the
advancing Russian armies was palpable. The joke of the season was that
the initials LSR for Luftschutzraum, or air-raid shelter, actually stood for
Lernt schnell Russisch, learn Russian quickly.

The largest air-raid shelter, surrounded by rubble and anti-aircraft
batteries, was the vast ferroconcrete Zoo bunker, but because it was always
overcrowded it felt claustrophobic. Candles on the floor measured oxygen,
and when they went out, children were lifted to shoulder height. The
bunker was lit with dim blue lights that flickered constantly. Condensation
dripped down the walls. The lavatories went unflushed because the water
mains had been hit. The smell became so overpowering some put on their
gas masks. Outside, in the Tiergarten, teenage girls had sex with strangers
because they wanted to lose their virginity before the Russians arrived.
The Red Army had 6.7 million men massed along a front which stretched
from the Baltic to the Adriatic, and already the stories of German women
being raped in their tens of thousands were filtering through.

The Ministry of Propaganda did nothing to play down the rumours of
mass rape. On the contrary, Goebbels reasoned that it would harden the
resolve of Berliners to fight to the death. By this stage of the war, sex was
being linked to death as a matter of routine by the Nazis. And not just on
their own people. They dropped leaflets over the advancing American
troops showing naked blonde women on one side and a picture of a
crippled GI on the other. The message read: 'Gentlemen prefer blondes,
but blondes don't prefer cripples.' Variations on this showed GIs having
sex with women in the shadow of the Grim Reaper.

In Berlin, the impulse to have sex was not restricted to teenage girls. A
sense that the Götterdämmerung – the twilight of the gods; their ultimate
destruction in a battle with the forces of evil – was upon them made
everyone feel morality and decorum were now pointless indulgences.
They wanted to fornicate, get drunk and spend all their money while they
still could. Most Berliners had dropped the Heil Hitler greeting in favour
of *bleib übrig* – 'survive'. A rumour that Hitler himself had succumbed to

madness did not help matters. His New Year message had made no mention of the fighting on the Western front and a story began to circulate that this was because the message was pre-recorded – and that since recording it the Führer had gone insane. This rumour was fuelled by his disappearance from public. In fact, on 17 January, he retreated into his bunker where, apart from three brief appearances again on the surface, he remained until his death.

The Joyces even turned to drugs to escape the hellish scenes in Berlin. They took opium together, which was available over the counter at chemists, so long as the customer said it was for stomach ache. Margaret also took it with her sometime French lover Jean, who was a journalist. 'Spent the night with Jean and he gave me opium,' she noted in her diary. Four days later the inevitable entry came: 'Quarrelled with Jean.'

William's relationship with Margaret was still stormy and he described in his diary how she would regularly walk out on him, only to return a few days later. In addition to Jean she had also been sleeping with Pablo de Pedraza again. One night, after Pablo was wounded in a bombing raid, Margaret bandaged him. It was at this point that he told her he had a wife back in Madrid. Margaret did not mind.

William doesn't seem to have minded either. On 25 January he noted: 'In view of military situation, decide a truce with Margaret.' A fortnight later he twisted his ankle in a tank trap while staggering around drunk in the Potsdamer Platz. Margaret had offered to guide him because she knew he suffered from night-blindness, but he had been too proud to accept. The injury left him with a limp that plagued him until his dying day, which was now less than a year away.

His death wish grew worse and in this he seems to have been in tune with the Old Man, as he liked to call Hitler. Down in his bunker Hitler had ordered that the panzer reserves on the Vistula front be moved forward, despite warnings from his senior staff that this would bring them within range of Soviet artillery. Those around Hitler began to wonder whether he subconsciously wanted to lose the war.

Whom the gods would destroy they first drive mad. Joyce was by now producing six scripts a day and was beginning to suffer from mental and physical exhaustion. In fact he seems to have been close to a nervous breakdown. He took to singing in the air-raid shelters and collapsing in fits of hysterical laughter. On one occasion, after he had been drunkenly

trying to teach Jean the Frenchman some English songs, he was ordered
out of the Zoo bunker by an imposingly tall air-raid warden. A scuffle
ensued. Joyce came away from it with a bleeding lip; the warden, a black
eye. Joyce shouted at the huddled Berliners who watched the fracas. He
then buckled in a heap of uncontrollable giggling, struggling for breath.

Two days later he was issued with a document notifying him he was
to be charged by the German authorities with 'sub-treason'. The warden
had reported him. Joyce thought this hilarious: both the British and the
Germans, it seemed, considered him a traitor. Reflecting on his situation
to Margaret he said: 'I ain't nobody's darling, except yours!' Dietze was
annoyed at his flippancy and warned him that he was in serious trouble –
not even his status as a broadcaster would help him if he was found guilty
of sub-treason. His crime was essentially 'causing an affray' but even
listening to a foreign radio station was a serious offence. If Joyce's particular
act of sub-treason was deemed to 'endanger the defensive power of the
German people' it would carry the death sentence.

The climate of suspicion and paranoia in Berlin was fuelled by the
Volksmeldedienst, the People's Reporting Service, intended to turn every
German into a spy. Berliners were encouraged to report any of their
neighbours who were being unpatriotic or defeatist. If you sat in an air-
raid shelter and asked out loud whether it was all worth it you could
expect to be reported. People did still talk openly but only after a quick
look over the shoulder, what became known as the *Berliner Blick*. In the
first months of 1945, 5,600 Berliners were arrested by the Gestapo for
being Volksschädling, an enemy of the people, and beheaded. On the first
day of February, a court official arrived at the Funkhaus and handed Joyce
a summons ordering him to appear for preliminary examination before
a judge at the People's Court. This gave Joyce pause for thought. To
Berliners, the People's Court had become synonymous with its President,
Roland Freisler, the sadist who had screamed abuse at the 20 July plotters
before sentencing them to be hanged by piano wire. Goebbels had filmed
their excruciating deaths so that Hitler could watch the executions at his
leisure.

But the gods were again playing with Joyce for their sport. On the
morning of 3 February, before his case came to trial, US bombers mounted
an exceptionally heavy raid. It left three thousand Berliners dead. It also
badly damaged the Reich Chancellery, the Gestapo headquarters in the

Prinz–Albrecht–Strasse and the People's Court. Freisler was killed. Joyce's records were buried in the rubble. The warden who was the chief prosecution witness against Joyce was also killed in the bombing. Case dismissed.

That same day, Stalin, Churchill and Roosevelt met in Yalta for the conference that would decide the post-war map of Central and Eastern Europe. It soon became apparent that Stalin was the more skilful negotiator of the three. He bugged the rooms where the British and American delegations were staying, took the chair so that he could pit Roosevelt against Churchill, and managed to sound reasonable as he demanded 'spheres of influence' that would protect his vast borders. But already the geopolitical map of Europe was being shaped by the huge numbers of Eastern Europeans who were on the move, fleeing West through the snow as the Russian T-34s churned up the earth behind them. Around fifty thousand German refugees were arriving by train at Berlin's Friedrich-strasse Bahnhof every day.

The food shortage in Berlin was by now chronic, hence a new popular saying in the city: 'The fighting will not stop until Göring fits into Goebbels's trousers.' Joyce, who used to pride himself on his 'well-fed appearance', became almost delirious with hunger. He arrived at the last possible minute, sometimes drunk, for his broadcasts, and during the cold Berlin winter, with the heating system in the Funkhaus irreparably broken, he sat in front of his microphone shivering and starving in his overcoat, muffler and worker's peaked cap, an image which bore little resemblance to the Bertie Wooster monocle and topper of Lord Haw-Haw folklore.

That month, a kindly official warned Margaret that some foreign employees of the Reichsrundfunk were arranging to have false passports made in anticipation of the inevitable. She and William would be well advised to do the same. When she mentioned this to her husband he was unimpressed. 'Soldiers can't run away,' he said, 'so why should we?' Wagnerian that he was, William had become obsessed with the idea of staying in Berlin to man the barricades for the coming Götterdämmerung. He took to heart Goebbels' edict that Berlin would be defended until the last man and the last bullet. Indeed, he added his own gruesome twist to this, telling Margaret that he would be keeping two bullets, one for her, one for him. He had come to regard Berlin as a living entity. One afternoon, as he and Margaret, both covered in brick dust, negotiated a heap of twisted metal girders in the street, he stopped and said sadly: 'I can't bear to see the city dying. She is dying and will never be saved.'

Perhaps Joyce knew that the time was fast approaching when it would be impossible to leave Berlin anyway. Trenches and tank traps were being dug in front of their apartment. Trams that had broken down were being overturned to make barricades. Goebbels had just declared that leaving Berlin without a travel permit was tantamount to desertion. He himself had no intention of leaving, and while Hitler paced his bunker, refusing even to look outside, Goebbels, as was his habit, visited the victims of bombing, gaining considerable popularity among Berliners as a result. Joyce noted that the true hero of the Götterdämmerung is 'the gallant little doctor'.

Eva Braun was also proving herself to be brave in the face of the Allied onslaught. When Hitler told her she must leave Berlin she refused. Eventually, on 9 February, she was evacuated to Berchtesgaden with her sister Gretl, and Martin Bormann himself was sent to make sure she got on the train. But few places in Germany were now safe from Allied bombing. Four days later, the British and Americans levelled Dresden, reducing one of Germany's most beautiful and historic cities to rubble. Goebbels called it a terror attack and for once he was not exaggerating. Some thirty thousand refugees were caught up in the firestorm. Goebbels, enraged, argued that for every German civilian killed at Dresden a British prisoner of war should be executed in reprisal. He was overruled.

In Berlin civil disquiet was becoming a way of life, for Joyce at least. In his diary entry for 23 February he described another incident in the air-raid shelter in which he had a row with an 'old devil' who would not make room for him to enter the cubicle. Joyce asked him if he belonged to the Reichsrundfunk and threatened to have his pass withdrawn, at which the man vanished. A few nights later he records: 'Trouble at the Zoo Bunker. Another bloody V official pushed Margaret. M kicked him good and hard and I intervened.' A few days later: 'Margaret cries when SS officer insults her in bunker when she was locked out and I storm and rave and a doctor intervenes to comfort her. Is it possible to get on with these people? I wish I knew how. Afraid I created a bad impression by shouting "pigs" and "swine". But I hate to see Margaret insulted.'

Often the bunker was the only place where William could write his diary. One night, shortly after the air raid sounded, he saw a young woman at the entrance to the bunker 'crying most pitifully' because the guard would not let her in. 'They say that volks will make trouble if they do, because she has not the proper papers,' Joyce noted, 'a disgusting sight.' On another night when there was a 'never ending' air raid overhead he became so hungry he wrote: 'I could almost eat the fucking bunker.' He decided drink, tobacco and food were 'the main desiderata' of his life. Their lack was affecting his work: 'Sorry to harp but there is some connection between physical satisfaction and mental effort,' he wrote. Occasionally he tried to make light of the shortages and the dangers: 'These days will soon be over which is why I mean to eat and drink what I can get. I am not in the least perturbed. Quite calm.' But he may have been trying to convince himself as much as anyone. 'Go to Club 7.30 and wonder on way if RAF will cut my drink off. How exciting. Shall I make the Club? Shall I not? We shall soon see.' A few days later he wrote: 'My hunger is now so intense I doubt whether I can wait to go into the town. I could do with a smoke now. I wonder what is wrong with my mental condition? Is it fatigue, over work, ill health or what? Went home with Margaret and a bottle of red wine she got from our dealers. Good.'

The tone of what he called his 'Jerry Calling' broadcasts had grown melancholic. Contrary to the folklore, his later broadcasts were not so much bilious as bleak. They had become political essays, largely concerned with warning Britain about the Soviet threat. There was a tone of grim dignity, weariness and obstinacy about them. Perhaps he was feeling a little humbled.

Certainly he had bouts of feeling sorry for himself. As he noted in his diary on 27 February 1945: 'Sleeping badly. Foot hurts. Let the future look after itself. My blessed superiors don't or won't realise that after 5½ years a steady writer needs certain amenities. One might think that writing was plumbing.'

The Russians, the people whom Germans had been taught to think of as subhuman Mongol hordes intent on raping, looting and butchering their way across the Fatherland, had crossed the Oder and were now only forty miles from Berlin. While most Berliners were still hoping the Anglo-American forces would reach Berlin before them, William and Margaret found neither prospect appealing. If the British arrived first they would both be tried for treason, assuming they weren't summarily lynched instead. If the Russians took Berlin, it would almost certainly mean Margaret would be raped.

William felt frustrated that he could no longer summon the words to record his impressions of Berlin. 'We are used to living in ruins, but about the ruins of ruins there is something almost funny,' was the best he could manage. A pall of yellow smoke and plaster dust veiled the city, drawn into the air from bombed buildings. Streets were blocked by rubble and there was glass underfoot everywhere. Some claimed they could hear the Russian guns. Joyce dismissed such people as 'suffering from auditory hallucinations'. Nevertheless, women began committing suicide rather than be captured alive.

On 28 February Joyce acknowledged that he was past his best as a propagandist. 'Ruefully wonder whether I would ever have made my present reputation by my present standards. I think not. But what with bombs and bust ankle it is not surprising I'm not on top form.' His relationship with Margaret was, as ever, swinging from romantic to tempestuous, sometimes in the same evening. 'Walk with Margaret in twilight. Swan on river, owl on tree. Dinner at Club. Discourse quite happily on English literature. Early alarm – and this meant only one schnapps after dinner – more fool me. Unfortunately, had a terrible row with M when we got home. I was helping her make the bed and for some reason she infuriated me. Shook her. She wanted to leave the flat but I wouldn't let her. She slept in the front room but at about three I carried her into the bedroom. Most unpleasant!'

The next day, Margaret was in vengeful mood. 'Margaret now threatens to "punish" me for last night by going for a time to KE str [a girlfriend's flat]. I apologise to her but I resent the KE idea very greatly, after all, she is not blameless and she ought to learn to control her temper. In the present circs, I am not amenable to blackmail or intimidation or reprisals on her part.' Margaret didn't carry out her threat and came home 'in a sulk' to find her husband in elegiac mood, his powers of speech having temporarily returned. 'Last night I commented to M on the strange beauty of the bare, whitish, gently wind-swept streets. They take, in the abstract, a blue tinge from the twilight and then, against the sky, the leafless trees are silhouetted. I feel deeply moved and recover my old strength.' On 3 March he had also recovered some of his humour. In reference to the tobacco shortage he wrote about himself simply: 'I is sad.'

Berlin was disintegrating before their eyes, not just the buildings but the infrastructure and the civil-defence systems. The 'wailing winnie' near the Joyces' apartment no longer functioned because of the shortage of electricity, or rather it no longer worked during the daily 'saving hours' when supplies were cut off. Portable sirens had to be deployed in the street instead and if one was walking to the station and heard it they would go back to warn the other to head for the shelter.

Eva Braun returned to Berlin. Her fate was symbolically linked to that of Nazi Germany, as indeed were the fates of Lord and Lady Haw-Haw. The Third Reich was collapsing around their heads. Death was stalking them. Yet, in his diary entries, Joyce preferred to avert his eyes from the bigger picture and chart instead his day-to-day routine, a fact he seems to have been embarrassed about. 'They hardly ever have a sweet in the Club now. Pity. I crave for sugar. I wish I could write greater thoughts in this diary but frankly it is at present largely on animal plane. Lunch is a hell of a time coming today.' He described how he would have races with Margaret to the Club, one taking the train, the other the tram. He also wrote constantly about his disrupted journeys and his disillusion with the incompetence and officiousness of Berliners – 'The crowds at the station though still under control are getting more irritable. More pushing and shoving – of course there are far too many passengers in Berlin.' The problem, of course, was that fewer trains were running because of the fuel shortages, and because of the flood of refugees there were more passengers. The tempers of commuters were frayed. An exchange Joyce records in his diary was typical: 'Old bugger in train starts lecturing me on how I should stand. I shut him up – what uncouth Yahoos one meets!'

His 'grossly prosaic diary' meanwhile helped him in the Berlin traffic. 'Almost the moment I start to write, something moves.' One constant annoyance at work was 'the loss of the cable' to the transmitters and this would become a recurring theme for Joyce in his post-war letters, a metaphor for being out of communication with Margaret.

He would also write at length about the weather and about office politics at the Funkhaus. 'Hesse, the bastard, has been and gone and done it! This incredible wretch has torpedoed months of our propaganda and practically all our diplomatic chances by letting the British believe that we will let the Russians in.' One cause of tension seems to have been a colleague he had clearly had an on-and-off affair with for some time, Ruth. 'Ruth yowling for me nastily. She wants to make trouble. The soured conceited nincompoop. Of course she has lost all sense of proportion and is definitely neurotic . . . I was well out of that noble liaison much as I liked it at times, she still seems to bear a slight resentment, however sub conscious. We should never have been able to live together (literally interpreted) for even a week. I should furiously resent being paraded as a catch and on most personal matters her outlook is very different from mine. As to A [name unknown, another colleague he seems to have had an affair with], who wrote to Margaret, she is a louse of lice not fit to be at large. One of the most treacherous bitches I ever met. I think I am luckier in the marriages I did not contract than in those I did. Exception was Mary [Ogilvy, the student he had had an affair with in 1929, when working as a tutor] with whom I am sure success would have been certain. Too late now. Anyhow Margaret and I pull together, if not always in the same direction – war is war.'

Whether or not they were pulling together they seem to have still been sleeping with each other because, on 8 March, William hinted in his diary that Margaret might be pregnant: 'Margaret illish – belly, heart, head. I wonder why? At intervals she is quite well. Hm! We shall see.' The same day the London *Star* ran a story that Joyce was planning to claim Irish nationality and had been in negotiation to buy a house in Galway. This was not true. However, there was a plan for the Joyces, along with all the Funkhaus staff, to be evacuated from Berlin. Dietze had decided to move the whole English-language service to Apen, near the Dutch border. Giddy with hunger, Joyce reacted angrily. His dreams of a heroic last stand, of a grand Wagnerian apocalypse in which he died in glory alongside his Führer in Berlin – the Führerdämmerung – were shattered. He soon resigned himself to the move, though, and became sentimental at the thought of leaving Berlin, and the Club.

'13 March. Dietze insists on our going to Apen as "anything may happen" but we don't want to. We don't want to leave the Club behind. Margaret does not want to come. Like me, she values the Club cellars . . . Dismay among the staff. Poor Margaret is crying. She could not believe that it would ever come to this. Poor darling has worse surprises in store for her. Now we are going to reap the whirlwind.'

William could not believe he was about to pass his last hours in Berlin, either. 'Despite its swine and despite the heartaches it has brought me, Berlin is a composite part of my life,' he wrote, 'and I do not yield it up gladly. I do not weep, like Margaret, but I feel deeply. I shall be lonely for Berlin even as I was for London, perhaps more so.' On their last visit to the Club they were nearly killed in a bomb explosion but both were too full of schnapps and burgundy to care unduly. 'I believe a bomb fell quite near,' Joyce later recorded, 'but I was indifferent to it. Was really drunk. Margaret left me, nearly had a scene at Potsdamer Platz. Thank heavens I did not. Bashed myself badly coming home.'

Margaret's diary for the same day was, as usually, more laconic: 'Packing imminent. Lunch at Club. Said goodbye S.O.B office. Last dinner at Club. Quarrelled with W and came home alone. Miserable. Miserable.'

William awoke next morning 'feeling sorry' for himself. 'Left leg badly hurt and face a mess. I regret my exit from Berlin should be so undignified. Naturally the reason for my scars is obvious to anyone who knows my little habits. Made up with Margaret who was not really responsible for what she did last night. Drink, although she stands it better than I, had a bad effect on her. She will miss it in Apen even more than I. However, she may be better for the lack of it.'

Leaving Berlin filled him with a gnawing discontent. 'I still love England,' he wrote in his diary, 'and hate to think that I am to be regarded as a traitor to her, which in my own opinion I am not. I am deeply sorry for Germany: but I can see how the whole ghastly situation has come about.'

On 14 March, the day after two and a half thousand Berliners died in air raids and another hundred and twenty thousand found themselves homeless, the Joyces were evacuated to Apen. Himmler ordered the evacuation of the concentration camps threatened by advancing troops. Sick inmates were to be killed, the rest force-marched. Bormann flew to Salzburg to look at mines for hiding Nazi loot. Hitler issued his 'scorched-earth policy' to destroy everything that could be of use to the Allies as the Germans retreated. This included bridges, railways and factories, as well as broadcasting equipment. Albert Speer, the Armaments Minister, thwarted him, refusing to issue explosives for the demolition.

The Funkhaus was covered in a shroud of plaster dust, broken glass and shrapnel. The Joyces stood at its entrance and watched dolefully as lorries began carting away teleprinters, typewriters, scripts and gramophone records. They were being taken to the train station. 'Our last sight of Berlin,' Joyce wrote in his diary. 'Naturally M cried . . . Wish I had her more time. M of course has Mrs Thing. It seems that I have become a human contraceptive.' As they drove to the station on this their last day in Berlin they happened to see Christian Bauer, the man they had met on their first day in the city five and a half years earlier. They waved, but he did not notice them.

At the station Margaret went in search of coffee for everyone, but the 7 p.m. train arrived early, and as the Funkhaus team were loading up their equipment it started to trundle off. Everyone jumped on except for Margaret who now appeared at the far end of the platform carrying a tray of steaming mugs. Leaning out of the window, William shouted: 'You'll be all right, Meg. There's another!' In his diary he scribbled: 'Margaret left behind. Terribly worried.'

SIXTEEN

'The situation is so grave I should hate to take it seriously.'

Not only Margaret but also some of the Funkhaus equipment had been left on the platform in Berlin. She managed to get a seat on the next train two hours later, lugging the equipment with her. Like everything else in the Third Reich, the train seemed to be rotting from the inside out: the mahogany panels in its coaches were scratched and the varnish on them flaky. The brass ashtrays had been removed, with their broken screws left in the windowsills, and what remained of the carpets were spotted with cigarette burns. The journey to Apen was grindingly slow, through dense pine forests and darkened stations. When she eventually arrived, she was greeted with a cheer by a few of the Reichsrundfunk staff who had come to meet the train. 'Town crowded,' Margaret observed in her diary. 'So unhappy.'

The Joyces were billeted in two attic rooms, one of which had a Puffing Billy heater, fuelled with coal and named after a type of steam train because of its long funnel-like chimney. The landlady was a woman whose husband was away in the army. 'I am tired of Hitler,' the landlady sighed resignedly. 'I just want this war to be over.'

From the absence of noise compared to Berlin, the war might well have been over. There were no bombs, guns or cars. There was the occasional swell of a plane engine overhead but no air-raid sirens accompanying it. As soon as they unpacked, the Joyces reported for work. Already the sound of clicking teleprinters was coming from the makeshift studio in the Bahnhofshotel. Engineers had quickly installed a transmitter outside, and the *Germany Calling* broadcasts were able to resume that night. After work, the Joyces fell into bed exhausted, but the unaccustomed tranquillity kept them awake.

After a few more days of stillness their spirits improved and their old good humour returned. They felt safe there, and, against advice, went for a stroll in the middle of a country road, only to find themselves suddenly deafened by the noise of a fighter engine behind them. William had to push Margaret into a ditch and jump in after her. As they looked up they saw a Spitfire disappearing. A couple of days later they noticed the ornaments rattling, not an earth tremor but bombing in nearby Bremen. The war was catching up with them again.

William wrote his next diary entry while sitting in a woodland clearing. He was feeling better disposed toward the world. 'As I write I can hear the droning and purring of many planes . . . Feel much better, get up 8.45, excellent rolls for breakfast, new bed comes. I love this place. I'm sure my health will greatly improve if the diet remains the same. In Berlin I was literally starving.'

Whether his mental health would improve was another matter. The last year of the war had exaggerated certain of his character traits: his impulsiveness, single-mindedness and lack of empathy. But he also showed himself to be prone to mood swings and unable to delay gratification. Certainly the optimistic tone of his diary did not last long. On 20 March he wrote: 'Suffering from chronic flatulence. I am not a cow and I am eating food I was not trained to digest in such masses. The food is vanishing from here, too. 1000 refugees all coming, so bang goes our larder.'

To escape, Joyce retreated into reverie about lost lovers. 'I think much of Mary [Ogilvy] and fifteen years ago – that magic evening at Princes Risboro! Ah well, I am cut off from that life anyhow and as I told M on Sunday night, I have nothing left to live for. If only I could spend my last days drinking, smoking and eating, the least I think that I deserve. My employers are mean, undiscerning buggers.' The following day he returned to his theme: 'Think of Mary more than ever. I'm sure she sometimes thinks of me and loathes me.' By day he watched in awe as hundreds of Flying Fortresses overhead fended off attacks from German fighters. The sky, he noted, looked like it had been thrashed with a cat-o'-nine-tails. 'It is clear that the bloody war is lost unless a dozen miracles happen, which they won't, I fear. Sad but true we have made a complete balls of it!'

Lack of alcohol was still his main complaint. 'A week without drink. Hell, I'm in training for clink! It is a bastard.' Margaret was being 'irritable, rude and lazy', he wrote. 'I suppose she is not well, doubtless she feels rotten and discouraged, well we both need tobacco badly, but alcohol much more.' He heard from Sammy, the man in charge of the secret station, that Margaret was being allowed to visit Berlin to collect their remaining possessions and buy extra supplies of alcohol and tobacco. William could not accompany her because he was needed at the microphone. 'Lucky buggeress,' he wrote. 'How I envy her.'

24 March 1945 was a black day for Germany. As William put it: 'The Yankees have crossed the Rhein at Oppenheim. Pop goes the weasel. Shan't be long now. The situation is so grave I should hate to take it seriously. I could have warned the Old Man against most of his mistakes before he made them. But I have not even shaken hands with Goebbels. The anomaly is known as the Führer Prinzip – God save the mark! If we lose this war the formula "Ja mein Führer!" is largely responsible.'

As the tongue returns to a cavity in the tooth, so William's thoughts returned to the treason charge he knew he must face. 'Today I have sad and haunting memories. I yield nothing of my political opinions, nor do I believe that I have acted wrongly. But I hate the idea of dying as England's enemy – or being despised by those amongst whom I was once regarded as an ardent patriot. A damned nuisance.' The next day he walked by a grave yard and watched a suicide's funeral. 'Horses draped in black looked queer and sinister. Damn it. I wish I could go out like a man – with plenty to drink and food and cigars.'

On 27 March, William saw Margaret off at the station. As soon as her train left for Berlin he began to worry. 'I should not have let her go. It is four years today since we parted [her trip to Danzig]. Evil omen. May God bring her safely back. If, of course, Apen is going to be cut off it is very well that she is gone. Better that way than the other. But I trust she will rejoin us in happiness. Well. This is life that one can and must breathe in with both nostrils. Place seems very empty without Peggy [Margaret] with whom, despite all, I am still obviously very much in love.'

That evening, as the wind howled and buffeted outside 'like a 1000 bomber raid', William sat in front of a fire, toasting bread and reading *Richard II*. He had heard that all the trains from Oderling to Apen ceased from midnight and, feeling anxious, he resumed his diary. 'Have foreboding. Shall I see M again? The end is near. I now begrudge every hour she is away from me. I am sorry I sent her but I trust in God to restore her to me. It is only about Margaret I am worried. For myself I do not care. How my mind and body burn for her when she is away and not safe. That sort of love must be quite pathological, especially after all that has happened between us. I always took her back. I hope she will realise before the end what she meant to me . . . I feel bitter because there was no need for this all-consuming tragedy . . . I cannot bear to think of M suffering. However, we must be brave and trust in God, little as we have done to deserve his favour. We are the victims of *hamartia* for, sure as fate, England will have to fight Russia and our principle will be vindicated in the end . . . I still love England and hate to think that I am to be regarded as a traitor to her, which in my own opinion I am not. I am deeply sorry for Germany . . . I have one consolation: If M does not return I need not live long.'

Margaret managed to get on the last train back to Apen from Oderling. William was beside himself with relief. In her diary Margaret wrote enigmatically that just before leaving Berlin she met 'a nice major who gave me cigarettes and schnapps.' It is tempting to speculate what he might have asked for in return. In Berlin in March 1945 a cigarette cost five marks and a prostitute cost fifty, the same price as a loaf of bread.

The people of Apen, they noticed next day, were rubbing swastika graffiti from their walls and burning pictures of Hitler. The Apen bank had only 4,000 marks left. 'We are twice as rich as it!' Joyce mused. They were asked to dig trenches and build barricades but they spluttered with indignation at the request. 'Trenches forsooth!' Joyce said. 'Bows and arrows! If I can do nothing more valuable than that at this juncture I ought to be buried.'

It looked as if they would soon have to be moved on from Apen, too. The radio station staff were each given three months' salary in advance – to all intents, it was severance pay, a clear indication that the end was near. Goebbels, in a gesture of gratitude that was surprising given his more pressing concerns in Berlin, sent a priority message on the teleprinter to Dr Hesse at Apen: 'The Joyces are at all costs to be kept out of Allied hands.' Perhaps the 'gallant little doctor' was feeling guilty about having stalled for a whole year before granting them their German citizenship in 1940. More likely, this was a final reward for services rendered, just as Maxwell Knight's tip-off had been five and a half years earlier.

It was decided that William and Margaret should be transferred by car to Hamburg and then, with false papers, spirited away by U-boat to Ireland (a neutral country which had dismissed the Second World War as 'the emergency'). As they drove through the night, they saw the front line, a distant glow of red. William squeezed Margaret's hand but said nothing. They nearly ran into some panzers camouflaged by branches at the side of the road, then their driver told them that he was not allowed to drive beyond the district of Bremen so he would have to drop them off there and they would have to catch a train for the remainder of the journey to Hamburg. To William's bemusement and frustration, it seemed the bureaucratic Germans were still following their rules obsessively. Progress on the train was slow because whenever planes flew overhead it stopped and the passengers ran out and took cover. 'Feel bored and sleepy,' William scribbled in his diary. 'So dirty and shabby, I amuse an SS man. Am I really so funny looking! On the journey, Margaret seems to have collapsed entirely. I am sorry, but half of it is fear. Personally I couldn't fear anything after what I have endured.'

What should have been a short journey took nine hours. Hamburg, they noticed, smelled sickly sweet: an arid combination of gas, smoke, bodies putrefying in rubble, and dust from pulverized bricks. With carpets of glass covering the pockmarked streets, infestations of rats and shops empty behind stacks of sandbags, it looked like Berlin. Buses were no longer running. There were craters everywhere. The streets were littered with burnt-out vehicles and the carcasses of horses.

The city was a blackened shell that had never recovered from the firestorms caused by the heavy RAF bombing raids of the summer of 1943. Half of its housing stock had been completely destroyed and only twenty per cent of its buildings and dockyards were undamaged. 'This city must have been lovely before it was bombed,' Margaret noted in her diary. 'Hate the English for bombing!'

Hamburg had been Germany's second largest city, with a population of nearly two million. Yet after just three nights of bombing in 1943, fifty thousand people had been left dead – more than were killed in London in the whole of the war – and a million had fled the city to live in the neighbouring provinces. Coal and coke supplies stored in houses had contributed to the inferno that summer. They had taken weeks to extinguish. Those who made it to shelters were poisoned by carbon monoxide, suffocated and then reduced to ashes as though in a crematorium, which was indeed what each shelter proved to be. Now a stream of haggard, terrified refugees were trudging back into the city, fleeing the Red Army advance from the East, and the people of Hamburg were waiting nervously behind shuttered windows for the British to arrive. They were the lucky ones: the ones who would fall into Anglo-American hands.

A suite had been booked for the Joyces at the imposing Atlantik Hotel, known as the 'White Castle on the Alster', situated as it was on the banks of the Aussenalster. It had come through the bombing relatively unscathed and the menus, the Joyces noticed, included a footnote: 'The possibility of an air raid forces us to ask our valued guests for immediate payment.' At the Atlantik they were to await instructions about the U-boat. They kept an 'emergency suitcase' of luggage with them at all times. While they waited, Lord and Lady Haw-Haw resumed their broadcasting careers, working from the Hamburg Funkhaus, one of the few buildings in the centre of the city that hadn't been hit. Angular, modern and white, it had a large clock tower and a tree outside it, a peculiarity in such a treeless, apocalyptic landscape.

They worked more closely than they had been doing in Berlin and Apen. Now, indeed, they were more like equal partners, according to one colleague, Edwin Schneider. 'They shared an office which contained two small typewriters sent especially from Berlin. Mr and Mrs Joyce also used one of the studios in the bunker as an office and they had a typewriter there, too!'

On 13 April, they were sitting in a restaurant overlooking the harbour when there was an explosion nearby. 'This doesn't sound good,' William shouted above the noise. 'Drink the wine up before it gets blown off the table.' They had only just opened the bottle and were reluctant to waste it. As they drained the last drop, the windows of the hotel restaurant were blasted in and they were covered in tiny shards of glass. William grabbed their suitcase and pushed Margaret towards the corner of the room just as a wall collapsed opposite them. William stood over Margaret, shielding her as a bright white flash filled the room: another blast. After this, white with plaster dust, they felt their way to the cocktail bar which was serving as a shelter and found themselves surrounded by German officers, including a general in a gold-braided greatcoat, pyjama trousers and bare feet. The shivering, barefoot general did not strike them as looking undignified, only chilly. In his diary that night Joyce merely noted: 'A mosquito attack. Told M to hold on to her glass. Crash, crash, crash.' Holding on to glasses was a private joke of theirs, a reference to the champagne they spilt the night they got engaged in Mayfair eight years earlier.

As they emerged from the restaurant they saw a corpse on the road. It had no limbs and its cranium was lolling open in a pan smeared with blood. 'An interesting sight,' Joyce later reflected in his diary. 'If we had been passing 20 minutes earlier we should have shared his fate. Ah well, I can think of worse ways of dying. This book is nearing its end and I am wondering if there will be any need of a second volume.'

However grim life was in Hamburg, it was better than in Berlin, where thousands had now taken permanent refuge in a subterranean world of tunnels and shelters. Marshal Zhukov was about to launch his great offensive on the city with 2.5 million troops, 41,600 guns, 6,250 tanks and 5,500 aircraft. On 12 April the Berlin Philharmonic gave its last performance: Beethoven's Violin Concerto, Bruckner's 8th Symphony and, appropriately, Wagner's *Götterdämmerung*. The orchestra was like the quartet that continued playing as the *Titanic* went down. After the performance, it was said, Hitler Youth members stood in uniform with baskets of cyanide capsules, offering them to members of the audience as they left. Albert Speer, Admiral Dönitz and Nicolaus von Below, Hitler's Luftwaffe adjutant, declined the offer and walked in silence across the flattened Potsdamer Platz back to the Reich Chancellery.

That day Roosevelt died. The ever-optimistic Goebbels telephoned Hitler next day and said: 'My Führer, I congratulate you! Roosevelt is dead. It is written in the stars that the second half of April will be the turning point for us. This Friday, 13 April. It is the turning point!'

It was. Belsen and Buchenwald were liberated soon afterwards and the full horror of the Nazis' attempt to exterminate the Jewish race was brought to light. As British troops reported what they had found at Belsen, Germans in nearby Hamburg convinced themselves that the stories about living skeletons and piles of corpses couldn't be true. The Joyces were among those in denial about it. Indeed, they dismissed the news as enemy propaganda. Presumably, they didn't hear Richard Dimbleby's heartbreaking eye-witness report for the BBC, otherwise they could have been left in no doubt that the news was accurate. 'I picked my way over corpse after corpse in the gloom, until I heard one voice raised above the gentle undulating moaning. I found a girl, she was a living skeleton, impossible to gauge her age for she had practically no hair left, and her face was only a yellow parchment sheet with two holes in it for eyes. She was stretching out her stick of an arm and gasping something, it was: "English, English, medicine, medicine", and she was trying to cry but she hadn't enough strength.' Dimbleby's report ended with the words: 'I have never seen British soldiers so moved to cold fury as the men who opened the Belsen camp this week.'

On 16 April, as Zhukov's offensive began, Joyce again noted in his diary that Margaret had 'Mrs Thing'. It seemed a sign. She had been trying to get pregnant. Joyce now figured it would be for the best if she didn't conceive. 'It is very fortunate that either she is impregnable or I am impotent.' He meant infertile, but as the father of two, he knew that was not the case. The arrival of 'Mrs Thing' put a further strain on their relationship. Margaret began mocking her husband and he in turn criticized her. She then, in a heroic act of displacement, went off to have her perm done at a Hamburg hairdresser's that was, by some miracle, still open. 'I very much want to get drunk tonight,' William confided to his diary. 'M complains that she is overworked when in reality she is only suffering from a mixture of laziness and fright. She always wants to be clever and is too clever. Her cheap repartee is derogatory to her own dignity. I may be most unjust but much as I love her subjectively I find her objectively not merely difficult but almost impossible. Very badly brought up.'

A few optimistic Germans in Hamburg believed there would be a counter-offensive on the Führer's fifty-sixth birthday, Friday 20 April, one using his much-vaunted 'new secret wonder weapons'. Others joked that, as the Americans charged to the Elbe, optimists should learn English; pessimists, Russian. Hitler, now completely deranged, learned neither. Such was his distance from reality, when he heard that the Ministry of Propaganda had received a direct hit, he told Goebbels that he would soon build him another one.

In Berlin, Göring, Ribbentrop, Dönitz, Keitel, Himmler, Speer and Jodl met at the half-wrecked Reich Chancellery for a noon appointment with Hitler to celebrate his birthday. He told them that the Russians were about to suffer their bloodiest defeat. They nodded politely but soon departed to discuss their evacuation plans. Goebbels, one of the few leading Nazis planning to stay in Berlin with Hitler, broadcast a speech to mark the Führer's birthday. Ribbentrop announced at a dinner for diplomats that night that 'Germany has lost the war but still has it in her power to decide to whom she loses.' She did not, as it happened.

That day the Joyces went to the Gestapo headquarters in Hamburg to pick up two false passports in the name of Herr and Fräu Hansen. The officer who handed them over could not look them in the eye. Joyce guessed that the plan to get them onto a U-boat had come unstuck – the Germans must have realized that the chance of a submarine making it out of the Hamburg estuary, past the Royal Navy ships and RAF planes that were guarding it, was negligible. The Joyces appreciated the irony: they may not have made it to their submarine, but, by accepting false papers, they had become what Germans colloquially called 'U-boats', people whose identities were concealed below the surface. Margaret kept repeating her new name under her breath to try and remember it.

The British were only five miles away and the Gestapo were preparing to evacuate, along with the German army. Hamburg was not going to be defended. Even so, William decided to keep his Wehrpass, made out in his real name, as a precaution against being arrested by the retreating Germans and mistaken for a deserter.

On 21 April, Field Marshal Model shot himself and his army surrendered en masse. In his diary William wrote: 'D [Dietze] seems very melancholy today. The big news is the siege of Berlin into whose suburbs the Russians have entered. Poor old Berlin! Goebbels calls for a last ditch defence.' The next day he woke up thinking about Ireland and wondering if escape was still possible. 'In any case I shall be glad when this damned war is over. No alcohol, tobacco or food. Life would be better in penal servitude. How grateful I shall be to get a rest from the mental work, if only in the condemned cell.'

Three days later, on his thirty-ninth birthday, he had given up hope of escape. 'A queer birthday. It has been suggested that I should disguise myself as a soldier and Margaret as a Flakmaddam. Mad!' In her diary,

Margaret airily scribbled: 'Fat Will's Buffday. Could not get him a present. Damn this place. Funny to be so near the English. For it is so quiet.' In private William was describing Hitler's plans to defend Berlin as 'lunatic', but in his *Germany Calling* broadcast that day, being the professional hack that he was, he cast Hitler and Goebbels as heroes manning the barricades. 'The Führer has given the ultimate proof of his good faith, of his devotion to the cause of the West, by taking the great and momentous decision that henceforth what forces Germany possesses shall be concentrated on the imperative task of defending not only Germany but also Europe against the onslaughts of the Red Army and the infamous power of destruction it represents. The Führer has taken his post in Berlin, side by side with the Commissioner for the Defence of the Capital, Dr Goebbels, and he is directing the fanatical resistance of the tough and valiant Berliners in the fight for every street corner, every heap of ruins, every cobblestone in the city, greater than ever in the invincible majesty of its ruins. Even at the height of this crisis, the greatest of our modern era, I am as convinced now as on the day when I arrived in Germany in August 1939 that there can be no security for Britain, nor safety, I would even say no hope, without an independent German Reich strong enough to prevent the Soviet monster from swallowing the West. Without Germany,' he concluded, 'there cannot long be an England.'

He got drunk that night and scrawled in his diary: 'The beginning of true knowledge is certainly self knowledge, but in most cases, providentially, it is the end.' He signed himself 'Confucius W Joyce aus Brooklyn.'

The next day, as the Russians and Americans met on the Elbe at Torgau, effectively cutting Nazi Germany in two, William wrote: 'I get two cigars. Coffee, cigars and schnapps in one day. Hip hip hurray. The staff at the radio have weird ideas about what will happen after the surrender. They think, poor dears, that they will be allowed to carry on as if nothing had happened. Some have been solemnly wondering whether we should serve under the British. Chance would be a fine thing. We have several plans but I doubt if any of them will work. However I am not worried. If I cannot dodge the bill I must pay it.'

On 27 April the Russians entered the Berlin district of Charlottenburg and took control of the Funkhaus. The next day, in Italy, Mussolini was reported captured. Slipping into the language of his beloved chess, Joyce observed: 'The major pieces are being taken.' Then came, for him, 'the bally limit'. Reuters had reported that Himmler had offered unconditional surrender to the West but not to the Russians. The offer was refused. All would be over when Berlin fell, Joyce noted. The southern redoubt was a myth. The Old Man would either be killed or commit suicide. There were rumours that Goebbels had been killed. And there were early reports coming over the wire that Mussolini's body was being spat upon in Milan. 'Ugh!' he wrote. 'Filthy business. Wish, in a way, I was in Berlin.'

Margaret, too, was disturbed about the news of Mussolini and his mistress, thinking that her own fate might not be dissimilar. She confided to Edwin Schneider that she didn't know whether they would swing from a lamppost or die of starvation in an Allied camp. 'English crossed the Elbe at Luneberg,' she wrote in her diary. 'BBC confirmed Mussolini murdered and gave gloating description of how he was hung and then his body thrown in Milan square and riddled with bullets – and the BBC calls these people patriots.'

In Berlin even trams that were still working were being filled with brick and rubble and tipped on their sides to make barricades. Zoo animals were running wild. Few buildings had roofs. Vehicles were burning in the road. Retreating German soldiers were riding bicycles or driving confiscated hay carts pulled by horses. There was a continual thunder of artillery in the air. The bloated bodies of deserters were hanging from lampposts and trees everywhere. It was such a commonplace sight that, in one case, boys played games with the unfortunate 'traitor', twisting him by his legs, winding the rope and then spinning the body. The soldier was naked, save for his underpants. The sign around his neck explained that he had been caught trying to burn his uniform.

Hitler even had Eva Braun's brother-in-law executed for treachery in the Reich Chancellery garden. He would have liked to execute Göring and Himmler as well, as he now believed that they had betrayed him. In his madness the Führer seemed to want to kill everyone around him. Indeed, his self-identification with the German people had reached such psychotic levels, he wanted the whole German population to share in his suicide.

Many did. An estimated hundred thousand Berlin civilians were killed by shelling and summary execution during the battle. The carnage as the Russians overran the city was unspeakable. Mangled dead and wounded lay in the streets alongside decomposing corpses. Young women wore make-up in a futile attempt to age themselves and put off Russian rapists. Six thousand civilians preferred suicide. Eerily, the same number of Berlin Jews had taken this option rather than face 'resettlement' between 1941 and 1943.

As the Red Army reached the Tiergarten, Hitler married Eva Braun. After this, a sexual fever gripped the labyrinthine Führerbunker. Secretaries had sex with SS guards on desks. A half-naked general was seen chasing a signalwoman. Dozens and dozens of bottles of champagne were drunk. A corrupt and genocidal regime was in its final, hellish death-throes. Magda Goebbels was to lead her six children into the bunker and poison them before playing cards and poisoning herself. Goebbels, too, was about to kill himself. With poignant timing, Dachau concentration camp was being liberated by the US Third Army. The thirty thousand inmates still clinging on to life there were saved.

There were bacchanalian scenes in Hamburg, too. Shop-keepers ignored orders to ration alcohol – reasoning that if they didn't sell it, it would only be drunk by British troops when they arrived in a few days – and the city became one big sexually charged party. Some people drank themselves into a stupor. The Hamburg Rundfunk was no exception and there was something pagan about the bonfire lit there on 30 April. Members of staff stood around it drinking and tossing onto it scripts, tapes, files and records. The mood was dampened when an official from the Propaganda Ministry arrived and said that he believed that Goebbels and Hitler were dead. Hitler had married Eva Braun, they were told, just before he died in action on the Berlin streets. It was a final lie. As the Red Army had launched its assault on the Reichstag, Hitler and Eva Braun took cyanide, then Hitler shot himself. Their bodies were carried out of the bunker, doused with petrol and burned.

When he heard this rumour, Joyce muttered, 'My work is over,' and refilled his glass. He drained it and filled it again. A macabre end-of-term party ensued, in which every last food ration and every last bottle of alcohol at the station was consumed. People ate, drank, laughed, kissed, groped and gave toasts. It was the end of the war; the end of the Third Reich. They were celebrating not their defeat but their survival.

Barely able to stand, a maudlin and drunk William Joyce went to the studio to record his infamous 'last broadcast'. In his final performance he played the rueful prophet whose messages had gone unheeded and, to our ears, his final slurring words are an uncomfortably accurate prediction of the coming Cold War. Half of Europe was about to be ceded to Stalin, a tyrant whom history would judge to be on a hideous par with Hitler. Nevertheless, had the recording engineers not been drunk as well, they would probably have stopped the recording. There were long pauses in it. At times Joyce raised his voice to a shout then lowered it to a whisper, as though running on weak batteries. Alone in his studio, he banged the table for emphasis, and lost his train of thought several times. The talk lasted for ten embarrassing minutes, but had an oddly moving and dignified sign off. (The italics show the random words he emphasized.)

'This evening I am talking to you about [pause] Germany. *That* is a concept that many of you may have failed to *understand*. Let me tell you that in Germany there still remains the *spirit* of unity and the *spirit* of strength. Let me tell *you* that here we have a *united* people *who* are modest in their wishes. They are not *imperialists*. They don't want to take what doesn't belong to them. All they want is to live [pause] their own simple lives [pause] *un*disturbed by outside influences. That is the Germany that we know. [Pause] I can remember when I cast my [pause] memory back to 1932 and 1931, *I* can remember how *every*thing that could be done to stimulate the *hatred* of England against Germany was done. I remember how my old friend said: "*What* shall we do with this man Hitler? He wants [pause] Poland. He wants Czechoslovakia. What shall we do if he wants more than that?" Now *it* does behove you to think, at the moment, *how* much Stalin has taken and *how* much Stalin wishes. I ask you to remember that in 1939, in August, the only question was that of bringing Danzig back to the Reich. No more, and no less. What a *small* problem that was in comparison with those that confront us today. Surely if only we had had the common sense [pause] to agree that the German people of Danzig should go back to the Reich then we might have had peace. We might have avoided all the terrible sacrifices of the last five and a half years. We might have avoided the *hatreds* which can only be very gradually repaired.

'Now I say to you, my English listeners, the trouble is this: Germany, if you like, is not *any more* the chief factor in Europe. Germany maybe, I may be wrong, I will only say, the German armies have been in many battlefields defeated, but I ask you how could it have ever been possible for England to maintain a front against Soviet Russia unless [pause] she had the help of the German legions? That is a question which may perhaps be debated and discussed ad infinitum. I cannot promise that I can give any solution to it tonight. I can only say that *if* England *and* Germany together had decided to preserve the welfare of this continent, then I should have hope. Then, I should *be* happy. An optimist. But so far as I can see, the policy of England has been [pause] to allow Germany to sacrifice the very last, ultimate end of her resources in an attempt to stay the Bolshevik attack. If I am right, then I can only say that the people of Britain deserve what they get in the future.

'I speak now personally. I want to talk to you of what I *know* and what I feel. I have always hoped [thump] and believed that in the last resort [thump] there would *be* an alliance, a combine, an understanding between England and Germany. Well, at the moment, that seems impossible. Good. If it cannot be, then I can only say that the whole of my work has been in vain; [pause] I can only say that I have, day in and day out, called the attention of the British people to the menace [pause] from the East which confronted them, *and* if they *will* not hear, if they are determined *not* [thump] to hear then I can only say that the fate that overcomes them in the end will *be* [long pause] the fate they have merited. More I cannot say.

'Now in this the most serious time of our modern age, I beg you to realize that the *fight* is on. You have heard something about the Battle of Berlin. You know that there a tremendous world-shattering conflict is being waged. Good. I can only say the men who have died in the Battle of Berlin have given their lives to show that *whatever* else happens Germany will *live*. *No* coercion, *no* oppression, *no* [thump] *measures* of tyranny that any foreign foe can introduce will shatter Germany. Germany *will* live [pause] because the people of Germany *have* in them the secret of life: endurance, will and purpose.

'And therefore I say to you, in these last words, you may not hear from me again for a few months. I say, [pause] *es lebe Deutschland*! [pause] Heil Hitler. And farewell.'

Almost as much as the death of Hitler, this final recording came to symbolize the end of the war in Europe. In his last diary entry, William was uncharacteristically emotional. 'On this tragic day the death of Adolf Hitler was reported. Feel lonely, though Margaret is splendid. What a night. Drink, drink, drink. I shed tears as I left the Funkhaus. I fear I made a recording of an improper speech but what it was I don't know. I was under the influence. Was given good bottle of wine as I left. Splendid. Leave Hamburg between three and four in the morning.'

After this, Lord and Lady Haw-Haw were driven away by two SS officers to the small German town of Flensburg from where, the plan was, they would be smuggled across the German–Danish border and into neutral Sweden. It was reported in the *Daily Telegraph* on 1 May that: 'Haw-Hic!-Haw forgot his lines. He could not even remember where he was broadcasting from. There was a long pause before someone kicked him and he said "Hamburg" with a loud hiccup. "Ah well it will soon be over now," he sighed drunkenly.' In fact Joyce's final talk was never broadcast so the *Telegraph* reporter couldn't have known what he said in it, although he does seem to have somehow captured the spirit of it. Perhaps he had managed to track down one of the engineers from the Funkhaus.

English soldiers marched into the Hamburg radio station two days later and found it almost completely empty, except for Joyce's last recording, which, over the years to come, was played many times by the BBC.

On 4 May a British officer made a broadcast from the same microphone Joyce had used: 'This is Germany calling, calling for the last time from Station Hamburg. And tonight you will not hear "Views on the News" by William Joyce. For Mr Joyce, Lord Haw-Haw to most of us in Britain, has been most unfortunately interrupted in his broadcasting career and at present has left, rather hurriedly, for a vacation – an extremely short vacation if the Second British Army has anything to do with it – maybe to Denmark and other points North. And in his place this is the BBC calling all the long-suffering listeners in Britain who for six years had to put up with the acid tones of Mr Joyce speaking over the same wavelength I am using to talk to you now. I am seated in front of Lord Haw-Haw's old microphone or rather the microphone he used in the last six weeks of his chequered career, and after tonight's great news of the surrender of the German forces [in the north], I wonder what Lord Haw-Haw's views on the news are now.'

The man making that broadcast was none other than Lieutenant Geoffrey Perry. Perry had recently been with the British troops who liberated Belsen and had told his mother in a letter: 'What I saw today was the result of the most terrible bestiality ever devised by human beings claiming to be civilised.' Three weeks later, with his memories of Belsen still vividly fresh, Perry was Joyce's nemesis.

PART 4

TRIAL

'The spring is wound up tight. It will uncoil of itself. That is what is so convenient in tragedy. The least little turn of the wrist will do the job ... The machine is in perfect order; it has been oiled since time began, and it runs without friction. Death, treason and sorrow are on the march; and they move in the wake of storm, of tears, of stillness. Every kind of stillness. The hush when the executioner's axe goes up at the end of the last act ... Tragedy is clean, it is restless, it is flawless. It has nothing to do with melodrama – with wicked villains, persecuted maidens, avengers, sudden revelations and eleventh-hour repentances. Death, in a melodrama, is really horrible because it is never inevitable.'

Jean Anouilh, *Antigone*

SEVENTEEN

'Have you anything to say why the court should not give you judgement according to law?'

As William Joyce reached the top of the steps at the back of the dock, the court froze into silence. He was shorter than everyone had imagined, an impression exaggerated by the two unusually tall police officers escorting him. He looked around the courtroom calmly, and acknowledged with raised eyebrows his friend Angus Macnab and his brother Quentin who were sitting together in the public gallery – Margaret was not present as she was still a prisoner in Brussels.

Joyce bowed stiffly to the judge, Sir Frederick Tucker, who sat in a high-backed chair, the sword of justice in its jewelled scabbard fixed to the oak panel behind him. He then sat down and stared at the jury. It was Monday 17 September 1945, the first day of what would become known as 'the trial of Lord Haw-Haw'.

Mr Justice Tucker looked imposing in his scarlet robe, with its neckband of white linen, deep cuffs and sash of dark purple taffeta. He had heavy-lidded eyes, a Roman profile and an expression of weary scepticism. If he was feeling the strain of presiding over such a high-profile treason trial he was not showing it. Perhaps it helped him to know that he had already decided Joyce was guilty. He had, after all, been the judge who described Joyce as a traitor during the Wolkoff–Kent trial in 1940. (Later, when Joyce heard about this, he remarked: 'It is reassuring to find that 'Ucker did not approach the trial in a state of what might be called, for lack of a better phrase, mental virginity.')

Joyce looked healthier than he had done the last time he appeared in public, three months earlier. His head was no longer painted green with scalp ointment, for one thing, and he had put on half a stone in weight. He was wearing a blue shirt and dark blue tie, and the navy blue suit he had had made in Berlin. It was still held together with tape, his buttons having been confiscated. ('I must disappoint you by admitting that there are no arrows on my suit,' he later wrote to Margaret, 'although much tape in lieu of buttons. They have me taped!')

Rebecca West, who was sitting in the press gallery, perched forward in her seat and observed her subject for the first time. 'His voice had suggested a large and flashy handsomeness,' she noted, 'but he was a tiny little creature and not handsome at all. He was a not very fortunate example of the small, nippy, jig-dancing kind of Irish peasant.'

The clerk stood up and read from a piece of paper. 'William Joyce, you are charged, in an indictment containing three counts, with high treason.' The first count was that between 18 September 1939 and 29 May 1945 he, being a British subject, 'did traitorously adhere to the King's enemies in parts beyond the seas' by broadcasting propaganda. In the second count it was charged that he, on 26 September 1940, being a British subject, adhered to the King's enemies by becoming naturalized as a German subject. And in the third count he was charged with broadcasting propaganda between 18 September 1939 and 2 July 1940, a period in which his British passport was still valid. The clerk paused before asking: 'Are you guilty or not guilty?'

There was an expectant hush, then the prisoner answered, 'Not guilty.'

Joyce had no intention of denying that he committed the acts alleged, he merely denied that he had a duty of allegiance to the King and so could not be guilty of treason.

The jury was sworn in.

Sir Hartley Shawcross, the newly appointed Attorney-General, was leading the prosecution. An erudite, youthful and dapper-looking man, he was eleven years younger than Gerald Slade, the bald, beady-eyed teetotaller in wing collar and Edwardian moustache who was leading the defence. As Joyce was apparently guilty until proven innocent, Slade had the harder task.

Finding a jury that was not already prejudiced cannot have been easy. There would scarcely have been a single man or woman in England who had not thought or spoken of Haw-Haw as a traitor in the past six years. And if the members of the jury were unprejudiced before walking into the Old Bailey, they would have needed wills of iron not to become so after the Attorney-General's opening address.

'The prisoner who is in your charge is William Joyce,' Shawcross began in a velvety baritone, 'and today, nearly six years since he first entered into the employment of the German Broadcasting Corporation, he comes before you on what is the gravest crime known to our law, upon an indictment for treason. It would be idle to shut our eyes to the fact that some of us may know, or think we know, something about this case. We may in times past have read about this man in the newspapers; we may have discussed his activities – and indeed his activities were notorious enough; it may even be, perhaps in those dark days of 1940 when this country was standing alone against the whole force and might of Nazi Germany, that some of us may have heard, or thought we heard, his voice on the wireless, attempting to undermine the morale of our people. And perhaps at that time some of us formed feelings of dislike and detestation at what he was doing. And perhaps later on some of us heard with a not altogether unnatural satisfaction that he had been apprehended and was to be brought to trial. If anyone of you had feelings of that kind about this man I ask you, as I know you will, to cast them entirely from your minds.'

Shawcross had deftly reminded the jury what it was they were supposed to be putting from their minds. It was a masterly combination of an appeal to put aside prejudice while at the same time reinforcing it. 'I dare say,' he continued, 'that in the years to come in the pages of history it will count for nothing what happens to William Joyce in the course of this trial. He will leave no mark upon those pages. But it may count for a great deal that we who are concerned in this trial comport ourselves in accordance with the best tradition of English law, unprejudiced by any preconceived notions, coldly and dispassionately.'

Although he approached this, his first trial at the Central Criminal Court, with 'a definite feeling of awe', the young Shawcross proved himself to be adept at presenting facts in such a way as to steer a jury. When describing Joyce's arrest, for example, he said that the arresting officer 'with perhaps more mercy than many people would have shown' had shot Joyce *in the leg.*

'Now,' he went on, 'not everyone who assists the King's enemies is capable of committing the crime of treason. A German soldier fighting in the uniform of his country may be made a prisoner of war, but he cannot be convicted of treason, for he would be fighting for his own people and his own country and be under no debt or duty of loyalty or faithfulness to the British Crown. Only those can be convicted of treason who owe a duty of loyalty and faithfulness to the British Crown; only those can be convicted of treason who, in the language of our law, owe a duty of allegiance to the Crown, and the first thing that you must have prominently before your minds is: *did this prisoner owe a duty of allegiance to the British Crown?*'

This was the crux of the case.

Shawcross then made the point that the words with which a British passport opens are not idle. He read them out: '"His Majesty's Principal Secretary of State for Foreign Affairs requests and requires in the name of His Majesty all those whom it may concern to allow the bearer to pass freely without let or hindrance, and to afford him every assistance *and protection* of which he may stand in need."' In a foreign country, Shawcross explained, be it friendly, neutral or belligerent, Joyce's passport entitled him to be accorded all the protection due to a British subject. 'Nor were those rights insignificant even in Germany, even in time of war. In Germany, William Joyce, as the holder of this British passport, was entitled to all those rights which by international law one belligerent power owes to the subjects of another. Those rights Germany could disregard only at her peril.'

Shawcross argued that in those circumstances Joyce had 'not merely clothed himself with the status of a British subject; he had, so to speak, enveloped himself in the Union Jack, secured for himself the greatest protection that he could secure.' He noted that when Joyce applied for a renewal of his passport war was just days away. 'No doubt thinking, however mistakenly, that he was deserting the sinking ship, he left this country for Germany.'

The Attorney-General maintained that it was because Joyce was a British subject that he had his great value to the Germans. 'Members of the jury, in his work book, a record which was to be kept of his employment, under the heading "special qualifications" is the word "English". I cannot tell you, for I do not know, whether that means that

15 and 16. He also grew a toothbrush moustache.
Margaret didn't seem to mind. Indeed, five days after his divorce
papers came through that year, she married him.

17. William and Margaret Joyce the day after they married in 1937. They did
not go on a honeymoon, preferring to canvass for the BUF in Shoreditch.

18. (*a to c*) In keeping with her
celebrity status, Margaret Joyce posed
for a swimwear photo-shoot at the
Olympic Stadium in Berlin in 1942.

19. Lady Haw-Haw at the microphone
with a Nazi officer. Margaret was paid
almost as much as her husband, and
MI5 considered her to be just
about as much of a traitor.

HAW-HAW ON ANY NIGHT OF THE WEEK

"Where is the *Ark Royal*?"
"Where IS the *Ark Royal*?"
"*WHERE IS THE ARK ROYAL*?"

20. Lord Haw-Haw as imagined
by the *Punch* cartoonist 'Fenwick',
who illustrated Jonah Barrington's
spoof book on Haw-Haw.

"Where IS the *Ark Royal*?"

21 and 22. P. G. Wodehouse and Ezra Pound . . .
two literary giants who were compared to Lord Haw-Haw.
Both were accused of treachery after broadcasting
propaganda for the enemy.

Der Führer

hat mit Erlaß vom heutigen Tage

der Sprachleiterin

Margaret Joyce

in Berlin-Charlottenburg

die Kriegsverdienſtmedaille

verliehen.

Berlin, den 1. September 1944.

Der Staatsminiſter
und Chef der Präſidialkanzlei
des Führers und Reichskanzlers

23. Margaret Joyce laughing at the
microphone. In her broadcasts she often
compared the lot of the British housewife unfavourably with that of the
German housewife.

24. Margaret was notoriously flirtatious
and promiscuous. Throughout the war
she had an on–off affair with an
aristocratic German intelligence officer,
Nikolaus von Besack.

25. Margaret Joyce's Civil Merit Medal,
signed by Hitler in 1944.

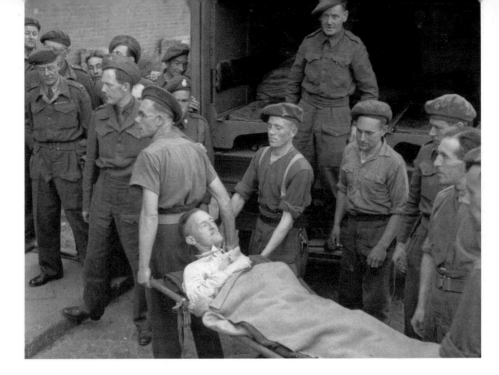

26. Joyce being carried into hospital after being shot. News of his arrest had filtered out and soldiers crowded around the ambulance, hoping for a glimpse of him.

27. The newly appointed Attorney-General Sir Hartley Shawcross led the prosecution in the Joyce trial. Joyce nicknamed him 'Hot Cross Buns'.

28 and 29. William and Margaret Joyce after their capture . . .
'WE'VE GOT HAW-HAW!' was the headline in the *Star* on 29 May 1945.
'CAUGHT IN MANHUNT: WIFE, TOO'.

30. Members of the public –
some legal-minded, some
voyeuristic, others merely
curious – began queuing at
2 a.m. for a place at the second
day of the trial.

31. Margaret Joyce in 1954,
her final year in Germany.
Since her release from a
German internment camp
six years earlier she had been
working as a secretary for a
Hamburg food company.

his special qualification was that he would speak English, or that he was English, but you will probably have little doubt about this, that it was because he was a British subject that he had his great value. They wanted him to broadcast as a British subject to his own people in the hope, the vain hope, that he might undermine the morale of his own people and seduce some of them from their allegiance to the British Crown.'*

As Shawcross set out the central argument of the prosecution – that allegiance was synonymous with protection – Joyce listened with increasing respect, impressed by the lucidity of his argument. In his perverse way, he seemed to enjoy the legal debate, fascinated by the nuances and pedantry. Like all prisoners in the dock, he had been given foolscap sheets to write on. As the silks flicked through heavy volumes and quoted passages, Joyce made notes on these with a pencil and frequently passed them down to his counsel. He also tore off irregularly shaped pieces and covered them with large handwriting, so large that it could be read by people sitting in the gallery. He smiled. He nodded. He stood up when asked, and according to a report in the *Mirror*, sat 'unconcernedly, hands folded'. It might have been that, on an unconscious level, he wanted to lose, because if he was executed as a traitor to the Crown that would make him what he had always hoped he would be, and which he sometimes lied that he was: a British subject. Perhaps he was busy turning an inevitable defeat into a symbolic victory, as he had attempted to do in his later broadcasts. He was a skilful propagandist, after all.

His OTC application of 1922 and his British passport application of 1933 were brought into the court and read out. Prosecution witnesses were called from the OTC and the passport office and were cross-questioned by the defence. It emerged that Joyce's passport had been renewed on 24 August 1939, at which time he was on the Special Branch arrest list. Slade asked Harold Godwin, the witness: 'Am I right in saying that one year is the minimum period for which a passport can be renewed?' The point behind this question was that if Joyce had only wanted the passport renewed in August 1939 in order to leave England and reach Germany, he would of necessity have had to apply for a whole year's

---

* Bechhofer Roberts noted in the Old Bailey Trial Series: 'This last suggestion is rather hard to follow. Surely, one may think, Joyce's value to the enemy, apart from his undoubted skill and wit as a commentator, was his perfect command of English rather than his national status?'

renewal. The passport officer on the witness stand became distressed – the court record noted that 'the witness became indisposed'. When Godwin regained his composure he agreed that, in practice, a year was indeed the minimum.

The next witness called was to provide the single piece of evidence on which the prosecution case rested. It was Albert Hunt, the Special Branch officer who claimed to have recognized Joyce's voice on the radio some time in the autumn of 1939. When asked if he could be more precise he said: 'To the best of my recollection it was during the first month after the outbreak of the war.' When asked if he could remember anything he heard the prisoner's voice say, Hunt said: 'Yes. He said that Dover and Folkestone had been destroyed.' When cross-examined he added that he had never actually talked to Joyce, but had heard him give talks in public before the war.

The main problem for the prosecution was to try to prove that the Treason Act (1351), amended 1945, could be stretched to cover the activities of an alien working in a foreign country. For as long as he lived under the protection of British law, Joyce owed allegiance to the monarch, as any foreigner does in such circumstances. But the moment he left the country, whether for Germany or anywhere else, the protection and the allegiance ceased. And this was the case for the defence.

On these grounds, Slade argued that all charges should be dropped immediately. There was no more justification in a British court trying Joyce – an American citizen by birth – than there would have been for trying Ezra Pound, the American poet who broadcast for Mussolini. Even America didn't have the right to try Joyce, Slade continued, because, by the time the United States entered the war, Joyce had become a German citizen. Neither Britain nor America had any call upon Joyce's loyalty. 'I submit to your Lordship as a matter of law that there is no case to go to the jury on any of the three counts, the subject matter of this indictment.'

Slade went further. 'With regards to counts 1 and 2, I am now submitting to your Lordship that there is not even prima facie evidence to go to the jury that William Joyce is or ever has been a British subject. Nationality is a question of status, and status must be in every case a question of mixed fact and law. My submission to your Lordship really comes to this, that, if I am Chinese, by screaming from the housetops fifty thousand times that I am a British subject I do not become one; secondly, by swearing on oath that I am a British subject, or by a statutory declaration, I do not become one. And it makes no difference whether I make those statements because I honestly believe them to be true or whether I make them for some ulterior motive of obtaining a British passport. I cannot alter my status, nor can I create a status by anything which I can do. In other words, it takes two people at least to make status: the person who is the subject, and the Crown in this country who by act of parliament or otherwise at common law confers that status upon persons.'

When Slade then went on to talk about passports and status, the judge interrupted him. 'I don't want to stop you, Mr Slade, but I am finding it a little difficult to follow because, at the present moment, there is no evidence as to where this man was born.'

'The birth certificate, my Lord,' Slade said, holding up the item in question.

'That is no evidence yet,' Tucker said. 'It is a birth certificate. It only becomes evidence when there is some evidence of the identity of the person referred to in the certificate. I merely know that there is a docu- ment in existence which purports to show that somebody was born on a certain day.'

'My Lord,' Slade said patiently, 'in my respectful submission, that has been put in as having been acknowledged by William Joyce to be his property and is quite clearly referring to his own birth certificate.'

'Very well,' Tucker said with a nod.

Slade continued until the court was adjourned. The first day had gone well for the defence. Joyce was later to note that the Attorney-General's emphasis on the prediction that his name would not go down to history struck him as being a little contrived. Shawcross had shown some initial brilliance of a grocery store variety, he concluded, but had later been reduced to embarrassment by Slade's argument.

Outside the court, bookies were offering odds of 6−4 that Joyce would be acquitted. Inside it, lawyers were laying odds of 50−1 on an acquittal. Shawcross was rattled and, as the court rose, he turned to one of his legal advisers, Professor J. H. Morgan, a distinguished constitutional lawyer who had been on Sir Roger Casement's defence team in his treason trial, and said: 'Could I have a word with you?' They went to the Crown Counsel's room, where the Director of Public Prosecutions, Sir Theobald Mathew, was waiting for them.

'Have we any chance?' Shawcross asked Morgan bluntly.

'No,' Professor Morgan replied. 'I don't think you have – not unless the judge is prepared to make new law.'

Slade meanwhile was passed an unsigned note: 'You can sub-poena the Special Branch on when Joyce left England. He was checked out at ports by Home Office emigration. A detention order under 18B was to have been served on him on 3 September, 1939. Weeks later the Special Branch found that he had been checked out of the country and that his wife had been, too.' The defence chose not to act on this tip-off.

The evening papers, meanwhile, whipped up a mood of hysteria about the trial. But there were those who did not need much persuading about Joyce's guilt. People who had lived through the 'invasion summer' of 1940 found it hard to forgive their tormentor. The awful dread and panic that had filled hearts as England stood alone between May and September that year had hardened to indignation and patriotism. Hitler, Göring and Goebbels had been remote cartoon figures who spoke in a foreign language English people didn't understand, but Lord Haw-Haw had been an enemy who spoke their language, and this traitor had been in their living rooms every night, goading them, scaring them, insulting them. He had seemed to know every detail of their lives. It had been as if, like some supernatural being, he had been running the war on the German side. In September 1945, two days before the trial began, the patriotic fervour was rekindled in London when Douglas Bader, that personification of RAF heroism, led a fly-past of Spitfires to commemorate the fifth anniversary of the Battle of Britain.

There may, of course, have been an element of 'Vichy guilt' among those who clamoured for Joyce to receive the ultimate punishment that September. Those who had vigorously supported appeasement before the war were now repudiating equally vigorously any suspicion of having held those views. Newspapers such as the *Daily Mail*, which had supported the Blackshirts, were now rabid in their denunciation of fascism and all its evil works.

There may, too, have been a sense that Joyce was a loose end that had to be tied up, or rather strung up, before people could get on with their everyday lives. Like the return of Eros to Piccadilly Circus that month – it had been taken down and stored away safely for the duration – the death of Lord Haw-Haw would mean a resolution of sorts, a return to normality for cold austerity London. On VE-Day, Churchill had said: 'The evil-doers now lie prostrate before us.' He had, as always, chosen his words carefully. And had Aristotle heard them, he would have known how to interpret their meaning: for order to be restored to the land at the end of a Greek tragedy, there had to be a cleansing, a catharsis. The tyrant had to die.

Yet this does not reflect the climate entirely. That September, the country was divided about what to do with Joyce. The mood for retribution was admixed with grey exhaustion, disillusionment and, after six years of anxiety, collective relief. There was a sense among some who followed the Lord Haw-Haw trial that there had been enough killing, and that little would be gained by an additional murder, albeit a judicial one. Besides, show trials were not the British way.

Several weeks had passed since the VJ-Day bunting had been taken down and now, for some, the victory was beginning to look hollow. The rationing that had been considered a necessary restriction during the war – with people turning 'the queue' into a national institution – was now beginning to cause resentment. Britain's pre-war gold reserves had been worth tens of billions of pounds; now the country was seriously in debt. The victorious British had lost part of their Empire, moreover, and were planning to give back the jewel in their crown, India. And even with Hitler gone the world still seemed to be in a precarious state. There were atom bombs now. And, in private, Churchill was predicting a Third World War with Stalin.

But there was also a mood of optimism in evidence. Britain may have been bankrupt but it was on the road to recovery. There were home-comings and family reunions. There was an end to blackouts. The sound of 'Moaning Minnie' (the air-raid siren) no longer pierced the night air. The evacuated children had returned. And as working-class Londoners emerged from the sooty Underground tunnels and air-raid shelters they demanded a revolution – an end to poverty, social injustice and unem-ployment. That summer they had got it when the first majority Labour government was elected with a landslide. Now a New Jerusalem was to be built by Clement Attlee: four million new houses; slum clearances; a welfare state that included a National Health Service and social security. In this utopian atmosphere, peace had to be equated with justice for all, even those suspected of treason.

The appetite for vengeance, then, was waning. Indeed if Joyce had stayed on the run for a couple of years it is doubtful whether there would have been the same public demand for his life as there was that month. As it was, members of the public – some legal-minded, some voyeuristic, others merely curious – began queuing at two in the morning for a place at the second day of the trial. But there was space for only twenty members of the public in the court. Journalists had spilled out of the press gallery into the public seats.

When the Black Maria carrying Joyce pulled up outside the Old Bailey, onlookers shouted: 'Where is the *Ark Royal*?' One spectator, an old man from County Galway, was ranting at the crowd. 'Joyce should be hanged for treason,' he shouted, 'he worked with the Black and Tans in persecuting the Irish when they were revolting against the English.' The crowd was amused by the eccentric logic.

Once he had been escorted to the court cell, Joyce was told that Slade had received an anonymous death threat overnight. If the silk got Joyce off, the note informed him, then he would be killed. 'Surely it would be more appropriate, in that case, to assassinate the Attorney-General,' Joyce observed coolly.

The court rose as Mr Justice Tucker entered and Slade was invited to open the day's proceedings. He attempted to prove, by producing a marriage certificate, that Joyce's father, Michael, had taken US citizenship. The judge decided that more evidence was needed. Slade then called Joyce's brother Quentin to the witness stand and said: 'You have, I believe, been able to find nothing dealing with your father's nationality?'

'No, nothing at all.'

'Do you remember an incident some years ago when certain documents were destroyed?'

'Yes,' Quentin said. 'I do.'

'About how long ago was that?'

'To the best of my recollection, about eleven years ago.'

'Who destroyed them?' Slade asked.

'My father destroyed them.'

'Just say yes or no to this question. Did your father tell you or give you the reason why he was destroying them?'

'He did.'

'Did you see him burn any of the papers?'

'I saw him burn a number of papers.'

'Did you notice anything about any of the papers that you saw him burn?'

'Yes, one,' Quentin said. 'It had an American eagle embossed on it, and I believe also there was a seal, a sort of red seal towards the bottom of the sheet.'

Quentin Joyce was not required to repeat in court the reason his father had given him for burning the family papers in 1934, but since the date coincided with Joyce's arrest at Worthing, it can be assumed that Michael Joyce had feared that if the police found out about his true nationality they would deport not only his son, who had a become a fascist nuisance, but also his whole family.

The judge accepted Joyce was American and so, in effect, ruled out the first charge, namely that from his first broadcast in 1939 to his last in 1945 he owed allegiance to the King and had traitorously adhered to the King's enemies.

Slade continued with more witnesses and then said: 'Before I address the jury perhaps your Lordship would be good enough to give some indication to us as to what matters there are for the jury to try?'

Tucker looked at Shawcross. 'Mr Attorney, perhaps you would assist me now by saying whether, having heard the evidence which has been adduced by the defence, you are going to invite the jury to come to the conclusion that this man was a British subject or not.'

'No, my Lord,' Shawcross said. 'I indicated as far as I properly could in opening that I was not going to press the point, and I certainly do not consider it my duty to invite them to do so.'

Tucker nodded. 'Very well, Mr Attorney, I think everybody must agree that the evidence which has been tendered really is overwhelming. That leaves us with Count 3 as the only effective matter which we have to deal with.'

The second charge – that on 26 September 1940 Joyce adhered to the King's enemies by becoming a naturalized German – had been dropped.

The first editions of the London evening newspapers went on sale before the court rose. They reported that Joyce had got off on the first two counts. 'A crowd of angry people gathered outside the door of the Old Bailey,' according to a *Daily Mail* report, 'following a rumour that William Joyce had been acquitted and would walk out of the court at any moment a free man.'

Shawcross, meanwhile, set out the case for Count 3. 'There is perhaps some comparison to be drawn between a personal passport and a ship's passport,' he said. 'A ship flying a particular flag, and with the pass of a particular country, is not allowed to dispute that it is of the nationality of that flag and of that pass. A passport itself, in my submission, is an extension into the realm of international law and diplomatic practice of the sovereign's protection, and once protection is seen to be the basis of allegiance, then, in my submission, there is no reason at all in principle to limit it to cases where the protection arises because of residence. I would invite your Lordship to say that it may arise because of birth, it may arise because of an oath of allegiance having been taken, it may arise because of some presence in territory, and equally it may arise in any other circumstances in which the alien concerned voluntarily places himself as a subject under the protection of the Crown.'

There followed a curt exchange between the Attorney-General and the judge.

'Here was a man,' Shawcross continued, 'who quite independently of any continuing residence was under a duty of allegiance because of the protection of the Crown with which he clothed himself.'

'Mr Attorney,' Tucker interrupted, 'the only overt act laid under Count 3 is the broadcasting, the evidence of the witness who said he heard a voice which he identified as that of the prisoner, saying that Folkestone and Dover had been destroyed, is it not?'

'There is the contract, my Lord—'

'The contract was dated much later.'

'Yes, my Lord, the contract itself referred to a later period, I respectfully agree – the Work Book [his employment record], possibly the award [Joyce's medal], although I do not think I can place much reliance upon that.'

'What is the date of the award?'

'1944. There is the Work Book and his statement. The Work Book gives 18 September as the date on which he entered into the employment of the [German] Broadcasting Corporation. Hunt did say in his evidence that although that was the only occasion when he remembered actually what the man had said, he heard him on a number of occasions before he came back to London on 11 December.'

The judge was satisfied with this. It was Slade's turn again. 'In my submission to your Lordship,' he said, 'an alien only owes allegiance to His Majesty the King so long as he is resident within the King's dominions.'

He then made the point that it was absurd to suggest that Joyce had 'left his family and effects in England', just because his parents and grown-up brothers and sisters remained here. He had no control over them. And his wife had gone with him to Germany. Further, Joyce had said in his statement that he had no intention of ever returning to England, indeed, to do so would be to put his head into the lion's jaw. 'Take one illustration,' Slade said. 'Ex hypothesi, as I say, Joyce is now an American subject. Supposing in August, 1939, when he left Great Britain, instead of going to Germany, he had gone to New York, his own country; and supposing America had come into the war against us instead of on our side; he would have been liable for service in the American army. Whatever he tried to do, if the passport lasted for a year, and it might have lasted for five years – it had an extension for five years – he would have committed treason against the country by fighting for his own country! There are other absurdities which I will deal with later; but in my submission, quite apart from all these, it is extravagant in the extreme to say that a man who, according to the case for the prosecution, left this country for the express purpose of committing acts which would be undoubtedly treasonable, if he owed allegiance, only left her temporarily, intending to come back, and put his head into the lion's mouth so that he could be sentenced to be hanged. That is the sort of extravagant suggestion, if I may say so, which is being put forward in this case.'

Slade's fourth point was that the issue of a British passport to an alien does not, of itself, clothe him with the status of a British subject. 'In 1940,' Slade noted, 'a Turkish holder of a British passport issued to him in Palestine was recommended by a London magistrate for deportation as an alien, and the recommendation was upheld by the Court of Criminal Appeal.'

Slade's fifth point concerned what would happen if a man had wrongly obtained a British passport. 'It would disqualify him from protection by the King's representative in a foreign country if he got into trouble. His passport would then be withdrawn, and protection refused; therefore he would owe no allegiance to the King.' Finally, Slade argued that no English court has jurisdiction to try foreigners for crimes committed by them abroad, except in the case of piracy. 'And the prisoner is not charged with being a pirate!' There were smiles around the courtroom at this. Court was adjourned.

That night William wrote to Margaret from Brixton Prison. He knew she would not receive the letter until after the verdict and so he asked her to forgive his compulsive levity and gallows humour. He referred to his circumstances being a little complex and said that he had not forgotten her parting salutation to him – 'Ireland forever!' – as he was being carried past her, on a stretcher. His tone was hopeful. 'And now, my darling, I have just returned from my business trip to the City. For these few days, dear, you would have been able to say that your husband was "something in the City". Of course, by the time you get this, the trial will be over and I shall either be awaiting the Appeal hearing, or else studying the alternative attack which success would bring. From experience, I know that it is misleading to judge a trial by the first day, which, ipso facto, belongs to the prosecution. Old Hot Cross Buns [Shawcross], at whom I have been inclined to jest, is certainly very able . . . This morning, we had plenty of blast; but I did not notice any Volltreffer [direct hit].'

It is intriguing to speculate on what MI5 made of this and other Joyce letters. During the trial, they read all his correspondence, including his lawyer's. Not only that, they copied it all, re-sealed it all and – illegally – passed it all on to the prosecution. For his part, Joyce seems not have minded unduly. 'For the censor's convenience, I shall try to refrain from over abstruse phraseology,' he wrote.

The third and final day of the trial began with Shawcross asking to have the words 'being a British subject' substituted by the words 'being a person owing allegiance to the Crown' in the first two counts. Judge Tucker asked a taken-aback Slade if he had any objection to that. 'To put it frankly, the point was mentioned to me two minutes ago,' Slade said, still reeling. 'Quite candidly, I have not had the opportunity of seeing any possible repercussion which might result.' Joyce by contrast showed no excitement, only curiosity.

The legal argument between Slade and Shawcross continued all morning until Mr Justice Tucker announced that he would give his ruling on their submissions after the luncheon interval. Court was adjourned until 2 p.m.

Back in the court cell, Joyce began another letter to Margaret. 'When Slade said: "And that baby, William Joyce, was the prisoner in the dock..." some of my Scotland Yard and MI patrons [he could have meant Military Intelligence by this, but more likely MI5] were hard taxed to restrain their smiles – and I have had to keep my face no more crooked than usual.' He praised the staff responsible for taking him to court and looking after him, calling them 'most chivalrous'. 'When I returned here, I had nearly a litre of the most exquisite chocolate-koko waiting for me. I don't want to dwell unduly on the excellencies of this tuition, but really, tho' I am not British, and tho' all my views remain unchanged, I much doubt if any other people in the world would, in like circs, treat me so well ... I can honestly say that I should not like to have missed the brilliant and intensive legal battle which began to rage shortly before lunch, when the evidence for the defence closed.'

After lunch, Joyce returned to the dock with his usual excess of tight-lipped military smartness. The court rose as the judge took his seat. There was a silence. Tucker cleared his throat. He was about to make one of the most controversial rulings in modern legal history. And it was to be against the defence.

'Mr Attorney and Mr Slade, I shall direct the jury on Count 3 that on 24 August, 1939, when the passport was applied for, the prisoner, beyond a shadow of doubt, owed allegiance to the Crown of this country, and that on the evidence given, if [the jury] accept it, nothing happened at the material time thereafter, that is, up to July 1940 when the passport expired, to put an end to the allegiance that he then owed.'

The judge had denied the jury the chance to decide for themselves if Joyce, as an alien in a foreign land, still owed an allegiance to the Crown. He, and he alone, had decided, in other words, that Joyce was 'British enough' to be convicted of high treason – as a man owing allegiance to the King of England, a status he had once claimed falsely. The judge had dismissed the truth and accepted the defendant's lie.

After this disaster, Slade addressed the jury in what he must have known was now a hopeless cause. Following the judge's ruling, the jury was merely left with the question of whether Joyce – as opposed to, say, Norman Baillie-Stewart or Wolff Mittler, the original Lord Haw-Haws – had broadcast propaganda in the first month of the war, the period when Hunt claimed to have heard him. Thanks to the hastily amended Treason Act (1945), which was given Royal Assent the day before Joyce was escorted back to the United Kingdom, it was now no longer necessary to have two witnesses for a charge of treason to be brought. One would do. This was fortunate for the prosecution because it only had one witness: the man Joyce called 'Unt.

Slade had grown fond of Joyce and he may have wanted to make a mockery of the trial at this point by arguing that everyone knew Joyce broadcast propaganda during the war – and, if called, Joyce would have been the first to admit it, as indeed he did in the statement he made after his capture. The only chance the defence had was to discredit Hunt's evidence. How could the Special Branch officer be sure it was Joyce he had heard? After all, what he had supposedly heard – that 'Dover and Folkestone have been destroyed' – was clearly so ridiculous as to be absurd. No news agency would want to squander its reputation for accuracy by broadcasting such an easily disproved claim – there hadn't even been a shot fired in France in the period referred to, let alone a major bombing campaign on the south coast of England. Hunt, Slade pointed out, didn't even know which station he had supposedly been listening to. And even if, for some bizarre reason, Joyce *had* said that 'Dover and Folkestone have been destroyed', was it treasonous to say a town had been destroyed? It would have been a false report, but does erroneous reporting constitute adhering to the King's enemies?

Slade addressed the jury, but his comments seemed to be aimed at the judge: 'If your Lordship pleases, then I ought to address the jury, I think, just upon this point. Members of the jury, the only point you have to consider, being directed as a matter of law that the prisoner *did* owe allegiance to His Majesty the King, is whether he committed the offence with which he is charged in what has been called Count 3 of this indictment. You have to consider whether the prosecution has proved beyond all reasonable doubt this one point, that it was Joyce who broadcast those words in the first month of the war.

'I cannot do better than to ask you to do what the Attorney-General asked you to do at the outset of this case, to put aside from yourselves prejudice altogether. As he so truly remarked, Joyce will be all forgotten after a nine days' wonder, but the way that justice is done in this country will not be forgotten. You may think that it is a tribute that, while we are now proceeding, at Belsen most of those Germans are being defended by British officers.

'I can well understand a person saying "Don't try him at all; shoot him without trial." You may think that would be one of the best things to do. But what I do say is: If you are going to try him, try him, and do not make a mockery of the trial. You, members of the jury, have, of course, a most difficult task. Joyce has been branded as Lord Haw-Haw; he has been branded as a traitor. Everyone talks of him as though he were already condemned and convicted, but you are here to try whether he is guilty or not.'

To use one of Joyce's chess analogies, this was the end game. The judge directed the jury to return a verdict of not guilty on counts one and two. On the third count he directed the jury that on 24 August 1939, when the passport was issued, the prisoner 'beyond a shadow of doubt' owed allegiance to the Crown, and that nothing happened during the material time to end that allegiance. Referring to the inevitable appeal he said: 'I may be wrong; if I am I can be corrected.' When the judge then warned the jury to consider very carefully their verdict, because a person found guilty must be sentenced to death, Joyce put up his hand and touched his neck with a look of wonder.

The jury retired to consider their verdict at 3.37 p.m. and returned at 4 p.m. According to Rebecca West, they looked as if they had been out for a cup of tea. Joyce stared at each juror in turn. As instructed they found him not guilty on counts one and two. Tucker looked at the foreman of the jury and asked: 'How do you find on the third count?'

'Guilty, your honour.'

Joyce stood stiffly to attention. The clerk of the court said: 'Prisoner at the bar, you stand convicted of high treason. Have you anything to say why the court should not give you judgement according to law?'

A crackle of excitement passed through the court. Would this be the moment when Joyce finally gave vent to his famous voice? Throughout the trial the garrulous orator had said just two words: 'Not guilty.' The prisoner made as if to speak then checked himself, shook his head and clicked his heels together by way of reply.

At the end, his silence was as powerful as his voice had been. According to a report in the *Daily Telegraph*, Joyce then watched 'in fascination' as the judge laid the black cap over his wig. 'William Joyce,' he intoned, 'the sentence of the court upon you is that you be taken from this place to a lawful prison and thence to a place of execution, and that you be there hanged by the neck until you be dead; and that your body be afterwards buried within the precincts of the prison in which you shall have been confined before your execution. And may the Lord have mercy on your soul.'

The chaplain said: 'Amen.'

Macnab buried his face in his hands and sobbed loud enough for the court to hear.

After sentence was passed, Joyce pursed his lips, then he managed a thin smile and gave a quick wave to his brother Quentin – this was interpreted by the press as 'a Nazi salute'. He then gave a low bow to the judge, clicked his heels again, turned and walked down the steps from the dock.

Quentin Joyce was in tears as he walked from the court out into the mild autumn air. Head, the solicitor, tugged on his sleeve and said: 'It's the appeal that matters, you know.' Quentin nodded: 'Yes, I know. The appeal's everything.' A large crowd was waiting silently outside the court, behind a row of parked cars. A small band of Joyce's supporters gathered together in a knot just inside the main entrance to the court. After they had wiped their faces and composed themselves, they went outside and dispersed.

Later, in his cell, Joyce was having regrets about not speaking at his trial. 'It is true that I snapped noiselessly when the clerk asked me if I had anything to say as to why sentence of death should not be passed upon me,' he wrote to Margaret, 'but that was only because the evil old bladder-of-lard-faced weasel did not allow me an instant in which to make my intended formal reply to the effect that I was leaving the case in the hands of my counsel. I thought of interrupting the judge and demanding my undoubted right to make a reply: but my contempt for the judgement, combined with a somewhat belated respect for my own dignity, kept me silent. I might have created a sensation, not by wilting but by some aggressive demonstration. But through my head there kept running Marvell's lines [on Charles I]: "He nothing common did or mean, Upon that memorable scene." And so the conclusion was quite decorous. Whether I bore myself becomingly is for others to judge. But I do believe that I did nothing to shame me in the eyes of my lady: and I am therefore content. It gave me no small degree of satisfaction in the dock at the Old Bailey to see that His Lordship, complete with vampire chapeau, after once meeting my eyes, read his precious sentence into his desk.'

EIGHTEEN

'The entrance they are free to choose, but not the exit.'
(*Faust*, Part 1)

When Heather, Joyce's seventeen-year-old daughter, heard the news, she was devastated. She had secretly listened to her father's broadcasts during the war – when she was supposed to be doing her homework – as a way of feeling close to him. And at school she had felt a certain lateral bond with him because the other children had taunted her in the playground with chants of 'Germany Calling!' Perhaps as a consequence, she had been having recurring dreams about him. She asked her mother if she and her sister Diana could visit their father in prison: 'He will be so pleased to see us grown up,' she said. But Hazel Piercy, as she now was, cautioned against it. She also persuaded her daughters that it wouldn't be a good idea to write to him either. Her last words on the subject were: 'Poor little swine! Why did he get himself into this mess? He won't show his fear, you know. He's always very brave.'

Hazel was right. In fact, Joyce seems to have made up his mind to enjoy the structure of life afforded the condemned prisoner. He played many games of chess with his guards. He even, so he said, took pleasure in washing up his own crockery. And where once he and Margaret had scoured Berlin looking for soap, now he took delight in being able to use his favourite brand: Lifebuoy. Prisons are in some ways odd places, he wrote. But he could not grumble at his. His days were being pleasantly passed.

While a cell was being prepared at Wandsworth Prison, Joyce was transferred temporarily from Brixton to Wormwood Scrubs – this he called his 'knight's move', in other words he went from A to B via C, as a knight moves on a chessboard. He was escorted to a cell, a metal door was clattered shut behind him, and a key was turned noisily in the lock. Then a small hole opened in the door and a warden peered in. He had been put on suicide watch. Except for this he was mostly left alone to read books. The various prison libraries were reasonably well stocked with the classics and they also included a foreign section which enabled Joyce, as he put it, to 'keep in practise'. He particularly enjoyed *The Screwtape Letters* by C. S. Lewis (letters from a senior to a junior devil called Wormwood).

He was also now allowed a pint of beer or stout a day, plus ten cigarettes – a privilege of the condemned man. 'I hate to tell you but must,' he wrote to Margaret. 'Today I had some really good beer! Twas my first 'cohol since May. Of course, it cannot be equated to wine or schnapps: but, none the less, I enjoyed it.' When not reading, playing chess or drinking, he would write letters. The day after sentence was passed he tried to make light of the proceedings. He told Margaret not to worry and that his only concern in the whole Gothick drama was the fear that she would be upset and frustrated. That day, he added, he just wanted to caress his old Mother-Sheep's woollen coat. As ever, the extremes of Joyce's personality embraced the contraries of pertinacity and amiability, immaturity and tenderness.

The only real change to his routine since his sentence of death was that he was no longer allowed to read newspapers. This was no bad thing, because now that the case was no longer sub judice, the press was busy making up for lost time. When told about the coverage, Joyce said drily that he missed the papers but could reconcile himself to their absence.

The *Daily Mail* wrote: 'Never was punishment so richly deserved. Of all the creatures who served Hitler's gang, none was so detested as this man, who sought to weaken the resolution of the British people in the face of a mortal enemy. It matters not to the ordinary man whether he could claim American or German citizenship. He betrayed the country that sheltered him.'

A more measured *Daily Telegraph* leader noted: 'The case will make legal history as establishing for the first time certain conditions under which an alien may be condemned for treason, and it may possibly suggest to Parliament the desirability of legislation further qualifying the duties and liabilities of persons holding British passports. Why William Joyce should have elected to requite in this detestable manner the country whose hospitality he had enjoyed for many years, and whose protection he sought at the passport office, is still something of a mystery, and is not much elucidated by the diffuse statement which he made after his arrest and which was read out in court. His conduct, as described in evidence, betrays not a single redeeming feature, and no verdict has ever been more in accordance with the evidence.'

The Times, a paper that had supported appeasement, commented: 'Having been indicted in this country he was – and remains – entitled to the full benefits of the impartial processes of the law courts; but the verdict of the jury on the facts will be recorded with public approval. The fact that Joyce was technically an alien cannot in any degree lessen in retrospect the detestation and contempt which his conduct provoked.'

Although the media was gloating about Joyce's comeuppance, there seems to have been a feeling of unease among the *bien pensants* that his trial had been more about vengeance than justice. After all, the conviction was decided not by a jury of twelve good men and true but a single judge who had already declared the defendant guilty even before the trial began. Joyce had supported an evil tyranny, that was true, but that did not mean his trial should be rigged. Such trials, it was argued, were for dictatorships. As the barrister J. W. Hall asserted in his contemporaneous account of the trial: 'I have found, with a universal reprobation of Joyce's conduct, an almost equally universal feeling, shared by lawyers, servicemen and civilians, that the decision was all wrong, and that an unmeritorious case has made bad law. The feeling, and it is, I believe, strong and widespread, is not so much that Joyce, having been convicted, should be reprieved, but that he should not have been convicted. If one treats the sensation-mongers who stand outside a prison during an execution with the contempt they deserve, it is, I think, fair to say that the conviction of Joyce has caused more disquiet than satisfaction in the minds of the public.'

The historian A. J. P. Taylor echoed this sentiment, arguing that Joyce had been convicted 'on a trumped up charge'. 'The charges against Joyce were not proved in court. It was not shown that he had retained his passport once he was in Germany, nor was any satisfactory evidence produced that he had broadcast for the Germans during the period of the passport's validity. He had of course, as he would probably have admitted if asked, but that was beside the point.' He concluded that Joyce 'excited amusement, not alarm'. And that 'his real offence was to have attracted to himself the mythical repute of Lord Haw-Haw.'

Gerald Slade KC was inundated with letters concerning the trial. A reporter from the *Evening News* called upon Head, Joyce's solicitor, and inquired if those letters were menacing or hostile. When told that 95 per cent of them were in favour of Joyce, the reporter said: 'Oh! But we can't print that!' Joyce was delighted by this anecdote when it was related to him.

Members of the public in their hundreds wrote to King George VI, Clement Attlee, the Prime Minister, and James Chuter Ede, the Home Secretary, appealing for clemency. The file of letters, telegrams and petitions was several inches thick and was immediately deemed 'classified'. Some of these people must have been campaigners who always appealed against a death sentence on principle, as a matter of course. But others may have been feeling guilty for having listened to Lord Haw-Haw, and for starting the rumours about him: they hadn't thought what was essentially a national joke would end like this.

One cable read simply: 'Can you reprieve Joyce? He did no harm: he amused a great number of people.' Another read: 'I listened often to his broadcasts and never heard him say a word against England, the King or the British Empire. He only attacked the politicians who, he concluded, were dragging the country to ruin. He warned this country of the result of letting loose the Red Army in Europe, a warning which appears to have a solid foundation.'

The Duke of Bedford was among the petitioners: 'I gather Joyce has never been charged with betraying military secrets,' he wrote. 'I must say that I feel his execution would be an act of quite unjustifiably vindictive severity involving a not inconsiderable degree of hypocrisy as well.'

It was unclear whether Margaret would require the same kind of petitioning. MI5 was still open to the prospect. On 26 September, one of its officers, Major Wakefield, concluded that she had indeed committed treason. 'As a married woman she is unable to divest herself of her British nationality by an act of naturalisation,' he wrote in a briefing paper. 'A married woman can only lose her British nationality by a marriage which automatically confers on her the nationality of her husband . . . as a British subject she would have presumably committed an act of treason by taking German nationality in wartime.'

For her part, Margaret would glibly refer in private to 'my treachery', but she doesn't seem to have seriously considered herself a traitor. She and William were now writing to each other every day, over four sides of prison paper – their daily ration. They would draw each other pictures, address each other by their pet names of Old Ram and Mother-Sheep, and make allusions to bleating and to Margaret's sheep-like ears being straight and brave, as oppose to floppy and defeatist. On 26 September, for example, William wrote to thank his darling Mother-Sheep for the fine crest she had drawn. It showed a proud-looking Ram. This, he mused, should be called a woollen coat of arms. To know that she was keeping her ovine ears erect, rather than allowing them to flop dejectedly down, was enough to make him feel contented, he added. And he consoled her with the thought that the peers upon whom they might have to depend gave tribute to the Woolsack.

At times Joyce was lyrical in his letters. In one he wrote that it was dusk again and the loveliness of the shadows was throwing a celestial spell over the forbidding scene from his cell window. (As he was looking out, so, according to the *Daily Mail*, local residents were looking in, or at least they could see the light in his cell. 'And these people get a kick from looking. It is a great satisfaction to them to know that under this light sits William Joyce, the man whose voice they so often heard jeering and taunting over the German radio during the dark days of the London blitz.')

It is not easy to square the man who wrote these often poetic and playful letters with the repulsive anti-Semite, wife-beater and hate-filled soapbox psychopath of reputation. But as A. K. Chesterton had once said: 'When he put aside his jackboots, Joyce could emerge as a humble person, not without charm and with a delicate sense of irony.'

That said, the letters did occasionally offer glimpses of his pompous, self-justifying, callous side. On 27 September he wrote to Margaret about the latest reports concerning what he mistakenly called 'Belsen-Buchen-wald' (he meant Bergen-Belsen), trying to offer an explanation for the atrocities which, it was now more fully emerging, had gone on there. 'It was certainly not the best type of man who sought employment as a KZ [concentration camp] official, but probably the worst . . . If we picture them organising merely to keep a hostile political or criminal substratum alive, in the teeth of the enemy's bombing campaign, we can, perhaps, by induction, reach the idea of something which, if not exactly Belsen, would nonetheless not be Brixton. I see that, according to one allegation, though there was no food in Belsen, there was plenty in the Wehrmacht institution nearby. Now the British seem to think that this food could simply have been moved to Belsen. We know that before this end could have been attained, several plots against the Führer and perhaps even a minor civil war would have been needed: but that is something which the Briton would have no hesitation in disbelieving. Nor will the defendants ever be able to explain why the food could not have been moved. Then, imagine a [German official] dealing with incipient typhus, aided by a doctor who wrote articles on the thesis that smoking makes women sterile or that it is fatal to drink water after eating fruit. My dear, Germany is always a wonderland, but sometimes – alas! – a blunderland.' The only hope for the Germans, he believed, was that the occupying British army would share Margaret's opinion of them: and once the Germans had become familiar to them they would realize that most people in England still lived a much more comfortable life. To the Joyces it was painful that ordinary Germans, who they believed had no adult complicity, had to carry the mark of the concentration camps.

This argument, that if 'criminals' had died in the concentration camps it must have been due to a combination of typhoid and problems of supply and control during the last days of the Third Reich, was, of course, the standard lie trotted out by Nazis either in denial or out to save their own skins after the war. It is telling that Joyce refers to Belsen which, though a place of unbelievable horror and brutality, was not actually a death camp in the sense that Auschwitz-Birkenau was. Even so, it is debatable whether Joyce would have fully comprehended the terrible magnitude of the holocaust, given that he had been in prison since the end of May, with limited access to newspapers. He would have missed the shocking news footage which had been playing on cinema screens, and most of the revelations about the scale and the manner of the genocide only emerged during the Nuremberg Trial that autumn, during which time he had no access to newspapers.

Wandsworth Prison was a mid-Victorian building with a facade of dark stone derived from the town hall in Florence. It was divided from the main road by a nursery garden with thin streams trickling under miniature bridges. When Joyce was moved there on 28 September, he became prisoner Number 3229. 'As you will notice from the superscription, I am no longer Brixton Bill,' he wrote to Margaret, 'but Wandsworth Will. The alliterative effect is preserved.' His cell was thirteen feet by seven and was in E Wing. It had a high Victorian grille window with a limited view of a distant tree which Joyce promptly claimed as 'our tree' – his and Margaret's. In his imagination he would meet her there every evening at twilight.

His brother Quentin and his devoted friend Angus Macnab began making regular visits. Visiting time was three o'clock and he had to converse with them through a wire-mesh grille, across a table. The idea was that the grille would prevent his guests handing him an iron file, or a capsule of cyanide. Joyce likened the 'visiting box' to a rabbit hutch. (It must be assumed that Knight, or one of his fellow spooks, was bugging Joyce's prison conversations, as he had bugged Mosley's.)

On 2 October, Joyce revealed in a letter to Macnab that his time in prison had helped him examine his life and come to some self-knowledge. 'I know that if it is God's will that I should survive my present danger, I shall be far better for my experiences since last May. Indeed, without them, I shall be regrettably poor. I have the feeling, founded or unfounded, that every minute of experience in these months has had its value and that nothing has been left to chance.' He was confident, moreover, that if the law was properly interpreted, the Old Bailey conviction would be quashed. 'As I awaited sentence in the dock I had to think with an inward laugh, of Dryden's lines: "What weight of ancient witness can prevail / When private judgement holds the public scale."'

Miss Scrimgeour, his old patron, also visited him in prison. His letters to her were more formal than those he wrote to other friends: 'I feel no satisfaction but cannot quite restrain my contempt for those who would hang me for treason. Had I robbed the public or impeded the war effort by profiteering on munitions, a peerage would now be within my reach, if I were willing to buy it.' In a later letter to her he wrote that he would be an impoverished man if he did not bear his hardships lightly. There could be no greater reward, he said, than for a man to be condemned to death for his principles. After all, millions had perished for they knew not what. He said something similar to his friend Father Edmund: namely that any idiot could die, or fade away if in the army, but it took a true man to live to some purpose.

He claimed that while he did not mind being on remand at Brixton, he preferred his present status as a condemned prisoner at Wandsworth, joking that a civil servant of his rank was not entitled to anything better. This was a black joke indeed because sanitary conditions in all of London's prisons at that time were dire, with infestations of vermin and cockroaches commonplace. Perhaps the bravado was for Margaret's benefit. He asked her not to worry about his personal comfort. It would be impossible for him to write too highly of his conditions. The food was splendid. He had plenty of books, English and German. 'And I have been amusing myself by reading Shakespeare in Dutch. We have much chess and in the evening I generally have a mug of beer and a good smoke as I discuss philosophy with the chaplain, a very charming man who gives me the pleasure of his company very often. Really prison is the only place apart from my Jesuit school where I have seen any attempt to apply psychology consistently and sensibly.'

Of his impending appeal he wrote that what little Caledonian blood he had advised him not to make any plans for the more pleasing outcome. Mistress Fate, he added, did not like to be teased gently; she would rather be put over one knee and given a sound spanking. He could not see darkness, but even if he could, he would sooner that than be disloyal to his country in broad daylight. His optimism was remarkable – even he seems to have thought so – but it was probably only a defence mechanism. He was, he acknowledged, filled with an irrational sanguinity. But he insisted that he had not conjured this feeling up as a recompense. It was there: and he could not purge himself of it even if he would.

However, it may have been that he was, again, putting on a brave face to spare Margaret's feelings. He was undoubtedly concerned about how she was taking the news of his death sentence, and extremely worried that she, too, might have to face a treason trial. It may also have been that he made light of his situation out of pride and stubbornness. Either way, by the beginning of the new month, the tone of his letters became relentlessly jovial and deadpan – he referred wryly to a British passport being a life-insurance policy – and they were full of deliberate misspelling, such as jellus for jealous. His spelling was ruined by Middle English, he wrote in one letter (dropping the 'g' and one 'l' from the word). He imagined that October (which he spelled with a 'k') would be a lively month, though he could not complain about September being mundane. He mused upon how the authorities need not fear his influence on the public (spelled with a 'k') – because as a politician he now ranked with the Cretaceous marine reptiles. And when he received an invitation to a birthday reception for the exiled former 'King' Vladislaw of Poland, he pretended not to know what the correct form dictated. Although he was not normally a timorous man, he mused, he could not summon the nerve to ask the governor for the afternoon off. He regularly used the phrase 'Haw-Haw!' in his letters, as when, for example, he wondered whether by landing in Britain and residing there for a time afterwards, Rudolf Hess might have placed himself under the protection of the King – an allusion to his own trial. Sir Hartley Shawcross was leading the prosecution team at Nuremberg and Joyce suggested that his best bet would be to slip a British passport into the luggage of each of the defendants.

A newspaper cutting that Margaret sent him about his 'irresolute smile in court', made him smile, he wrote, though not without resolution. He speculated that any perceived lack of resolve was a consequence of his not wearing his dentures. He wondered whether that afternoon somewhere in England they were being proudly shown off to a garden party. If they were, he hoped they would bite the guests. It wasn't just his confiscated dentures that had been taken by souvenir hunters. His Cross of War Merit had been stolen, too, but he doubted that he would be allowed to wear it in his present situation, anyway – if he did, he quipped, it would make a good subject for Bateman (famous for 'The Man Who . . .' series of cartoons in *Punch*).

The letters revealed Joyce's sense of humour, then. They also suggested a certain self-awareness. He asked forgiveness for his tendency to be loquacious, for example, and for Margaret to pardon him for drawing an ink blot. It had no particular connotation, he wrote, it was just that he had found himself with a shortage of ink and so had suddenly had an urge to be profligate with what he had left.

Forgiveness was a recurring theme in the letters. Much on his mind was the thought that he had landed Margaret in trouble and that during their time together in Berlin he had treated her badly. Towards the end of the war, he explained, he had been exhausted – how exhausted, only she could guess. But he accepted that he was merely finding excuses for not having shown her more consideration. And in answer to a letter from her in which she apologized for her own quick temper, he counselled that she should never admonish herself for being grumpy. If she was, it was his fault. He knew that he was so impossible to live with he could, within a matter of days, turn the most beatific and placid woman into a ravenous wolf foaming at the mouth with rabies.

Perhaps his letters were pure escapism. After all, he did not dwell on an incident which must have brought home to him the brutal reality of his situation. While reading a book one afternoon he was given a reminder that, throughout history, treason was the crime most abhorred by the English. His fellow inmates began howling like wolves, raging against his presence. According to his guard, Joyce heard the riot, lifted his eyes from his book and forced them back again. Finally he put his book down and said hesitantly: 'These people are not calling out against me, are they?' The guard gave an evasive reply, but later, while Joyce was exercising in the prison yard on his own, the answer came. Prisoners spat at him and threw objects from their cell windows, along with patriotic insults. Four prisoners were punished. It emerged during the investigation that there had been a plot among the prisoners to rush the guards 'and get Lord Haw-Haw'.

If Joyce was rattled he was determined not to give those who taunted him – inside prison, and outside in the press – the satisfaction of seeing him so. The closest he came to acknowledging his unpopularity was when he noted in a letter that he knew people would be wallowing in the thought of him being forlorn, despised and covered in spit, but that he didn't care.

On 13 October he sought to reassure Margaret that she wouldn't also be tried for treason: if the Treason Act came up they would take it en passant. He seemed to be implying that he had something up his sleeve. He used another chess analogy with regard to the appeal: as in chess, he noted, a demarche that was premature often impaired a later attack. He hinted about a deal with MI5 – that if he did not mention his past association with them, they would not press for a prosecution of Margaret – though it is not clear what if any contact he had with the Security Service while in prison. He prided himself on judging that MI5 would take good care of Margaret. The Service, he wrote, 'does not suffer from "coetaneous sesqui-pedalianisme!"' Margaret may have been wondering in her letters why he hadn't played his MI5 card, because he asked her not to regret his discretion on the subject. He would rather be set alight, he wrote, than walk as a free man who had shown himself to be a cowardly sneak. He urged her to take blankets if they were offered and that when she was chilly she should squeal (spelled with 'kw' instead of 'qu' – if he used the correct spelling, he added, she might take it the wrong way, in the light of their legal position). He also noted, somewhat cryptically, that if MI5 received a royalty from every novelist – Knight? – who took its name in vain it could found a library for the blind. This was an allusion, presumably, to the Service's tendency to turn a blind eye to the question-able activities of some of its members. Then a few days after that he reflected that MI5 had some marvellous officers but that the pertinacity of others exceeded their wisdom. On balance, he reflected, the Secret Service was 'top-hole'.

It might have been that the Home Office was looking for an excuse not to prosecute Margaret anyway, because if she was brought to trial and the case against her collapsed – because a jury rejected the same evidence it had hanged her husband upon – then it would not look good. After all, if she was deemed to be German or American by marriage, then her husband must ipso facto have been German or American, too.

Joyce seems to have constructed his own imaginary world, a bubble of self-regard and adolescent fantasy in his Wandsworth cell. In it he built himself up as the hero in his own Greek tragedy. He referred to his approaching nemesis. He suggested to Margaret that he was glad she had not been called as a witness at his trial because mixing tragedy and farce was frowned upon by the ancient Greeks. Regarding his fevered walk to the scaffold, he advised her that, like Siegfried, they should bind fast the helm and ride.

As Lord Haw-Haw he had required an outward acknowledgement of his treacherous deeds, even if that did come in the form of notoriety. Clearly he had now come to the view that a glorious martyrdom would be preferable to ignominious imprisonment, or suicide. His mind was concentrated, no doubt, by the execution, on 24 October, of another traitor, Quisling. Joyce heard this news at the same time as that of the Nuremberg Trial was reaching his ears. He argued that a great many people took themselves too 'bloody' seriously and that if you committed suicide you were admitting that your beliefs were false – and that would be a tragedy in the Greek sense.

Before his appeal date, MI5 recorded, Joyce had received 'Fifty-eight letters from people expressing admiration, good wishes and friendship. A further twenty-three letters from eccentrics, thirteen of them anonymous.' One seemed to be pulling the leg of the Prison Services by suggesting William had been given improper access to a telephone during his incarceration. Another sent a bottle of rat poison. On the eve of his appeal hearing, Joyce laughed about how a madman had stormed Head's office and demanded to take over the case. The offer had been declined.

The Court of Appeal in the Strand was a square room lined with leather-bound volumes in blue, green and red. Part of the roof had been removed by a bomb blast, so there was, according to Joyce, an atrium effect. The appeal, which began on 30 October, was presided over by Lord Caldecote – whom Joyce promptly nicknamed Old Bandicoot. Joyce enjoyed his journey from Wandsworth Prison to the Strand because it took him through some of his old haunts, Battersea Rise and Clapham Common. They seemed familiar, he noted afterwards. For his appearance in court, according to one observer, he wore 'wide flapping trousers, brown shoes that were split, a black jacket and a pyjama collared greyish shirt that was held together clumsily by a tightly fastened black tie.' There was room only for a handful of spectators, including Joyce's friends. The counsel for both sides sat facing three judges, while Joyce was to one side. He was amused to discover that he was close enough to the judges to hear them snuffling like pigs. As he revealed in a later letter, he wished that Margaret had been with him at that moment so that they could have joked about how like a farmyard the court was.

Rebecca West was again among the spectators. 'Prisoners in the dock laugh more freely than is generally imagined,' she observed. 'Judicial jokes which so often annoy the newspaper reader are to them an opportunity for relaxation. But Joyce's amusement at his own appeal was more subtle than that. One of the judges on the bench was most picturesquely comic in appearance and might have come straight out of the *commedia dell' arte*. William Joyce watched him with delight; and he followed the legal arguments with an unusual detachment, once nodding in approval when a point was decided against him.' John Mayes, another onlooker at the appeal, noted that Joyce 'held his head high, with a smile of indifference.'

Joseph McLeod in his BBC report of the proceedings described Joyce as being 'quite aloof and probably the most self-possessed person in the court.'

The long contemplation of death seems to have given Joyce a dignity he had lacked in his previous court appearances. 'It could be recognised when he turned his eyes on the spectators who paused to look at him before they went up to their seats in the gallery,' West noted. 'At the Old Bailey he had soon come to recognise those who were sitting through the whole trial, and it had entertained him to catch their eyes and stare them out. At the court of appeal he gave spectators an inquisitive and gentler eye.'

One glimmer of hope for Joyce came in the form of the concept of a dual-nationality passport. As Macnab explained in a letter to Margaret: 'I haven't W's permission but as the matter is now so near I feel justified in mentioning the find. It is a dual nationality passport belonging to a friend of mine. It proves that under some circumstances a British subject having a valid British passport containing no false statements, can bear arms against the King of England without being guilty of treason. Also that when in the country of his other nationality he gets no protection from the British Crown and is not relieved of his allegiance to the other country. It follows that the Crown demands from William, while in Germany and a foreigner, a higher degree of allegiance than it demands from one of its own subjects.'

But Slade was not permitted to offer new evidence or new arguments. And due to high treason having only one possible sentence, he could only appeal the conviction, not the sentence itself. He based the appeal on the premise that Mr Justice Tucker had been wrong at the trial in his interpretation of the law and his direction of the jury. British law could not try a foreign national for an offence committed abroad, he argued. There was no evidence that between 18 September 1939 and 2 July 1940 Joyce sought or obtained any protection from his British passport. But that was an issue for the jury alone to decide, not the judge who had directed the jury. The fact that the King was unable to offer protection to Joyce in Germany, that Joyce was an American citizen and that Joyce never intended to ask for protection, meant that as no protection was asked for, no allegiance was owed in return. 'An alien's allegiance ceased when he left the country,' Slade concluded. 'The fathers of English legal theory are either right or wrong. If they are right, Mr Justice Tucker's ruling must be wrong.'

Joyce took in a blood-red sunset on the drive back to Wandsworth. Twilight was always his favourite time of the day and, back in his cell, he wrote to tell Margaret that he had tried to share the moment with her. Her absence that day had wounded him, he wrote, but he had checked himself. He could not afford to be soppy. But he asked her not to assume that because his writing was restrained he was being cold and unemotional.

On 2 November he acknowledged that the appeal didn't seem to be going in his favour, indeed he noted that he might have the distinction of being the only villain condemned to death twice for the same act. He also revealed that he had become annoyed in court when Old Bandicoot, as he called the judge, had stammered while reading. But this feeling had passed, to be replaced by a more philosophical disposition. He reflected that everyone had to die at some time and so it was a duty to live in such a way that you could, if it came to it, meet death in a cheerful spirit. Referring to the internment the Joyces would have faced had they not gone to Germany, he reflected that they would be worse off if they had had five years of Brixton and Holloway instead of their glorious Fatherland.

While awaiting the verdict of the appeal judges, Joyce indulged in an endearing flight of nonsense about a cyst his wife was complaining of and which she had named Cyril. 'The cyst occupies a higher place than the mere abscess in the eruption hierarchy,' he wrote. 'When you have had a cyst, you are entitled to boast of it, particularly if you do not say where it was. It originates with a rebellious local gestalt, demanding not, like a tumour, complete autonomy, at a quite irregularly constituted Borough Council. I should think that a little more calcium in the blood stream is indicated. Anyway, I shall be glad to hear the last of Cyril the Sod!'

On 7 November, Joyce heard from the Governor of Wandsworth Prison that his appeal had been dismissed. He was also told the date for his execution had been fixed for a fortnight's time, Friday 23 November at 9 a.m. That morning he joked that he had been handed a document that was like a certificate from an Indian university, one which recorded that the candidate had failed his degree. It was the formal declaration that his appeal had been dismissed. He also joked that he was by now getting used to being a professional eater of *Henkersmahlzeit*, the condemned man's last meal.

In the *News Chronicle* the next day there was a story under the headline 'THE MEN WHO DON'T BELONG'. It was about Lieutenant Perry, the man who had broadcast from Joyce's microphone after he vacated it in Hamburg, and who later shot him. The article pointed out that, under English law, many soldiers serving in British uniforms were not British subjects and they should be naturalized. Lieutenant Perry was given as an example of this. 'Lt Perry's real name is Horst Pinschewer, a German who will be an "enemy alien" again when he is discharged.' It went on to point out that if Joyce had arrested Perry, rather than the other way round, Perry would have been a traitor. Joyce was tickled by this story when Quentin related it to him.

He delighted in the fact that Perry had developed a discrimination complex because he was being treated in England as a German. He imagined Perry carping that he had shot Haw-Haw, so why would no one take him in and cloak him in Haw-Haw's Union Flag? Joyce said he felt something approaching fondness for Lickorish, but he didn't like Perry, not because he timidly shot him – he didn't mind being shot – but because Perry's bearing was unpleasant.

Due to the important questions of law involved in the Joyce case, the Attorney-General now granted permission for an appeal to be heard before the House of Lords, the highest court in the land. Joyce was encouraged by this. He also took comfort from a letter he was shown from a distinguished lawyer. It stated that if the sentence of death passed upon him was not quashed at appeal, it would be 'a blot on British justice'.

Unknown to William, secret plans were afoot to bring Margaret over to London so that she could visit him before his execution. On Monday 19 November, two plain-clothed MI5 officers landed in Brussels, escorted her to a waiting plane, flew with her to Croydon airport and then drove with her to Hendon. There she was formally refused permission to enter the country by immigration officers, on the grounds that she was 'an undesirable alien'. This technicality meant that she could then be legally arrested by Special Branch and taken to Holloway Prison. The press had not picked up the scent and any embarrassing questions concerning her ambiguous nationality had been avoided – or so MI5 mistakenly thought.

Holloway Prison, like so many buildings in 1945 London, was bomb-damaged. When she arrived there, Margaret went through a procedure known as 'reception'. This meant that for an hour she was locked in a wooden box that was painted a dirty cream colour and covered in graffiti. It was so cramped that when she sat down, on a fixed seat, her knees touched the door. There was no window but light came in from the wire-netting roof of the box. The wardress walked behind her as she was taken to a cell with a damp and lumpy mattress on the floor, canvas sheets and a chipped enamel chamber pot. The adjoining wing led on to a garden which contained two condemned cells and an execution chamber.

Margaret's transfer meant that the letters she had written to William had been delayed by a week. This lacuna – or 'loss of the cable' – upset him and he was beginning a letter to her discussing his concern about it when the Governor entered his cell. 'But – whoops . . . much excitement – the Governor has just been in to tell me that you are in England – and that you are coming to visit me – Ol! Ol! What joy!'

The first visit took place on 20 November. To avoid the press, Margaret had to be smuggled out of 'the Murderess's Gate' in the back of a car. It was an emotional encounter. They hadn't seen each other for half a year. At first they locked eyes across the table in silence, then William began to talk almost in a gabble. They were separated by the wire-mesh grille, so they were unable to hold hands. And this must have been hard for them because of all the sensory deprivations, to be deprived of touch is perhaps the most severe.

As soon as visiting time was over, William wrote Margaret a letter. He was full of remorse that he had dominated the conversation. 'I felt I just had to talk and keep on talking or burst,' he wrote. 'Words cannot describe my joy at seeing my darling friend, my beloved wife, again. It would be useless, at the present stage at least, to attempt to express my feelings. There was so much I wanted to say, there was so much I wanted to hear from you, dear: and I do hope you will forgive me for taking the floor as I did.' He had, he confessed in a postscript, been haunted by the thought that he might never see his wife again.

NINETEEN

'My beloved – do, I beg, forgive me for having spoilt your life.'

The date of William Joyce's execution had passed. 'There is certain humour in being alive after the time appointed for one's execution, ni?' he wrote to Margaret when he realized this. 'Of course, it is not a novel experience, but is still a trifle uncommon. Let us, however, stop talking shop.'

He couldn't resist making jokes about his situation, though. When his warders noted he had a slight sore on his neck, they asked him whether he was all right. He replied: 'Pretty good now, but I fear the neck might give me cause for complaint at a later date.' (This anecdote was related by Macnab. There was a variation on it told by Chesterton, in which Quentin visited him one afternoon with a bandage around his neck – it had swollen up due to a glandular problem. Joyce said with mock disapproval: 'Fancy coming to see me in that condition! Don't you know necks are a very sensitive subject in this quarter?')

His good humour was one of the reasons why his guards had come to regard him as a model prisoner. Indeed he had won something of a fan club for himself. As one of the warders put it: 'Joyce is a wonderful man ... smiling and courteous, never depressed, never out of temper, always thinking of others, apologising for causing us trouble. We all love him here – there has never been a prisoner like him.' (It was rumoured that he had scratched a swastika on his prison wall, which was not the sort of thing a model prisoner would do. But this may have been another myth. After all, rumours and myths followed Joyce like flies wherever he went.)

In her cell in Holloway, Margaret was showing similar blithe unconcern: she had taken up sewing again to pass the time, was reading the *Oxford Book of English Verse* and was allowed to wear her own clothes. Although she was still not permitted visitors, she was able to send and receive letters. One from the elderly Miss Scrimgeour was especially sympathetic. 'It must have been trying not to be allowed to see him in private: touch him, even clasp his hand. Even I felt that when I visited him.' Another from Macnab, who signed himself Master, tried to cheer her up by referring to the 'naughty fascists', such as himself, who had been detained under Regulation 18B during the war. He also tried to distract her by teaching her some Arabic, Sanskrit and hieroglyphics. He finally broached the delicate subject of William's morale: 'It was only on Saturday the eleventh when he had just been informed of the number of days he had left, failing the fiat [the appeal to the Lords], that his iron composure appeared to be slightly shaken, and then it was entirely on your account. Fortunately the press never got hold of that.'

On 30 November, her mother, Mabel White, wrote to her on dark blue notepaper from 18 Princess Road, Crumpsall, Manchester. Margaret's parents had moved there from Carlisle before the war and her father was now employed in a chemical works in the city. Mabel's touchingly simple letters reveal that she was an educated woman – she wrote in a looping copperplate – but also that she was provincial, God-fearing and unable to express her emotions. At the time of writing she would have had every reason to suppose that her daughter would also be tried for treason. But her letters showed a very British reluctance to confront this issue. Instead she tried to distract Margaret with family news about her maiden aunts, Daisy and Maud, their 'fag lady' and the family pets. Tellingly, Ernest White did not write any letters. It may be that he wanted to disassociate himself from his infamous daughter, perhaps worried that his own fascist past would catch up with him if he didn't. Even Mabel had denied all knowledge of her daughter's activities. A few months earlier she had been quoted in the *Daily Mirror* as saying: 'We still love our daughter. We didn't have a wireless set or perhaps we might have learnt where she was, from her traitor husband's broadcasts.' Given that their daughter had been announced as 'Margaret Joyce also known as Lady Haw-Haw' this seems unlikely, but perhaps when they moved to Manchester they didn't mention to their new neighbours that they had a daughter, or if they did they chose not to add that her married name was Joyce.

'My darling,' Mabel wrote, 'I waited to hear where you were. I could not believe you were in Holloway prison; it is such an awful address for my own dear girl. We were not given a chance to see you and buck you up . . . Dad and I have been thinking of you all the time, dear, and we do feel proud of your pluck.' She then told her daughter that they had a new Border collie puppy which 'has already half-eaten the hearth rug' and was making life hard for Fluff, their Persian cat. Margaret's father had taken up a pipe 'which is much better for him.' She ended: 'I am trusting you will find happiness in the long run. Cheerio, dearie. Chin up. Hope you like the cigs. Your loving mother.'

Judging by the airy language Margaret used in her own letters and diaries, she *was* keeping her chin up, or at least choosing to make light of her predicament. This can be seen in her conversations with Joyce, too, some of which were recorded for posterity by MI5. When, for instance, she heard that one of their former colleagues, Walter Purdy, had been charged with treason, she flippantly said of him: 'Dotty, of course. He didn't have much brains. But they are raking them in, aren't they!'

There were more to rake in than many in England suspected. History usually relates that William Joyce was working more or less alone in his treacherous crime of broadcasting propaganda for the Nazis. In fact, as we have seen, there were forty British subjects at it (not including Joyce). Purdy, a Royal Navy seaman from Barking, Essex, was one of the worst offenders. He joined the British Union of Fascists at sixteen, was taken prisoner in June 1940 and began broadcasting in August 1943 continuing until May 1944. He also betrayed prisoners' escape plans in Colditz and informed on a British agent there.

After Joyce, the best known of the British renegades broadcasting for the Nazis were Norman Baillie-Stewart, the original Haw-Haw, and John Amery. Baillie-Stewart had been captured in the Austrian Alps after the war dressed in lederhosen, disguised as a goat herd. He was sentenced to five years' imprisonment on the charge of aiding the enemy. He had claimed that he was a British agent who had been given credibility by a fake trial in 1933 and planted in Germany in 1937 to win the Nazis' confidence. He become a radio speaker, he claimed, so that he could intercept code messages.*

Amery's Old Bailey trial on 28 November 1945 lasted just eight minutes. When asked how he pleaded to the charge of high treason he stunned the court by answering: 'I plead guilty to all counts.' It amounted to suicide. If he pleaded guilty he must be sentenced to death; there was no alternative for high treason. And there could be no appeal. The judge asked him if he understood the implications of his plea. He said he did. 'You now stand a self-confessed traitor to your King and country,' the judge said, 'and you have forfeited the right to live.' When the clerk of the court asked Amery if he had anything to say before sentence was passed, the thirty-three-year-old answered: 'No, thank you.' The attendant placed the square black cloth on the judge's head, but the judge did not deliver the death sentence. Instead he leant forward and asked: 'You do not want to say *anything*?' Amery said: 'No, thank you, sir.' Afterwards a prison psychiatrist examined Amery and concluded that he had a 'severe and long-standing case of psychopathic disorder of the type at one time called "moral insanity" or "moral imbecility." '

Amery was moved to the death row at Wandsworth, and so had his old rival Joyce as a neighbour. When Joyce heard about the Amery trial he declared it a severe blow. Whatever he might have said about the chap in the past, he had acted with courage on this occasion, he said. Faced with such a tragedy, it was no time to be petty. Assuming that Amery would be petitioning the Home Secretary, Joyce asked one of the guards to wish him luck on his behalf.

In a letter to Joyce, Margaret wrote that she felt sorry for Amery.† The British public seems to have felt more sympathy for Amery's popular and distinguished family. One theory was that he had pleaded guilty to spare them any more embarrassment.

As his appeal to the House the Lords loomed, Joyce made it clear that he would not retract his original statement. And he advised Margaret not to retract hers. 'Morally, if not legally, it is highly pertinent that we firmly

---

* Baillie-Stewart ended his days in Dublin as a travelling salesman of cowboy boots. He drank himself to death in 1966.

† Although Margaret's prison letters to William were destroyed in accordance with government regulation immediately after his execution, MI5 quoted from them selectively in its reports.

believed ourselves to be serving the best ultimate interests of the British people – a fact which was appreciated and respected by the best of our German chiefs. And it was always our thesis that German and British interests were, in the final analysis, not only compatible but mutually complementary.' Nevertheless he was worried about her. His only concern, he claimed to his friend Aubrey Lees, was for the fate that might now befall his wife. But there was no question that he would renege on any deal that had been made, officially or unofficially. To Father Edmund, he implied that he could not surrender his wife's life to save his own.

He also made it clear that he would not go back on his stated position regarding the Church. Although Joyce believed in a Christian God, he was still a lapsed Catholic and pressure was mounting upon him, from both Macnab and Margaret, to return to the bosom of Rome before his execution. But he was stubborn on this matter. He had, he said, little patience with 'canonical jiggery pokery'. More to the point, he had not forgiven the Catholic Church for its treatment of his Anglican mother – and, besides, he had forged a friendship with the Protestant chaplain at the prison. He made light of his predicament to Margaret, also known as Mother-Sheep: he didn't want her to think that he was rushing back into the pen merely because the lupine predators were becoming too inquisitive.

When, during a prison visit, Macnab begged him to see a priest he joked that he had got into enough trouble with bogus passports without trying to get one into Heaven. Anyway, he had embraced a new religion of sorts, gestalt theory, a belief in the fundamental interconnectedness of all things in the universe. In his letters to Margaret, he wrote at length about this complex idea, even though during the Berlin years he had sometimes called her 'a half-wit'. He must have known his lofty philosophizing would be lost on her. Perhaps he included it anyway for the sake of posterity, a testament that he guessed would be given a wider circulation.

Quentin Joyce, meanwhile, began raising a 'fighting fund' to pay for copies of the record of the Old Bailey trial for use at the Lords appeal, as well as for other expenses above those covered by Joyce's legal aid grant. A couple who described themselves as 'living below the Plimsoll line in Kensington, seeking to preserve the bygone decencies', sent a cheque for £50. A Suffolk farmer sent ten shillings for a 'very brave gentleman'. Joyce told Macnab that he felt overwhelmed and embarrassed by such generosity from strangers.

On 28 November, after another visit from Margaret, William returned to his Greek tragedy theme: he wrote to tell her that she had looked very pretty and that the Greek chorus had been there when she visited. She had transported the prison into something affirmative for him – the place he now felt most at home in London.

MI5 was still censoring his correspondence, with whole paragraphs being blacked out with ink. Yet he managed to drop in occasional cryptic references to a deal with the Service regarding Margaret. The more he reflected upon what he called the Iron Curtain between them, the more he understood why the authorities wanted to keep as quiet about her trip as possible. One deliberately indiscreet remark in the right ear might give rise to an uncomfortable situation for the authorities, he observed. Two days later he joked that MI5 might be suffering from suppressed-memory syndrome, having spent so long living in the shadows. He suggested that it should be called the Shy Intelligence Service, and he smiled as he thought of an example in his Russian primer: 'He is moving about amongst the lies. He must be a spy (or a traitor)!' In this context he referred to a skeleton in the cupboard (characteristically spelling skeleton with 'll' and an 'ing' before the 'ton'), and teased about MI5 developing an understated sense of humour.

At one point he made an allusion to the SIS – at that time an autonomous department within the Foreign Office, based at King Charles Street – being much distressed about his case. He appreciated it, he said. On 6 December he took up the MI5 theme again: it had been a convenient refuge for enemies of the state, he suggested. He also imagined that if he came forward and said that he was a British double agent, he doubted that the spymaster – Knight? – would write and complain to the authorities that he was an impostor.

Although Maxwell Knight was still in charge of B5(b) he had slipped off the radar in terms of his contacts with Joyce. There were several unnamed MI5 officers present at his Old Bailey trial, but there is no record of Knight having visited Joyce in prison. Then again, presumably there wouldn't be. Perhaps if there was a deal made between the two men, it took the form of a gentleman's agreement: Joyce's silence in return for Margaret's freedom. Perhaps also there was an understanding that if Joyce didn't speak at his Old Bailey trial, there might be an accommodation made – a word in the right ear – when his case later came before the

Lords. That way, the press and public demand for a conviction would have been met in the courts, but the actual execution would have been avoided – and, honour served, Joyce could be deported quietly back to Germany, as a German citizen. This would explain Joyce's nonchalance about his predicament, and his confidence, as expressed time and again in his letters, that the Lords would find in his favour. Perhaps he felt that, on an unconscious level, they might feel a certain esprit de corps with Lord Haw-Haw.

The hearing in the House of Lords began on Monday 10 December. There was a heavy mist that morning and the ghostly blackened shell of St Thomas's Hospital was barely visible across the Thames. By now Joyce must have been coming to appreciate the extent of the bomb damage in London and the reason why so many Englishmen resented his broadcasts. Even the Palace of Westminster was bomb-damaged, which was why the Lords were temporarily sitting in the Robing Room used by monarchs for their coronations, and for the State Opening of Parliament.

William wrote to Margaret to point out that few members of the public would be permitted to attend the appeal, but among those who could would be 'a special friend and my brother. Q showed me his pass – a grandiose document with Lion and Unicorn, to be returned to the Lord Chancellor's Office. He is to enter through the Norman Porch! So with you in Warwick Castle [Holloway] and me in the Queen's Robing Room, it will be an historic week. For one edition [of the newspapers] at least, Nuremberg is in the shade.'

Presumably the 'special friend' was Macnab, but he may have been referring to the eighty-year-old Miss Scrimgeour. Although she was bowed with arthritis, she attended every day of the Lords hearing, travelling up from Sussex on the train. Since his mother's death, Joyce seems to have looked on her as a mother: and since her brother's death, Miss Scrimgeour had looked on Joyce as a son. She knew his faults, she told him one day, but loved him nevertheless.

Half joking, half in earnest, Joyce told his warders how much he enjoyed making his ceremonial entrance into the Mother of Parliaments, with its red leather seats, thrones and frescoes. For once, he looked well groomed. The prison warders had arranged for him to have his shirt and suit pressed, a kind gesture that thrilled him. But his pallor was noticeably yellow from prison and as he stood in the diplomatic box, in one corner of the Robing Room, surrounded once again by four tall policemen, he looked puny. The spectators spilled out of the room into the surrounding corridors. To Joyce, members of Parliament, Commons and Lords, looked like an animal collection past its best: with legs bent, eyes running, hairless heads and moth holes in their pelts. Microphones had been rigged up so those unable to see the proceedings were able to hear them, with a thin thread of sound being spun under everyone's feet by invisible speakers. He could not even be seen by the press, but a large number of peers could see him and there were dozens of curious MPs crowded round the entrance, too. Joyce stared at them and they at him. 'A beer baron crowded up to the edge of my box and all but examined me with a magnifying glass,' Joyce later wrote. 'Was he afraid of losing a potential customer, I wonder?'

William Joyce's entrance wasn't quite as grand as that of the Lord Chancellor (Lord Jowitt, who had been the prosecutor in the Wolkoff–Kent trial). His Lordship was wearing a long black silk gown with a train carried by an attendant. On his head was a full-bottomed wig, its white curls lying in rows on his shoulders. He sat on a throne at a table in the broad aisle which ran down the middle of the chamber. The four appeal judges – Lords Macmillan, Wright, Porter and Simonds – followed behind wearing lounge suits. They sat either side of Lord Jowitt, and because they were all in their seventies and eighties, it was a bitterly cold day and there was no fuel to heat the House of Lords, they were given steamer rugs to drape over their knees.

Peers who had arrived late slipped in to listen. Some had brought along their eldest sons, who according to an ancient custom were allowed to sit on the steps of the dais beneath the thrones. All listened keenly as Shawcross and Slade did battle once more, their arguments swinging back and forth all morning. Occasionally there were adjournments while attendants brought out tea trays for the shivering judges.

The prisoner was amused by the eating arrangements at lunchtime. He had to eat with a spoon and fork – knives being forbidden to condemned men. Sadly, he reflected, the House offered to open its cellars but 'regulations again inflicted upon me that "unkindest cut of all". Still, the offer was something. And my custodians most chivalrously confined themselves to H_2O.'

The following day, the Home Secretary, Chuter Ede, called an emergency meeting at the Home Office. It partly dealt with an earlier meeting that had been held during Joyce's initial trial. According to the minutes: 'At the meeting on 18 September, the Cabinet decided that should William Joyce be found not guilty by the Court of Trial, he should be interned as an undesirable enemy alien and held in custody until the position should be reached on his disposal. I decided to make a deportation order against him with a view to his deportation to Germany, of which country he is a national. In case his appeal succeeded, the deportation order is still in force and, in the event of the House of Lords deciding that Joyce is not guilty, I propose that the deportation order should be enforced and that Joyce should be immediately detained pending his removal to Germany.'

Joyce would no doubt have been honoured to know that he had been the subject of a Cabinet meeting. He would have been pleased, too, to learn that in Moscow the Kremlin was busy bringing pressure to bear on the British Ambassador regarding his case. The Soviets had been critical of the way the Anglo-Americans had conducted themselves at the Nuremburg Trial and had been monitoring the progress of the British treason trials for any signs of liberal weakness. As an MI5 memo phrased it that week: 'We are worried about what the Russian reaction might be if the Lords quash his conviction.' Joyce had become a player on the international stage.

On the final day of the Lords appeal, Joyce wrote: 'Today was the most dramatic of the hearing. Slade did very well this morning in replying to Hotcross. He finished at 1pm and then the Lord Chancellor said: "The House will adjourn till 3 o' clock." So then I thought: "Ha! 'Tis signed, sealed, and now only has to be delivered." Our retiring room overlooks the Thames and Lambeth Bridge. It was a wonderful afternoon – crimson sun on the water, mist, leafless trees, a picture which stirred my heart with memories of the *Heimat*. We played nap till nearly three, and then arose from our be-coroneted chairs. I thought of the Wilhelmsplatz and, looking at the arches, felt that perhaps I had a little more Norman blood in me than some of the peers whom I have seen during the past few days.'

According to some sources, Mosley held a rally for his followers in a London hotel that afternoon, which cannot have helped Joyce's cause much. Joyce's old friend Captain Gordon Canning, who had just bought a bust of Hitler from the German Embassy auction sale for £500, was said to have attended. Even without that, the atmosphere in Parliament Square was tense. Special Branch officers, anticipating that the Lords would quash Joyce's conviction, were waiting outside the Palace of Westminster when the hearing reconvened at 3 p.m. There were rumours that Joyce had been taken back to Wandsworth because it would be awkward if he was acquitted and had to be rearrested on defence-regulation charges – not only awkward but illegal because arrests could not be made on the premises of Westminster, but would have to be done outside in the square in public view, with a potential for a riot or an escape. The rumours proved unfounded: Joyce was still there, making an entrance.

He described the moment he returned to the Robing Room after the lunchtime adjournment: 'Through a laneway of Commoner ghouls, I marched into the House, where a number of noble ghouls had assembled in joyous anticipation of the kill. I bowed to the L/C who gravely acknowledged and who then called on Counsel to stand. He curtly said: "We require a little more time to consider this case and shall give judgement on Tuesday morning at 10.30." The *continuere omnes ora intentique tenebant* attitude of the assembly dissolved into a ripple of surprise, and the ghouls picked themselves up and slunk out of the House like schoolboys "creeping unwillingly to school". Of course, I don't class all present as ghouls: I was referring not to those who attended *durchaus* [throughout] but to the "last-nighters", those, who in the days when peers hunted foxes instead of less reputable animals, would have said that they meant to be "in at the kill".'

West described his departure from the House that afternoon: 'He held his chin high and picked his feet up, as the sergeant majors say, and though he held his chin so very high that his face was where the top of his head ought to have been and though his feet flapped on his weak ankles, his dignity was not destroyed, but was made idiosyncratic, his very own. It appeared that there could be such a thing as undignified dignity. That he was a civilised man, however aberrant, was somehow clear before our eyes, and mournful. At the House of Lords he had gone past comparison, looking at us from a territory whose clocks kept another time, and listening to the striking of an hour that had not yet struck us.'

The postponement must have been hard for Joyce dangling on the abyss and many lawyers felt a reprieve was appropriate now simply because the torment of his trial followed by a failed appeal followed by a postponement of a second appeal was inhumane. Some cited the practice in English law of commuting a death sentence to life imprisonment, if a third appeal, to the Lords, failed, and if several months had passed since the initial sentence of death.

Joyce was told by the Governor on the Monday morning that he was not permitted to attend the House of Lords the following day for the judgement. 'I suppose,' he wrote to Margaret, 'that the police do not want me to be there. In the event of an unfavourable decision, the trip would be useless; and should the result be otherwise, well, it might, in their opinion, be easier to spirit me away from here than from the House of Lords. I draw no inference, of one kind or another, from the news. I was allowed to attend the CCA judgement, and it did me no good: so let us hope for better luck this time. I should actually have liked to hear the judgement, whatever it may be: but still, I am not too disappointed. Frankly, I think that with all these crime waves, the police want to save themselves trouble. But I know that Q and [Macnab] will be surprised to discover that I am missing. So will the Press! But the disappointment of the journalists will not cause me any lack of sleep.'

At what point does it become unusually cruel to offer a condemned man hope only to dash it again? That was a question that many legal minds were considering as the Lords foregathered once more at 10.30 on the morning of Tuesday 18 December 1945. Only three of the appeal judges were in attendance, the fourth having issued instructions that his judgment be read out to the Lords on his behalf. As was traditional, the Lord Chancellor only voted in the event of a stalemate between the four judges. The first stepped forward and declared that he upheld the sentence and would give his reasons another day. The second said the same and added that he also spoke on behalf of the third who shared his judgement. He concluded with the words: 'In common with the rest of your Lordships, I should propose to deliver my reasons at a later date.' Joyce was outnumbered and, so, doomed to die.

The fourth judge to step forward was Lord Porter. He had an unexpected statement to make. 'In the present case a reasonable jury, properly directed, might have considered that the allegiance – between crown and subject – had been terminated. Against the mere receipt of the passport there has to be set the fact that its possession was at least desirable, if not necessary, to enable the accused man to proceed to Germany from this country; the fact that it was not found in his possession again, or anything further known of it; his statement as to his intention of becoming naturalised in Germany; and his acceptance of a post from the German State. At any rate these were matters for a jury properly directed to consider. They were not directed on them and, as I have stated, in my view they were told that the matter was one of law and not for them . . . Apart from this, the principle that questions which are rightly for the jury should be left to them, and that a proper direction should be given is, as I think, also of great public importance: the one matter concerning this country only in the exigencies of war, though then no doubt it is of vital importance; the other is a necessary element in the true administration of the law in all time of peace. If the safety of the realm in war times requires action outside the ordinary rule of law, it can be secured by appropriate measures such as the Defence of the Realm Act, but the protection of a subject or foreigner afforded through trial by jury, and the due submission to jury of matter proper for their consideration, is important always, but never more important than when the charge of treason is in question. For these reasons I would myself have allowed the appeal.'

Lord Porter, then, had decided that a miscarriage of justice had occurred, but had been out-voted. However, this majority had not always been so clear-cut. Lord Beaverbrook was told by Lord Jowitt, the Lord Chancellor, that initially the four Lords were divided. In such a case Lord Jowitt would have had to cast a deciding vote. After lengthy discussion one of the two for acquittal changed sides and by a majority of three to one the decision was taken to reject the appeal. The reason for this change of mind was simple, and it had nothing to do with law. Beaverbrook remarked to Jowitt that public opinion would have been outraged by a verdict of not guilty. Jowitt agreed, adding that 'public opinion had to be taken into account'. It was law by lynch mob.*

The Lord Chancellor moved backwards down the floor of the House and halted at the Woolsack. He stretched out his hands to the peers on each side of the chamber and bade those vote who were content with the judgement. When this was done he said, 'The contents have it,' and gathered up his gown and strode from the chamber. Quentin Joyce, wrapped in a muffler, shouted out after him: 'William Joyce is innocent!' A scrum of reporters was waiting outside. Macnab, tall, thin and bespectacled, approached them and, in his easy cultivated voice, said: 'William

* Beaverbrook was told this in 1952, according to the *Daily Telegraph*, 27 February 1995.

Joyce was calm when I saw him at the weekend. In fact he was in excellent spirits and was discussing quite objectively and with all his old brilliance the psychology of the four judges. He was wonderful. But I must leave you now. I must go and tell my wife what happened. My name? Angus Macnab. And please do not spell it M-c-N-a-b. The correct spelling is M-a-c-n-a-b.'

For Joyce the tension of waiting for the result of the Lords appeal must have been unbearable. He knew the Lords were meeting at 10.30 in the morning, but by the afternoon he still had not been told the result. He began his daily letter to his wife: 'It is now approximately 14.00 hrs and I have been expecting ever since 11.00 to hear the Lord's decision. I suppose that I shall be told nothing till a copy of the judgement arrives, presumably by courier. Well, I do not mind admitting that I am curious to know the result. If it is unfavourable, I can meet it in the right spirit: if it is good, so much the better! But I shall be glad when the suspense is over. I am wondering if I shall be allowed to have any visitors this afternoon: for perhaps they might not be permitted to see me till the Great Document has arrived. I suppose that by this time, the news has been imparted to you, dear: and I sincerely hope that it did not prove too much for you.'

In the cell, the two prison officers in attendance sprang to their feet as they heard the Governor's footsteps approach. Joyce stood up, too. 'The Lords have rejected your appeal, I'm afraid,' the Governor said. Joyce's long game of chess with the British legal system was at an end. This was checkmate.

Two minutes later Joyce calmly resumed his letter. 'Well – the Governor has just told me that my appeal has been dismissed. So that is that! At long last, the suspense is over, and except for your dear sake, I am pleased. For it was, in itself, an indignity to sue and plead before my enemies, to observe their pretence at fair play, not serving to mask their determination to liquidate me. Now, quite naturally, at this harsh moment, all my thoughts go out to you, dear: and I curse myself for not having allowed you to go your way in 1941, I needed you absolutely: that is my excuse, not my justification. But now – alas! – there is nothing I have to offer you except my non-material being for all time. Please do not take what I write amiss. I know your feelings – as I know my very own: but death would be the simplest matter in the world if it did not leave you in such a predicament. My beloved – do, I beg, forgive me for having spoilt your life. You know that it was fated to happen. That is my excuse. But now, at least, I can show, I hope, that you gave yourself to a man – and not to a craven weakling.'

In Sophocles' play, Oedipus is seen as holy, not despite of but because of his guilt, or rather his full recognition of it. In a Greek tragedy it is good for a man to understand the nature of man, how guilty he is. There is a kind of redemption in the act of recognition itself. But in some circumstances there can be no saving from retribution: there can only be refuge for the hero in stoicism. And through his humiliation and death he is able to assert a human dignity which would not otherwise have been within his compass. So it was that Joyce explained to Lees that he saw himself as a player in a Wagnerian opera. He wanted his death to be grand, sombre and selfless, he told his friend, adding that he did not want to take refuge in heroic pathos.

That afternoon he wrote his will. He also left instructions that, should there be a memorial service, he would like the 'Horst Wessel' song, Grieg's 'Morning' from *Peer Gynt*, and Siegfried's funeral music from Wagner's *Götterdämmerung* to be played at it. His loyal solicitor Head visited him and told him that the Lords intended to give their reasons for the dismissal of the appeal only after he had been executed. It was another example of the cruelty of the judicial process: having already faced, in effect, three death sentences, he was now never going to hear why his last chance for a reprieve had gone. And it was telling that the Home Secretary did not think it necessary to wait and see whether passages in their Lordships' opinions might afford some ground for the exercise of clemency.

Walter Purdy's trial at the Old Bailey ended that same day. He was found guilty of high treason and sentenced to death. During the trial he had claimed that he had made an attempt to assassinate William Joyce, the man who had recruited him. When Joyce heard this he noted, with extraordinary gallows humour, that if this were true, Henker (hangman) Pierrepoint should write to the newspapers complaining about Purdy's attempted breach of trade-union practices.

At Wandsworth Prison the following morning, the famous Albert Pierrepoint came for John Amery, a young traitor he would later describe as the 'bravest man I ever hanged'. Amery greeted him with the words: 'Mr Pierrepoint, I have always wanted to meet you, though not, of course, in these circumstances.'

TWENTY

'How easy still it proves in factious times
With public zeal to cancel private crimes'

John Dryden

Quentin Joyce visited Wandsworth Prison on the day John Amery was hanged. In an attempt to lift his brother's spirits he told him that a full transcript of his trial was to be published as part of the Old Bailey Trial Series, a claim to immortality of sorts. He also held up to the visitor's cage an editorial from that day's *Manchester Guardian*. It was devoted to the Law Lords' appeal and opined that Joyce's treachery was motivated by a consuming ideology. It gave the condemned prisoner some satisfaction. 'One can say that this document [Joyce's British passport], which he ought never to have possessed, has been the deciding factor in Joyce's sentence. One could wish that he had been condemned on something more solid than a falsehood, even if it was one of his own making. At the same time, leaving the sphere of law for that of common opinion, here was a man who chose to leave us at the outbreak of war to do all he could from enemy soil to sap our resolution when it was being tested most. It would have seemed extraordinary to the majority here, and still more so to our allies on the Continent, if this man had escaped. Yet one may still wonder whether the death sentence is appropriate. Joyce – and Amery, for the cases have much in common – held strongly certain opinions which were once shared by many who walk untouched among us. He carried his opinions, which he never hid, to their logical conclusions. We detest those opinions and may feel that he ought to be restrained from ever again advancing them, which would be a worse penalty for a man like him than death. Even in these days of violence, killing men is not the way to root out false opinions.'

It revived Joyce's flagging self-esteem. 'Nobody would expect the *Guardian* to go the whole hog,' he wrote, 'but what I like is the rather chivalrous recognition of the fact that I have stood by my beliefs. For this alone, I must retract the many unkind remarks that I have made about the paper.'

The *Manchester Guardian* article seems to have galvanized the intelligentsia because, the following morning, George Orwell made a comment in reference to it: 'The hunting down of petty rats is largely the work of bigger rats.' When Joyce heard that even *Freedom*, an anarchist newspaper, had come out with an article strongly in his favour, he wrote some nonsense verse and, by way of explanation for it, joked that the unexpected support from the anarchists had disturbed his mental balance.

Margaret visited William that afternoon and he told her that she looked beautiful in her sorrow and that he was glad she was able to laugh at his rotten jokes. But his frivolity masked an anxiety that she might be taken back to Brussels before his execution. He petitioned the Governor that afternoon to ask if she could remain in the country. The Governor informed him soon afterwards that the Home Office had agreed she could stay. 'Well, darling,' Joyce wrote that evening, 'you were superb – as I knew you would be. How proud of you I am, I cannot very well say. But you gave me a feeling of exaltation which will be with me to the end . . . The Governor has just informed me that it is not proposed to send you back to Brussels until after close of play . . . And the dear, sweet, nice Sheriffs, bless their little stars, have fixed 3 January as the festive day. I shall survive my Annus Mirabilis: and that was one of my sekret ambitions – It is the end of my fateful year, and I take a sort of mischievous pride in having seen it through . . . It does not seem as if I should learn the reasons for their Lords' decision. Curiouser and curiouser – but, to me, not very disturbing. For the reasons are bound to be irrelevant. Sorry to have announced the date, beloved, but I thought it best to tell you as soon as I could.'

In her Holloway cell, Margaret received another letter that day, from her mother. 'Daddy and I are broken hearted, knowing of your terrible ordeal. We are thinking of you all the time. Try and keep your courage and the Lord will help you bear it. William is a brave man and is far more anxious about you and about your future than he is about himself. If you think we can see you tell us and we will be on the first train we can get. The enclosed cigs are from Aunt Daisy.' A few days later Mabel wrote: 'I think the only alternative for William would have been long imprisonment which would have been prolonged torture, especially to such an active man of his splendid brain power. God bless you, dear, and everybody who is kind to you. We will always pray for you. The last thing Dad and I say every night, ever since you went away, is God bless Margaret.'

She also received a letter from an emotional Macnab, who had clearly convinced himself that the appeal to the Lords would be successful. 'For you there is wonderful pride to have been the partner well beloved of such a man. And for those honours you pay a terrible price, in this poor life, no more. But ask yourself truly, whether you would change lots, now, with the happy contented wife of a British public school stockbroker. Would you? If I could have offered my wretched carcass in exchange for that peerless understanding and those gifts now lost to the world, I should be most willingly dead ere now. With all my love, dear wife of my brother, Master.'

At Wandsworth Prison, meanwhile, Joyce's sister Joan came to visit. She was in tears and, in a reversal of roles, the condemned prisoner felt obliged to try and cheer her up. The poor thing was crying, he wrote afterwards, but he comforted her with the thought that it was easier to breed Joyces than to string them up. When she said that now she did not want to give up her maiden name, he told her to hyphenate it with her husband's name. Then he realized that she was already Brooke-Joyce, and so she would end up with a title like that of a firm of old and reputable lawyers.

Margaret visited him on Christmas Eve. That night as he sat drinking a pint of beer and smoking a cigarette he wrote her a letter: 'My beloved wife, dearest cousin – *Dominus tecum et cum spirituo uo!* I had said that I would conspire to pretend that the *Weihnachten* were not with us: and, in the main, I will try to adhere to that resolution – hard though such adherence may be. And this morning, I must admit, I have had poignant feelings, for reasons which I need not mention ... When you have recovered from the sickening shock, you will begin to rejoice at all that was good and beautiful in our mortal time together here.' He described places in Galway he had visited in boyhood and to which he had hoped to take his wife one day. Then he wrote: 'I know my faults and am sorry that I have made others, you in particular, suffer for them. At least, I am painfully aware of my own former smallness in personal dealings. "Nymph, in thy orisons, Be all my sins remembered."'

Margaret was allowed to visit him again on Boxing Day. Afterwards he wrote: 'I ask to be forgiven for my somewhat crude *galgenhumor* [gallows humour] but it is not quite unintentional. Too much of it would probably be as intolerable as you found my jesting amidst a hail of bombs. But often, by looking at the unpleasant squarely and laughing at it, we deprive it of certain not very desirable characteristics with which tradition had invested it. The death which a man suffers by one sudden means or another is usually infinitely more comfortable for him than his birth was for his mother.' He asked her if she would try and write as much of his life story as she could, with help from Angus Macnab and Quentin. He ended with a quotation from Dryden: 'How easy still it proves in factious times / With public zeal to cancel private crimes.'

On 28 December he was in romantic mood. It was, he wrote, a damp, cool and brooding morning: but Margaret's visit the previous evening had made it better than a warm day in June. The following afternoon he wrote and apologized for introducing too much gloom into her last visit, but concluded that being lachrymose in moderation brought no mischief. He told her that after he died she should go to Ireland, where his spirit would walk with her in the Galway sunshine. In a poetic flourish he added that when she stood on the storm-tossed bluff, looking down at the boiling sea below, she would hear his voice and feel him near to her. He enclosed a lock of his hair. It was not as fair as it used to be, he noted, but that was because it had to be cut from a place where there was a palpable growth.

On a visit on New Year's Eve, Margaret reassured her husband that she didn't think him a pig. He thanked her for her magnanimity. He did not deny his transgressions, he wrote afterwards, indeed he was ashamed of them, but he was glad that she really did seem to absolve him of them. Her forgiveness, he said, calmed his mind.

He explained to Margaret why he seemed self-possessed at their meetings. 'When, in days to come, dear, you look back upon these sessions try not to think of me as stiff, callous, academically precise, and generally unemotional. It has been necessary and will be particularly necessary at our last interview to keep the ears straight. But I admit to you now, dear girl, that there have been times when the sheer emotion of my love for you has nearly overcome all else. Not now, but later, I want you to reflect that beneath the crust was a yearning tenderness. It was perhaps a long time before you found out that I could be soft-hearted: and, in that respect, you know me far better than anybody else ever has done.'

Joyce sensed the point of no return was upon him and it enabled him to see things plain. This, he finally understood, was what Greek tragedy was about: *pathos* leading to *anagnorisis*; the realization of the unthinkable. He knew he had been afforded a moment of leisure to compose himself and reflect upon his life before it was taken from him, and he sensed that this, in a strange, existential way, was a privilege. After all, only the condemned man is permitted to know the exact time of his death. Macnab noticed an aura of calm around Joyce when he paid a final visit to his old friend on 2 January: 'Without pallor, his flesh seemed to have a quite transparent quality. Being with him gave a sense of inward peace, like being in a quiet church.'

Even his enemies would have had to admit that Joyce handled the hope and despair of his final days with equanimity. Moreover, he seems to have achieved a degree of redemption through his long, courageous walk to the scaffold. Those who observed him as his execution date approached – the chaplain, the governor, his guards – all agreed he had wit on his tongue and was courteous, gentlemanly and brave to the last. They would not have known that he had reason to feel grateful for one small mercy: his marriage was ending on a happy note. Margaret and William had reconciled; left nothing unsaid. Perhaps it was simply a matter of them always getting on better when they were forced to be apart, when each could idealize the other. It is possible that William was taking comfort from the thought that he had, in the end, been able to prove his love for his wife with a bargain, his life for hers.

In another area of his life, too, the wheel was coming full circle. Joyce's former tutors at Birkbeck College, who remembered him as a likeable and hardworking student, sent a message to the Governor of Wandsworth Prison on the eve of the execution. 'We do not condone his later activities,' it read, 'but we recall him as we had known him and, if it is within the rules, we would like you to tell him that we wish him well.'

William began another letter to Margaret. 'I never asked you if you wanted to receive posthumous letters. The question was too indelicate, even for me: but I assumed your wish. For I think you are sufficiently strong now to overcome the grief of this blow, and that your faith will triumph over tears.' At this point he stopped writing because Margaret had arrived for her final visit.

How do you say goodbye to someone you love when you know you will never see them again? Judging by the letter William resumed writing soon after Margaret had gone, there is not much you can say. 'Oh! My dear! Your visit. With no words can I express my feelings about it: I want the "children" [his siblings] to be able to take leave of me, of course, as they will this afternoon: but now I am anxious to die. I want to die as soon as possible, because then I shall be nearer to you. With the last glimpse of you, my earthly life really finished . . .' He told her he would die with a picture of her face imprinted on his mind, and he tried to persuade her that whatever words he had spoken during her visit they were heartfelt. He wanted to make things easier for her, but she could see how sentimental he was becoming, and he thought that unless they ended the visit when they did his resolve not to cry would collapse.

This touching letter was in contrast to the note he handed Quentin when he visited: a final parting message by Lord Haw-Haw, intended for publication. 'In death, as in this life, I defy the Jews who caused this last war: and I defy the power of Darkness which they represent. I warn the British people against the aggressive Imperialism of the Soviet Union. May Britain be great once again; and, in the hour of the greatest danger to the West, may the standard of the *Hakenkreuz* [swastika] be raised from the dust, crowned with the historic words *Ihr habt doch gesiegt* [You have conquered nevertheless]. I am proud to die for my ideals; and I am sorry for the sons of Britain who have died without knowing why.'

As a grave was being dug in the prison grounds, Albert Pierrepoint and his assistant drew up in a car at the main gates. It was 4 p.m. They unpacked their equipment then went to weigh and measure the condemned prisoner. Joyce had weighed nine and a half stones when he had arrived in the United Kingdom in June and he was now exactly one stone heavier. Pierrepoint measured him as being precisely five foot five and three-quarter inches. The executioner then noted in his logbook that the prisoner's build was 'spare but muscular'. He calculated that a drop of seven foot six inches would be needed to do the job. Pierrepoint then tested the apparatus with a bag of sand – and, perfectionist that he was, he left the bag hanging overnight to stretch the rope. He took pride in his work and was scathing about the amateurism of rival executioners. And he had a point. The American assigned to do gallows duty at Nuremberg proved himself inept, leaving Ribbentrop flailing in the air for twenty minutes.

The execution chamber was in the next room along from Joyce's cell, so he would, presumably, have heard the trapdoor being tested. The 'cold meat shed', as it was known, had been constructed in 1916 using three cells, one above the other. The top floor contained the beam with two floor traps through which hung chains for attachment of the ropes. The first floor contained the trapdoors and lever – which was always pushed, not pulled – and the ground-floor cell was 'the pit'. Two other ropes hung down for the warders to hold onto as they stood on planks over the drop to support the condemned man. The chamber was clean and tidy; the wooden floor was even varnished.

As the daylight waned, Joyce looked through his small prison window at the leafless branch of 'his tree', which was all he could see of the natural world. It was his link with Margaret, he believed, a link between heaven and earth. He looked unagitated as he had a final shave and, afterwards, as he studied his face in his metal shaving mirror, he ran his finger over the scar on his cheek.

The Governor then entered his cell, delivered the message from the Birkbeck tutors, told him there would be a delay of an hour in the morning – he would be hanged at nine not eight – and asked if he had any last words. Joyce explained that he had already imparted them to his brother. His next visitor was the prison doctor. He offered Joyce a sedative which he accepted. Even with this, not surprisingly, the prisoner slept fitfully.

In the cold grey dawn of 3 January 1946 the ponds outside Wandsworth prison had frozen over and a thin icy fog shrouded Joyce's tree. The condemned man rose at 6.30, had a cup of tea, changed from his prison uniform into his blue serge suit and washed his face. He had communion with the chaplain at 8 a.m.

A crowd of three hundred people had gathered outside Wandsworth Prison. There were women with shopping baskets, men in suits and overalls, and children on their way to school. Some were wearing black.

Others were stamping their feet and clapping their hands around themselves to keep warm. A war veteran with a bulldog on a lead told a reporter that he had walked all the way from Tooting. Two men had travelled down from Glasgow for the event. A yellow van from Movietone News was parked near the gates, the camera on its roof trained on the imposing front gate. To prevent demonstrations, several detachments of policemen had been deployed. A small noticeboard in a glass case was hung on the door. Inside it was pinned a bulletin saying that the sentence of death passed on William Joyce was to be carried out that morning at nine o'clock.

At 8.30, Joyce wrote a letter, neatly, with a steady hand. 'Beloved Freja, – in this last hour of my early life, I confirm all my vows to you and promise never to leave you. I have just received Holy Communion and we prayed for you. This morning the spirit of St Paul is strong upon me. I will not write much more. The letter which you left yesterday was the most marvellous I have ever received. Just before my last escort comes, as it soon will, I shall send you a message of love by my tree.' He repeated the quote he had given Quentin. 'I gladly and proudly give the example my old chief demands. "*Wir haben doch gesiegt!*" I salute you, Freja, as your lover for ever. Seig Heil! Seig Heil! Sieg Heil! Your Will. [Yp-Baa!] With all my kisses. 8.36.'

The time was underlined. Curiously, with twenty-four minutes to go, he then wrote to Angus Macnab, the friend he always insisted upon calling John. Perhaps his letter to Margaret took less time to write than he anticipated. But it could be that, on an unconscious level, he wanted to write his last letter to the other love of his life. 'Beloved John – I have now so far moved away from all earthly things that the remaining minutes of my life seem like tenants who have not paid their rent. Thank you for your devotion to me and above all for your prayers. More I shall not write, save to say that when we meet again, we shall regret nothing that has happened now.'

Twenty minutes before the execution, the High Sheriff arrived at the prison and proceeded with the Governor and the medical officer to Joyce's cell where Pierrepoint and his assistant were already waiting with the chaplain and two prison officers. The party of eight stood in a tense semicircle facing the door, rocking back and forth on their heels, no doubt, and checking their watches. On the pediment of the main entrance outside, the gold hands of the blue-painted clock approached the hour. A man in the crowd removed his hat and stood to attention. Joyce looked out of his window one last time and sent Margaret a message of love by his tree. He can be imagined waiting there in his cell: his mouth dry; his heart palpitating; yawning tensely, as those awaiting execution are said to do. At one minute to nine the Governor opened the cell door and informed Joyce it was time. Pierrepoint entered the cell, loosely pinioned Joyce's wrists behind his back with straps★ and delivered his customary calming line: 'Follow me, sir, it'll be all right.' Joyce followed. His bullet wound and his twisted ankle had left him with a stiff and awkward gait and, as he covered the fifteen paces to the adjoining room, escorted by an officer on either side, he looked down at his wayward leg and smiled. Even now, his sense of humour had not deserted him. The prison clock began to strike nine. His feet were positioned on 'the drop' on a marked spot so that they were directly across the division of the trapdoor. He would not have seen the noose, as it was concealed in the white hood that the hangman drew over his head with the words: 'I think we'd better have this on.' Pierrepoint's assistant pinioned Joyce's legs. The lever was pushed, Joyce took what he had once called 'his last leap in the dark' and the rope sprang taut. The tied hands went white. The body went still. Between entering the execution chamber and the drop taking place nine seconds had elapsed. Those present knew because the prison clock had just finished striking the hour. The only sound now was the creaking of the rope as it swung. The medical officer proceeded to the pit and examined the body to make sure Joyce was dead. The shed was then locked so that, as was customary, the body could remain hanging for one hour.

At eight minutes past nine a prison guard opened the small glass case hung on the gate and pinned up two bulletins: one was the High Sheriff's declaration that the prisoner had been hanged, the other was the medical officer's declaration that he had examined the prisoner's body and found him to be dead. The three hundred people who had gathered to see that

---

★ This was to give just the suggestion of restraint. Pierrepoint had once hanged a German who had struggled ferociously and since then he had always pinioned his clients. That prisoner was a foreigner, Pierrepoint explained in his memoirs, adding that he had noticed that Englishmen took their punishment better than foreigners. This, then, would be a symbolic test of whether the man he was about to hang was an Englishman or not.

minute shred of ceremony went up for a closer inspection. On the roof of the Movietone van the camera focused in on the scene. Three men wearing flannels and sports jackets stepped behind a frost-covered shrubbery into the prison nursery garden and raised their arms in a furtive Nazi salute. At a West Brompton Catholic church a mass was being held with six of Joyce's friends in attendance. The Very Rev Father Johnson, Macnab's local priest, had timed it so that the communion took place at exactly nine o'clock.

That afternoon, as the first editions thudded onto the newsstands, it was reported that Lord Haw-Haw's legs had trembled – and this was deemed proof of his cowardice. William Joyce would not have expected anything less. No wonder he had looked down at his leg and smiled.

EPILOGUE

A Greek tragedy holds up a warning example which, if heeded, will save other men from error and its penalty. That at least is the theory. In practice we, the audience, tend to want to distance ourselves from the tragedies we watch. We try to objectify the people in them; think of them as one-dimensional figures who have nothing in common with us. Perhaps this is why it suits our national purpose to think of William Joyce as a devilish caricature and an aberration, rather than an unwelcome but psychologically complex product of his time.

Joyce's story is undoubtedly a dark one. Had Germany won the war he would not have been elevated to the status of tragic anti-hero. On the contrary, he would probably have become a ruthless, seedy and vengeful gauleiter in an occupied Great Britain. But his trial and execution gave him, as he himself recognized, an unexpected and belated dignity. Prison life had suited him. It had allowed him to come to an understanding with his wife and to delude himself that his had been a perfect marriage. It also gave him a chance to recover his health, not least because he was eating properly and could no longer get drunk every day. It represented a period of calm and contemplation after the traumas of the Battle of Berlin.

The conditions of his Faustian pact, if that is what it was, were met in full. After his execution, his corpse was taken to the prison mortuary where, ghoulishly, the jurors from his trial had assembled to view it. A coroner pronounced that 'death was due to injury to the brain and spinal cord, consequent upon judicial hanging'. (It was rumoured that, as Joyce's body dropped, the scar on his cheek ripped open, 'leaving a second uglier mouth' – but this seems unlikely as the rope was attached to his neck, not his face, and there is no mention of it in the coroner's report.) The gold bridgework on his teeth was then removed: a 'valuable' to be sent to his widow along with his watch, signet ring and wedding ring. (The bridgework is now in a private collection. Indeed the collector is wont to place it in the hands of unsuspecting guests to his house, after first asking them to close their eyes.) As was customary, Joyce's body was buried at midnight in the prison yard in an unmarked grave – plot eighty-seven – without a member of the clergy present. The grave was dug to a depth of six feet, and he was laid on top of a murderer who had been executed five days earlier. Their corpses were separated by a layer of charcoal. The next day, in accordance with prison regulations, the letters he had received from Margaret – all 140 or so of them – were destroyed.

It was announced on 6 January, three days after his death, that a new Treason Act was to be drafted because the old one was out of date. Exactly one month later, when the Lords finally gave their reasons for dismissing Joyce's appeal (on the same grounds, it turned out, that his first appeal had been dismissed), *The Times* wrote a weary leader on the subject: 'If present normal procedure makes it possible for execution of a capital sentence to precede the recording of the grounds on which the final judicial appeal has been dismissed, would it not be well that this procedure should be altered?'

Joyce had gone to his grave without ever hearing the legal reasoning that ultimately condemned him. 'This attracted some criticism of the Home Secretary and surprised me a little,' Sir Hartley Shawcross wrote in his memoirs. 'I feel it was a mistake . . . I always considered that of the Law Lords concerned, Lord Porter was the most learned and responsible . . . After its conclusion, the case became the subject of much public discussion and some argument among lawyers. The general opinion among the less informed at all events, which is to say the great majority – was that Joyce's execution was not fair . . . It is of the greatest importance that the public accept the law is fair. Mea Culpa in this instance.'

It might be expected that the controversies of Joyce's life would not be ended merely by his death. Many lawyers now came forward to register their discontent with the whole Joyce trial, arguing that at best it was tendentious and brought the law of treason into disrepute, at worst it had been an instrument of vengeance that had stained the soul of the nation. A letter to the *Telegraph* in which one leading silk, Mr N. Long-Brown, took another, Mr J. P. Eddy, to task was typical: 'It seems unfortunate that

Mr J. P. Eddy should select the trial of William Joyce as a fair illustration in which to take pride in the expedition associated with the administration of British Justice. Most lawyers regard this case as a blot on British justice. I have myself heard a judge say that had the case not been so rushed it is doubtful if the man would have been executed. It will be remembered that had Joyce not forgotten to post back his British passport from Germany in 1939 he could not have been convicted. He was not a British citizen and had obtained his passport illegally. Mr Eddy seems proud of the fact that Joyce was a executed "before the House of Lords had given its reasons for dismissing his appeal". More a matter for shame one would have thought, especially in view of what Lord Porter said in his judgement.'

What Lord Porter had said, in effect, was that Mr Justice Tucker had no business taking away from the jury the decision about whether Joyce owed allegiance to the crown or not. The jury might well have decided Joyce was guilty anyway, but we will never know. They might, moreover, have been wise to decide that – a case of wrong crime, right verdict. And strange though it may seem, Joyce might well have agreed with that. As West wrote: 'He thought England was right in hanging him. He would have taken it as proof of our national decadence if we hadn't.'

Joyce had, after all, made himself an enemy of his own adopted country at a time of war. But again, either way, that decision was for the jury to make, not the judge. According to Rebecca West, the moment Tucker made his ruling 'it meant that Joyce was going to die, and his death would be recorded in legal history as the most completely unnecessary death that any criminal has ever died on the gallows.' She meant it was unnecessary because Joyce was the victim of his own and his father's lifelong determination to lie about their nationality. Had he not applied for a British passport he wasn't entitled to, and had he left England for Germany on the American passport which was rightfully his, no power on earth could have touched him. In a tragedy the anti-hero is often hoist by his own petard. In Joyce's case he was obsessed with the idea of Jews being aliens, and was so determined not be one himself that he lied to obtain a British passport. But there was an even greater irony about his trial and execution: it finally seemed to make him what he had always wanted to be, an Englishman. By definition, only an Englishman can be hanged for treason against England.

At his trial Joyce had been told by the Attorney-General that history would not remember him. Shawcross was only half right. Lord Haw-Haw is still a household name after more than half a century. For British tabloid newspapers, this title is a useful short-hand. It implies treasonable activity without stating it overtly, and libellously – George Galloway MP, the former *Daily Mirror* editor Piers Morgan and the American documentary maker Michael Moore are just three of the controversial figures who have had the name applied to them by the press in recent years. In the case of Michael Moore, the *Sun* bestowed an even grander title: 'The Lord Haw-Haw of the War on Terror'.

Four days after he had been sentenced to death, Joyce protested to Margaret that he realized the consequences of arrogance and now accepted the moral value of humbling one's self. Even so, he archly dismissed the chance that Shawcross's name would outlast theirs. He claimed that being widely recognized or known to historians did not matter, but that he understood instinctively that he had not been absent from the stage of the world.

William Joyce cast a long shadow over the lives of the people who knew him. Indeed many who played a part in his story went to their graves with only one claim to dubious fame: their association with him. His Lord Haw-Haw persona had been invented by Jonah Barrington and, in a way, he was hanged for that good joke. But so, in another way, was Barrington. In old age, the journalist lamented: 'Haw-Haw hangs round my neck like the "buried-alive" Prelude hangs round Rachmaninov's. It was all I was remembered for.' When both Lord Porter and Captain Lickorish died their obituaries opened with their Joyce connection. Lieutenant Perry, who had been with Lickorish at the time of Joyce's capture, went on to have a successful career in publishing, launching *Family Circle*, the supermarket magazine, but he is still only known as 'the man who shot Haw-Haw'. Hazel, Joyce's first wife, and her second husband Eric, moved to Canada to escape their past with Joyce. She died there in 2001. Angus Macnab and his wife Katherine went to live in Spain, where they had three children. They lived in the charming Plaza de Santo Tome in Toledo and there received a number of distinguished visitors from England, including Evelyn Waugh. Macnab worked as a translator, taught English and wrote two books on Islamic medieval Spain and one on bullfighting. Shortly after his death in March 1977, his internment file was shredded by MI5, and, as

Francis Beckett, the son of Joyce's friend and colleague John Beckett, has written: 'If anyone outside MI5 knew the truth about Joyce's connection with the security services, their role in his treachery, and the nature of the warning and any guarantees he may have recovered from them, it was Macnab.'

Eduard Dietze, Joyce's Mephistopheles, did not have the problem of having to leave England. He wasn't even allowed in. He was arrested shortly after Joyce but released on condition that he would never again enter Britain. He returned to German broadcasting in 1950 and became a television executive. But before he died of a heart attack aged fifty-one a decade later, he manage to slip into England one last time, to commentate on Royal Ascot for German television.

P. G. Wodehouse, on the other hand, never set foot on British soil again and if he had done he would probably have been put on trial for treason. Although Sir Theobald Mathew, the Director of Public Prosecutions, had decided against prosecuting him after the liberation of Paris in 1944, two years later he changed his mind. A recently declassified memo of a 1946 meeting between an MI5 officer and Sir Theobald reveals that his case was re-evaluated. 'The Director said that he now takes the view that, if Wodehouse ever comes to this country, he should be prosecuted,' the officer recorded. 'In view of the observations by Lord Justice Tucker that the motive which prompted the broadcast was immaterial, he thought that the authorities should now bring Wodehouse to trial and leave the jury to decide the question of his guilt or innocence.' This change of mind had been prompted by the discovery of documents in the former German Embassy in Paris which detailed 'suspicious payments' made to Wodehouse and his wife Edith. One letter from the German Embassy requested that Wodehouse's French villa in Le Touquet be well kept 'in view of the propaganda value of his work'. The transactions were seen to 'strongly suggest' that Wodehouse was working for the German Embassy. But MI5 also noted that the Germans may simply have been transferring the author's funds left behind in Berlin when he moved to France in 1943. Suggestions of treachery have outraged fans of Wodehouse, who insist he was simply naive. The payments were probably either royalties or maintenance, they argue, because the Germans didn't want their world-famous prisoner to die in their hands. The financial affairs of P. G. Wodehouse during the war, moreover, were such that his wife had to sell her jewellery, and they had to borrow money to eat. Royalties were all that kept them going and were funnelled through the German Foreign Office, which would account for the mysterious payments.

The case of Wodehouse reveals much about the hysterical climate in which Haw-Haw was prosecuted. How ironic that the author of Bertie Wooster, the character to whom Lord Haw-Haw had so often been compared, should have been accused of the same crime as William Joyce. The British authorities, moreover, would not have made such a fuss about Wodehouse's broadcasts had they not been busy putting together a case against Joyce: they knew it was going to be hard to make a treason charge stick purely on the grounds of someone making broadcasts; they also knew that if they were seen to turn a blind eye to Wodehouse's misdemeanours, then that would weaken their case against Joyce. In this curious way, then, the fates of Wodehouse and Joyce were linked: each contributed to the other's downfall.

The gentle Wodehouse, of course, didn't have a treacherous fibre in his body, yet he never fully regained his reputation after the war. In 1955, he became an American citizen. And in 1975, he was awarded a knighthood, which the Queen Mother, a devoted fan, wanted to travel to New York to present in person, or so it was said. The British government vetoed the idea. A few weeks later, at the age of ninety-three, Wodehouse died.

Ezra Pound was not so lucky. On 5 May 1945, having been indicted on charges of treason two years earlier by a federal grand jury in Washington, the poet was arrested in Italy and handed over to US Counter-Intelligence. He was taken to a top-security camp for defectors in Pisa, where he was detained in a specially constructed cage in the open – *plus ça change*. He had searchlights trained on him at night to keep him awake. His belt and braces were confiscated and no one was allowed to speak to him. After three weeks he began suffering hallucinations. He was transferred to the sick bay where he began work on *The Pisan Cantos*. Later that year he was flown to Washington but was deemed 'insane and mentally unfit for trial'. Even in that condition he proved himself to be a bigger man than Joyce, in as much as he was able to admit he was wrong – not only wrong but ashamed and dismayed about the Nazi treatment of the Jews. He spent the next twelve years in a mental institution. 'An insane asylum is the only place I could bear to live in, in this country,' he said. He died in Venice in 1972 at the age of eighty-seven.

The various literary figures whose stories overlap a little with Joyce's – Wodehouse, Pound, Priestley and Wheatley – were not overshadowed by him. And neither was Shawcross. If anything, he tried to play down his success as a prosecutor at the trial. In his memoirs, he wrote that the Joyce case 'remains in my mind as one of which I am not specially proud . . . It was pure theatre . . . most listeners regarded Joyce as so fantastic as to be funny.' When he died in 2003 at the majestic age of 101, his obituaries led on his work at the Nuremberg Trial. They also made much of his opposition to capital punishment and his use of the phrase 'we are the masters now', which arose when he was putting through a bill to increase trade union power. He was appointed President of the Board of Trade in 1951 but resigned as an MP in 1958, at which time he was christened Sir Shortly Floorcross by the columnist Bernard Levin. Shawcross was created a life peer the following year and in 1983 crossed the floor one last time to join the Social Democrats.

Understandably, in his final days, Joyce gave some thought to how, or if, he would be remembered. On her prison visits he gave Margaret biographical details which she would later weave into her own unpublished memoirs. His life would make a 'great' saga, he mused. Frank Capra certainly thought so and wanted to make a movie about Joyce's life. He even got so far as to cast Alec Guinness in the lead, but the project never came to fruition.

There are no blue plaques on the various houses in which Joyce lived in London, and local residents were not amused when, a few years ago, it was suggested that one be put up on the house in Oldham where he stayed when he first arrived from Ireland. The windows of the corner tenement block in Brooklyn, New York, where Joyce was born are boarded up. It is in a dangerous neighbourhood now. There is a solitary shop opposite which, curiously enough, sells wigs, but there are few other signs of civic life. On the main door of the block itself there is a notice advertising 'violence awareness classes'. On top of it there is a pole from which a large Stars and Stripes flaps. Not surprisingly, there is no commemorative plaque on the side of this building, either.

Hanging from the rafters of a heritage centre in County Mayo there is an exhibit labelled 'Lord Haw-Haw's Cradle'. It came from the pub which

Joyce's grandparents ran in Ireland. The only other public commemoration of his life hangs on the wall of a gentleman's lavatory in a pub next to Wandsworth Prison. It is a framed 'Capital Punishment Act 1868' notice signed by the governor of the prison on 2 January 1945: 'The sentence of the law passed on . . . found guilty of murder will be carried into execution at . . . tomorrow.' The name 'William Joyce' has been handwritten in the first space and the time '9 a.m.' in the second. The word 'murder' has been crossed out and replaced with 'high treason'. It was quite an unusual crime.

In fact, pace Shawcross, Joyce did secure a place in history, as the last civilian to be hanged in England for high treason. (Private Theodore Schurch was hanged for treason at Pentonville Prison on 4 January 1946, after a court martial.) The 'last traitor' honour would have fallen to Walter Purdy, but he was given an eleventh-hour reprieve and his sentence was commuted to life imprisonment. He served nine years then changed his name to Robert Wallace Pointer and worked as a quality-control inspector in a car factory in Essex. He died from lung cancer in 1982. But until recently there was still a possibility that someone might deny Joyce his modest place in the history books – because although the death penalty was abolished in 1964, the punishment remained a theoretical possibility for treason, piracy with violence, and mutiny in the armed forces. In 1999 Jack Straw, the Home Secretary, finally abolished capital punishment, with no exceptions. The gallows at Wandsworth had been dismantled seven years earlier, having been tested every six months until then using a sandbag. They are now an exhibit at the Prison Service Museum, Rugby. Today the former execution chamber at Wandsworth is a TV room for inmates.

Freud said that biographical truth was not to be had, and if we did have it, we would not know it. Perhaps, then, the truth about Joyce died with him, and also with Maxwell Knight. That the rogue spymaster shared a name with one of the more complex pieces on a chessboard seems achingly appropriate. What little evidence there is seems to suggest that, in the first few months of the Phoney War, Knight regarded Joyce as an undercover option he was keeping open. Then Joyce unwittingly provided Knight with a means to trap Wolkoff and Kent. After that, the Knight–Joyce connection had to end. In 1945, Knight all but admitted that he had fabricated the whole story about Wolkoff using the Italian diplomatic bag.

Just before Kent was deported back to the United States, Knight went to visit him in prison. 'Kent maintains that he had no idea that Anna Wolkoff was going to transmit information which she had obtained from him out of the country, via del Monte at the Italian Embassy,' Knight wrote in his MI5 report of the meeting. 'I feel forced to record that I am now prepared to believe Kent.' A couple of months later, in an interview with Henry J. Taylor, an American reporter, Ambassador Kennedy made the same admission: 'Kent's reported friendliness with the Russian girl, Anna Wolkoff, had its place in his attitude, but apparently she didn't have safe and regular channels into Germany.'

With the war against the Nazis over, Knight become increasingly obsessed with the Soviet Union, specifically with the idea that a communist spy ring had infiltrated MI5. But he was no longer taken seriously by his colleagues – indeed, they ignored the numerous reports he wrote on the subject. Knight was by then regarded as paranoid and unstable and, even though his theory was proved right in 1951 when Guy Burgess and Donald Maclean fled to the Soviet Union, his reputation within the Service never recovered. He left MI5 a few years later and embarked upon a successful second career as a naturalist on radio and television. He soon became a household name, proving especially popular with children, and was awarded an OBE. In 1967 he published *How to Keep an Elephant*, a guide to keeping off-beat pets. The following year he wrote a sequel: *How to Keep a Gorilla*. Knight died of pneumonia on 27 January 1968, at the age of sixty-eight.

The question about whether Knight and Joyce cut a deal to spare Margaret from prosecution remains unanswered. But Joyce's silence looks suspicious. He never once mentioned in his defence that he had worked for MI5 in the 1930s, or that he was only able to get to Berlin at the start of the war thanks to a tip-off from a senior figure in MI5. Nor did he mention, as seems to have been the case, that Knight had sent him coded letters after he arrived in Germany and that, while in Germany, according to the question in the House of Commons, Joyce received payments of £10 month from 'the British government'. In fact Joyce said just two words at his trial – 'Not guilty' – which, for a famous orator, was a little perverse. What he is recorded as saying, to Commander Burt, the man who charged him with treason and escorted him back to England, was:

'My wife had nothing to do with anything I did. I know you won't try and pin anything on her.'

If a deal was done, then MI5 kept its side of the bargain. Although she had, as she admitted in her statement, broadcast enemy propaganda consistently throughout the war, Margaret Joyce was not charged with treason. This twist seems the more remarkable when it is considered that all the other British female broadcasters working in Berlin were so charged, even though they had mainly been announcing rather than commentating. Margaret Bothamley, who had been living in Germany before the war and had been married to a German, was found guilty of treason and sentenced to a year in prison. Dorothy Eckersley pleaded guilty to treason and was given a year's hard labour. Pearl Vardon was given nine months. Nearly all the men who had worked at the Funkhaus received between five and fifteen years in prison. As has been seen, P. G. Wodehouse only escaped prosecution by never returning to England. In fact, of the thirty-two renegades caught at the end of the war, Margaret was the only one not to be charged.

The day after her husband's execution, Lady Haw-Haw wrote from Holloway Prison to her brother-in-law, Quentin. She had been told she was to be returned to the Continent and this at least ruled out the possibility of her being tried for treason at the Old Bailey in the immediate future. She noted that her destination was unknown to her, but she presumed it was Brussels. She hoped that the hanging hadn't been too 'gruesome' for Quentin. She had managed to bear up, she explained, only because her husband had been so strong at the end. She asked her brother-in-law to look after her pictures and scrapbooks until she knew her fate, but added that she would take William's letters with her on the plane, as she valued them more highly than anything else she owned. She also asked if the newspapers had been 'beastly' about William and apologized for writing such a 'nightmarish' letter. She added that she was sure Quentin would forgive her – on the grounds that she was writing the letter while dangling half out of bed, with her packing only half done and with her mind 'half loopy'.

The following day she was driven from the prison, under armed escort, to Croydon airport for a 9 a.m. flight back to Brussels. She was shown on the passenger list as Margaret Schmidt and, for the purposes of the immigration authorities, she completed an alien's embarkation card in the name of Margaret Jones and declared herself to be of German nationality. After six months of being held in solitary confinement without charge she was being set free, or so it seemed. She was accompanied by T. M. Shelford, an MI5 agent. 'During the journey she outwardly showed herself to be cheerful, but it was apparent that she was endeavouring to conceal somewhat strained emotions,' Shelford wrote in his report. He also noted, with evident concern, a comment she made about the prospect of being held in solitary confinement without charge for another six months. 'I have formally submitted meekly to the treatment meted out to me during my detention, fearing any apparent untoward conduct on my part might adversely affect my late husband's case. I now intend to demand my rights even if it leads to a decision to charge me with the same offence as my late husband. If I am charged I will stress that I never intended to return to England having taken the decision to leave.'

When she landed back in Brussels, the airport authorities realized who she was and tipped off the press. The following day a story appeared in *Le Soir* – 'Mme Joyce, femme du traître anglais' – suggesting that she was to be freed in Belgium. This, as far as the newspaper was concerned, was not a welcome prospect. Although MI5 had agreed not to charge her with treason, a question mark was still hanging over her freedom. It would be embarrassing and potentially dangerous to have a symbolic figure such as Lady Haw-Haw roaming around post-war Europe at will, especially as she seemed to be stateless. 'Mrs Joyce is British by birth,' an MI5 memo noted. 'She did not acquire American nationality, or lose her British nationality by her marriage to William Joyce, an American subject. William Joyce obtained German naturalisation in 1940. It is not known whether his wife was included in his naturalisation, and all efforts to trace the German records have been unsuccessful. But German law provided that the naturalisation of the husband extends to the wife.'

But if she was German, then her husband must have been German, too, which was a bit embarrassing, given that he had just been hanged for being British. And if she was an alien, by virtue of her husband being a naturalized German, that would mean she would have to be interned as a security subject, as a matter of course, when she was returned to Germany, because it was occupied by the British. And if she was interned this would go against MI5's agreement not to 'punish her further'. What to do?

On 24 January 1946, Margaret wrote to Colonel Brooke-Booth, the head of the Intelligence Bureau in Brussels, requesting that she be allowed to go to Ireland to study philology. 'As apparently no decision regarding my future has yet been reached I should like to give my reason for not wishing to be forced to return to Germany as a condition of release. Owing to the strong measures taken against those in any way connected with the public services of the Third Reich, there would probably be an understandable disinclination to assist me.' She ended her letter with a veiled threat. 'Although I have no desire for any political activity, and no interest whatsoever in British politics of any kind, were I resident in Germany there would always be the likelihood of my being drawn into the inevitable reaction against occupation and the possible reaction against continued Soviet encroachments, with both of which tendencies I feel a natural sympathy which would be greatly increased by direct contact with the conditions from which they will spring.'

This letter worried Brooke-Booth and he passed it on to Colonel Cussen at MI5. Cussen in turn wrote a memo to the Home Office: 'It would be most undesirable for Mrs Joyce to come back to the United Kingdom. The penultimate paragraph of Mrs Joyce's letter is a good illustration of her frame of mind, and it would be deplorable if she should become available to fascist elements here as a stalking horse of some nuisance value. The best way of preventing this is to secure that she is safely disposed of elsewhere.'

A very British compromise was reached: it was decided that a decision on Margaret's future would be postponed until 'feelings were less strong'. So it was that Margaret Joyce was put on a passport black list, again, and sent to Germany as a displaced person, to No. 5 Civilian Internment Camp at Paderborn in the Ruhr. This was supposed to be a temporary measure but the problems she presented as a symbolic figure would not go away. On 1 July 1946, a question was asked in the House of Commons about her status: namely, was she British or German when the Home Office briefly granted her admission to the United Kingdom in November the previous year? Mr Hyde answered that she had been an alien, 'having thrown in her lot with Germany' – she had also been 'one of the dangerous Nazis'.

Matters were complicated further by the intervention of her solicitor, Head. He wrote to the Home Secretary pointing out that she had never changed her British nationality because, under British law, she did not become an American citizen when she married Joyce. And a British subject cannot acquire the nationality of an enemy state during time of war. This was an interpretation of the law which conflicted with MI5's. Clearly it was a grey area, legally. Either way, the *New York Times* was tipped off about this twist and began a series of reports that were sympathetic to her case.

They made little difference. Margaret languished in the internment camp for two years, spending her time reading and writing letters, diaries and notes for her memoirs. She befriended a British army officer, John Alfred Cole, to whom she told her life story in a series of interviews. Quentin kept in touch with her by post and she became popular with the other internees, teaching them English and organizing games for them to alleviate the boredom. The British press eventually picked up her story in 1947 and was in a more forgiving mood. A reader from Hampshire, a Mr W. L. Sinclair, wrote a letter to *The Times* complaining about Margaret's unfair treatment. 'It would appear that laws can be altered to satisfy the blood lust of officialdom,' he concluded.

On 16 September that year, the British Intelligence chief in Germany wrote to the Home Office: 'We suggest that you reverse the decision that Mrs Joyce is a German national and arrange to repatriate her as a British citizen unobtrusively to her parents in Manchester at the first opportunity. We request authorisation for this as her continued presence in the British Zone, whether in or out of internment, is a source of increasingly grave embarrassment.'

When a Home Office official replied that there were no plans to reverse the decision and that she should be released as a German, the intelligence chief tried again: 'Is there an inconsistency between this decision [to classify her as German] and the sentence passed on William Joyce? Are we not having the best of both worlds by declaring that Joyce was not, but his wife was, a German national? The decisive factor was that it was in Mrs Joyce's own interest to assume German nationality as otherwise she would be liable to trial for high treason.'

The attempts by British Intelligence to get Margaret out of Germany become increasingly desperate. 'The world press is taking a keen interest in her,' the intelligence chief warned the Home Office on 26 September, 'in particular the American press. There is little doubt but that the object of the latter is to offer Mrs Joyce a large sum for her life story which could be used as another stick to beat the British on the grounds of: "You hanged her husband as an Englishman, but you banish the wife as a German. This is British justice." It will undoubtedly become a cause célèbre. Attempts to obtain accommodation and employment for her in the British Zone as you suggest have previously failed and no one will take charge of what they consider to be dynamite. It is therefore probable that, having no friends and no possibility of employment, she will drift into subversive activity. There are circles in Germany who would be only too willing to use the prestige of her name.'

After this, Margaret became the subject of dozens of letters between Sir Alexander Maxwell at the Home Office and Sir Brian Robertson of the Foreign Office. Eventually, it was decided between them that after two and a half years of internment without trial Margaret should be released immediately, as a German citizen. But neither the Home Office nor the Foreign Office had allowed for Margaret's wilfulness. She refused to sign her release papers and denied having ever made any claim to German citizenship. An anxious Maxwell took this to mean that she was planning to sue: 'If Mrs Joyce were admitted to the UK by right as a British citizen, the Home Secretary would have to be prepared to explain why, when she was brought to England to see her husband before his execution, she was detained in Holloway as an alien. She would then be able to claim for damages for wrongful imprisonment.'

Another compromise was found. She was to be deemed a 'German but stateless and British born', and she wouldn't have to sign any release papers.

On 1 January 1948, Margaret gathered her few possessions together – souvenir hunters had left her with little, her one remaining valuable, a gold monogrammed pocket watch, having now also been liberated – and took the train to Hamburg, a free woman. Well, almost. She was placed in 'Provisional Category III' which meant, according to one MI5 memo, British Intelligence would 'keep an especially careful eye on her'. Her final categorization would rest with a local GDP (German Denazification Panel). Hauntingly, Hamburg now looked like a giant construction site, its skyline dotted with cranes. Margaret hardly recognized the city, but at least she didn't feel a complete stranger there. She moved into 13 Bottgerstrasse and, within days, changed her name to

Margaret Brooke-Joyce (Brooke being William's mother's maiden name). She found work as a translator and supervisor for an international food-stuffs company, the Deutsche Maizena Werke, where she soon became a popular and cheerful member of staff.

The woolly-headedness which her husband often used to comment upon was still in evidence. On 19 December 1951 she sent a letter to one of her former bosses, Dr Erich Hetzler, Sammy, the man who had run the secret station which had broadcast as NBBS.

> *My dear Erich,*
>
> *Damn it – and I had such a good conscience – I was sure I'd answered your last letter! When I was over in England, Quentin gave me a book in which he had made notes of Will's last messages to his friends over here. Quentin had never dared to send it but had waited till he could give it to me.*
>
> *"For Dr Hetzler. I regret never having said good-bye to him in Berlin, but my failure to do so was deliberate because I could see the tragedy coming and I had no wish to take a final leave of him after such a happy association and deep friendship. Tell him I was true to the Hakenkreuz till the end and I salute him with the Deutsche Grüss Heil Hitler."*
>
> *I thought you would like to have his message at last, although it is just about six years since it was given. He began probably that day – the 19th December – to put his affairs in order, for it was on the afternoon of the 18th that we heard, he in Wandsworth and I in Holloway, that the appeal had been dismissed and he was to die.*
>
> *Ever yours, Margaret.*

Not long after writing this she tracked down Nicky and the two rekindled their affair. But then she discovered his second wife was pregnant. Heartbroken, and still childless herself, the unfortunately nicknamed Mother-Sheep left Nicky, the Honorary Sheep, for good. As she put it in her own inimitable style: 'Besack left me flat for good and all – his wife had a baby mitten in den Vorbereitungen zur Scheidung (my German is as bad as ever). That was too much for me and I at last believed all the people who told me he was rotten – it left rather a hole in my Steele!'

Despite her erratic German, she wrote a paper on German refugees which was published in Germany in 1952. She still felt like a refugee herself and never settled. In 1955 she reapplied for British citizenship, was quietly granted it and returned to England. She visited Quentin but found that her old friends and haunts had long since disappeared. She began drinking heavily, and while sitting in a pub one day met Donald John Alban May, a thin, middle-aged accountant turned construction auditor who worked for a company based in Casablanca. May, the son of a school caretaker, was a convicted fraudster – a minor offence, he had impersonated an officer – and he still liked to dress up. His favourite uniform was that of an RAF air marshal and, such was his patriotism, he had a flag-pole in his garden from which he flew a union flag. He seemed a colourful character and, more than anything, Margaret hated being bored. The two were married in Gibraltar, on 28 December 1962. She was fifty-one, he forty. They bought a house together: 29 Dunraven Road, Shepherd's Bush, West London, and after a lifetime spent on the move it was Margaret's last home. In an interview in 1964 she told a reporter that 'I still love Britain – more than ever, in fact. It is the only really civilised country.'

Margaret was still gregarious but she had trouble with her teeth and this made her want to socialize less that she used to. In March 1966, without telling her husband, she visited Heather, William's eldest daughter from his first marriage, and gave her the 144 letters Joyce had written from prison. She feared that, what with the market for such things among morbid collectors, Donald May would try and sell them if he found out about them. On 19 February 1972, at the age of sixty, Margaret Joyce drank herself to death. Under 'cause of death' her death certificate reads: 'heptic cirrhosis due to chronic alcoholism.'

Lord and Lady Haw-Haw had both, in the end, contrived their own downfall. As Rebecca West wrote: 'Iago was a gentle child compared to their suicidal selves.'

Within a few weeks of his wife's death, Donald May sold some of her personal effects to a couple from Birmingham who specialized in collecting medieval instruments of torture, as well as ropes and gadgets used for public executions. The memorabilia he sold included photographs, post-war diaries, scrapbooks and the lock of hair Joyce had given her – items that had somehow escaped the souvenir-hunters over the years. Such lack of sentimentality suggests that Margaret's relationship with her second husband had become strained towards the end. Perhaps May simply needed the money; he was an alcoholic, too.

Four years later, after a long campaign by Heather, the then Home Secretary Roy Jenkins agreed to allow William Joyce's body to be exhumed and re-interred under a spreading yew tree, just outside Galway, the place where he had claimed he was born. Some two hundred people turned up at the Protestant section of Bohermore Cemetery to watch; something about Joyce's tragic story must have touched the Irish soul.

Joyce was an eccentric who liked to spell things his own way. He was also a pedant with a first in English. It seems appropriate, then, if a little cruel, that there are two mistakes in the inscription on his white marble gravestone in Galway. 'I am the resurrection and the life. Dona eis requiem. William Joyce 23 April 1906–3 January 1946.' He was born on 24 April – even his passport got the date right – and there should be two 'r's in resurrection.

PEMBROKE BRANCH TEL. 6689575

CHRONOLOGY

1906, 24 April – William Joyce born in New York

1909, November – WJ moves to Ireland with his family

1911, 14 July – Margaret White born in Manchester

1921, 8 December – WJ moves to England

1923, 6 December – WJ join the British Fascisti Ltd

1924, 22 October – WJ is attacked with a razor at a political rally and is left
    with a scar on his cheek

1927, 30 April – WJ marries Hazel

1927, June – WJ graduates with a first from London University

1928, 30 July – WJ's first daughter, Heather, is born

1931, 20 July – WJ's second daughter, Diana, is born

1933 – WJ joins British Union of Fascists and becomes Mosley's deputy

1933, 4 July – WJ applies for a British passport

1936 – WJ and Hazel divorce

1937, 13 February – WJ marries Margaret

1937, 11 March – WJ sacked from BUF

1939, 27 August – William and Margaret arrive in Berlin

1939, 1 September – Germany invades Poland

1939, 3 September – Britain declares war on Germany

1939, autumn – Lord and Lady Haw-Haw make their first broadcasts

1939, 17 December – *Graf Spee* scuttled

1940, 21 February – Construction of Auschwitz begins

1940, 9 April – Germany invades Denmark and Norway

1940, 10 May – Churchill replaces Chamberlain

1940, 18 May – Tyler Kent arrested

1940, 27 May to 4 June – Evacuation of Dunkirk

1940, 10 June – Italy declares war on Britain and France

1940, 14 June – Germans enter Paris

1940, 10 July – Luftwaffe raids south of England: Battle of Britain begins

1940, 2 September – US gives UK 50 destroyers

1940, 26 September – William and Margaret granted German citizenship

1940, 12 October – Hitler postpones Operation Sea Lion. Blitz of London begins

1940, autumn – *Twilight over England* published

1940, 10 November – Margaret first announced as Lady Haw-Haw

1941, 11 April – Tobruk cut off

1941, 10 May – Rudolf Hess flies to Scotland

1941, 27 May – The *Bismarck* sunk

1941, 22 June – Germany invades the Soviet Union

1941, 12 August – William and Margaret divorce

1941, 19 September – Hitler decrees all Jews must wear yellow star

1941, 14 November – The *Ark Royal* sunk

1941, 7 December – Japan attacks Pearl Harbor

1942, 11 February – William and Margaret remarry

1942, 27 May – Heydrich assassinated (dies 4 June)

1942, 30 May – First thousand-bomber raid on Cologne

1942, 21 June – Germans take Tobruk

1942, 23 October – Montgomery attacks Rommel at El Alamein

1942, 12 November – Allies retake Tobruk

1942, 9 December – Margaret introduced by her own name

1943, 2 February – Germans surrender in Stalingrad

1943, 16 May – Dambusters raid

1943, 25 July – Fall of Mussolini

1943, 13 September – Italy surrenders

1943, 13 October – Italy declares war on Germany

1944, 16 February – 800 aircraft bomb Berlin

1944, 6 March – First daylight bombing raid on Berlin by USAAF

1944, 8 March – USAAF sends 1,800 bombers to Berlin

1944, 6 June – D-Day

1944, 13 June – First use of flying bombs

1944, 20 July – Hitler assassination attempt

1944, 25 August – Paris liberated

1944, 17 Sept – The Battle of Arnhem begins

1944, 14 October – Forced suicide of Rommel

1944, 16 December – Battle of the Bulge begins

1945, 27 January – Auschwitz liberated by Russians

1945, 31 January – US Army crosses into Germany. Red Army reaches the river Oder, fifty miles from Berlin

1945, 14 March – William and Margaret evacuated from Berlin

1945, 15 April – Belsen liberated

1945, 30 April – Hitler commits suicide. WJ makes last drunken broadcast as Lord Haw-Haw

1945, 23 May – Himmler commits suicide

1945, 28 May – William and Margaret captured on Danish–German border

1945, 26 July – Attlee replaces Churchill

1945, 7 August – US drops atomic bomb on Hiroshima

1945, 19 September – WJ found guilty of treason and sentenced to death

1945, 7 November – WJ's appeal dismissed

1945, 18 December – Law Lords dismiss appeal

1946, 3 January – WJ executed aged thirty-nine

1946, 5 January – Margaret deported to Germany and interned

1948, 1 January – Margaret released

1962, 28 December – Margaret marries Donald May

1972, 19 February – Margaret dies an alcoholic in London aged sixty-one

1976, 18 August – WJ's body re-interred in Ireland

BIBLIOGRAPHY

Unpublished primary sources

Much of the information quoted in this book comes from the Public Record Office at Kew (now part of the National Archives), especially material relating to MI5, the Home Office, the Cabinet Office and the Foreign Office. The main files are TNA-PRO KV 2/250 (which includes William Joyce's Berlin diary) and KV 2/346 (which includes Margaret Joyce's Berlin diaries). Other material is quoted from KV 2/245–250 passim, KV 2/253, KV 2/346, KV 2/543–545 passim, KV 2/826, KV 4/117, HO 45/22405, HO 45/25690, HO 144/19069, HO 144/22454, HO 283/40/22, FO 945/783, FO 371/11384, FO 371/64689, FO 1030/33, FO 1060/49 and FO 370/6877.

(The copyright in the wartime diaries of William and Margaret Joyce, as well as their broadcasts, William Joyce's book *Twilight over England*, and Margaret Joyce's correspondence from Belgium and Germany during the 'War period' was extinguished under the Enemy Property Act (1953) (1&2 Eliz c52). The statements of William and Margaret Joyce, as well as Joyce's passport application, are Crown copyright.)

From the National Archives of Australia: CRS A 981/1, item 'Fascism 3'.

Unpublished biographical notes about Joyce made by Angus Macnab and A. K. Chesterton (these are held at the Sheffield University Library Special Collection).

William Joyce's prison letters (copies of which are held by his daughter Heather Iandolo).

BBC Monitoring Service Reports, which include transcripts of Joyce's broadcasts. (These are held at the Imperial War Museum and at the National Archives, Kew, and are BBC property and copyright.) Also BBC WC R28/121/ SNE to C (P) 4 April 1940.

Home Intelligence Reports on Opinion and Morale by the Ministry of Information, 1940–44.

'Public and Private Opinion on Lord Haw-Haw', Mass Observation's Weekly Intelligence Service, 1940.

The information quoted from among others Heather Iandolo, James Clark, Geoffrey Perry, Francis Beckett, John Hope, Dame Vera Lynn, Tully Potter and Terry Charman comes from interviews with the author in 2002, 2003 and 2004.

Published primary sources

Andrew, Christopher, *Secret Service*. London, 1985.

Beckett, Francis, *The Rebel Who Lost His Cause: John Beckett, MP*. London, 1999.

Beevor, Antony, *Berlin: The Downfall 1945*. London, 2002.

Bergmeier, Horst and Lotz, Rainer, *Hitler's Airwaves: The Inside Story of Nazi Radio Broadcasting and Propaganda Swing*. London, 1997.

Bewley, Charles, *Memoirs of a Wild Goose*. Dublin, 1989.

Booker, J. A., *Blackshirts on Sea*. London, 1999.

Burt, Leonard, *Commander Burt of Scotland Yard*. London, 1959.

Cole, J. A., *Lord Haw-Haw and William Joyce*. London, 1964.

Doherty, M. A., *Nazi Wireless Propaganda: Lord Haw-Haw and British Public Opinion in the Second World War*. Edinburgh, 2000.

Fitzgeorge-Parker, Tim, *The Biography of Brigadier Roscoe Harvey*. London, 1987.

Flannery, Harry W., *Assignment to Berlin*. New York, 1942.

Goebbels, Josef, *The Goebbels Diaries, 1939–1941*. London, 1982.

Griffiths, Richard, *Fellow Travellers of the Right: British Enthusiasts for Nazi Germany 1933–39*. London, 1980.

—— *Patriotism Perverted*. London, 1998.

Hall, J. W. (ed.), *Notable British Trials: The Trial of William Joyce*. London, 1946.

Hennessy, Peter, *Never Again: Britain 1945–51*. London, 1992.

Joyce, William, *Twilight Over England*. Berlin, 1940.

Kenny, Mary, *Germany Calling: A Personal Biography of William Joyce/Lord Haw-Haw*. Dublin, 2003.

McCrum, Robert, *Wodehouse. A Life*. London, 2004.

Masters, Anthony, *The Man Who Was M: The Life of Maxwell Knight*. Oxford, 1984.

Miller, Joan, *One Girl's War*. Brandon, 1987.

Mosley, Diana, *A Life of Contrasts*. London, 2002.

Mosley, Nicholas, *Beyond the Pale*. London, 1983.

Perry, Geoffrey, *When Life Becomes History*. Oxford, 2002.

Pierrepoint, Albert, *Executioner: Pierrepoint*. London, 1974.

Porter, Bernard, *Plots and Paranoia*. London, 1989.

Richie, Alexandra, *Faust's Metropolis*. London, 1998.

Roberts, C. E., *The Trial of William Joyce*. London, 1946.

Rutledge, Brett, *The Death of Lord Haw Haw*. New York, 1940.

Shawcross, Lord Hartley, *Life Sentence: The Memoirs of Lord Shawcross*. London, 1995.

Shirer, William, *Berlin Diary*. New York, 1941.

Simpson, A. W. B., *In the Highest Degree Odious*. London, 1992.

Smith, Howard K. *Last Train from Berlin*. London, 1942.

Taylor, A. J. P., *English History 1914–1945*. Oxford, 1965.

Weale, Adrian, *Renegades: Hitler's Englishmen*. London, 2002.

Weeks, David, *Eccentrics*. London, 1995.

West, Rebecca, *The Meaning of Treason*. London, 1949.

White, John Baker, *It's Gone for Good*. London, 1941.

—— *True Blue*. London, 1971.

Newspapers and magazines

Action – 1933–38

Daily Express – 1939–45

Daily Mail – 1932–45

Daily Mirror – 1939–45

Daily Telegraph – 1934–76

Life – 1940

Manchester Guardian – 1934–45

People – 1939–45

The Times – 1934–45

Select bibliography

Allen, Martin, *The Hitler–Hess Deception*. London, 2003.

Anonymous, *A Woman in Berlin*. London, 1955.

Baillie-Stewart, Norman, *The Officer in the Tower*. London, 1967.

Baker, David, *Ideology of Obsession, A. K. Chesterton and British Fascism*. London, 1996.

Balfour, Michael, *Propaganda in War 1939–1945*. London, 1979.

Barrington, Brendan (ed.), *The Wartime Broadcasts of Francis Stuart*. Dublin, 2000.

Barrington, Jonah, *Lord Haw-Haw of Zeesen*. London, 1940.

Bearse, Ray, and Read, Anthony, *Conspirator: The Untold Story of Churchill, Roosevelt, and Tyler Kent, Spy*. London, 1991.

Benewick, Robert, *The Fascist Movement in Britain*. London, 1972.

Boelcke, W. A., *The Secret Conferences of Dr Goebbels: the Propaganda War 1939–1943*. New York, 1970.

Boveri, Margaret, *Treason in the 20th Century*. London, 1961.

Bower, Tom, *The Paperclip Conspiracy*. London, 1987.

—— *The Perfect English Spy*. London, 1995.

Calder, Angus, *The Myth of the Blitz*. London, 1991.

Carlton, Eric, *Treason: Meanings and Motives*. Aldershot, 1998.

Carpenter, Humphrey, *Spike Milligan*. London, 2003.

Charman, Terry, 'The number one radio personality of the war: Lord Haw-Haw and his British audience during the phoney war'. *Imperial War Museum Review*, no. 7, pp. 74–82.

Cockett, Richard, *Twilight of Truth: Chamberlain, Appeasement and the Manipulation of the Press*. London, 1989.

Cross, Colin, *The Fascists in Britain*. London, 1961.

Curry, David, *A History of the Security Service: 1909–1945*. London, 1998.

Edwards, John Carver, *Berlin Calling*. New York, 1991.

Ettlinger, Harold, *The Axis on Air*. Indianapolis, 1943.

Forester, C. S., *Fatal Fascination, a choice of crime*. London, 1964.

Gilbert, Martin, *Churchill: A Life*. London, 2000.

Goldhagen, Daniel, *Hitler's Willing Executioners: Ordinary Germans and the Holocaust*. New York, 1996.

Gombrich, E. H., *Myth and Reality in German War-Time Broadcasts*. London, 1970.

Gottlieb, Julie V., *Feminine Fascism: Women in Britain's Fascist Movement, 1923–45*. London, 2002.

Gross, Leonard, *The Last Jews in Berlin*. New York, 1982.

Grundy, Trevor, *Memoirs of a Fascist Childhood*. London, 1998.

Hastings, Max, *Bomber Command*. London, 1979.

—— *Armageddon: The Battle for Germany, 1944–45*. London, 2004.

Hayward, James, *Myths and Legends of the Second World War*. Stroud, 2003.

Herzstein, Robert, *The War That Hitler Won: Nazi Propaganda*. London, 1979.

Hickman, Tom, *What Did You Do in the War, Auntie? The BBC at War*. London, 1995.

Holmes, Colin, *Anti-Semitism in British Society*. London, 1979.

Jowitt, Earl, *Some Were Spies*. London, 1954.

Keegan, John, *The Second World War*. London, 1997.

Kershaw, Ian, *The Hitler Myth: Image and Reality in the Third Reich*. Oxford, 1989.

—— *Hitler: 1889–1936*. London, 1998.

—— *Hitler: 1936–1945*. London, 2000.

—— *Making friends with Hitler: Lord Londonderry and the Roots of Appeasement*. London, 2004.

Langley, D., *Roosevelt and Churchill: Their Secret Wartime Correspondence*. New York, 1975.

Leech, Clifford, *Tragedy*. London, 1969.

Leon, R. W., *The Making of an Intelligence Officer*. London, 1994.

Lewis, D. S., *Illusions of Grandeur: Mosley, Fascism and British Society 1931–1981*. Manchester, 1987.

Longmate, Norman, *How We Lived Then: A History of Everyday Life During the Second World War*. London, 1971.

Lucas, F. L., *Tragedy in relation to Aristotle's Poetics*. London, 1928.

McCutcheon Raleigh, John, *Behind the Nazi Front*. London, 1941.

Martland, Peter, *The National Archives Secret History Files: Lord Haw-Haw*. London, 2003.

Mitford, Nancy, *Pigeon Pie*. London, 1999.

Mosley, Oswald, *My Life*. London, 1968.

Muggeridge, Malcolm, *Chronicles of Wasted Time*. London, 1973.

Muir, Kate, 'The Englishman who felt Nazi Germany calling', *The Times*, 3 May 1991.

Murphy, Sean, *Letting the Side Down: British Traitors of the Second World War*. Stroud, 2004.

Nicolson, Harold, *Diaries and Letters 1930–1964*. London, 1980.

O'Donoghue, David, *Hitler's Irish Voices*. Belfast, 1998.

Orwell, George, *The Road to Wigan Pier*. London, 1962.

Otto, Heinrich, *Germany Calling: Lord Haw-Haw's Radio War. Facts, Figures, Stories about William Joyce*. Melbourne, 1987.

Pincher, Chapman, *Their Trade is Treachery*. London, 1981.

Pryce-Jones, David, *Unity Mitford: A Quest*. London, 1976.

Pugh, Martin, *Hurrah for the Blackshirts. Fascists and Fascism in Britain Between the Wars*. London, 2005.

Rees, Philip, *Fascism in Britain*. Hassocks, Sussex, 1979.

Roberts, Andrew, *The Holy Fox: A Life of Lord Halifax*, London, 1991.

—— 'Double-Barrelled Traitors of 1941'. *The Spectator*, 23 January 1993.

—— *Eminent Churchillians*, London, 1994.

Scruton, Roger, *Death-devoted Heart: Sex and the Sacred in Wagner's Tristan and Isolde*. Oxford, 2004.

Seabrook, David, *All the Devils Are Here*. London, 2002.

Selwyn, Francis, *Hitler's Englishman: The Crime of Lord Haw-Haw*. London, 1987.

Silvey, Robert, *Who's Listening? The Story of the BBC Audience Research*. London, 1974.

Sinclair, W. A., *The Voice of the Nazi, being eight broadcast talks given between December 1939 and May 1940*. London, 1940.

Skidelsky, Robert, *Mosley*. London, 1981.

Smith, Naomi Royde, *Outside Information*. London, 1941.

Speer, Albert, *Inside the Third Reich*. London, 1970.

Sprout, Iain, *Wodehouse at War*. London, 1981.

Stafford, David, *Roosevelt & Churchill, Men of Secrets*. London, 1999.

Steiner, George, *The Death of Tragedy*. London, 1961.

Thurlow, Richard, *Fascism in Britain 1918–1935*. Oxford, 1987.

Todd, Nigel, *In Excited Times: The People Against the Blackshirts*. Whitley Bay, 1995.

Turner, E. S., *The Phoney War*. London, 1961.

Weale, Adrian, *Patriot Traitors*. London, 2001.

Weeks, David, *Eccentrics*. London, 1995.

West, Nigel, *MI5: British Security Service Operations 1909–1946*. London, 1981.

West, W. J., *Truth Betrayed*. London, 1987.

Wheatley, Dennis, *Stranger than Fiction*. London, 1959.

—— *The Young Man Said: Memoirs 1897–1914*. London, 1977.

—— *Drink and Ink: Memoirs 1919–1977*. London, 1979.

Wilson, A. N., *Hilaire Belloc*. London, 1984.

Winterbotham, Frederick, *The Nazi Connection*. London, 1978.

INDEX